T0328809

Finance, Intermediaries, and Economic Development

This volume includes ten essays dealing with financial and other forms of economic intermediation in Europe, Canada, and the United States since the seventeenth century. Each relates the development of institutions to economic change and describes their evolution over time. Several different forms of intermediation are discussed, and these essays deal with significant economic and historical issues.

Stanley L. Engerman is Professor of Economics and History at the University of Rochester. He is the co-editor of *The Cambridge Economic History of the United States* (1996, 2000).

Philip T. Hoffman is Professor of History and Social Science at the California Institute of Technology. He is the co-author, along with Jean-Laurent Rosenthal and Gilles Postel-Vinay, of *Priceless Markets* (2000).

Jean-Laurent Rosenthal is Professor of Economics and Associate Director of the Center for Global and Comparative Research at the University of California at Los Angeles. His books include *Fruits of Revolution* (1992).

Kenneth L. Sokoloff is Professor of Economics at the University of California at Los Angeles. He is co-editor of *The Role of the State in Taiwan's Development* (1994).

Finance, Intermediaries, and Economic Development

Edited by

STANLEY L. ENGERMAN
University of Rochester

PHILIP T. HOFFMAN
California Institute of Technology

JEAN-LAURENT ROSENTHAL
University of California, Los Angeles

KENNETH L. SOKOLOFF
University of California, Los Angeles

CAMBRIDGE
UNIVERSITY PRESS

CAMBRIDGE UNIVERSITY PRESS
Cambridge, New York, Melbourne, Madrid, Cape Town, Singapore,
São Paulo, Delhi, Dubai, Tokyo, Mexico City

Cambridge University Press
The Edinburgh Building, Cambridge CB2 8RU, UK

Published in the United States of America by Cambridge University Press, New York

www.cambridge.org
Information on this title: www.cambridge.org/9780521147415

First published 2003
First paperback printing 2010

A catalogue record for this publication is available from the British Library

Library of Congress Cataloguing in Publication data
Finance, intermediaries, and economic development / edited by Stanley L. Engerman...[et al.].
p. cm.
"Papers first presented at a conference 'In data veritas: institutions and growth in
economic history.' held in honor of Lance Davis at the California Institute of
Technology, November 6–8, 1998" – Pref.
Includes bibliographical references and index.
ISBN 0-521-82054-5
1. Financial institutions – Congresses. 2. Economic development – Congresses.
I. Engerman, Stanley L. II. Davis, Lance Edwin.
HG173 .F4882 2003
332.1 – dc21 2002031366

ISBN 978-0-521-82054-7 Hardback
ISBN 978-0-521-14741-5 Paperback

Contents

List of Contributors

Stanley L. Engerman, University of Rochester

Larry Neal, University of Illinois at Urbana-Champaign and NBER

Stephen Quinn, Texas Christian University

Eugene N. White, Rutgers University and NBER

Phillip T. Hoffman, California Institute of Technology

Gilles Postel-Vinay, EHESS and INRA-LEA

Jean-Laurent Rosenthal, University of California, Los Angeles

Angela Redish, University of British Columbia

John B. Legler, University of Georgia

Richard Sylla, New York University and NBER

Kenneth A. Snowden, University of North Carolina at Greensboro

Naomi R. Lamoreaux, University of California, Los Angeles and NBER

Kenneth L. Sokoloff, University of California, Los Angeles and NBER

Dianne Newell, University of British Columbia

Robert C. Allen, Nuffield College, Oxford

Michael Bordo, Rutgers University and NBER

Michael Edelstein, Queens College, CUNY

Hugh Rockoff, Rutgers University and NBER

List Of Contributors

Preface

This volume contains papers first presented at a conference, "In Data Veritas: Institutions and Growth in Economic History," held in honor of Lance Davis at the California Institute of Technology, November 6–8, 1998. In addition to the presenters, also attending, as formal or informal discussants, were Karen Clay, Robert Cull, Price Fishback, Albert Fishlow, Stephen Haber, John James, Shawn Kantor, Zorina Khan, Margaret Levenstein, Rebecca Menes, Clayne Pope, and John Wallis. The Introduction and the Afterword were written by the editors at a later date. We wish to thank Frank Smith from Cambridge University Press and the two anonymous referees for the Press for very helpful suggestions.

We wish to acknowledge the administrative help of Susan G. Davis and the financial help of the Division of the Humanities and Social Sciences, California Institute of Technology, in the conference arrangements. In preparing the final manuscript we were aided by the Department of Economics, University of Rochester; the Department of Economics, UCLA; and the Division of the Humanities and Social Sciences, California Institute of Technology. In the process of publication, we benefited from the editorial work of Michie Shaw of TechBooks, the copyediting of Carol Sirkus, and the preparation of the index by Kathleen Paparchontis. But most of all we gained from the scholarship and enthusiasm of Lance Davis.

Introduction

One of the striking changes accompanying – if not helping to cause – economic development is the dramatic increase in financial transactions among firms and individuals, sometimes directly between borrowers and lenders, sometimes involving third parties (financial intermediaries).[1] Over time these third parties played an increasingly important role. In part it is because the type of intermediaries who appeared early on (brokers, banks, stock markets) grew more numerous; and in part it is because of the introduction of totally new institutions (legal institutions and informal rules of behavior) and totally new organizations (savings and loan associations, investment trusts, and central banks). In most societies this expansion of financial intermediation fueled higher rates of savings and investment, more rapid growth of the capital stock, and a higher rate of economic growth.

The big question here is how financial intermediaries facilitate investment. Lance Davis has long maintained that intermediation acts both on supply, the magnitude of investment funds, and demand, the choice of projects these funds will support. In the early stages of growth, the key issue lies in mobilizing the available savings rather than increasing its amount. Mobilization occurs when savers increase the relative size of their financial holdings. The decision to do so depends on financial institutions that provide savers with information and diminish the risk they bear. Such a task is not easy, for savers appear to be creatures of habit. Davis has gone so far as to argue that savers must actually be taught to hold financial claims (Davis and Cull 1994). Similarly, when economies begin to develop, they experience structural change. Resources must, therefore, flow to new sectors and new regions in the economy, and investment must be reallocated. Here financial intermediaries play a critical role in allocating funds to different projects, particularly to new

---

[1] The correlation between financial deepening and economic growth has long been established. Summary information for a number of countries was compiled by Goldsmith (1969).

firms or those dependent on external finance. Information, of course, plays an important role. Intermediaries specialize in information gathering and must acquire the information about the quality of investment projects and perform other services for entrepreneurs. If financial intermediaries are successful in their twin tasks of mobilization and allocation, then capital will flow from savers to entrepreneurs, from parts of the globe where returns are low to parts of the globe where they are higher. Here Davis has put considerable emphasis on the public and private rules that govern financial intermediation and on the interaction between government regulation and private institutional innovation (see Davis and Huttenback 1986; Davis and Cull 1994; and Davis and Neal 1998). It is studying these rules that allows us to understand why some forms of financial intermediation have been successful although others proved to be failures.

Success comes from a subtle interplay between government and the private sector. On the one hand, financial markets can easily fail or fall victim to panics. If the government can intervene in a way that reassures savers and makes them believe that financial intermediaries deserve their trust, then financial crises will have only temporary effects, and the development of capital markets will continue almost unabated. But if the government acts with too heavy a hand, then, as Davis and Gallman (2001) emphasize, it will stifle financial innovation and obstruct the allocative role played by financial intermediaries. Innovation is particularly important here, for it often brings on failure and thus a greater temptation for the government to intercede.

Lance Davis's investigations of financial intermediation have been very broad-ranging, including not only examination of interest rates and rates of return (Davis 1965) but also the study of the amounts of funds transferred. Beyond interest rates, he has also devoted considerable attention to measuring capital flows and their economic return over the long run (Davis and Gallman 1978), thereby raising questions about the evolution of the rules that structured the movement of capital. Research on such questions made Davis one of the first to stress the importance of political economy for understanding both domestic and international financial structures and the relationship between financial development and economic growth (Davis and North 1971; Davis and Huttenback 1986). The collections of essays we present here all follow Davis's lead in going beyond questions about prices and quantities to questions of institutions.

Such an emphasis on political economy has much relevance in economics today. To begin, consider the empirical debates raging over the role of transparency and legal origins in financial development (e.g., La Porta et al. 1997; Beck, Levine, and Loayza 2000; Rajan and Zingales 2001). The authors engaged in this debate have used recent data on economic and financial performance and long-term indicators of financial development to ask what role institutions play in growth. They have certainly asked important questions, such as why is economic growth slower in developing countries that inherited a French legal code or in countries with limited European settlement or in countries with a legacy of extreme inequality or abundant land relative to labor? (Acemoglu, Johnson, and Robinson 2001; Engerman and Sokoloff 1997; La Porta et al. 1998). But the recent data alone cannot answer these questions; it can only help frame them. The answers have to come from a long-term focus that is the stock-in-trade of economic historians. They and other scholars with the long-term focus that these issues demand can begin to address these questions. In the same fashion, debates about financial systems ask important questions that can only be answered with a historical perspective. Currently, scholars are fond of contrasting British and American financial systems that rely heavily on equity markets with German ones that favor banks (e.g., Calomiris 1995; Guinnane 2002). The last decade of the twentieth century was a heady time for the United States and other stock exchange-based economies, and it might seem reasonable to decide, therefore, that equity markets are superior to banks, even though Germany's difficulties probably have more to do with the costs of unification than with the fluctuations of its banking system. Yet, before German and Japanese financial structures are confined to the historical dustbin, we should bear in mind the stellar long-term performance of both economies during the long period from 1870 to 1990. Which financial system is better at promoting long-term growth, even with fluctuations, is thus still an unsettled question, and answering it will necessarily involve economic history. It also will have to take into account political economy and do so in two ways: first, because governments bear much responsibility for the original structure of financial institutions; and second, because governments are themselves major consumers of financial resources and their thirst for debt is almost unquenchable.

This volume follows Davis's call for research on the role of financial institutions and intermediaries in economic development, although it does not provide final answers to all the questions he has raised – a task that would take far more than a single volume. In particular, the volume takes a broad view of finance and intermediation, as it examines changes in England, France, Canada, and the United States over the past several centuries. A first set of essays probes the evolution and impact of differing financial institutions in two European countries. Larry Neal and Stephen Quinn analyze the role of bankers and merchants in the development of London as a major center of European finance in the seventeenth century. They put special emphasis on the innovation of private and decentralized clearing systems in London. Philip T. Hoffman, Gilles Postel-Vinay, and Jean-Laurent Rosenthal then focus on the competition during the first half of the nineteenth century between two important Parisian financial intermediaries, bankers and notaries. They argue that this competition drove innovation and risk taking in the financial system. Angela Redish next describes the importance of the mortgage market in Ontario, Canada, in the first half of the nineteenth century. Dianne Newell sketches the developing west coast salmon cannery industry in the late nineteenth and early twentieth centuries, with stress on the means and mechanisms of intra- and inter-ethnic entrepreneurial borrowings. John Legler and Richard Sylla evaluate the performance of the stock market in the U.S. South after the Civil War. And the final paper in the Americas section, by Ken Snowden, deals with the initial rise and collapse of a financial institution of more limited scope but of great importance to local economic development in the United States – savings and loan associations.

Together, this group of essays stresses the role of private enterprise in the development of financial markets. All the chapters take the legal and political context as given and downplay the role of political and administrative reforms. They in fact imply that what enabled private initiative was not reform but rather benign public neglect – public neglect in the context of a relatively stable legal and political structure. In this setting, financial innovation took place when new intermediaries appeared or old ones delved into new areas of finance. Both Neal and Quinn and Hoffman, Postel-Vinay, and Rosenthal go even further: They point out how financial crises, far from always being disasters for financial markets, can sometimes generate responses that promote financial innovation. One broad implication of their research and of the other essays in this first group is, therefore, a call for a new direction in current research on institutions, particularly legal ones. In particular, the legal factors that scholars currently devote so much attention to are in fact unlikely to explain the secular evolution of financial markets in developed economies. Prior to World War II at least, North America and Northwest Europe grew despite different legal regimes and despite periodic bouts of political and economic instability. Economic growth was widespread because politicians in these countries recognized how important finance was, and they, therefore, allowed a broad array of private financial intermediaries to operate. This broad array allowed the financial sector to quickly respond to new challenges as the economy developed

The second set of essays in the volume deal with a broad view of finance and intermediation. We now recognize that capital flows are quite complex processes. We must begin by acknowledging that nonfinancial assets have had a significant effect on economic change and that they are often transferred through channels other than banks or brokerage houses. Hence, it is worthwhile to integrate the study of financial markets with the study of other asset markets. In a different vein, the development of financial institutions also entails a significant role for politics. Governments are after all important borrowers or lenders, and thus they care directly about financial markets. Moreover, governments provide the regulatory framework for asset markets, and they tend to get more involved with these markets as economic development proceeds. At the same time, governments can use fiscal policies to redistribute incomes among individuals, as well as political units, leaving an impact on relative economic growth and distribution and affecting the demand in asset markets. As a result, governments can either promote private asset markets or discourage them.

The major issues in the second set of essays relate to the transmission of assets, broadly defined. Two of the essays focus on the private sector. In the first, Naomi Lamoreaux and Kenneth Sokoloff examine intellectual property rights. Their essay, which takes up an understudied aspect of the market for technology, underscores the importance of trade in patents among individuals and firms, both directly and with the assistance of specialized intermediaries. In the case of the market for technology, intermediation arose to facilitate the transfer of new technologies from inventors to those firms best positioned to commercially exploit them. But that market was based on the government's patent system. In a similar vein, Eugene White describes how the Paris Bourse emerged in the eighteenth and nineteenth centuries. Early on this market focused on privately held government securities, but the government continuously intervened to limit innovation by the Bourse. The government intervention, in turn, reduced the importance of the stock exchange in the French economy. The final two papers place the government even closer to center stage: Robert Allen describes the role of finance in Soviet economic development between 1928 and 1939, explaining the battery of measures put in place by the central planning authorities to raise investment rates in manufacturing. Finally, Michael Bordo, Michael Edelstein, and Hugh Rockoff focus on how the adoption of the gold standard during the interwar period promoted the existence of an important intangible asset, financial credibility.

This second group of essays highlights the tremendous complementarities between public and private institutions: For instance, a market for intellectual property rights can hardly exist without patents, but the value of patents, in turn, depends on private agents and institutions. They also emphasize the uneven relationship between private and public institutions when it comes to finance: The government exerts tremendous influence on the structure of these markets, on the assets that get traded, and (at least in the twentieth century) on the direction of investment flows. Although the Soviet Union is clearly an extreme case, in the twentieth century most governments rich or poor have intervened heavily in capital markets via development banks, capital flow restrictions, or distortionary taxation. Issues of monetary stability, public and private institutional coordination, and investment flows are often thought to be modern problems, but as these essays show, they have a long history, even before globalization.

If this volume has any single lesson, it is that finance and intermediaries are critical to the process of economic growth. Intermediaries make possible more effective exchange in an economy; they also create developed markets that link nations together via flows of capital. To succeed, however, the intermediaries must inspire confidence in savers, a difficult task given the obstacles to creating and maintaining trust. Among the many obstacles are macroeconomic risks like inflation, government intervention, limitations of the legal system, and microeconomic hazards – not least of which is the fear that the intermediary will exploit his position of trust for his own benefit. Hence, the economic history of these intermediaries is often two faced, extolling their virtues on the one hand but also assailing them for the crises they provoke on the other. Although many observers have complained about the instability that banks and other financial intermediaries have periodically caused, instability is an inherent part of the process of growth, and we must not forget that these intermediaries have been a key element in the process of economic growth in those countries lucky enough to have achieved it.

Stanley L. Engerman
Philip T. Hoffman
Jean-Laurent Rosenthal
Kenneth L. Sokoloff

Bibliography

Acemoglu, Daron, Simon Johnson, and James A. Robinson. "The Colonial Origins of Comparative Development: An Empirical Investigation," *American Economic Review* 91 (Dec. 2001): 1369–1401.

Beck, Thorsten, Ross Levine, and Norman Loayza. "Finance and the Sources of Growth," *Journal of Financial Economics* 58 (Oct./Nov. 2000): 261–300.

Calomiris, Charles W. "The Costs of Rejecting Universal Banking: American Finance in the German Mirror, 1870–1914," in *Coordination and Information: Historical Perspectives on the Organization of Enterprise*, eds. Naomi R. Lamoreaux and Daniel M. G. Raff. Chicago: University of Chicago Press, 1995, 257–315.

Davis, Lance E. "The Investment Market, 1870–1914: The Evolution of a National Market," *Journal of Economic History* 25 (Sept. 1965): 355–99.

Davis, Lance E., and Larry Neal. "Micro Rules and Macro Outcomes' the Impact of Micro Structure on the Efficiency of Security Exchanges, London, New York, and Paris, 1800–1914," *American Economic Review* 88 (May 1998): 40–45.

Davis, Lance E., and Robert J. Cull. *International Capital Markets and American Economic Growth, 1820–1914*. Cambridge: Cambridge University Press, 1994.

Davis, Lance E., and Robert Gallman. "Capital Formation in the United States During the Nineteenth Century," in *The Cambridge Economic History of Europe*. Vol. 7, pt. 2, eds. P. Mathias and M. M. Postan. Cambridge: Cambridge University Press, 1978, 1–69, 495–503, 557–61.

———, and Robert Gallman. *Evolving Financial Markets and International Capital Flows: Britain, the Americas, and Australia, 1865–1914*. Cambridge: Cambridge University Press, 2001.

Davis, Lance E., and Robert A. Huttenback. *Mammon and the Pursuit of Empire: The Economics of British Imperialism*. Cambridge: Cambridge University Press, 1986.

Davis, Lance E., and Douglass C. North. *Institutional Change and American Economic Growth*. Cambridge: Cambridge University Press, 1971.

Engerman, Stanley L., and Kenneth L. Sokoloff. "Factor Endowments, Institutions, and Differential Paths of Growth among New World Economies: A View from Economic Historians of the United States," in *How Latin America Fell Behind: Essays on the Economic Histories of Brazil and Mexico, 1800–1914*, ed. Stephen Haber. Stanford: Stanford University Press, 1997, 260–304.

Goldsmith, Raymond W. *Financial Structure and Economic Development*. New Haven: Yale University Press, 1969.

Guinnane, T. "Delegated Monitors, Large and Small: Germany's Banking System, 1800–1914," *Journal of Economic Literature* 40 (March 2002): 73–124.

La Porta, Rafael, Florencio Lopez de Silanes, Andrei Shleifer, and Robert W. Vishny. "Law and Finance," *Journal of Political Economy* 106 (Dec. 1998): 1113–55.

———. "Legal Determinants of External Finance," *Journal of Finance* 52 (July 1997): 1131–50.

Rajan, Raghuram G., and Luigi Zingales. "The Great Reversals: The Politics of Financial Development in the Twentieth Century," National Bureau of Economic Research Paper 8178, Cambridge, MA, March 2001.

I

FINANCIAL INTERMEDIARIES IN EUROPE

I

Markets and Institutions in the Rise of London as a Financial Center in the Seventeenth Century

Larry Neal and Stephen Quinn

Informal networks are an important technology in financial development, and successful formal systems have usually replaced previously successful informal systems. Recent examples in the U.S. include the development of venture capital firms and the rise of NASDAQ from the previous over-the-counter market for small capital equities. For earlier examples, Lance Davis has highlighted the importance of personal relationships for effective financial intermediation in the early national development of the U.S. economy. The Savings Bank of Baltimore, while drawing on the deposits of numerous small investors, was owned by the wealthy few of Baltimore, the 134 original incorporators responsible for electing annually the twenty-five directors who oversaw the daily operations of the bank. Over time, the bank became professionally managed, maintaining an arm's length relationship to the borrowing needs of its stockholders.[1] For New England textile mills, which borrowed both short and long term from a wide range of intermediaries and individuals in the period 1840–1860, Lance Davis also found that individual lenders often reappeared in a given firm's accounts as the source of special loans in times of crisis, often at higher rates than were enforceable under usury laws.[2]

In addition to the evidence of important personal, presumably informal, relationships on both the savings and the investment sides of financial intermediation in the early U.S. economy, Davis noted a number of English precedents. Savings banks in the U.S. were typically based on the ideas of the national savings banks formed in Britain after the Napoleonic Wars. Also, the varieties of lending sources available to New England textile mills

[1] Peter Payne and Lance E. Davis, *The Savings Bank of Baltimore, 1818–1866: A Historical and Analytical Study* (Baltimore: The Johns Hopkins Press, 1956): Chapter IV. In special cases, however, Johns Hopkins had access to renewed and enlarged loans, sometimes at favorable rates, so that personal connections still mattered.
[2] Lance E. Davis, "The New England Textile Mills and the Capital Markets: A Study of Industrial Borrowing 1840–1860," *Journal of Economic History* 20 (March 1960): 1–30.

all had their English antecedents, from trade credit extended by merchant houses to loans by country banks to mortgages from individuals.[3]

The effectiveness of the English-style intermediation depended on an integrated financial system within which each component could contribute its comparative advantage. Integration was secured through a deep, highly liquid, market for bills of exchange in London that mobilized short-term credit. An integrated market for short-term, essentially mercantile, credit arose in England and in Northwest Europe well before an integrated market for long-term credit or bonds. Davis noted a similar situation in his study of New England textile mills, where he found that interest rates charged for short-term loans moved together regardless of the location or category of lender, whereas long-term rates varied widely depending on the institutional and legal constraints inhibiting the respective lenders. English, and eventually Scottish, industrial development also relied initially on short-term credit extended via inland bills of exchange that used London as a domestic hub in the eighteenth century. The inland bill of exchange, in turn, was an offshoot of the prior success of London as an international hub for foreign bills of exchange. By the end of the seventeenth century, this bill market reached from London to the rest of Europe and across the Atlantic. Although the bill market would become formalized through discount houses and Bank of England branches after 1825,[4] the system began informally long before through a network of merchants and bankers that connected London to the world economy.

International credit market integration in the late seventeenth century required the ability to take advantage of favorable exchange rate differentials with regard to geographic location (London, Amsterdam, Paris, and others) and media of exchange (bills of exchange and bullion). London-based bankers acquired this ability by using a network of merchants and bankers that spanned nations, religions, and trade specializations. This network was more diverse than the kin groups, religious connections, or guilds that had supported the rise of international trade during the Middle Ages. Members of the London network were bound by financial interaction revolving around the banking center of London. By using bills of exchange written between a banker and his agent, merchants became stakeholders in the monitoring and enforcement of agency relationships. The efficacy of the network, however, did vary with the nature of a nation's legal system. We find that the autocratic tendencies of France diminished the credibility

---

[3] Larry Neal, "The Finance of Business during the Industrial Revolution," in *The Economic History of Britain*, vol. 1, 1700–1860, 2nd ed., eds. Roderick Floud and Donald N. McCloskey (Cambridge: Cambridge University Press, 1994): 151–81; and Stephen Quinn, "Finance and Capital Markets" in *The Cambridge Economic History of Britain*, vol. 1, 1700–1860, 3rd ed., eds. Roderick Floud and Paul Johnson (Cambridge: Cambridge University Press, forthcoming).

[4] W. T. C. King, *History of the London Discount Market* (London: George Routledge & Sons, 1936).

of agents, whereas the Dutch and English commitment to international commercial law strengthened overseas enforcement.

With information flows crisscrossing Northern Europe, London-based bankers could successfully specialize in the supply of international financing. Merchants both secured the system for the bankers and benefited from the services provided by the bankers. Essential to the character of London's emerging financial system was the lack of a singular institution to coordinate information. A substantial network was in place as early as 1670. By the founding of the Bank of England in 1694, London did not require a Dutch-style exchange bank to support the system of international payments. Instead, the Bank of England was designed along the lines of the other fractional reserve banks that already formed a close-knit network within London. At the turn of the eighteenth century, no single bank in London dominated the market for bills of exchange. Rather, deepening channels of finance enmeshed the bankers of Lombard Street with agents in various ports and the many merchants who connected them.

Examining the ledgers from the late seventeenth century of Edward Backwell, the preeminent goldsmith–banker at the time, we find that Backwell relied on the existing network of foreign merchants to connect himself to overseas agents. The goldsmith made merchants his stakeholding partners in the process of moving funds and monitoring the behavior of his primary agents with whom he held covering balances in foreign currencies. With his arrangement of primary agents and multiple monitors, Backwell and other London bankers were supplying bills, offering discounts, and arranging bullion shipments by 1670. Although London was not yet the banking center that would come to dominate international finance, it was creating a new style of banking and payment system that would form an integral part of the financial revolution. The English system was oriented to an active market in bills of foreign exchange, a market that was unregulated but disciplined by English law, based on existing law merchant for dealings in goods. Even after the establishment of the Bank of England, this payment system continued to flourish, focused increasingly on Amsterdam and Hamburg rather than Paris or Madrid. In the merchant-controlled cities of London, Amsterdam, and Hamburg, the law merchant governed the settlement of disputes arising from protested bills of exchange. In the royal cities of Paris and Madrid, by contrast, the often-arbitrary law of the monarch could disrupt the web of credit that supported the prospering trade of Western Europe.

We then find that the practices of arbitrage[5] in foreign exchange, making foreign payments that took advantage of minor fluctuations in

---

[5] "Arbitrage" in this period meant comparing exchange rates on foreign bills of exchange to find the cheapest means of payment. Only since World War II has it come to mean simultaneous buying low in one market and selling high in another market, implying riskless profit taking. See the extended discussion in Geoffrey Poitras, *The Early History of Financial Economics, 1478–1776* (Cheltenham, UK: Edward Elgar, 2000): 243–50.

cross-exchange rates from the mint par ratios, were already emerging in the Restoration period of London, well before the revolution in public finance that occurred after 1688. Again, the evidence is taken from the complex payments arranged by Edward Backwell among his agents in Cadiz and Amsterdam. By the middle of the eighteenth century, Postlethwayt's *Universal Dictionary of Trade and Commerce* could devote many pages to describing these payment alternatives taken by London merchants. That this system survived the systemic shocks of several major wars and the financial crisis of 1720 testifies to the inherent durability of trade networks when credit and payment networks sustain them. It is the credit nexus established in the seventeenth century, more so than the preceding kinship, religious, or political nexuses, that sustained the long-run development of trade relationships in Northern Europe.

Finally, we examine in detail how enforcement procedures in case of credit default could be invoked in the London–Amsterdam nexus by contrast to the arbitrary rules set in Paris. The evidence derives from the systemic crisis that affected all of Europe with the collapse of both the Mississippi bubble in France and the South Sea bubble in England. In the general collapse of the European payments system, a diamond merchant in Amsterdam tried to force payment by another merchant banker in Amsterdam of bills drawn on him by a goldsmith-banker in London. At the same time, the Amsterdam diamond merchant had to deal with default by a merchant–banker in London. The different procedures followed in the two cases of default and the different outcomes that emerged in London and Amsterdam demonstrate the long-run viability of the merchant-oriented legal system. The "bubbles" episode was a defining moment for the competing systems of London and Paris – thereafter in the eighteenth century, financial relationships flourished between London and Amsterdam, with spillover to Hamburg and the Baltic, while the French and Mediterranean connections languished.

Networks

As networks of European trade developed, with Amsterdam at the center, the supply of bills of exchange became a viable commercial specialization, not only in Amsterdam but also at each of the outlying nodes. Bills of exchange were orders to pay in a foreign port in a foreign currency at some time in the future. Bills were similar to modern travelers' checks, and were the dominant means of international payment in the early modern era. Instead of merchants arranging all the elements needed for a bill, third party intermediaries supplied credit or other services. This innovation in financial intermediation liberated individual traders from the costs of maintaining foreign contacts, settling their offsetting accounts, acquiring credit information on foreign traders, and other costly activities. As the number of merchants who dealt with foreign markets within Europe increased, the value added by the suppliers of financial intermediation became greater. In London, at least, these services became concentrated in bankers. From the middle of the seventeenth century, these bankers were transforming from goldsmiths to purely financial businesses.

The supply of international services required agents in foreign ports. The principal–agent problem faced by London-based bankers was of particular importance because the city was evolving into a new kind of hub for international finance, a hub without an exchange bank. An exchange bank like Amsterdam's held specie deposits on which bills of exchange could be written.[6] Such banks brought many advantages to suppliers of bills. The transaction cost of settling bills was reduced by the clearing of accounts within the bank (in banco); risk was also reduced because default meant expulsion from the bank. Both of these features – reduction of transactions cost and reduction of default risk – enjoyed increasing returns as more merchants participated in the exchange bank. Because the Exchange Bank acted as a clearinghouse for international payments, it centralized information of default and orchestrated ostracism of the defaulter. The city of Amsterdam required all bills of exchange above 300 guilders to be processed through the city's exchange bank, so network economies of scope were enjoyed.[7] Indeed, funds on deposit at the *Wisselbank* enjoyed a persistent premium (*agio*) over circulating coins.[8]

The differences between London and Amsterdam translated into divergent paths of development. Founded in 1609, the Amsterdam Exchange Bank replaced the paper notes then being issued by cashiers and money changers.[9] As a result, the development of Amsterdam's private banking system appears to have been constrained for a century.[10] In the absence of an exchange bank, London developed a strong banking system. Individual bankers supplied deposits, means of payment, lending, and money changing.[11] As a group, the bankers offered mutual acceptance and systemic monitoring.[12] To offer overseas services, London bankers had to arrange a network of international monitoring without the benefit of a centralized institution. A measure of

---

[6] J. G. van Dillen, "The Bank of Amsterdam," in *History of the Principal Public Banks*, ed. J. G. van Dillen (The Hague: Nijhoff, 1934): 73–123.

[7] W. D. H. Assar, "Bills of Exchange and Agency in the 18th Century Law of Holland and Zeeland," in *The Courts and the Development of Commercial Law* ed. Vito Piergiovanni (Berlin: Dunaker and Humbolt, 1987): 103–30.

[8] J. McCusker, *Money and Exchange in Europe and America, 1600–1775: A Handbook*, (Chapel Hill: University of North Carolina Press, 1978): 46–51.

[9] Pit Dehing, and Marjolein 't Hart, "Linking the Fortunes: Currency and Banking, 1550–1800," in *A Financial History of the Netherlands*, eds. Marjolein 't Hart, Joost Jonker, and J. L. van Zanden (New York: Cambridge University Press, 1997): 43.

[10] Dehing and 't Hart, "Linking the Fortunes," 43–4.

[11] R. D. Richards, *The Early History of Banking in England* (London: P. S. King & Son, 1929): 23–4.

[12] S. Quinn, "Goldsmith-Banking: Mutual Acceptance and Inter-Banker Clearing In Restoration London," *Explorations in Economic History* 34 (October 1997): 412.

London's success in this regard was that when the Bank of England was founded in 1694, it was as a fractional reserve, note-issuing bank patterned on existing banks. The London financial system had developed to the point that the new corporate bank was not created to dominate the London bill market or act as a clearinghouse.

Individual London bankers could handle their foreign contacts in a variety of ways. The most secure arrangement was to send an employee abroad. However, such employees were expensive to maintain and were limited to primary markets only.[13] An alternative was to retain correspondents on a for-fee basis. This scheme reduced costs relative to maintaining employees. For an individual banker in London, the cost of placing employees in numerous continental cities was prohibitive. Because goldsmiths ran shops with only a few apprentices or clerks, the agent-based system was adopted.

The archetypal principal–agent relationship was based on merchants who agreed to accept each other's bills for a fee and then settle the balance by creating an offsetting bill.[14] "In such cases, Amsterdam merchants accepted bills drawn on them for the account of others and covered themselves by redrawing."[15] Transaction costs were kept low because offsetting bills meant specie did not have to be transported. Vesting overseas agents with fiduciary power, however, created the risk of misbehavior. Kinship or religious ties were often insufficient to cover the wide network of commerce that had developed by this era. Creation of reputation effects by repeated business was another important tool. Agents with much to gain from future business were less likely to cheat. When the goldsmith–banker Edward Backwell set up a web of foreign agents, he usually concentrated his foreign business on only one correspondent per city. In this way, the banker generated considerable business with a trusted agent. Building this reputation was a service that Backwell supplied to customers who could not manage such levels of activity on their own.

Concentrated business, however, still left risk for the banker. The London banker had to be aware of trouble before punishment could be pursued. The arrangement would be more effective if news of malfeasance could be spread to damage the agent's reputation with other principals. London-based bankers needed to generate a flow of information sufficient to extend reputation effects to a network of bankers and merchants. In this way, a default to one member became known and punished by the whole. By the middle of the eighteenth century, such reputation effects were well established.

---

[13] J. Price, "Transaction Costs: A Note on Merchant Credit and the Organization of Private Trade," in *The Political Economy of Merchant Empires*, ed. J. D. Tracy (Cambridge: Cambridge University Press, 1991): 279.

[14] L. Neal, *The Rise of Financial Capitalism* (New York: Cambridge University Press, 1990): 5–9.

[15] Price, "Transaction Costs," 283–84.

The conduits for this information were merchants. Seventeenth century merchants passed information between ports constantly. One family firm was found to have saved 10,500 letters over the years 1668 to 1680.[16] The correspondence of merchants brim with all manner of information. News of market conditions, war, exchange rates, bankruptcies, and anything else of interest was routinely shared. The letters were saved because they formed a record of advice given, orders received, and actions taken. If a merchant had to explain why a shipment was lost, why a venture was unprofitable, or why he could not pay his bills, the letters could clear his good name. Published price currents complemented this effort by providing a third party record.[17] Even though Amsterdam was clearly the hub for distributing commercial information at this time,[18] London was able to exploit effectively the information channels that existed in northern Europe.

The financial side of this correspondence was the bill of exchange. Merchants saved copies of bills for the same reasons they kept letters. Unlike letters, bills represented payments, and merchants named in the bills became stakeholders in the payment process. A default, like a bounced check, affected all named parties. The individuals added by endorsement after the original bill was drawn were also dragged into any failed performance because, if the bill was not paid, everyone who endorsed the bill became liable. The Dutch developed transfer by endorsement in the sixteenth century specifically as a means to involve merchants in the quality of the bills they passed. The English adopted the system.[19]

By using merchants to pass funds to agents abroad, bankers like Edward Backwell took advantage of the incentives that bills created. When the banker accepted or wrote bills involving his foreign agents, his ledger clearly named the merchants involved. For example, on March 28, 1670, the banker Edward Backwell drew a bill of exchange ordering Henry and Charles Gerard to pay William Jarret 2,080 guilders.[20] The Gerards were Backwell's agents in Amsterdam. Should the Gerards have failed to pay as ordered, Jarret would become a party to the dispute. Similarly, any merchant to whom Jarret transferred the bill to would also become involved. Jarret had clear

---

[16] H. Roseveare, *Markets and Merchants of the Late Seventeenth Century* (Oxford: Oxford University Press, 1987), 14.

[17] C. Gravesteijn and J. J. McCusker, *The Beginnings of Commercial and Financial Journalism* (Amsterdam: NEHA, 1991), 43–53.

[18] Woodruff D. Smith, "The Functions of Commercial Centers in the Modernization of European Capitalism: Amsterdam as an Information Exchange in the Seventeenth Century," *Journal of Economic History* 44 (December 1984): 985–1005; and Michel Morineau, *Incroyables Gazettes et Fabuleux Metaux* (Cambridge: Cambridge University Press, 1985).

[19] J. Rogers, *The Early History of the Law of Bills and Notes* (Cambridge: Cambridge University Press, 1995); and J. M. Holden, *The History of Negotiable Instruments in English Law* (London: Athlone Press, 1955).

[20] Royal Bank of Scotland, London, Backwell Ledger S, 1670–71, folio 41.

incentive to know that the bill was honored and settled. The merchants had a stake in monitoring Backwell's agent and would spread word of default to their colleagues.

We also know London bankers and their agents used a large number of different merchants for each port to send and receive bills. Although the banker might want to move large sums overseas, individual merchants wanted small bills in line with their smaller transactions. Thus, a number of merchants were used, which thickened the credit nexus and supplied multiple monitors for each agent. The effect was strengthened by integrating different religious and geographic communities. Each group added its internal system of monitoring and reputation to the whole. For example, on October 15, 1669, Backwell paid Abraham Doportos for a bill drawn and sold by the Gerards in Amsterdam to Simon Nunes Enriques and Simon Soares of Hamburg.[21] On August 23 of the same year, Backwell paid Jo. Patters for a bill drawn by the Gerards on Jo. Vandercloet of Rotterdam.[22] George and Robert Shaw of Antwerp drew bills on Backwell by way of Engeld Muyhuk, Albertus Lunden, Barnardo Bree of Brussels, and Bartholomew van Berchen of Bruge.[23] Backwell had a wide range of merchants also moving between London and Middleburg, Hamburg, Cadiz, Seville, and Paris.

The problem with a diverse body of merchants was passing news of default on to others and organizing collective action. Here banks in London helped solve the problem. In Amsterdam, the city's Exchange Bank monitored and enforced all bills clearing through the city. In London, the system of individual banks mimicked the same role. Word of an agent's behavior would pass back to the banker through the injured merchant and protested bill. The banker then passed word to the numerous other merchants who held accounts in London. The banker also had a regular channel to the other bankers in the city via regular, bilateral clearing arrangements.[24] The web tightened further because merchants banked with more than one shop. For example, on July 13, 1669, Backwell paid Sir John Frederick and Company for a bill drawn by the Gerards in Amsterdam after passing through the shop of another goldsmith–banker, John Lindsay.[25] A number of other London bankers also appear in the process of moving bills to Backwell.

Use of multiple merchants per banker and multiple bankers per merchant expanded the network's ability to spread information. For example, the Gerards of Amsterdam received bills from Backwell from over twenty different merchants over the twelve months from March 1670 to March 1671. Default by the Gerards would spread to a large number of merchants that

---

[21] Backwell Ledger R, 1669–70, folio 481.
[22] Backwell Ledger R, 1669–70, folio 63.
[23] Backwell Ledger S, 1670–1, folios 76, 328.
[24] Quinn, "Goldsmith–Banking," 418–24.
[25] Backwell Ledger R, 1669–70, folio 62.

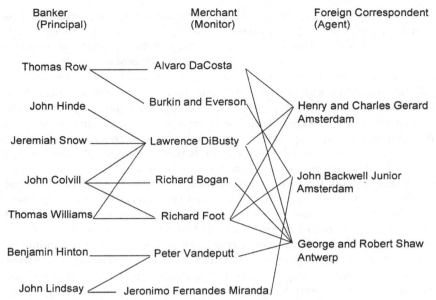

FIGURE 1.1. An Example of the Connections between Bankers, Merchants, and Foreign Agents in 1670
Source: Edward Backwell's Ledger S, 1670–1, folios 24, 92, 326, 337, 379, 383, and 442.

would expand the scope of damage to the Gerards' reputation. Also, these merchants often banked with more than one goldsmith in London. Again, these contacts would spread knowledge of improper behavior. Figure 1.1 connects seven merchants that presented bills from the Low Countries to Backwell in London and then transferred their resulting credit on the banker's ledger to other goldsmith–bankers. These examples are very exclusive because they do not consider the many merchants who presented bills to Backwell but did not bank with him. Such bills would have been settled by cash, note, or some other form of payment, rather than by ledger credit. More, the examples in Figure 1.1 also do not include merchant transactions with goldsmiths other than Backwell (listed in Backwell's ledger) who were not directly associated with a bill of exchange. Merchants banking with Backwell regularly transferred funds to other bankers. Even under these restrictive terms, a substantial number of goldsmith–merchant–agent connections existed in the year 1670.

The British East India Company also used the same arrangements. When engaged in continental bullion purchases in 1675, the East India Company used the same agents as Backwell: the Gerards in Amsterdam; the Banks in Hamburg; Rowland Dee in Cadiz; and Benjamin Bathurst in

Seville.[26] Moreover, the company used numerous prominent merchants and London goldsmith–bankers to pass the funds.[27] The strong similarities between the banker and the East India Company in their payment procedures suggested this was common practice in seventeenth century London.

Another common element between the East India Company and the goldsmith–banker was that covering balances with agents. In contrast to a correspondent relationship premised on credit, both the company and the banker regularly built up balances with their agents in advance of drawing bills payable by those agents. This was an expensive arrangement because neither operation earned interest on funds placed abroad. However, when the East India Company or Edward Backwell sent a bill, the agent already owed that amount. Covering balances made an agent's failure to honor a bill a failure to retire debt rather than a failure to extend credit. One benefit was that the agent would not have to create an offsetting bill, so the likelihood of acceptance would increase. A second benefit was that not honoring an order to pay backed by a debt was a more serious matter than failing to extend credit. By analogy, today a credit card has more latitude in denying funds than a demand deposit. The law regarding debt was well advanced by the seventeenth century, whereas that binding agents to credit-granting commitments was less clear.[28]

The potential problem of establishing that an agent in Amsterdam actually owed a principal in London was mitigated by the use of merchants to transfer funds. Merchants witnessed the transfer of funds and had incentives to see that those transfers were honored and remembered. Merchants formed the spokes and bankers the hub of the London network. The flow of information was necessary for London-based bankers to conduct overseas finance.

Arbitrage

The incentive for bankers and merchants to cooperate in operating the web of credit and information lay in the profits to be earned, and shared, in the arbitrage of foreign exchange. For example, bankers could offer bills between pairs of ports to capture favorable exchange rate differences. By increasing demand for bills denominated in weaker currencies and increasing the supply of bills denominated in stronger currencies, banker networks created a flow of funds that narrowed exchange rate differentials. Whereas the integration of eighteenth century exchange markets has been quantitatively established, data to perform similar tests for the seventeenth century are not available.[29]

---

[26] India Record Office, London, East India Company Ledger 1673–5, L/AG/1/1/6.
[27] East India Company Ledger 1673–5, L/AG/1/1/6.
[28] Assar, "Bills of Exchange and Agency"; and Rogers, *Early History*.
[29] E. Schubert, "Arbitrage in the Foreign Exchange Markets of London and Amsterdam During the 18th Century," *Explorations in Economic History* 26 (January 1989): 1–20; and Neal, *Rise of Financial Capitalism*.

In place of market data on exchange rates, we use the accounts of leading banking firms to show that bankers and merchants took advantage of differences between direct rates and cross rates throughout the network of leading European ports well before 1700. This, incidentally, shows that the origins of international market integration arose well before 1700 and before the revolution in English public finance in the 1690s.

A network of agents was necessary for taking advantage of exchange rate and cross-exchange rate opportunities. More, such networks could provide spatial economies of scale. The marginal effect of adding one more information node to a network increased geometrically with the increased size of the network. Adding Hamburg to a London–Amsterdam network added two cross connections: Hamburg–London and Hamburg–Amsterdam. Adding Paris to the Hamburg–London–Amsterdam network would add three links and so on. Each new link expanded the returns from the fixed investment embodied in existing nodes and opened new cross-market opportunities. The profits to be shared among participants engaged in effective arbitrage maintained the cohesion of the credit network as it expanded.

With regular correspondence, dealers in bills of exchange would know when differences in rates developed between ports. "When such local disequilibria occurred it was natural for the more adventurous dealers to practice arbitrage – dealing with a third centre whenever rates on a second centre might prove more advantageous."[30] Henry Roseveare found that the London merchant Jacob David moved his funds from Amsterdam to Antwerp to take advantage of cross-rate imbalances in 1676.[31] More, David did this on the advice he had received by letter from his underwriter, Claude Hays. At other times, David routed funds via Amsterdam and Venice on the way to Hamburg.[32]

Edward Backwell engaged in similar arbitrage behavior at an even earlier date. Much of Backwell's foreign transactions involved supplying funding for the English fleet provisioned out of Cadiz. Backwell provided banking services to the famous diarist Samuel Pepys and other purchasing agents for the Royal Navy.[33] For example, on February 9, 1671, Backwell drew bills due on Rowland Dee, Junior, of Cadiz for 15,000 pieces of eight (£3,375). Dee's account with Backwell recorded payment of the bill to Sir Hugh Cholmely at 20 days sight, value of Samuel Pepys. Because of his various agents, the banker could also supply bills directly between Spain and the Low Countries. After supplying the Royal Navy with silver and honoring bills drawn in London by Backwell, Rowland Dee balanced his accounts with the banker by drawing bills both on London and on Backwell's agents in Amsterdam.

---

30 Roseveare, *Markets and Merchants*, 53.
31 Roseveare, *Markets and Merchants*, 593.
32 Roseveare, *Markets and Merchants*, 593
33 Richards, *Early History of Banking*, 74–5.

FIGURE 1.2. An Example of Arbitrage between Cadiz and London via Amsterdam in 1670
Source: See note 34.

In the twelve months starting in March 1670, Dee drew £6,000 worth of bills directly on London. The Cadiz agent drew an additional £3,769 worth of bills on the banker's agents in Amsterdam and £4,474 on the goldsmith's agents in Antwerp.[34]

The timing of Dee's bills, however, was most important. Rowland Dee switched from drawing bills on London to only drawing bills on the Low Countries in the Fall of 1670. This would have benefited Backwell in London. Through the summer of 1670, Dee drew bills on London at a rate of 48.5 pence/peso (2 month bills). When Dee switched to Amsterdam and Antwerp in September and October, the Dutch schellingen had already appreciated against the pound by two and a half percent since May (34.6 Sch/£ in May to 35.5 in September). When the Dutch schellingen reached 36 to the English pound in October of 1670, Dee's pesos-via-Holland were only costing Backwell 47 English pence a piece instead of the 48.5 they had during the summer.[35] That was a 3 percent gain. With the winter of 1670–1, the Dutch rate strengthened relative to Spain as well, so the cross-rate differential favoring the Low Countries was eliminated. In February of 1671, Rowland Dee resumed drawing bills directly on London. Figure 1.2 presents a schematic of Backwell's arbitrage behavior.

The ability to switch financial channels was evident. Merchants and bankers had the means to capture favorable cross-rates. Moreover, the information the network provided would have been essential to successful manipulation of exchange rate differentials. Eric Schubert has described arbitrage between markets for bills as uncertain.[36] From the perspective of pricing bills, uncertainty entered into the demand for bills. Consider a

---

[34] Backwell Ledger S, 1670–71 with Dee in Cadiz, folios 300, 320, 593, 595; Gerard in Amsterdam, folios 41, 443, 444; Shaws in Antwerp, folios 76, 328, 573.

[35] The calculation was (117 grooten/ducata)(0.72533 ducata/peso)(0.08333 schellingen/grooten)[1/(36 schellingen/£)](240 pence/£) = 47.15 pence/peso. Denominational relationships from McCusker, *Money and Exchange*, 44, 61, 99–100, 107.

[36] Schubert, "Arbitrage."

market for bills in London. Information regarding the supply of pounds would be apparent to all parties in London. The demand side, however, was comprised of agents for merchants in Amsterdam and other cities wanting to buy pounds with their schellingen, pesos, and so on. For those trying to price a bill in London, information on actual demand would be as old as the latest ships crossing the channel. Expectations of demand arriving from foreign ports would play a discriminating role. A supplier of bills in London with better information about conditions in Amsterdam would have an advantage. "Good manners, if not explicit instructions, required merchants in most European centres to keep their customers informed of the current rates of exchange."[37] The better the information, the faster markets would tighten the weave of cross-rates. The same information was also essential for financial speculation as well. The implicit rate of return on bills was speculative because it relied on re-exchange.[38] The return to *dry exchange*, meaning rolling over the value of a bill into a bill due back at the initial port, depended on the exchange rate in the foreign port when the first bill fell due. Information from abroad reduced the risk of speculation by improving estimates of where foreign exchange markets were moving.

The network also aided the flow of bullion. In late 1669, Backwell drew down some of his account with the Gerards of Amsterdam by having the agents buy bullion and coin. On the banker's behalf, the Amsterdam agents acquired Spanish pistoles and pieces of eight, French crowns, Venetian ducats, and Dutch rixdollars, along with ingots and bars of silver and gold.[39] Market integrating arbitrage between bills and bullion required both access to and knowledge of foreign markets with Amsterdam being the key market.[40] Thus, the network of bankers and merchants provided the means to connect the many European markets for bills of exchange, gold, and silver. The question remains, how could this credit network survive repeated shocks inflicted on it by the succession of wars, revolutions, and financial crises that characterized the rest of the seventeenth century and the eighteenth century?

Enforcement

A detailed example of enforcement in action was provided by the surviving correspondence of an Amsterdam diamond merchant, Bernard van der Grift, with his principal client in London, Lord Londonderry (Thomas Pitt, Jr.)

---

[37] Roseveare, *Markets and Merchants*, 592.
[38] R. De Roover, "What is Dry Exchange? A Contribution to the Study of English Mercantilism," *Business, Banking, and Economic Thought* (1974): 183–99.
[39] Backwell Ledger R, 1669–70, folios 64, 481–2.
[40] S. Quinn, "Gold, Silver, and the Glorious Revolution: Arbitrage between Bills of Exchange and Bullion, "*Economic History Review* 49 (August 1996): 474–82.

in the years 1720–5.[41] Van der Grift was trying to collect sums owed to Londonderry by John Law, the result of a tremendous loss suffered by Law in speculating against stocks traded on the London stock market.[42] From Paris, Law had instructed his agent in London, the goldsmith–banker, George Middleton, to pay Londonderry in Amsterdam.

To make this payment, Law told Middleton to draw five bills on his Amsterdam agent, the representative of the French *Compagnie des Indes*, Abraham Mouchard. Middleton drew the bills as he was instructed, tendered them to Londonderry as partial payment of the sums owed Londonderry by Law. Londonderry then endorsed them to his agent in Amsterdam, the diamond dealer Bernard van der Grift. In each bill, Middleton asked Mouchard to pay a stated sum in Dutch bank currency to Lord Londonderry based on value received from John Law. Londonderry, in turn, endorsed it to his agent in Amsterdam, van der Grift, so that van der Grift could receive the sum and credit it to Londonderry's account with him. Middleton would write a letter of advice to Mouchard, explaining the source of funds from Law that Mouchard should use in making the payment, while Londonderry wrote to van der Grift explaining how and when he wanted the funds used for his account. Mouchard was expected to accept the bill when van der Grift presented it to him. After signing his acceptance on the bill, it would become a negotiable instrument in Amsterdam, and van der Grift could discount it for immediate cash or hold it for the two months usance allowed to Mouchard to raise the sums and pay off the bill. Londonderry had made acquaintance with van der Grift while acting as the overseas agent for his father, Thomas Pitt, Sr., also known as Governor Pitt, perhaps the wealthiest diamond merchant in London. One of the largest capital transfers of the time ultimately had to be made through the credit network previously established by traders, in this case diamond merchants in London and Amsterdam.

Earlier in the year 1720, Londonderry had sent van der Grift five bills drawn on Mouchard by John Lambert, another goldsmith–banker of the time. In his letter of June 14 to Londonderry, van der Grift explained that Mouchard had not accepted the bills for payment. Instead of protesting the bills with a notary public in Amsterdam as the first step in pursuing legal remedies against Mouchard, van der Grift this time simply returned the bills as unpaid and unaccepted to Londonderry. Here he was simply following

---

[41] This correspondence is found in a bundle of letters in Chancery Masters Exhibits at the Public Record Office in London (C108/420). All dates on van der Grift's letters are Gregorian calendar, New Style, and correspond to eleven days earlier in Britain, still on the Julian calendar, Old Style.

[42] Details of this episode are in L. Neal, "George Middleton: John Law's Goldsmith-Banker, 1727–1729," in *Entrepreneurship and the Transformation of the Economy (10th–20th Centuries)*, eds. Paul Klep and Eddy van Cauwenberghe (Leuven: Leuven University Press, 1994); and L. Neal, "'For God's Sake, Remitt Me': The Adventures of George Middleton, John Law's Goldsmith–Banker, 1712–1729," *Business and Economic History* 23 (Winter 1994): 27–60.

Londonderry's instructions, who had suspected the bills might not be covered by funds Lambert had on account with Mouchard.

When van der Grift received the new set of bills drawn on Mouchard, this time by Middleton, he was naturally concerned for his client Londonderry. Despite his reservations about the ability of both Middleton and Mouchard to carry on payments in this manner, van der Grift promised to pay the bills Londonderry drew on him "on account of the value, and credit I have for your Lordship, (and I assure your Lordship on no other accounts)."[43] Wanting to keep the continued business of Londonderry, his principal in London, van der Grift was volunteering to pay out his own cash to Londonderry's creditors whether or not he received cash from Mouchard. All he asked was that the bills drawn by Middleton on Mouchard be dated payable before the bills Londonderry drew on van der Grift, a reasonable precaution in the uncertain circumstances of the time. Van der Grift intended to cover his payments on Londonderry's behalf by drawing on money owed him in London by a Lewis Johnson and to have this remitted to him via bills of exchange. It would be in Londonderry's interest to help out van der Grift in collecting the sums owed him by Johnson, if any difficulty arose in completing that contract.

As matters developed, van der Grift found in October 1720 that his speculations on South Sea stock with his agent in London, Lewis Johnson, had come to nought. Johnson had stopped payments on bills drawn on him. Nevertheless, van der Grift insisted that he could continue to meet Londonderry's drafts on him through other balances he had owing to him in London. But now Londonderry became van der Grift's agent in London to help resolve his claims on Lewis Johnson. Meanwhile, van der Grift continued to pay off Londonderry's partners in Amsterdam by accepting bills drawn on him by Londonderry, given that this time Mouchard had accepted the bills drawn on him by Middleton. Both sets of accepted bills were negotiable instruments, but van der Grift was holding on to the bills accepted by Mouchard. Given the general knowledge in Amsterdam of the payments difficulties Mouchard was facing as his source of funds in Paris dried up, any discount of one of Mouchard's accepted bills would have incurred a heavy risk premium as well as a hefty interest charge, given the general shortage of credit in Amsterdam.

So far, all that required appeal to enforcement mechanisms, whether formal or informal, was van der Grift's claim on Lewis Johnson, which he wished to use for making payments to Londonderry in London. To initiate proceedings against Johnson while still maintaining a flow of payments to Londonderry, van der Grift suggested that Londonderry send him back the protested bills of van der Grift on Johnson and sell £1,000 of South Sea stock that van der Grift had bought earlier through Londonderry. To maintain

---

43 Public Record Office (PRO), Kew, London: Chancery Masters Exhibits, *Pitt v. Cholmondeley*, C108/420, Letter of September 24, 1720.

Londonderry's business, van der Grift had earlier sent Londonderry funds to buy shares in the rapidly rising stock of the South Sea Company, which were still being held in London by Londonderry on van der Grift's account. He assured Londonderry that even if Londonderry didn't sell the stock now, because of its low and falling price, he would remit Londonderry immediately against it, in effect pledging it as collateral for whatever payments Londonderry made on his behalf, "for his honour."[44]

In his letter of October 29, van der Grift gave Londonderry his first hint of the coming trouble with Mouchard. He noted first that the only way Mouchard was getting the means to make payment on the bills drawn on him was by gold continually sent to him from France in monthly shipments, which he pawned immediately into the *Wisselbank* (Exchange Bank). There was no silver being sent nor any other form of exchange with France, either to or from Amsterdam. While Mouchard had a considerable amount of coffee and indigo in his warehouse, that was being held on account of the French Compagnie and was not available to Mouchard either to be sold or pawned on his account. And the bills he had accepted earlier and was supposed to pay the day before had not yet been paid.[45] All this information on Mouchard's affairs was readily available to all concerned bankers and merchants in Amsterdam and could be easily confirmed by Londonderry from London.

In the next letter of November 1, 1720, van der Grift enclosed his protests on three of the bills on Mouchard that Mouchard had accepted, but not paid when due. While Mouchard appeared to van der Grift to be an honest man, if the Compagnie in France did not continue to support him he would not be able to pay the large amount of bills he had already accepted. A week later, van der Grift was informed by Mouchard that the gold he had received from the Compagnie in Paris was much less than he needed and expected. There were hundreds of bills running on him, so if he failed there would be serious trouble in Amsterdam, as two of the very best houses in Amsterdam had already stopped payments on their accepted bills.[46]

To give Londonderry some assurance about Mouchard, van der Grift persuaded Mouchard to give him some bills due to Mouchard over the coming month. Even though van der Grift was apprehensive whether these bills in turn would be paid, he felt it was "better security than none at all." The bulk of his letter of November 12 was taken up with his reasoning how to deal with his defaulter in London, Lewis Johnson, and giving instructions to Londonderry how to act as his attorney in resolving that matter. Van der Grift proposed to pay out cash to the people owed by Londonderry in Amsterdam, but then have them return the accepted, but unpaid, bills drawn

[44] Ibid., Letter of October 22, 1720.
[45] Ibid., Letter of October 29, 1720.
[46] Ibid., Letter of November 8, 1720.

on Lewis Johnson back to London with a counter protest. As van der Grift would have then paid off the obligation of Lewis Johnson, he would become Johnson's creditor in London, and have legal standing to sue Johnson in London courts and possibly force him to be declared a bankrupt. It was more the threat of bankruptcy and imprisonment rather than the practice that van der Grift desired. In this way, he could force Johnson to make a full account of what he could pay.[47]

As conditions worsened in France, especially for the personal circumstances of John Law, van der Grift found himself in the middle of yet another transaction between Londonderry and his father. This time, Law had directed Middleton to draw bills on his agent in Hamburg, Alexander Bruquier, and give them to Governor Pitt as payment for his share in the wager. The Governor, in turn, sent them to his trusted agent, van der Grift, to collect on his behalf in Amsterdam. Bruquier had informed Middleton by letter that he had accepted the bills for payment, but van der Grift knew that he had not accepted them until the second time they were presented. There was no negotiation of bills between Hamburg and Amsterdam at the time, because of the systemic financial crisis then enveloping all of Europe. So there was a problem how to return payment to Governor Pitt's account with van der Grift in Amsterdam even if Bruquier paid in Hamburg. Van der Grift proposed to send the bills accepted by Bruquier to a friend of his in Hamburg, Lucas Backman, whose character he vouched for, for re-exchange back to van der Grift in Amsterdam (Letter of November 26, 1720). In this way, Backman would end up being paid by Bruquier in Hamburg, Governor Pitt would be paid by van der Grift in Amsterdam, after the intermediate steps of van der Grift creating a claim on Backman and Backman discharging it with a bill drawn on van der Grift. The contract among the principals, Pitt and Bruquier, would be completed by Bruquier paying out in Hamburg and Pitt receiving payment in Amsterdam. The intermediaries, van der Grift and Backman, would receive commissions for their services and some interest derived from the exchange rate spreads in Amsterdam and Hamburg. In short, van der Grift was recommending that Governor Pitt rely on the proven network of merchant credit built up over the years rather than trusting to the new network of agents established by John Law on behalf of the French Compagnie des Indes.

Regardless of this side play, Londonderry still needed to pay off his father and his powerful partners in Amsterdam for their part in the wager with Law. He evidently proposed that van der Grift pawn some of the merchandise of his that lay unsold in Amsterdam to pay the bills Londonderry had drawn in turn on van der Grift. Van der Grift dismissed this course of action, noting that prices of such goods had fallen dramatically and so sale or pawn of the

---

[47] Ibid., Letter of November 12, 1720.

goods would not begin to cover the sums required to honor the bills drawn by Middleton on Mouchard. Rather, he recommended that Londonderry return the protested bills on Mouchard to Middleton, who would then be obliged to reimburse Londonderry, just as van der Grift had reimbursed the Amsterdam partners of Londonderry when Lewis Johnson had defaulted in London.[48] Van der Grift evidently did not perceive that Middleton, in turn, was about to fail at nearly the same time Londonderry would have received his letter.

But Middleton's desperate situation in London, reflecting that of John Law himself in Paris, became clear when the next post brought a batch of bills drawn by Middleton on Law's agent in Genoa, M. Chavigny. Van der Grift agreed to send the first bills to Genoa to get them accepted, but asked Londonderry to send the seconds endorsed to van der Grift. These bills he would hold until usance was nearly up before sending them to Genoa. This way, he would get the shortest dated bills possible, which would be the most secure for payment back in Amsterdam. Meanwhile, it became ever clearer that Mouchard would not be able to pay the bills accepted by him. Van der Grift was growing tired of his procrastination and repetitive excuses, so he recommended, finally, initiating legal action. As with Lewis Johnson in London earlier, this legal action was intended to frighten Mouchard to exert himself more seriously to make payment if at all possible. Otherwise, Mouchard could be made bankrupt and imprisoned.[49]

Before taking van der Grift's advice, however, Londonderry had to cope with the shock of Middleton's stoppage of payments on December 13 (in London, but December 24, Christmas Eve, in Paris and Amsterdam). Middleton himself wrote to van der Grift, to explain that the dismissal of John Law in Paris had made it impossible for him to cover any of Law's bills in expectation that Law could eventually reimburse him.[50] From Paris, Londonderry sent van der Grift a power of attorney that enabled him to put Londonderry's name to the unendorsed bills Londonderry had already sent to Amsterdam. Van der Grift noted that this unusual method, apparently recommended to Londonderry in Paris, was not lawful in Amsterdam, so he suggested instead that Londonderry endorse the second copies of the bills and send those to him in Amsterdam. Even so, these bills would be no good if Mouchard still had no funds on account for John Law.[51]

The next ploy by Mouchard was to suggest to van der Grift (and to Londonderry) that Mouchard draw bills on the Compagnie des Indes in Paris payable to Londonderry's agent in Paris, Sir John Drummond. French law, however, required such bills always to state clearly that "value was received" by the drawer of the bill. A bill of exchange drawn on Paris could

[48] Ibid., Letter of December 3, 1720.
[49] Ibid., Letter of December 20, 1720.
[50] Coutts & Co., Archives, London, Letter Book 'O–14', Foreign Letters 1720. f. 509.
[51] PRO, Chancery Masters Exhibits, Letter of January 14, 1721.

be declared null and void if the drawer could not provide proof that he had received value corresponding to the amount being drawn. This was the assurance provided in French law that the ultimate drawer would always be responsible for the amount paid out on his credit. English law was more flexible, requiring only that the original drawer be responsible ultimately for payment of the bill, without needing to demonstrate that value had been received for each bill. If van der Grift gave Mouchard either the bills drawn by van der Grift directly on Mouchard or bills drawn to Londonderry and endorsed to van der Grift, he would lose legal leverage on Mouchard under Dutch law in Amsterdam. He did not trust the Compagnie des Indes to pay in any case, as they had not been providing Mouchard with the necessary means to meet his obligations to date in Amsterdam.[52] Meanwhile, van der Grift had received payment for the bills drawn by Middleton on A. Bruquier in Hamburg, and he was remitting the proceeds directly to Governor Pitt. The well-established merchant lines of credit were being sustained to this extent at least in the midst of the financial meltdown of international capital markets in 1720. Ironically, one of the bills sent by van der Grift was drawn on Robert Knight, treasurer of the South Sea Company. Knight was under close investigation by a secret committee of Parliament inquiring into the collapse of the South Sea Company, and he was about to abscond to Brussels!

In the next month, van der Grift continued to inquire at least each post day at Mouchard's office to keep the pressure on him while his protested bills were in process of being sent to Londonderry. Londonderry then obtained a contra-protest on the bills from Middleton, who could claim rightly that he had been informed by his principal, John Law, that provision had been placed with Mouchard for payment of the bills. By mid-February, the contra-protested bills had been received back in Amsterdam by van der Grift, who was now ready to proceed with legal action against Mouchard. Van der Grift's lawyer used the contra-protested bills – endorsed originally by Londonderry to van der Grift and then accepted by Mouchard, protested by van der Grift and sent to Londonderry, who had them contra-protested by Middleton and sent them back to van der Grift – to obtain a prise de corps authorization from the Amsterdam magistrates. Once in effect, the prise de corps meant that van der Grift could, at his pleasure, have Mouchard arrested and put in prison. For the prise de corps to take effect, Mouchard had to be summoned three times before the magistrate. Within a week this was carried out and van der Grift now had the full force of Dutch law at his disposal to be used against Mouchard on behalf of Londonderry.

Nevertheless, it seemed to van der Grift the better part of wisdom to keep the threat of imprisonment as an option, rather than to exercise the prise de corps.[53] The course of action recommended by van der Grift was taken and seemed to have the desired effect of terrifying Mouchard. Van

---

[52] Ibid., Letter of January 17, 1721.
[53] Ibid., Letter of February 14, 1721.

der Grift reported that Mouchard was no longer to be found in his office, but was hiding in his home. Moreover, he had shown bad faith by first depositing some French bank bills with the notary who was holding the prise de corps and then taking the bills back. Despite this show of desperation by Mouchard, van der Grift still counseled patience. Mouchard repaid this kindness by hiding out in a friend's house, which moved van der Grift to recommend declaring him bankrupt and arresting him. This way he and Londonderry could seize what little effects remained in Mouchard's possession before he had a chance to dispose of all of them.[54] In the event, another creditor obtained a prise de corps against Mouchard and took out a statute of bankruptcy against him.[55] That creditor turned out to be Londonderry himself, a bit to van der Grift's surprise no doubt, but Londonderry then allowed Mouchard three months liberty to try to put his affairs in order and Mouchard gratefully accepted. Van der Grift noted that after Londonderry's liberty period expired, his original prise de corps would again be in force, so the ultimate threat of imprisonment would remain.

For the next several years, Mouchard's name only appeared every three months in the weekly letters by van der Grift to Londonderry on renewed extensions of the liberty he allowed to Mouchard from the prise de corps still outstanding against him. The prise de corps, never being exercised, finally lapsed by law one year and six weeks after its issue, but *sauf conduits* (safe conduct passes) were then issued repeatedly to protect Mouchard from the statute of bankruptcy. The affair finally ended in March 1724 as Law and Londonderry had come to a separate conclusion of Law's huge debt after intensive negotiations between the two principals in London. By the end of 1723, it appeared that Law would be recalled to France by the Duc d'Orléans, chief advisor to teenaged Louis XV, and allowed to resume possession of his estates and financial assets. Law pledged in turn 3,000 shares he held in the Compagnie des Indes toward payment of a final debt of £92,000 owed to Londonderry and associates. He then released all of his agents – in Amsterdam, Genoa, Hamburg, and London – of their obligations to pay the bills of exchange drawn on them. In the actual course of events, the Duc d'Orléans died in late 1723, the new ministers turned against Law, inducing his brother to turn against him and apparently seducing his wife to stay in Paris while Law languished in Venice. But that is another, unhappy, tale of the lack of honor among statesmen and aristocrats. It has no more bearing on our story of the network of credit established among the mercantile community of early modern Europe and the legal apparatus supporting it.

The legal procedures of protest and contra-protest on bills that were either not accepted or, if accepted were not paid, provided documentary evidence

---

[54] Ibid., Letter of March 4, 1721.
[55] Ibid., Letter of March 7, 1721.

of breach of payment. All parties to a bill also had to supply and preserve the supporting letters of advice with instructions from principals to agents and confirmation of actions taken sent back by agents to their principals. In the case study just presented, Londonderry was both principal and agent to van der Grift. It is unfortunate that Londonderry's letter book for the period is missing, but van der Grift was clearly the instructor in the relationship, patiently tutoring his new client in the ways of the mercantile world. Thanks to his expositions, we have been able to reconstruct the legal machinery available and used by merchants of the early eighteenth century. It was clearly in operation already by the middle of the seventeenth century.

Conclusion

To become an international financial center, seventeenth century London had to overcome at least one comparative disadvantage – the lack of a public bank, a central institution that processed bills of exchange. Such banks were essentially clearing houses for payments by foreigners using bills of exchange drawn on correspondents. Amsterdam's Wisselbank, established in 1609, was the most envied foreign example.[56] Despite considering many schemes to emulate the Wisselbank, London never created such an institution. Before 1688, the reason no doubt lay in the reluctance of merchants to put their specie assets at the potential disposal of a capricious monarch capable of seizing them for reasons of state. Only city–states governed by republican forms of government dominated by merchant interests, such as Venice, Genoa, or Hamburg, established such exchange banks in Europe. After the Glorious Revolution of 1688 in England, the Protestant monarch was more tightly constrained by the legislative power of Parliament.[57] Even then, it took the duress of war finance to persuade Parliament to establish a peculiarly British version of a public bank in 1694, the Bank of England. Unlike the Bank of Amsterdam, the Bank of London (as the Bank of England was popularly, and correctly, known in the eighteenth century) did not dominate the local bill market, it did not act as a large-scale clearinghouse, and no bills were required to pass through it.[58] Instead, the Bank of England was a fractional reserve, note-issuing bank committed to serving the English treasury. In place of a centralized institution such as the Wisselbank, London bankers had to arrange an informal network of mutual monitors

[56] J. K. Horsefield, *British Monetary Experiments 1650–1710* (Cambridge, MA: Harvard University Press, 1960), 94.

[57] D. North and Barry Weingast, "Constitutions and Commitment: The Evolution of Institutions Governing Public Choice in Seventeenth-Century England," *Journal of Economic History* 49 (December 1989): 803–832.

[58] H. V. Bowen, "Bank of England 1694–1820," in *The Bank of England, Money, Power and Influence 1694–1994*, eds. R. Roberts and D. Kynaston (Oxford: Oxford University Press, 1995), 14–16.

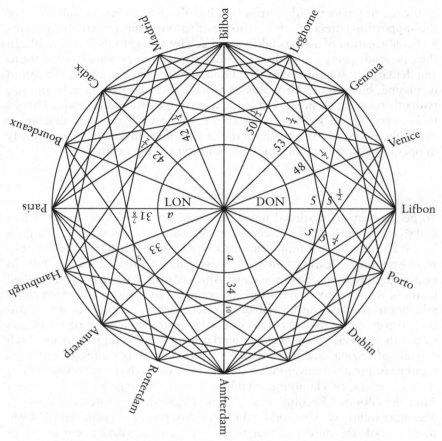

FIGURE 1.3. The Opportunities for Arbitrage Profits in the Exchange Network of Europe
Source: Malachy Postlethwayt, *The Universal Dictionary of Trade and Commerce*, 4th ed. (London, 1774). Reprinted New York: August M. Kelley, Vol. I, "Arbitrage." (1971).

operating through the foreign exchange markets to maintain a viable payments system. This was necessary to support England's growing overseas commerce and public expenditure.

Rather than clear all bills through an exchange bank, London bankers' bills were settled along with notes and checks via bilateral clearing between bankers.[59] The benefit for London's financial development was that the specie deposited in fractional reserve banks was recycled into market lending. In contrast, an exchange bank was required to maintain 100 percent backing

[59] Quinn, "Goldsmith–Banking."

for its deposits. Recycling deposits buttressed a resilient, market-oriented, domestic banking system in London. The cost, however, was that bills drawn on London lacked the firmer backing offered by bills drawn on Amsterdam. Further, because all bill traffic in Amsterdam was directed through the Wisselbank, any default there was immediately observed by all participants, and met by universal withdrawal of business from the defaulter. Defaulted bills in London, by contrast, required legal action to be initiated by the aggrieved individual, although the defaulter could continue to do business with other clients.

London bankers reduced their risks in dealing with international bills of exchange by creating a network of responsible agents overseas, each of whom owed a substantial part of his business to the London banking house, and therefore had every incentive to maintain his reputation for fair and prompt dealing with London. By the middle of the eighteenth century, London could be seen as the center of a complex web of possible payment procedures. Figure 1.3 replicates the illustration that Postlethwayt's *Universal Dictionary of Trade and Commerce* provided for the article on "Arbitrage," as the merchants of the time termed the process of selecting among alternative paths for settling accounts with foreign correspondents. The overseas agents of London bankers, in turn, were constantly monitored by a large number of diverse merchants, both British and foreign, who remitted bills of exchange between London and abroad in part to finance their trading activities. Confronted by a classic principal–agent problem, bankers on Lombard Street focused on establishing accounts with proven and reputable associates in Amsterdam, Paris, or Cadiz. As they widened their network of trade and credit, they rapidly outgrew the possibility of sanctioning opportunistic behavior of their foreign agents by religious or family ostracism or organizing collective action with other merchants in a foreign port against an expropriating prince or a mercenary merchant.[60] Both the London bankers and their foreign agents were subject only to the domestic law in each port. To enforce contracts across the resulting legal boundaries required the creation of enforcement mechanisms that were both informal and novel.

---

[60] A. Greif, "Reputation and Coalitions in Medieval Trade: Evidence on the Maghribi Traders," *Journal of Economic History* 49 (December 1989): 857–82; A. Greif, "Contract Enforceability and Economic Institutions in Early Trade: The Maghribi Traders Coalition," *American Economic Review* 83 (June 1993): 525–48; and P. Milgrom, D. North, and B. Weingast, "The Role of Institutions in the Revival of Trade: The Medieval Law Merchant, Private Judges, and the Champagne Fairs," *Economics and Politics* 2 (March 1990): 1–23.

2

The Paris Bourse, 1724–1814:
Experiments in Microstructure

Eugene N. White

How financial markets should be structured and regulated is one of the central questions of modern finance. Although theory provides some guidance, the microstructure of contemporary stock exchanges is sufficiently varied and complex that it is difficult to determine the optimal set of rules for an efficient marketplace.[1] During the formative years of the Paris Bourse [Stock Exchange], the government radically altered the financial architecture of the exchange several times. These changes provide a natural experiment to examine the importance of entry restrictions and the size of security issues for the delivery of liquidity. In contrast to the stock exchanges in London and New York, government, not private interests, created the Paris Bourse in 1724.[2] Initially, the Crown's role in the establishment of a stock exchange arose out of its financial difficulties and reflected the hope that an exchange would improve the market for government securities. From a bourse with a fixed number of brokers trading relatively small issues, the French Revolution produced a new exchange where large issues were traded by an unrestricted number of brokers. Napoleon altered this mix by reducing and limiting the number of agents in the market. The concern of successive governments about the microstructure of the bourse in an changing economic environment produced a continuing search for advantageous exchange rules. However, a liquid market was formed not only by the regulations and structure set by the government but also by the operations of bankers and other large participants, acting at least partly as market makers.

---

[1] See Schwartz (1988) and Schwartz (1995).
[2] For a comparison of the London, New York, and Paris markets in the nineteenth century, see Davis and Neal (1998).

Eighteenth-Century Public Finance and the Formation
of the Financial System

There were secondary markets for public and private debt long before the opening of the bourse, but the royal interest determined the organization of the bourse in its early years. The establishment of the bourse arose out of John Law's efforts to reform royal finances by altering the structure and marketability of government debt. The collapse of John's Law "System" defined not only the bourse but also the regulations governing the eighteenth century French financial system. Thus, although the activities of the brokers on the bourse were kept strictly segregated from other financial activities, their operations must be seen within the context of the whole financial system.

The War of the Spanish Succession (1702–13) was disastrous for the finances of the French Crown. By the time the peace treaty was signed, the debt had reached 3 billion livres or about eighteen years of royal revenues, and interest payments were two years in arrears. Most of the long-term debt took the form of irredeemable annuities with high rates of interest, ranging from 8 to 10 percent. This form of debt locked the state into the high payments, while annuity holders, unable to easily transfer securities, could not realize the capital gain from the fall in interest rates after the war. Overwhelmed by the burden of this debt, the Crown fell into a two-stage default.[3]

In the midst of this disaster appeared John Law, a Scottish financial adventurer. Searching for a plan, Louis XV's regent, the duc d' Orleans, decided to back Law. With the duke's support, he established the Banque Generale in 1716. Although Law had hoped to stimulate the economy with this new bank, it had a small capital, and its operation had little effect on interest rates. To manage the Crown's debt, Law established the Compagnie d'Occident in 1717. This new trading company had monopoly privileges in Louisiana. Law was able to generate confidence and improve the realm's finances by offering the public an opportunity to exchange depreciated state debt for shares in the company. The public's billets d'etat (government bonds) with discounts of 68 to 72 percent were accepted at face value by the company to buy stock, while the company agreed to receive lower interest payments on this debt from the Crown. A key component of Law's system was the conversion of fixed interest irredeemable debt into variable yield securities that could be easily traded.[4] All parties appeared to be better off: The public obtained a potentially more lucrative asset, and the Crown lowered its debt service.

The value of trading the company's stock rose as the company was awarded more privileges, including tax farms. It merged with the Compagnie

---

[3] Hamilton, 121–22.
[4] Neal, 13–14.

des Indes in 1719, adopting this name. Law's system and share prices gathered more momentum, thanks to the rising loans and note issue of the Banque Generale, now restructured as the Banque Royale with a monopoly of currency issue. The inflationary effects of this expansion led Law to attempt to control stock prices, interest rates, and the specie value of French currency on the foreign exchanges. The incompatibility of these policy goals produced the monumental collapse in 1720.[5] In the clean up that followed the liquidation of Law's System in 1721–2, the national debt was fixed at 1.7 billion livres. Although the face value of the debt returned to where it had been in May 1716, Law had succeeded in lowering the service charge. The state of government finance had been improved but at the cost of enormous damage to the Crown's reputation and credibility as a borrower.[6]

Law's disaster had consequences for both financial intermediaries and financial markets by discrediting banks of issue – such as the Banque Royale – and securities markets as institutions worthy of public trust. A crucial effect of Law's debacle was to halt the development of banks of issue, imposing a half century prohibition on banks that issued hand-to-hand currency. In the absence of chartered banks, three groups of financial intermediaries dominated the primary market for short- and long-term credit – financiers, notaries, and private bankers.

Government finance, especially short-term finance, was largely the business of the financiers. This category encompassed all persons involved in the financial operations of the Crown, including the officials operating the tax farms. These for-profit businesses issued short-term notes that financed their activities and hence the government.[7] Alongside of the money and capital market for the government, a well-developed market for private debt evolved in the eighteenth century. The notaries formed a financial network intermediating within Paris and across France and played an important role in the marketing and trading of royal debt.[8] Private bankers provided many commercial and investment banking services, supplying short-term credit to business, accepting deposits, and assisting with the placement of government debt and private equities.[9] A core function of a private bank was to assist its clients in making and receiving domestic and international payments, using bills of exchange.[10] In addition, bankers assisted their customers with their purchases and sales of securities and offered investment advice. Clients asked bankers to execute their orders, for which they paid a commission of

---

[5] Faure, Chapters XVIII–XL; Neal, Chapter 1; and Murphy, Chapters 5 and 8.
[6] Hoffman, Postel-Vinay, Rosenthal, "Les Marches du Credit a Paris."
[7] Bouvier, 306–9.
[8] Hoffman, Postel-Vinay, and Rosenthal, "What Do Notaries Do?"; "Private Credit Markets"; and "Les Marches du Credit a Paris."
[9] See Cope, Luthy, and Antonetti, n.d.
[10] Bouvier, 304–5.

1 percent, sending them on to brokers on the bourse.[11] Bankers maintained close ties to other financial intermediaries to facilitate their operations, and some bankers had family members who were brokers.[12]

Customers used the banks' services to speculate on fluctuations in the markets.[13] Clients could provide their own funds for purchases or they could buy on margin and have their banker give collateralized short-term loans to buy securities. The bank also could assist its customers if they wanted to enter the *marches a terme* [market for future delivery] for futures (fermes) or options (primes).[14] Although the bankers might take orders to buy or sell securities, they could not execute the trades as this was the exclusive right of the stockbrokers. Brokers might take their orders directly from individuals, but bankers seem to have received and transmitted many orders. As they provided many financial services, their customers may have found it easier to pay a slightly higher fee and let their banker handle this transaction. The volume of trades by banks seems to have been fairly high. Some records of the Greffulhe et Montz Bank show a very high level of activity, although it is not possible to separate trades made for customers and its own account.[15] Banks also served as depositories for their clients' securities. At Greffulhe et Montz, securities were held in its name for clients, crediting their accounts for coupon payments, a service important to foreigners investing in France.[16] Last, Paris bankers often took positions as administrators in the new stock companies formed in the 1780s. Although this was viewed during the Revolution and by later historians as evidence of their predatory character, it gave them a chance to control and monitor the behavior of corporations and ensure that the shareholders – the banks and their customers included – were not defrauded.

The only bank of issue to appear after the collapse of Law's System was the Caisse d'Escompte, or Discount Bank, established by royal decree in 1776. With a capital of 15 million livres, it was modeled on the Bank of

---

[11] Antonetti, n.d. 160–3.

[12] Bouchary, *Les Boscary*, 7–8.

[13] Speculators often tried to manipulate the markets. For detailed descriptions of some of these operations, see Bouchary, *Les Manieurs* I, 43–4; Antonetti, "Les maoeuvres," 577–97; Daridan, 43–4, 60–1; and Tedde, 9–12, 95–6.

[14] Antonetti, n.d. 163–7. Their operations could be quite modern and complex. For example, on August 19, 1791, Greffulhe et Montz sold a call option on 100 shares of Compagnie des Indes at the end of October and combined it with the purchase on October 3 of a call option on 100 shares for the same terminal date. In modern markets this operation would be termed a bullish vertical spread.

[15] During the last seven months of 1789, its three most active securities were the actions of the Compagnie des Indes, with 3.6 million livres bought and 2.7 million sold; the Emprunt de 125 Million, with 2.7 million bought and 2.6 million sold; and the actions of the Caisse d'Escompte, with 1 million livres each bought and sold. Antonetti, n.d. 163.

[16] Antonetti, n.d. 168, 173–4. By holding the securities on behalf of its customers, the bank could vote their shares and give them a consolidated voice in the affairs of a company.

England. Its principal function was to discount bills of exchanges and other negotiable notes at a maximum rate of 4 percent. Although its initial purpose was to stimulate industry and commerce, the Caisse d'Escompte became a banker's bank, providing a central place for clearing interbank claims and rediscounting the notes of the banking houses. This activity allowed the bankers to more easily manage new securities issues. Rather than depend wholly on their own capital for holding a new issue, they might obtain short-term credit from the Caisse.

The Agents de Change and Secondary Markets before the Bourse

Before the establishment of the bourse, the Crown had created privileged offices whose owners enjoyed the right to trade securities. In selling these offices, the Crown was following the model it had established for other professions.[17] The agents de change, or stockbrokers, evolved out of the medieval office of courtiers or brokers who traded in commodities as well as financial instruments. The growth of financial markets encouraged the specialization of activity; and "courretiers" de change appear to have been first recognized by royal edict in 1572.[18] Although the Crown created a monopoly by fixing the number of brokers in 1595, it altered the number over time, reflecting in part the fluctuating demand for securities.[19] From eight brokers for Paris in 1595, the number was gradually raised to thirty in 1638. The following year, they were given the name of agents de banque et de change.[20] Their function as securities brokers, as distinct from commodities brokers, was made explicit in 1684 when they were forbidden to handle merchandise.[21]

The Crown had attempted to use the agents de change as a source of credit. After suppressing the existing offices, the Crown created forty new hereditary offices in 1708.[22] Their individual finance – a security deposit or forced loan to the Crown – was set at 20,000 livres, paying a gage of 10 percent interest.[23] In addition, they were required to pledge an additional

---

[17] Doyle (1996).

[18] Edict relatif aux courretiers, tant de change et de deniers que de draps de soye, laines, toiles, cuirs et autres sortes de marchandises: de vins, bleds et autres grains: de chevaux, et de tout autre bestial. June 1572. [Edict relating to traders, including exchange and coin as well as silk wool, leather and other types of merchanise: wines, wheat and other grains, horses and all other kinds of beasts.]

[19] Arret du 15 april 1595.

[20] Arret du conseil. April 2, 1639.

[21] Reglement des 5 et 8 juillet 1684, article 16.

[22] Edit aout 1708 portant suppression des vingt offices d'agens de change a Paris, crees par l'edit de decembre 1705 et creation de quarante autres pareils offices pour la ville, a titre hereditaires. [Edict of August 1708 concerning the suppression of the twenty Paris brokers offices created by the edict of December 1705 and the creation of forty similar offices in the city, with a hereditary title.]

[23] Originally, the Crown had optimistically hoped to obtain finances of 60,000 livres.

1,000 livres, earning a gage of 5 percent. However, the Crown tried to raise additional funds of 20,000 livres from the agents de change in 1713.[24] When the agents de change failed to produce this supplement, the government lowered the increment to 10,000 livres the following year and compensated by creating an additional twenty offices.[25] Yet, the costs imposed on these royal offices exceeded the benefits for many potential agents de change, and only thirty-five of the total sixty offices were taken in 1714.

Early in their existence, the agents de change were formed into a corporation or *compagnie* by royal decree in 1638.[26] The corporation was headed by a syndic who was elected by the members once a year and who was assisted by an adjoint. The syndic served as the compagnie's official public representative and presided over the meetings of the compagnie that took place the first Tuesday of every month at five o'clock in the afternoon. The regimen of the compagnie, including religious services, were carefully prescribed to avoid the appearance of meeting to manipulate the market. Extraordinary meetings were prohibited in 1714, "to prevent the bad impressions given of the company."[27]

In the early eighteenth century, the Parisian securities market centered on Quincampoix Street. Trading was largely outdoors apparently without any formal system of recording quotations.[28] As the volume of activity increased, there was interest among some participants in establishing an official

[24] Edit mai 1713 qui attribue des augmentations de gages aux quarante agents de change de Paris, en les obligeant de verser vingt mille livres, au denier vingt, et en donnant aux presteurs de la somme un privilege special sur lesdites augmenations et sur les prix desdits offices. [Edict of May 1713 that sets the increase in the security bonds of the forty Paris brokers and obliges them to deliver 20,000 livres, at 5 percent, and gives the lenders of this sum a special privilege on these increases and the price of their offices.]

[25] Declaration du Roy 13 juillet 1714 ordonnant que les agents de change de la ville de Paris seront tenus d'acquerir 10,000 livres d'augmentation de gages, au lieu de 20,000 qui leur avaient este attribuees par edit du mois de mai 1713 et leur interdisant d'associer avec eux aucume personne. Edit novembre 1714, portant creation de vingt nouvelles charges d'agens de change a Paris. [Declaration of the King July 13, 1714 ordering the Paris brokers to provide 10,000 livres of increases for their security bond instead of the 20,000 that they were required by edict of May 1713 and forbidding them to contract with anyone else. Edict November 1714 on the creation of twenty new broker offices for Paris.]

[26] Arret du Consel portant creation de dix nouveaux offices hereditaires en sus des vingt existant. December 1638. The most important edict governing the corporation was issued on October 2, 1714, Reglement des quarante conseillers du Roy, agens de banque, change, commerce et finances de Paris, pour l'election des syndics et pour la reception des officiers, fait a l'assemblee, tenue en leur bureau de la place du change. [Order in Counsel for the creation of 10 new hereditary offices. December 1638. Regulation of the forty royal counselors, agents in banking, exchange, commerce and finance in Paris, to the election of syndies and their reception by the assembly held in their offices in Exchange Place. October 2, 1714.]

[27] October 2, 1714, Article 2.

[28] Bigo, *Les bases historiques*, 154.

centralized place to trade. They hoped that an organized exchange would make markets more liquid and thus attractive to their customers.

As the state regulated the brokers, suggestions were naturally directed to the Crown. The first well-defined proposal for a state-organized bourse was made by a trader, La Bartz, in 1708.[29] Writing to the controleur general Desmarets, he recommended the organization of an official securities market in the Hotel de Soissons for traders, financiers, and loan officers, under public surveillance and recording the daily prices. La Bartz's project was ignored, and there appears to have been little interest in establishing a bourse until the securities markets came alive under Law.

By reviving interest in government debt and creating new securities, which appeared to offer extraordinary capital gains, the volume of trading under Law's System soared. Property owners along Quincampoix Street leased all available space to speculators. The prince of Carignan built and rented 150 wooden stalls or shacks in his hotel's gardens. Although the record is not clear, the agents de change's monopoly of trading does not appear to have been respected. Furthermore, there is evidence that some brokers took advantage of their customers, receiving an order for a fixed price but then executing it at a better price and pocketing the difference.

In an effort to uphold the rights of the agents de change and more important to protect his system, Law issued an decree on March 22, 1720, that prohibited all assembly on Quincampoix Street and the operation of any office for the purpose of trading. Chased from the street, the unregulated traders took refuge in the nearby cafes and carbarets where they carried on their business. Law then issued a second ordinance on March 28, 1720, that set fines and prison sentences for those trading clandestinely. In spite of these threats, it appears that unofficial, unregulated trading continued vigorously in the stock of the Compagnie des Indes, bills of exchange, and other securities.

When the market began to falter, Law was willing to use any means to bolster the value of the stock market. He attempted to draw in the unofficial market and sponsored a bourse. Decreed on July 20, 1720, this bourse had an ephemeral existence. Opened in the Hotel de Soissons, trading on the exchange was to be conducted at 138 rented stalls. The hours of the bourse were set from seven in the morning to seven in the evening in summer and eight in the morning to five in the evening in winter. All unofficial trading was to be penalized by a prison sentence and fine of 3,000 livres. Tinkering with the market, Law suppressed the offices of the agent de change in August and replaced them with sixty new "commissions" that required no finance, only a deposit of securities.[30] Apparently, failing to serve its purpose, an October

---

[29] Saint-Germain, 134.

[30] 30 aout 1720 arrest du conseil d'estat, portant suppression des soixante offices d'agens de change, cries par les edits dos mois d'aout 1708 et novembre 1714 et qui ordonne qu'il sera establi soixante agens de change en vertu d'une nouvelle commission. [August 30, 1720, Order in Council of State for the suppression of the sixty brokers offices, created by the edicts

25 *arret* (stop) ordered the bourse closed on October 29 and created sixty new offices for agents de change who would henceforth handle securities without the benefit of a public marketplace.[31]

Once Law's System collapsed, the demand for the services of agents de change to buy and sell securities collapsed. The number of agents dwindled from fifty-nine in 1721 to thirty-seven in 1723. The Crown annulled the existing offices and created sixty offices with drastically reduced costs. Their finance now consisted of much depreciated state securities and a modest entry fee for new agents and an annual tax, the droit d'annuel.[32] This decree of 1723 was not significantly altered until the very end of the ancien regime. Thus, the Crown abandoned its efforts to use the offices of the agents de change as a source of revenue.

The Foundation and Structure of the Paris Bourse

The massive default by the state after Law's System collapsed left markets thin and securities prices volatile. Furthermore, the surge in trading and the increase in the number of traders during the System had spawned fraud and a distrust of brokers. Thus, the initial design of the bourse reflected general contemporary concerns about securities markets providing an institution that would perhaps improve the marketability of securities.

The bourse was established by decree on September 24, 1724, and the number of agents de change was set at sixty. The bourse was located on Vivienne Street. It was open from ten in the morning to one in the afternoon, every day except Sunday and holidays. For Paris, all secondary transactions in the money and capital markets – including equities, debt, and bills of exchange – that involved a broker were supposed to occur on the floor of the exchange. Individual investors could trade amongst themselves, recording the transaction with a notary, but they could not use a middleman.[33] Trading in contracts to deliver merchandise was permitted on the floor but also was allowed to continue outside the bourse in fairs and marketplaces.

The bourse was open to brokers, merchants, bankers, and other known persons living in Paris, although certificates could be issued to other Frenchmen and foreigners to gain access. Women were formally excluded.

of August 1708 and November 1714 and which orders the establishment of 60 brokers with new commissions.]

[31] Faure, 654.

[32] Almanach Royal, annees 1721, 1722, 1723. Edit portant suppression des anciens offices d'agens de change establis dans la Ville de Paris, et creation de soixante nouveaux offices d'agens de change, banque et commerce dans ladite ville, avec diverses modifications, janvier 1723. Vidal says that initally no offices were purchased. Vidal, 142. [Edict for the suppression of the old brokers offices established in the city of Paris and the creation of sixty new offices for brokers for securities, banking and commerce in the aforementioned city, with many changes, January 1723.]

[33] For details on this informal market, see Hoffman, Rosenthal, and Postal-Vinay, "Competition and Coercion."

Each authorized person was given a *marque* that identified him and gave him entry. In cases of fraudulent entry, the transgressor was immediately expelled, and if caught again was subject to imprisonment and a fine of 1,000 livres. Guards patrolled the streets to protect and secure the peaceful operation of the bourse.

Participants were permitted to trade in bills of exchange and promissory notes (billets au porteur and billets a ordre); but securities (effets et papiers commercables) were solely the business of the agents de change.[34] Initially, the only effets et papiers commercables exchanged on the bourse were shares of the Compagnie des Indes. In 1776, the shares of the newly founded Caisse d'Escompte were traded on the exchange. The stock market boom of the 1780s added several new companies.[35]

Although one agent was sufficient to act as a broker between the buyer and seller for any bill of exchange, billet au porteur, billet a ordre, or commodity, the exchange of effets commercables required two agents so that each party would be properly represented and protected by his or her own agents.[36] To keep the specialized activities of the agents de change segregated from the rest of the market, the Crown decreed the erection of a three-foot-high *parquet* in 1774, where only the agents de change and the police could enter. Each agent was required to maintain a *registre-journal*, subject to inspection, where he recorded each securities transaction. The agents were intended to be pure brokers and forbidden to trade on their own account. The commission for the trade of any security was set at 50 sols for every 1,000 livres or 0.25 percent, half to be paid by the buyer and half by the seller. For the trading of goods, the commission was set at 0.5 percent of the value of the goods exchanged.

These basic rules determined the Paris bourse to be an agency/auction market where the market professional on the floor of the exchange – the agent de change – acted solely as an agent or broker for his customers.[37] The agents de change had a legal monopoly as middlemen in the trading of listed securities; but as they were forbidden to trade on their own accounts, they could not act as market makers to stabilize prices. This rule seems to have been dictated by an abiding concern that the agents de change would not necessarily act in the best interest of their customers. Even before the establishment of the bourse, the Crown had controlled entry into the profession and strictly limited the number of agents de change and set the commissions

---

[34] The agents de change's monopoly was temporarily abrogated by a decree on February 26, 1726, that authorized free trading in all securities. Their monopoly was restored in December 1733.

[35] Mirabeau, *Denonciation*.

[36] Transgression of these rules was to be punished by a fine of 6,000 livres and the nullification of the contract if it was contested.

[37] Schwartz 1988, Chapter 2.

they could charge. In the thin markets of the period, the rule forbidding agents de change from trading on their own account seems to have been aimed at preventing them from benefiting from any superior information they might possess. Under this more restrictive regime, concerns about the honesty of brokers that had existed before eventually seemed to disappear, and contemporaries commented on the safety of the market.[38]

Rules for orders, trading, and quotation were strictly set. Any individual wanting to buy or sell on the exchange was required to deliver his or her securities or money to their agent at least one hour before the opening of the bourse. This rule, which had the effect of consolidating the flow of orders, would have helped to overcome in part a problem arising in thin markets where price discovery is difficult because the orders are fragmented, that is, orders arrive in the market at any time. Consolidation of orders helped to improve the liquidity of the market by increasing the probability that orders would be matched and by compensating for the absence of market makers. However, the consolidation rule limited investors flexibility as to when they were permitted to enter the market. When an investor decided to enter the market, he or she would typically gave his or her agent de change limit orders for the maximum price acceptable for a purchase or a minimum price for the sale of securities, although there was apparently nothing to prevent an investor from delegating authority to negotiate a price.[39] The price uncertainty of thin markets, where few trades are expected, might widen the buy and sell limit prices, just as it increases the bid–ask spread in dealer markets. Once trading began there was no further contact with the customers by the agents de change who were limited to trading on the floor. On the floor, when two agents discovered that they had mutually agreeable buy and sell orders, they would negotiate a price and execute the transaction, registering it in their journals.

The registre-journal of one agent de change, a M. Malpeyre, reveals part of the daily activities of an ancien regime stockbroker. Malpeyre received his office from the controleur general Turgot on July 15, 1775, and he gave up his office in 1787. The registre-journal records the name of the client, the other agent de change, the security, and the price, although it is often difficult to decipher his hasty handwriting. The journal only records the transactions in which an agent de change had a legal monopoly right to trade and so omits additional business in other financial instruments. Malpeyre took orders from both bankers and private customers, with some traders constituting a large share of his business. The volume of activity clearly grew over time for Malpeyre. In 1776, he recorded eighteen transactions in January, fifteen transactions in February, and sixteen in March. In contrast

---

[38] Martin, 67–8.
[39] In contemporary terms, "Iles limites qui lui ont ete fixees parle commettant." Martin, 64.

for 1783, Malpeyre executed sixty-one orders in January, fifty-eight orders for February, and fifty-seven for March.

Once a transaction was completed, agents de change were obliged to deliver the securities and money the same day. Initially, it was strictly forbidden to announce the price of securities aloud or indicate in any manner the price agreed on, apparently based on the fear that brokers might attempt to manipulate prices. For any such infraction, brokers were threatened with expulsion and a fine of 6,000 livres. However, a decree issued on March 30, 1774, permitted agents, and agents only, to call out prices for effets royaux. After the end of the market, the agents would retire to a room to record the market transactions that appeared on the official quotation sheet, the *côte officielle*. Only then could customers, who might have been kept waiting in the gallery for as long as a half or three-quarters of an hour, discover whether their orders had been executed. Unfortunately, there is apparently no extant information about the volume of trading on the Paris bourse. The only partial information is contained on the notes officielles that recorded each time a transaction caused the price to change.

Central to the operation of the bourse or any market is the process of price discovery. The price information created on the bourse was very valuable. The construction of the parquet, the rules governing the *cri*, and the written record of transactions prices were aimed at ensuring the information remained the private property of the agents de change until the end of the trading day. Disclosure of prices during the course of trading could have allowed individuals on the *coulisse*, or curb market, to legally make trades without the benefit of an intermediary. The decrees reaffirming the monopoly of the agents de change in 1740, 1781, 1784, 1786, and 1788 suggest that the informal market found ways to free ride on the public good produced on the exchange. This problem was described in 1789 by one contemporary in his depiction of the bourse:

a large and narrow gallery, one enters by a door at the far end; an iron railing separates the brokers from the public. Between the door and the railing is a space that the guards call the "curb." Very often, two parties will meet, wishing to transact in the hurley-burley, but only the more forceful will be able to get a word with his broker. The majority of the public is squeezed out and only hears what is happening in the "echos of the Bourse." This is the situation that is found by the crowd at the bourse, by the peaceful citizenry. They would wish that the brokers in charge of their orders would head upstairs and yell out the window the price of a security is such and such ...[40]

By the end of the ancien regime, the bourse was an important feature of the financial system. Although secondary markets for money and capital

[40] Martin, Chapter 6.

continued to operate outside its doors, the bourse provided a ready assessment of the government's management of its finances and the operation of new private enterprises.

The Agents de Change: Families of Specialists

The bourse that emerged during the ancien regimes was dominated by dynasties of brokers. Although the nature of their offices encouraged retention within the family, the long tenures of individuals and families represent an accumulation of experience. This human capital on the exchange helped to improve the delivery of liquidity and the flow of information.

The great bankers and financiers were public figures who influenced both politics and the economy; and historians have provided us with numerous portraits of these intermediaries. However, the less socially prominent agents de change have remained largely anonymous.[41] Nevertheless, the historical record does offer a silhouette of this group. The collapse of Law's System not only disrupted the capital markets but also threatened the agents de change as a privileged corps of officials. The Crown had granted a new monopoly of trading securities and all negotiable paper to the agents de change in 1724. Yet the weak demand for securities lowered the value of the offices of the agents and led to a suspension of the monopoly in 1726, allowing all merchants, traders, and bankers admitted to the bourse to trade any financial instrument. However, once the market revived, willing purchasers were again found for the offices. The monopoly was reinstituted with the number of agents de change lowered to forty in December 1733.[42] The number remained unchanged for four decades until revived interest in the market induced the Crown to increase the number of agents de change to fifty in June 1775. A new crunch reduced their numbers to forty in November 1781. The last change under the ancien regime was decreed on March 19, 1786, when sixty offices were constituted.

Over time, the Crown imposed some minimum qualifications on the agents de change. By the end of the ancien regime, agents de change were required to be twenty-five years old, French, Catholic, and of good reputation. They were forbidden to admit any lower class person into their business affairs, subject to imprisonment and a fine of 6,000 livres. In 1781, the government required that anyone aspiring to the office of an agent de change to have worked for five years in a banking or commercial house or with a notary.[43]

---

[41] One exception is Jean Boscary's book, *Les Boscary*. Unfortunately, Boscary focuses on the banking business of the Boscary clan and their activities during the Revolution, providing very little information on their activities as agents de change.

[42] Vidal, 142–43.

[43] Arret du Conseil d'Etat du 26 novembre 1781.

A brief picture of the agents de change may be gleaned from the annual list of agents found in the *Almanach royale*. Between 1724 and 1789, the *Almanachs* list 198 agents de change. Whereas this large number might suggest a high turnover of agents, there was a core of dedicated specialists and, indeed, family dynasties that gave considerable professional continuity to this part of the financial sector.

Many agents de change had long careers. In the period between the fall of Law's System and the French Revolution, one man named Dumain held office for a record forty-one years. Ten agents de change were on the bourse for thirty years or more, nineteen agents served for twenty years or more, and thirty-nine agents held office for ten years or more. Before the tumultuous 1780s when turnover rose, the average tenure of an agent de change was sixteen years.

The great continuity of this profession is found in the family dynasties of agents de change. Among the leading families that were in office at the end of Law's demise, the Dallee family was continuously represented on the bourse until 1786, the De Marine family until 1763, the Duris family until 1751, the Langlois family to 1760, the Mallet family until 1793, the Mey family until 1758, the Moret family until 1764, the Pignard family to 1770, the Prevost family by perhaps as many as five family members serving at different times until 1793, and the Raymond family until 1771. Other long-lived families on the bourse included the Atger family who spanned the years 1753 to 1793, the Autran family who covered 1781 to 1793, the Berger family from 1726 to 1786, the Boscary family from 1771 to 1793, the Derbanne family from 1785 to 1793, the Genevey family from 1785 to 1793, the Mehaignery family from 1760 to 1786, the Page family from 1764 to 1793, the Pasquier family from 1734 to 1763, and the Rocque family from 1734 to 1767. If one were able to tie these families to cousins and nephews with different surnames who served as agents de change, the dominance of long-lived families would be even more striking. Thus, although new men could enter the profession when an office became vacant, the compagnie des agents de change and the bourse was run by a well-established professional corps.

Given this continuity, turnover among office holders was low. Figure 2.1 shows the turnover of agents de change from 1724 to 1793. There is a fairly regular pattern with usually fewer than five agents de change entering or leaving office per year for most of the eighteenth century. There are increases in new agents following the creation of new offices in 1775 and 1786, but what is even more striking is the high turnover in the 1780s. The Crown's intervention in the market and the business of stockbroking caused agents to quit and newcomers to take their places. Taking 1787 and 1788 together, thirty-four new agents de change took office and twenty-one left. The peak of seventy-eight new entrants in 1792 represents the demise of the ancien regime with the termination of the agent's monopoly and the granting of free entry into the profession.

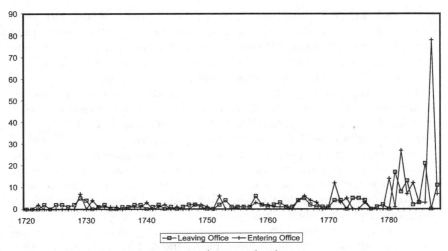

FIGURE 2.1. Turnover of Agents de Change 1720–1793
Source: Almanchs royale, Almanach nationale de France, 1720–93.

The Supply of Securities to the Bourse

Liquidity is partly a function of the size of a security issue. The heterogeneous character of government debt and the small private issues thus limited liquidity. Royal debt was the only type of long-term financial instrument traded on the bourse in the second and third quarters of the century. Thus, the livelihood of the agents de change was linked to the size of the government's deficits and the instruments chosen for financing the shortfall in revenues.

After the reduction in the debt following the demise of Law's System and the absence of any large wars, royal budgets were roughly in balance from about 1727 to 1740, with a few years of modest deficits. Significant and persistent deficits began in 1741 and continued until about 1750. Annual borrowing ranged from 24 to 56 million livres in this period. Unfortunately, there is a gap in budgetary information from 1750 until the beginning of the Seven Years War. Total gross borrowing for 1756 to 1762 totalled 849 million livres.[44] At end of the Seven Years War in 1763, the funded debt had risen to 1,960 million livres and the unfunded debt to 400 million livres.[45] Following the partial default in 1770 that again sharply reduced the debt burden, it appears that the budget was roughly in balance until the beginning of the American War for Independence.

The growing state debt was accompanied by a growth in private debt as well. The volume rose, and although the nominal interest rates remained

[44] Harris and Riley.
[45] Hamilton, 122–3.

stable, real rates fell. Total private debt in Paris rose steadily, with brief wartime plateaus, to more than 900 million livres in 1789, outstripping population or GNP growth. However, government borrowing had a strong effect on the private market and private borrowing appears to have been crowded out in wartime when government borrowing surged.[46]

During this period of gradual growth in the credit markets, the bourse began its operation. A window on the activity on the bourse is given by the côte officielle. The first extant côte officielle from the Bourse dates from 1751.[47] Initially the quotations were given twice a week, Monday and Thursday, but later they were supplied daily. These early côtes record primarily the transaction prices for effete publics, which were securities authorized by the Crown, such as the shares of the Compagnie des Indes, and for effets royaux, the direct obligations of the Crown, which included bonds, lottery tickets, quittances, and other obligations.

The most heavily traded security – as suggested by the number of quotations – were the shares of the Compagnie des Indes. The Compagnie's other obligations, the *billets d'emprunt* (loan certificates) or *emprunt d'octobre* (October loan). Five percent consols (4.5 percent after tax) created in 1745 were also traded. Royal lottery tickets were traded, as were rentes in the form of contracts on the "Hotel de Ville de Paris," contracts on the Caisse des Amortissements (Sinking Fund), 3 percent contracts on the "Royal Poste," 5 percent contracts on the revenue from the 10 percent tax. There were bills for advances (quittances) on Parisian and provincial tax receipts. The *billets des marchands* (short-term notes) were issued by the six great merchant corps of Paris, and bills of credit and bills of exchange on Paris were quoted on the côte, as well.

The partial bankruptcy of 1770 led to a reduction in the securities traded. Côtes for the years immediately following 1770 show no trade except in the stock of the Compagnie des Indes and the billets d'emprunt. The bankruptcy also led to the introduction of new issues that consolidated some of the government debt, including tax anticipation notes.[48] The outbreak of the American War for Independence vastly increased expenditures. Lack of confidence in the Crown's ability to manage its finances drove up yields on debt. Although wartime finance ministers carefully attempted to manage the governments resources, the Crown was dependent on borrowing. The total wartime borrowing is estimated to have amounted to 997 million livres for 1777 to 1782 out of total expenditures of 1,066 million livres.[49]

---

[46] Hoffman, Postel-Vinay, and Rosenthal, "Competition and Coercion;" and "Les Marches du Credit a Paris."

[47] Bibliotheque Nationale. Annonces, Affiches et Avis divers. 1751–1782 (V 28255) 1783–1815 (V 28264).

[48] White, "Was There a Solution?" 556–7.

[49] Harris, 240–2.

The capital market was thus flooded with new government debt. These were boom times for the bankers who assisted the Crown in floating new issues, assisted by the Caisse d'Escompte. The secondary markets also boomed. Much of the new debt was in the form of rentes viageres, or life annuities.[50] When the American war ended, borrowing by the Crown did not subside. By 1785, the Crown still had a deficit of 125 million livres.[51] The list of securities traded on the bourse expanded with these new issues. New loans were issued by the Crown in December 1782, December 1784, December 1785, and November 1787. The largest of these new royal issues was the lottery loan of 1784, which had a capital of 125 million livres. Also traded on the bourse was the Emprunt du domaine de la Ville (loan of the city), issued in September 1786 to construct a bridge in Paris.[52]

Long-term borrowing on the open market by the monarchy largely ceased in 1787 when there was no evident sign of improvement in government finances and the Parlement refused to increase taxes. However, a boom in the issue of private securities occurred in the middle of the decade. Except for the Caisse d'Escompte, founded in 1776, all new private companies were launched between 1783 and 1788. In 1783, the Caisse d' Escompte had a new issue of shares worth 3 million livres. The next year, a company to supply water to the capital, the Compagnie des Eaux de Paris was formed with an issue of 12 million livres. Reviving for a third time an old trading monopoly, the Nouvelle Compagnie des Indes was formed in 1785, and it issued 20 million livres of shares in that year and another 17 million in 1787. Three insurance companies were also created: the Chambre d'assurances contra les incendies (Bureau of Fire Insurance) in 1786 with a capital of 4 million livres, the Compagnie d'assurances contra l'incendie (Fire Insurance Corporation) in 1786 with a capital of 8 million livres, and the Compagnie d'assurances sur la vie (Life Insurance Corporation) in 1788 with a capital of 8 million livres.[53] The total private issues here was small, less than one year's borrowing requirement for the Crown. Yet, however modest their initial capital, the boom in stock prices was impressive. The shares of the Caisse d'Escompte surged from 3,000 to 8,000 livres and those of the Compagnie des Eaux from 1,200 to almost 4,000 livres in the postwar boom.

The Trade and Transfer of Securities

Trade in these public and private securities on the bourse could be cash, for immediate delivery, or (à terme), for future delivery. The latter was through timed payments, a futures market with delivery at the end of the current or

---

[50] Velde and Weir, 21–25.
[51] White, "Was There a Solution?" 560–5 and Table 3.
[52] Martin, 68–9.
[53] Crouzet, 51.

the next month. In the options market, a buyer could purchase a call option that gave the right to buy the security at a fixed price at a future date for a fee. Alternatively, a person could buy a put option, that is, the right to sell a security at a fixed price at a future date for a fee. The fees, or primes, would be paid at the time of purchase.

Although the côte officielle only recorded the purchases bought immediately, there were active futures and options markets. Speculators readily combined futures sales and purchases with call and put options, speculating that the price of a security would rise or fall by a certain amount. These types of operations would have been recognized by any modern trader, but as will be seen in a subsequent section, they were subject to manipulation and abuse because of the firm governance and government regulation.

Futures markets ordinarily play a role in pricing by tying together current and future prices. However, the existence of cash and futures trading in very thin markets may provide the opportunity for market manipulation.[54] Market corners occur when one or several individuals inconspicuously buy a large number of futures contracts so that their price is little altered, then buy heavily in the cash market, driving up the price and reducing the deliverable supply until futures contracts mature. The manipulators then can take delivery of the securities at a low price or force futures markets shorts to buy back their position at higher prices. To alter the result from private or government intervention, the Crown occasionally stepped in to cancel contracts, upsetting the proper functioning of the markets.

The operation of the market was further hampered by the difficulties encountered in transferring ownership of securities. Contemporaries made unfavorable comparison with the market across the Channel. In 1765, observers marveled at the simplicity of the British system for transferring ownership.[55] In France there were several cumbersome methods that added to transaction costs. One type of transfer required a notary to show that a security had been purged of any lien before it could be officially transferred. An alternative method, endorsement, replaced the original certificate with a title to the bearer by a lengthy process. In 1747, the controller general, Machault d'Arnouville, introduced a simplified method. Originally, it was limited to a few securities but gradually simpler methods were adopted for other securities.

Given these imperfections in the market, it is uncertain how efficient the bourse was as a secondary market. Scanning the côtes officielles, trading in any security does not appear to be heavy by modern standards. At most, there were a few transactions each day, and the total volume of trading is

[54] Edwards and Edwards, 333–66.
[55] Archives du Ministere des Affaires etrangeres: M.D., France, 1360.

unknown as records were not kept. They would only be recoverable from an examination of the registres of all agents de change, few of which have survived.

A customer's decision whether to buy or sell securities would be influenced by how easy it would have been to trade at the prices that he or she had observed in previous transactions. If all information about a security was contained in its price, then a single purchase or sale would not have a large impact; only new information should move prices. Prices and price changes are graphed for the shares of the Compagnie des Indes and the Caisse d'Escompte during February 1791 in Figures 2.2 and 2.3. Prices moved quite a bit but in discrete steps, of at most twenty livres for the Compagnie des Indes and 40 livres on a share of the Caisse d' Escompte. This suggests that potential customers could have relied on the market quotations for the previous day about the value of their securities.

The smooth movement of stock prices may appear to be puzzling as the agents de change were not permitted to act as market makers, only agents taking orders. It is easy to imagine that a large order imbalance could have occurred and prices could have gyrated. However, even if the agents de change did not act as market makers, the bankers might have taken on the role of market makers. The Paris banks often held substantial portfolios of securities, and they served on the administrative boards of companies. Given these positions, they could have easily smoothed out fluctuations to ensure a continuous market for their customers, and their heavy involvement in the market suggests that they traded frequently.

One of the most important characteristics that investors desire from a financial market is liquidity, which gives them the ability to buy or sell securities quickly with relatively little change in prices. In markets where trading is conducted by market makers who stand ready to buy or sell whenever the public wishes to trade, bid and ask prices are posted. The difference in price compensates the market makers for providing liquidity. The bid–ask spread thus reflects the trading costs or degree of liquidity.[56] Although the agents de change were not market makers, an implicit bid–ask spread could be calculated, and they could thereby obtain an idea of the size of the trading costs.[57] The results in Table 2.1 show the implicit bid–ask spreads for several securities in different periods, using data from the côtes officielles. The estimates for the Compagnie des Indes and the Caisse d'Escompte in 1791 reflect the microstructure in place between 1770 and 1791 when entry was limited by the fixed number of agents and the size of security issues were modest. As will be discussed later, following an examination of the microstructure for

---

[56] Campbell, Lo, and MacKinlay, 99–100.
[57] Roll, 1127–39. See also Campbell, Lo, and MacKinlay for some qualifications about the procedure, 134–8.

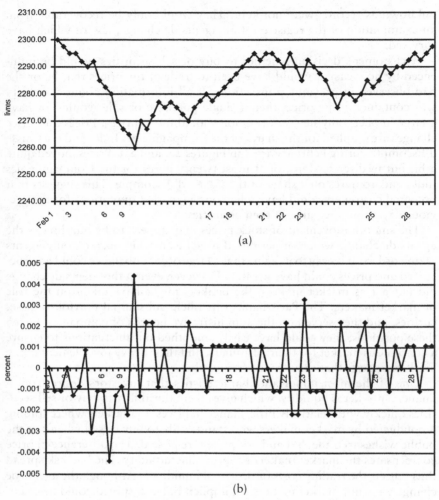

FIGURE 2.2. (a)Transaction Price of Compagnie des Indes Stock February 1 to 28, 1791, (b) Percentage Change in Price of Compagnie des Indes Stock February 1 to 28, 1791
Source: Côte officielle, 1791.

subsequent periods, the implicit spreads in 1791 show relatively low trading costs and high liquidity in spite of the lack of competition and small size of issues. Taken together with the price data and qualitative information on the behavior of bankers and brokers, it appears that customers were reasonably well served by the market.

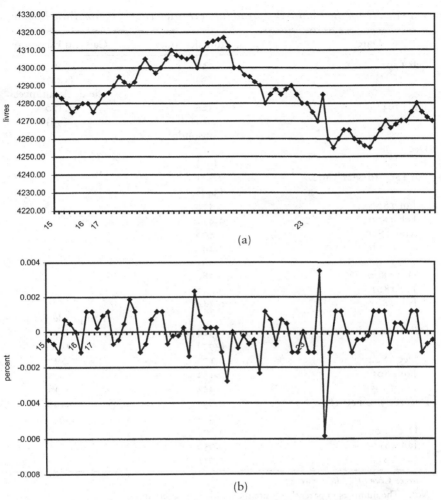

FIGURE 2.3. (a) Transaction Price of Caisse d'Escompte Stock February 15 to 28, 1791, (b) Percentage Change in Price of Caisse d'Escompte Stock February 15 to 28, 1791
Source: Côte officielle, 1791.

The Loss of Privilege

The financial crisis of the Crown in the 1780s forced ministers to seek additional sources of revenue. In their search for new funds to cover the deficit, they renewed their efforts, largely abandoned in the 1720s, to squeeze the agents de change for credit. In 1781, the government required all new agents

TABLE 2.1. *Implicit Bid-Ask Spread for Securities Traded on the Paris Bourse*

Date	Compagnie des Indes	Caisse d'Escompte
Feb 1791	0.056	0.067
	(63)	(128)
		Cie de Assurances
Jan 1793	0.326	0.370
	(76)	(98)
	5% Consolide	
Dec 1798	2.617	
	(90)	
Jan 1800 to Mar 1800	0.303	
	(344)	
Jan 1800	0.576	
Feb 1800	0.470	
Mar 1800	0.408	
Dec 1800 to Feb 1801	0.242	
	(613)	
Dec 1800	0.586	
Jan 1801	0.492	
Feb 1801	0.344	
		Banque de France
Dec 1804 to Feb 1805	0.314	0.102
	(377)	(104)
Dec 1804	0.173	0.147
Jan 1805	0.132	0.072
Feb 1805	0.452	0.113
Dec 1809 to Feb 1810	0.053	0.140
	(501)	(157)
Dec 1809	0.104	
Jan 1810	0.050	
Feb 1810	0.011	

Source: Côte officielle, 1791–1810.

Note: The numbers in parentheses are the number of observations.

de change to provide a bond worth 60,000 livres or 40,000 livres in specie, on which they would receive 5 percent interest.[58] The Crown seems to have judged correctly what it could squeeze out of the agents de change, as there were no more than the normal number of agents giving up their offices after the issuance of this arret (Fig. 2.1.) The boom in the stock market and the rising number of transactions on the bourse made it a very profitable occupation that could tolerate this new tax.

In desperate financial straits in 1786, the Crown took a more radical step and dissolved the existing offices and replaced them with old style hereditary

[58] Arret du conseil d'etat du 26 novembre 1781.

offices for sixty brokers.[59] Each office carried a finance or loan of 100,000 livres with a gage of 4 percent, later raised to 4.5 percent with the dixieme tax withheld.[60] This alteration produced a dramatic turnover (Fig. 2.1.) In 1786 and 1787, twenty-five agents de change abandoned their offices and were replaced with thirty-four new members.

Although the state had captured a loan of 6 million livres, the offices proved to be worth even more on the open market; and limited records show that they were sold for 180,000 to 190,000 livres in the next year.[61] The weakened financial condition of the Crown in 1788 forced the finance minister, Lomenie de Brienne, to consider various plans to reconstitute the offices at even higher prices. Under this threat, the agents de change offered to renounce their gages for a promise that the number of brokers would remain fixed – and the offer was accepted.

Like all the ancien regime's institutions, the compagnie des agents de change came under attack during the Revolution. The first sign of trouble was the dramatic declaration on the night of August 4, 1789, suppressing venal offices. Although other offices were liquidated in 1790, the agents de change aggressively protected their monopoly rights, petitioning the National Assembly. On March 17, 1791, freedom of occupation and profession was established and all privileged offices were abolished.[62] Officials' finances became part of the public debt. Any profession could be freely exercised by paying the license tax and following any regulations the government legislated. The brokers fought a rearguard battle, warning the National Assembly of the chaotic consequences of free entry into their profession.[63] Although the National Assembly permitted the brokers to continue their monopoly until April 15, 1791, the law was not modified.

The petition of the agents de change drew a scathing reply from the Jacobin, Francois Buzot, who challenged their contention that the government's credit and private fortunes depended on the preservation of their privilege.[64] His reply showed a remarkable change in attitude, at least for a portion of the public, placing his faith in a competitive market. He admonished the agents de change to forgo their privileges, assuring them that the market would support a regime of liberty. Furthermore, Buzot pointed out that in foreign countries, agents de change had no monopoly, no *brevet d'accaparement* [patent of monopolization].

59 Declaration du Roi, March 19, 1786.
60 This was a fairly high price compared to the most expensive offices, those of the receveurs generaux, which carried a finance of 500,000 livres. Doyle (1984).
61 Bien, 16.
62 Lois des 2–17 mars 1791.
63 Petition des courtiers de change a l'Assemblee Nationale, lue a la societe des Amis de la Constitution, March 30, 1791 (Archives nationales Ad XI 58).
64 *Moniteur Universel* 16 avril, 1791, Vol. VIII, 136–137.

The Assembly followed Buzot's advice and voted on May 6, 1791, to liquidate the compagnie and the offices of the agents de change and return their finances. On May 8, the Assembly set the new rules for brokers. Henceforth, to become an agent de change, any individual who was not employed by the government or in another line of commerce could pay the patente tax, take an oath of personal integrity, and become a broker. The commercial tribunals were to determine the commission charged by agents de change.[65] In a defensive action, the stockbrokers formed their own free company to defend their business. Yet, although the brokers unhappily faced a new regime, their customers seemed unperturbed. The banker, Greffulhe, wrote to a friend in 1791, "We do not believe that the loss of brokers' priveliges is regretted as they were not to be found in either Amsterdam or London."[66]

To the consternation of the established agents de change, free entry led to the appearance of many new brokers on the floor of the exchange. The *Almanach Royale* had reported there were a total of 50 brokers in 1787, 49 in 1788, 51 in 1789, 58 in 1790, and 57 in 1791. Then the dam burst: In 1792 the *Almanach* recorded 132 brokers and in 1793, 138 brokers. As Figure 2.1 shows, there were more than 20 agents who left office in 1791 but the total number of agents increased as 78 new brokers paid the patente tax and took the oath to compete in the new marketplace. Although there were many newcomers to the bourse as indicated by the new names in the *Almanach Royale*, most of the old guard did not abandon the bourse and some of the new names – Atger, Chabouillet, Derbanne, Lemire, and Soret – inscribed in 1792 belonged to established families of agents.

The destruction of the monopoly of the agents de change would presumably have been a momentous change, yet free entry into stockbrokering had apparently little effect on the business of the bourse. Figure 2.4 shows the price of each transaction for shares of the Compagnie des Indes for January and February 1793. There are a few spikes in the picture produced by data missing on some days, but they are little different from Figures 2.2 and 2.3 for 1791. It seems reasonable to conclude that allowing free entry did not alter the behavior of the leading agents de change on the market, nor of the bankers, who held large portfolios of securities and may have acted as market makers or at least as price stabilizers.

This early period of the Revolution permits an examination of the effects of free entry to the bourse when there was no change in the structure of the debt or other key features. Increasing competition should have lowered trading costs and improved liquidity. However, the estimates of the implicit bid–ask spread for January 1793 in Table 2.1 are higher than those for February 1791 when there was restricted entry. Assuming that these are

[65] Lois du mai 1791.
[66] Antonetti, n.d. 66.

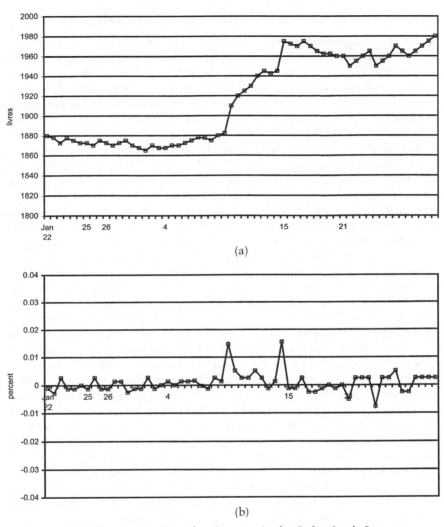

FIGURE 2.4. (a) Transaction Price for Compagnie des Indes Stock January 21 to February 28, 1793, (b) Percentage Change in Price of Compagnie des Indes Stock January 21 to February 28, 1793
Source: Côte officielle, 1793.

significant differences, the results suggest that the increase in the number of agents raised trading costs in spite of the increase in competition. One possibility is that the new agents, many of whom were apparently new to the business, lacked experience and did not cooperate well with the established agents.

The Revolution and the Financial Community

Although the agents de change, like other elite groups of the ancien regime, lost their privileges, many in the financial community initially welcomed the Revolution. They applauded and supported the reordering of royal finances and the introduction of a more laissez-faire regime. One agent de change turned banker, Jean Boscary l'aine, was elected to the Assemble Nationale de Paris for 1791–2.[67] Among the great bankers, the Le Couteulx family, for example, supported the new regime.[68]

The challenge to the Estates-General and then the National Assembly was to discover a politically acceptable solution to the financial crisis of the monarchy. When the Estates-General opened on May 5, 1789, the Crown was covering its deficit by borrowing from the Caisse d'Escompte. This vastly increased circulation of banknotes produced a run on the bank in September 1789, alarming the Assembly with the prospect of inflationary finance. To cover the deficit, a plan was offered to create state-issued paper money – the assignats – backed by the nationalized lands of the Church. The theory behind this scheme was that creating assignats to cover expenditures would not be inflationary. After being placed in circulation, the assignats would be eventually retired when they were used to purchase the lands.[69]

Even though they did not initially support the alternative proposal to create the assignats, most members of the financial community gave their approval. The continued weak state of government finance and the shifts in policy helped induce further economic crises and new opportunities for sharp traders. Inflation and economic uncertainty provided bankers with more opportunities to speculate in commodities, specie, and foreign exchange whose prices were subject to large and sudden shifts. These activities undermined government policy, and financial intermediaries were increasingly seen as threats to the success of the Revolution. The laissez-faire regime evaporated within two years when the revolutionaries proved themselves unable to solve the financial problems they had inherited from the ancien regime and were forced to rely on inflationary finance by issuing the assignats. When the government opted for price controls, confiscations, and a partial command economy, the existence of a free market on the bourse became a threat to the government's strategy. Traders and brokers were attacked as speculators and hoarders responsible for the falling value of the assignats and the bourse was closed on June 27, 1793.

On August 2, 1793 all those who had commerce with foreigners, including all bankers with international connections, were declared enemies of the Nation. The Convention voted to suppress all stock companies on August 24.

---

[67] Bouchary, *Les Boscary*, 7–8.
[68] Daridan, 171.
[69] White, "The French Revolution," 248–50.

On October 7, seals were affixed to the houses of all foreigners, bankers, and other persons with foreign trade or commerce in specie. Many bankers were jailed and their property seized. On May 8, 1794, the tax farmers were guillotined and the Republic seized their assets. Some bankers and agents de change subsequently shared the same fate, others fled.

By closing public institutions like the bourse, forcing the liquidation of the banks, and executing, exiling, and impoverishing many financiers, bankers, and agents de change, the Reign of Terror succeeded in smashing the financial system of the ancien regime. Even those bankers, like Le Couteulx and the Boscary, who survived the Reign of Terror and would later reestablish new banks and become agents de change had their portfolios of financial assets liquidated. If they preserved any wealth it was in the form of land or securities abroad.

Restructuring the National Debt

The failure to solve the fiscal crisis of the ancient regime was a driving factor in the radicalization of the Revolution. When the Convention opened on September 21, 1792 and began the final assault on the monarchy, most deputies were supporting a laissez-faire economic regime. Yet, the fiscal crisis of the state was not solved, and it grew worse with the war that had begun in April 1792. As financing the deficit became more difficult, the market economy was gradually abandoned. The National Assembly had offered a guarantee to the debt holders but in this deepening crisis, this promise was abandoned to cut nonwar expenditures.

Heading the finance committee in the Convention, Joseph Cambon presented a report on August 15, 1793, that recommended the creation of *Grand livre de la dette publique*. In this book, all the names of the owners of the new consolidated debt would be inscribed. All revenue below 50 livres were to be reimbursed. The ancien regime's process of payment and transfer were simplified. To the horror of the independently wealthy, Cambon eliminated all the special benefits and characteristics of loan contracts. The lottery loan of 1784, for example, was reduced to a simple 5 percent consol. The newly uniform debt was known as *inscriptions sur le Grand Livre de la dette publique* (book of public debt), or simply inscriptions. On May 12, 1794, Cambon engineered a forced conversion of the high yielding 100 million life annuities into 5 percent consols. All revenue under 50 livres were reimbursed. To receive payment, now in depreciating assignats, proof of residence was required to exclude enemies of the regime.[70]

The final chapter in the financial failure of the Revolution was the default on the government's debt on September 30, 1797. After ten years of

---

[70] Vuhrer, Chapter XIII.

promising to pay interest and repay the debt, the government acknowledged that it had failed and wrote the debt down by two-thirds. The 5 percent revenue, or as they became known, the tiers consolide, were then created; but even with this reduced burden, no payment in specie was forthcoming. An even vaguer promise was issued for the *bons de deux tiers* [two-thirds bonds] or *bons au porteur* (bearer bonds), which offered payment for the lost two-thirds and traded at huge discounts.

Reconstructing the Financial Markets

The Reign of Terror and the controlled economy failed dismally, with price controls and hyperinflation devastating both markets for goods and financial markets. The government gradually began to restore a market economy. The bourse was reopened briefly from May 20 to December 14, 1794, and then again on April 25, 1795. New regulations were decreed. Trade in bullion and foreign bills was legal but only on the bourse; no contract was valid unless made on the bourse. The committees of public safety and finance were delegated the task of appointing twenty-five agents de change, twenty were to be assigned to banking operations and negotiation in foreign bills in Paris, and five to the purchase and sale of specie. Still distrustful of the market, brokers were again prohibited from trading on their own accounts and trading in term payments. The law liquidating existing stock companies and prohibiting new ones was abrogated on October 21, 1795.[71] To encourage the reappearance of specie, the government made it legal to trade in gold and silver but only on the bourse.[72] On September 9, 1795, the bourse was closed because the government was embarrassed by the high price of a gold Louis, that showed the rapid depreciation of the assignats in the hyperinflation.[73]

With the end of paper money in sight, the government issued a decree on January 10, 1796, that ordered the reopening of the bourse on January 22.[74] This new bourse operated in the former church of the Petits-Peres, every day from one to three in the afternoon. It was open only to those who could show that they had proof of payment of the forced loan, although foreign merchants were exempted from this requirement on January 27. The effets commercables, which could only be traded by the twenty agents de change, were foreign bills of exchanges, gold, silver, and government securities. A clerk-crier announced in a loud voice the prices at the end of the market and

---

[71] Brumaire An IV, Loi abrogeant la loi du 26 germinal an II.

[72] Trading elsewhere carried a penalty of two years imprisonment and public exposure of the offender with the inscription on his breast "agioteur" and confiscation of his property.

[73] Fructidor an III. Arrete du Ministre de l'Interieur ordonnant la fermeture de la Bourse de Paris.

[74] 20 Nivose an IV. Arret concernant la tenue de la Bourse.

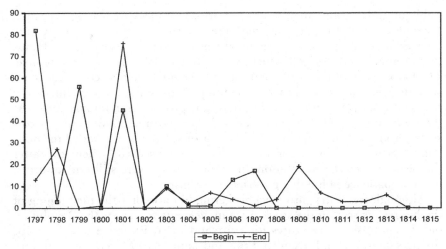

FIGURE 2.5. Turnover of Agents de Change 1797–1814
Source: Almanach nationale de France, Almanach imperiale, 1797–1814.

recorded them in a register. However, all the laws concerning speculation were to remain in force – hardly encouraging active trading.

Pronouncing itself scandalized by the fluctuations on the market produced by speculators, the government issued a new decree on February 21, 1796, to control speculation.[75] The bourse's operation was limited to one hour, between one and two in the afternoon. No one could engage in any trading without proof that he had the specie, assignats, or securities with him or deposited with an agent de change or notary and the transfer was required to occur within twenty-four hours. Any violation of these new rules would be treated as speculation and punished accordingly.

This restrictive regime did not endure long, and in 1797 free entry to the bourse was granted upon payment of a tax, the license, of 300 francs. The republican *Almanach* for the Year VI (1797–98) shows eighty-two agents de change were registered. Several of the pre-1793 agents who had survived the Reign of Terror brought their expertise, but the list of names shows a large number of newcomers. Furthermore, as Figure 2.5 shows, there was considerable entry and exit for the next several years, with new agents taking a chance of making a living by trading, while discouraged agents were leaving.

The côtes officielles of the bourse in 1795 reveal a market that was a shadow its former self. Bills of exchange on several foreign cities are quoted, and there are occasional quotations for specie in the form of coin and ingots. The two securities listed are the inscriptions sur la Grand Livre de la dette

---

[75] 2 Ventose An IV. Arret portant reglement concernant la Bourse.

publique and the bons au porteur. Quotations for these are scarce, indicating a very low level of trading. In 1796, the government promised to pay one-quarter of the revenue in specie; but only delivered promissory notes – bonds du 1/4 and bonds des 3/4, which were infrequently traded on the bourse. The bankruptcy of the 2/3's bonds in 1797 created the tiers consolide (consolidated thirds), a consol that seemed to promise solid future payment and the bonds des 2/3 again carried some vague promise of reimbursement. At the same time the Directory reimbursed short-term debts with *tiers provisoire* [promissory notes]. To this short list of securities was added the *bons d'arrerage* in 1798, issued for interest due on other securities. Ten years after the beginning of the Revolution, in 1799, rentiers were still not rewarded for their patience in holding government securities.

Although free entry into stockbrokering did not alter the functioning of the bourse, as seen in the stock price movements for 1793, the Revolution did. In contrast to the figures for 1791 and 1793, Figures 2.6 and 2.7 for the tiers consolide in December 1798 and January to March 1800 are very different. The changes in price between transactions are much more volatile. Prices in 1791 and 1793 moved less than one-quarter of 1 percent between transactions, but after the Revolution the average seems to be about 2 percent between transactions, with 3 and 4 percent not uncommon. There is much more volatility in the market. This contrast is particularly striking because the tiers consolide was much larger than the earlier issues – it had a nominal capital of 930 million francs in 1799 – and hence, had the possibility of more frequent transactions.[76]

In Table 2.1, the implicit bid–ask spread is extremely high for 1798, reflecting the low levels of liquidity in the market. Even after Napoleon arrived in power, the spreads remain relatively high for 1800 and 1801 compared to earlier periods. The large consolidated debt and the free entry into the market should have lowered trading costs. Whereas political uncertainty might have increased volatility month-to-month or sometimes day-to-day, it is hard to see how this could have raised within day fluctuations between transactions. One factor that may have reduced liquidity was the Revolution's destruction of the financial system and the bankers' wealth, in particular. The bankers were no longer in a position to act as market makers. Their portfolios of securities had disappeared. By expropriation and harassment, the Revolution destroyed the banking houses and their informal network that had encouraged a smooth operation of the bourse. The agents de change were now merely agents taking orders with no financial intermediary interested or able in making a market; informal market making seemed to have disappeared.

[76] Fachan, 131.

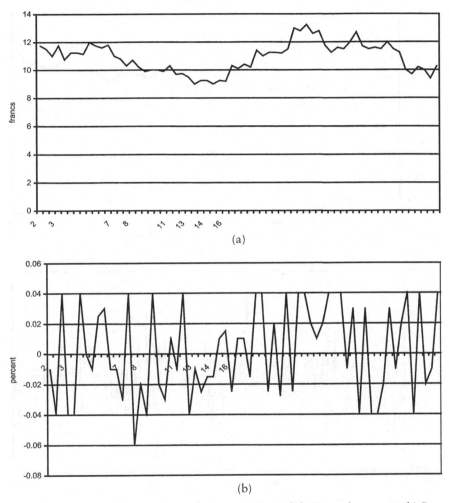

FIGURE 2.6. (a) Transaction Price of 5 percent Consolide December 1798, (b) Percentage Change in Price of 5 percent Consolide December 1798
Source: Côte officielle, 1798.

Reconstituting the Bourse

Napoleon's coup on November 9 (18 Brumaire in the revolutionary calendar) began sweeping changes, completing the Directory's reorganization of government finance. To restore France's economic prowess and establish order, Napoleon recreated many of the institutions of the ancien regime. Building on the efforts of the Directory, tax revenues increased and gradually

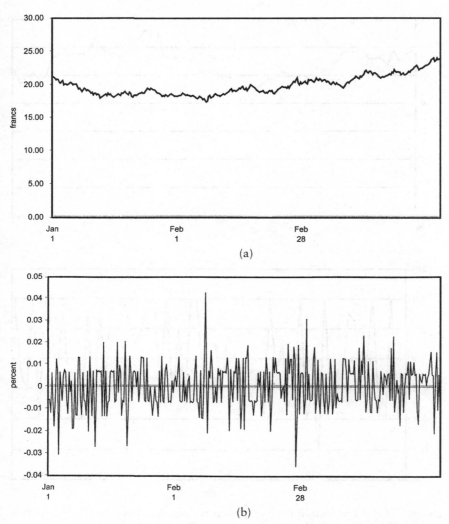

FIGURE 2.7. (a) Transaction Price of 5 percent Consolide Jan 1, 1800 to March 30, 1800, (b) Percentage Change in the Price of 5 percent Consolide Jan 1, 1800 to March 30, 1800
Source: Côte officielle, 1800.

the budget moved into balance. A sinking fund was established in 1799 and the Banque de France in 1800, while payment of interest on the debt in specie resumed in 1800 and the nation returned to the bimetallic standard in 1803. Concerned about what the price of the rentes – the tiers consolide – said about his government, Napoleon had a personal interest and took special advice in the design of a new bourse.

Napoleon's chosen expert was François Mollien, director-general of the Caisse d'Amortissement, who before the revolution had served in the tax farms administration and the office of the controleur general and whose wife was the niece of an agent de change.[77] Mollien's memoirs record an audience with the First Consul in June 1801.[78] In the silent presence of the two other consuls, Cambacères and Lebrun, Napoleon grilled Mollien on the subject of the Paris bourse for two hours. Napoleon saw public confidence in the newly created Consulate reflected in the price of the rentes, and he was fearful that speculation on the exchange could depress prices. Buoyed by the rise in the price of the rentes from 10 francs to between 40 to 50 francs, the First Consul announced that the newly created sinking fund should try to stabilize prices.

Napoleon launched into a tirade about the "hommes sans etat, sans capitaux, sans patrie," [men without rank, fortune, or country] who bought and sold a rente ten times a day seeking to become arbitrators of the market. While recognizing that some agents de change were honest, he criticized most as a "fouls d'aventeuriers qu'on appelle les agioteurs; les agents de change eux-mimes" [wild adventurers called speculators; the brokers themselves] for trading on their own account even though it was forbidden. The First Consul considered it absurd that for the simple payment of the patents tax, anyone could enter the business. He stated that he felt it necessary to restore the corporate discipline to the agents de change that they had been subject to before 1789. Instead of an annual tax, a finance fee should be required. Before admission to the profession, candidates should be judged by a jury of the leading agents de change as to their moral character and capacity to serve.

Although defending the brokers as honest, Mollien was not in favor of free entry upon payment of the patents and an oath. He told Napoleon, "Il n'est pas plus difficule de multiplier les hommes d'honneur parmi les gens d'affairs, qu'il ne l'a ete pour vous, general, de multiplier les braves dans les armees francaises. [It is no easier to increase the number of honest men in business than it is for you, General, to increase the number of brave men in the French army.][79] Mollien concurred with the need to restrict entry, suggesting that a bond of 100,000 francs be required and the number of agents be limited to sixty.

After Napoleon had made an unfavorable comparison of the Paris bourse to the Amsterdam and London exchanges, Mollien pointed out that these were much larger markets. He argued that government bonds in Paris were more volatile because the Paris market was thinner. One found small speculators on the bourse, willing to trade on wide fluctuations. Mollien attributed the higher volatility to the recent history of expropriations, violations of

[77] Brugiere, 215.
[78] Mollien, 250–79.
[79] Mollien, 250–78.

contracts, inflation, and other ills that kept merchants and bankers out of the market. The sharpest disagreement came over futures markets, where Mollien confronted Napoleon's desire to suppress them.

Napoleon challenged Mollien, asking if a man offers to sell a 5 percent rente for 38 francs in one month when the current price is 50 francs, does he not proclaim his lack of confidence in the government? Mollien responded that this transaction does not have an independent effect on public credit; but simply reflects it. Furthermore, if the seller is wrong, he is penalized. Napoleon then reminded him that the marches a terme had been prohibited before the Revolution. In response, Mollien carefully explained that futures markets are common for all sorts of goods, and there was no reason to exclude them from the bourse. He argued that one should not abolish bills of exchange simply because some merchants abuse them. If contracts were abused, then it is proper to take the case before a court of law, rather than ban them outright.

The result of this interview was the decree of 27 Prairial X (June 16, 1802), governing the bourse. Together with the law enacted on 28 Ventase IX (March 19, 1801) and the Code de Commerce in 1807, they determined the structure of the bourse under the Consulate and the Empire. The law of 28 Ventase IX and the Code de Commerce conferred on stockbrokers a monopoly of trade in government securities and other securities "susceptible" to being quoted. Securities not quoted on the official list were transacted on the coulisse and the quotation of foreign securities remained forbidden until 1823. Beyond these powers granted by the ancien regime, the Code de Commerce gave brokers the right to trade bills of exchange and other commercial instruments. They also divided the right to deal in specie with merchandise brokers. Agents de change were to be nominated through the filter of local committees and the Minister of the Interior to the Emperor who had the power to appoint eighty.

The agents de change alone had the right to act as middlemen, to verify quotations and testify before courts on questions about the quotations. They were to be paid a fixed commission and were forbidden to trade on their own account by the Code de Commerce. Other individuals usurping their functions were subject to a fine not in excess of one-sixth and not less than one-twelfth of a broker's bond. This market may be characterized as an agency/auction market, where the orders were consolidated by requiring customers to deliver them to their brokers in advance of the opening of the markets. Once again, agents de change were required to keep a journal-registre of their trades. Quotations were released after the closure of the markets. The bourse continued to operate in the former Church of the Petits-Peres until 1809 when it was moved to the Palais-Royal. Except for holidays, the bourse was open every day for trade in securities from two to three o'clock in the afternoon and for commercial operations from ten o'clock to four o'clock. The intent of the laws were explained by Jard

Panvillier, the reporter of Title V of the Code de Commerce: the agents de change must have the "perfect confidence" of the public. "They must not be allowed to expose themselves to the danger of compromising the interest of their clients by compromising their own fortune in a risky or unfortunate enterprise."

Trading on the Napoleonic Bourse

The Napoleonic laws drastically reduced the number of stockbrokers. The *Almanach National de France* for 1799–1800 reported that there were 106 agents de change practicing their trade. While the new law had permitted eighty brokers to be selected by Napoleon, he only found and appointed seventy-one honest agents de change on July 20, 1801. Of the total 228 agents de change during the Napoleonic era there were many newcomers, but agents from the ancien regime or members of their families reappeared. The *Almanachs* for the Consulate and the Empire show at least thirty family names also listed as agents de change before 1793. Of these survivors, Boscary, Breant de la Neuville, Lemire, Guesdon, Personnel Desbrieres, Pignard, Richard de Montjoyeaux, Mandinier, Mallet, and Rogues are notable for the many years of their service in both periods.

While the volume of activity and hence the demand for brokerage services continued to grow as transactions increased, it became much less attractive when a surety bond of 60,000 francs was required. The high rate of turnover of agents de change for the early years of the decade disappeared, as seen in Figure 2.5 when the cost of entering the profession soared. In 1805, when there were seventy-two agents de change as reported by the *Almanach Imperial*, Napoleon raised the bond to 100,000 francs. While the number of offices was increased to 100, after 1807 no new agents took office and the number of agents dropped steadily to forty-one in 1814.[80]

While markets were reestablished, complete freedom of enterprise and practice was still suspect. Not only was the monopoly of the agents de change established, but the marches a terme were regarded with suspicion. Initially, some restrictions were placed on futures markets, following the dictates of the First Consul. The law of 27 Prairial X required brokers to have in their possession securities for sellers and money for buyers when they went to trade. The design of this decree was intended to check transactions for future delivery by brokers. The marches a terme were not, however, repressed. The police observed and noted large operations of futures markets in the politically sensitive rentes.[81]

---

[80] The increase in offices was intended to offset the suppression of the commissioners who had assisted them. *Manuel des agents de change*, 243.

[81] Bouchary, *Les Boscary*, 42.

When the new regulations of the Compagnie des agents de change were proposed by the Minister of the Interior in 1808, the syndic, Jean-Baptists-Joseph Boscary de Villeplaine, felt obliged to once again explain the purpose and necessity of the marches a terme.[82] Boscary de Villeplaine pointed out that the Emperor's belief that the Code de Commerce's stricture that futures trades be conducted with the asset in possession applied to all markets was incorrect. This rule only applied to the property market. Furthermore, the marches a terme did not increase the short-term funds available for speculation. He plainly told Napoleon that the spot market was small, the banks handled all domestic commercial paper, and international financial transactions were virtually nonexistent. Thus, only the courtage earned from the marche a terme provided the agents de change with any income. The syndic had no objection to regulating the marche a terme and limiting it to two months duration, but he warned that attempting to ensure immediate possession for delivery would cause the securities markets to dissipate. The bold words of the agents de change's syndic may have stayed the Emperor's hand as no legislation followed.

The variety of assets traded on the Napoleonic bourse grew slowly. Gold and silver in ingots, bars, and coin had an active trade. From 1800 to 1814, the number of cities with quotations for thirty- and ninety-day bills of exchange on the côte officielle grew. The various types of securities created under the Directory to pay emergencies and arrears – the temporary rente, the 2/3s bond, the 3/4s bond, the 1/4 bond, the bond for arrears and the bond for the year VIII – were gradually consolidated into the tiers consolide, which became know as the consolide 5 percent, or the 5 percent consol. This financial instrument, with a capital of nearly one billion francs, was by far the largest issue. The only other issue that was frequently traded was the stock of the Banque de France. Initially, the Banque had a capital of 30 million francs when it was founded in 1800; in 1803 it was raised to 45 million francs, and in 1806 it reached 90 million francs. There were also several small issues, which traded infrequently: The Emprunt du Roi de Saxe, the Actions des Trois Ponts sur la Seine, the Canaux du Midi, d'Orleans, and the Loing. The low level of activity on the capital markets served by the bourse was paralleled by the quiescence in the market served by the notaries. In contrast to its heady pre-revolutionary growth, this private debt market was almost stagnant in the first decade of the nineteenth century.

The resurrected bourse had a rising volume of activity in the limited issues quoted on it. Although the new regime restricted the number of agents, there was less transaction-to-transaction volatility. Customers placing an order one day had good information from the close of the previous day available about the price that would be realized by their trade in the absence of any

---

[82] Bouchary, *Les Boscary*, 42–5.

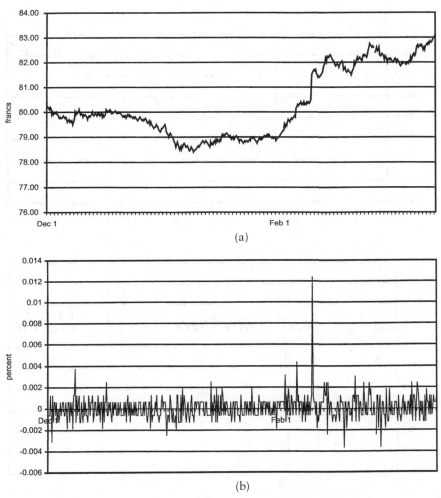

FIGURE 2.8. (a) Transaction Price of 5 percent Consolide December 1, 1809 to February 28, 1810, (b) Percentage Change in the Price of 5 percent Consolide December 1, 1809 to February 28, 1810
Source: Côte officielle, 1809–10.

"news" to the market. Figures 2.8 and 2.9 for the tiers consolide and the shares of the Banque de France for three months in 1810 show a substantial reduction in the change in prices from transaction to transaction, compared to earlier years. By 1810, the fluctuation was under one-quarter percent for the tiers consolide and the shares of the Banque. There is one identifiable piece of news for the period December 1809 to February 1810, which produced a big price spike. On February 5, the Viennese Court approved of the marriage

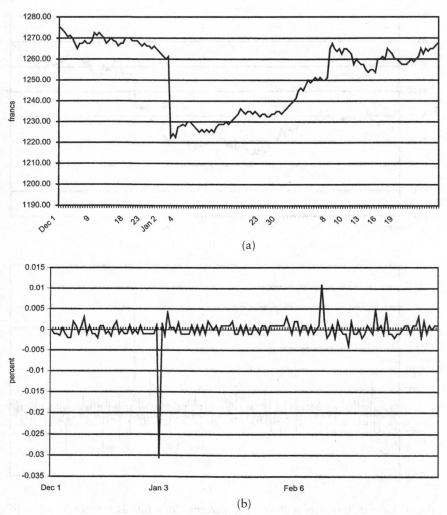

FIGURE 2.9. (a) Transaction Price of Banque de France Stock December 1, 1809
to February 28, 1810, (b) Percentage Change in Price of Banque de France Stock
December 1, 1809 to February 28, 1810
Source: Côte officielle, 1809–10.

of Archduchess Marie Louise to Napoleon, signalling improved relations
between Austria and France.[83] Given the approximate two-day travel time
between capitals, this must be the event that caused the jump in the tiers
between the last transaction on February 7 and the first on February 8. The

[83] Bertaud, 147.

large spike for the Banque de France appears to be some unidentified rumor from which the shares eventually recovered.

For the Napoleonic era, the estimated implicit bid–ask spreads in Table 2.1 for 1804 to 1805 and 1809 to 1810 are substantially lower than the spreads for the previous decade. They are approximately the same as the spreads for the ancien regime. The Napoleonic market, as represented by the 5 percent consol and the stock of the Banque de France, had the largest issues, but trading was handled by a restricted number of agents de change. This general narrowing of fluctuations and spreads means that the market had returned to the pattern of behavior observed before the Reign of Terror had ripped up the fabric of the financial system. This evolution is consonant with the recovery of banking. The Revolution had devastated Paris banking houses that had been intimately involved in the operation of the securities markets and market making. Their portfolios had been liquidated, and the bankers survived by fleeing abroad or hiding in the countryside, converting their assets into real estate or investing in foreign securities. Under the safety of the Napoleonic regime, bankers returned to their former role in the financial markets.[84] The reconstitution of the banking business was a slow process. Some bankers who had gone abroad, participating in the general capital flight to London, did not return, as war with Britain continued. Instead, new bankers came from the provinces, Switzerland, and Belgium.[85] Bankers like Boscary de Villeplaine played the market to acquire the capital necessary for a bank. On the eve of Napoleon's coup on the 18 Brumaire, Boscary de Villeplaine took all the funds at his disposal and invested them in the tiers consolide. This investment increased his fortune six-fold, allowing him to become a important player in the market.[86]

Conclusion

From the foundation of the bourse to the end of the Napoleonic era, the rules of the Paris bourse evolved following the dictates of the government. The result was a changing microstructure that provided varying degrees of liquidity depending on the rules of the market and the structure of the general financial system. On the eve of the Revolution, trading issues of modest size on the highly regulated bourse had evolved to a point where trading costs to the public were relatively low. The revolutionary upheaval changed the rules and consolidated the government debt, but the ruin of the financial inter-mediaries, who apparently served as market makers, prevented the market

---

[84] Although Napoleon's government occasionally intervened in the market, it was to counter embarrassing movements in the 5 percent consols, not a daily intervention as a market maker. Mollien, 343–56.

[85] Bergeron, 45–86.

[86] Bouchary, *Les Boscary*, 42.

from providing greater liquidity. Only the political stability under Napoleon that permitted the reemergence of the financial system allowed the bourse to once again provide its customers with a liquid market on which to trade their securities.

Bibliography

Almanach royale, Almanach national de France, Almanach imperiale, various years.

Antonetti, Guy. *Une Maison de Banque a Paris au XVIIIe siecle: Greffulhe Montz et Cie (1789–1793).* Paris: Edition Cujas, n.d.

Antonetti, Guy. "Les manoeuvres boursieres du controleur general Le Peletier des Forts et la reglementation du marche des valeurs mobilieres (1730)." *Revue d'Histoire du Droit* (1984): 577–97.

Bergeron, Louis. *Banquiers, negociants et manufacturiers parisiens du Directoire a l'Empire.* Paris: Ecole des hautes études en sciences sociàles, 1978.

Bertaud, Jean-Paul. *Histoire du Consulate et de l'Empire.* Paris: Perrin, 1992.

Bien, David D. "Property in Office Under the Old Regime: The Case of the Stockbrokers," in *Early Modern Conceptions of Property,* eds. John Brewer and Susan Staves. London: Routledge, 1993.

Bigo, Robert. *La Caisse d'Escompte (1776–1793) et les Origines de la Banque de France.* Paris: Presses Universitaires de France, 1927.

Bigo, Robert. *Les bases historiques de la finance moderne* Paris: A. Colin, 1933.

Bouchary, Jean. *Les Manieurs d'Argent a Paris a la fin du XVIIIe siecle.* Paris: Marcel Riviere et Cie, I, 1939; II, 1940; III, 1942.

Bouchary, Jean. *Les Compagnies financieres a Paris A fin du XVIIIe siecle.* Paris: Marcel Riviere et Cie, I, 1940; II, 1941; III, 1942.

Bouchary, Jean. *Les Boscary: Une famille d'agents de change sous l'Ancien Regime La Revolution Le Consul L'Empire et La Restauration.* Paris: 1942.

Bouvier, Jean. "Vers le capitalisme bancaire: L'expansion du credit apres Law," in *Histoire economique et sociale de la France* II, ed. Ernest Labrousse et al. Paris: Presses Universitaires de France, 1970, 301–21.

Brugiere, Michel. *Gestionnaires et Profiteurs de la Revolution.* Paris: Olivier Orban, 1986.

Butel, Paul. *L'economie francaise au XVIIIe siecle.* Paris: SEDES, 1993.

Campbell, John Y., Andrew W. Lo, and A. Craig MacKinlay. *The Econometrics of Financial Markets.* Princeton: Princeton University Press, 1997.

Cope, S. R. *Walter Boyd, A Merchant Banker in the Age of Napoleon.* London: Alan Sutton, 1983.

Courtois, Alphonse, fils. *Histoire des Banques en France.* Paris: Guillaumin, 1881.

Crouzet, Francois. *La Grande Inflation La Monnaie en France de Louis XVI a Napoleon.* Paris: Fayard, 1993.

Daridan, Genevieve. *MM. Le Couteulx et Cie banquier A Paris.* Paris: Editions Loysel, 1995.

Davis, Lance, and Larry Neal. "Micro Rules and Macro Outcomes: The Impact of Micro Structure on the Efficiency of Security Exchanges, London, New York and Paris, 1800–1914." *American Economic Review* 88 (May 1998): 40–45.

Doyle, William. "The Price of Offices in Pre-revolutionary France." *Historical Journal* 27 (1984): 831–60.

Doyle, William. *Venality: The Sale of Offices in Eighteenth Century France.* Oxford, Oxford University Press, 1996.

Edwards, L. N., and F. R. Edwards. "A legal and economic analysis of manipulations in futures markets." *Journal of Futures Markets* 4 (1984): 333–66.

Fachan, J. M. *Historique de la rente francaise.* Paris, Berger-Leurult, 1904.

Faure, Edgar. *La banqueroute de Law: 17 Juillet 1720.* Paris: Gallimard, 1977.

Hamilton, Earl J. "Origin and Growth of the National Debt in Western Europe." *American Economic Review* 37 (May 1947), 118–30.

Harris, Robert D. "French Finances and the American War 1777–1783." *Journal of Modern History* 48 (June 1976): 238–58.

Hoffman, Philip T., Gilles Postel-Vinay, Jean-Laurent Rosenthal, "Private Credit Markets in Paris, 1690–1840," *Journal of Economic History* 52 (June 1992): 293–306.

Hoffman, Philip T., Gilles Postel-Vinay, Jean-Laurent Rosenthal. "Competition and Coercion: Credit Markets and Government Policy in Paris 1698–1790." Mimeographed November 1993.

Hoffman, Philip T., Gilles Postel-Vinay, Jean-Laurent Rosenthal. "Redistribution and Long Term Private Debt in Paris, 1660–1726." *Journal of Economic History* (June 1995): 256–284.

Hoffman, Philip T., Gilles Postel-Vinay, Jean-Laurent Rosenthal. "Les marchés du credit a Paris, 1750–1840." *Annales HSS* 49 (janvier-fevrier 1994): 65–98.

Hoffman, Philip T., Gilles Postel-Vinay, Jean-Laurent Rosenthal. "What do Notaries do? Overcoming Asymmetric Information in Financial Markets: The Case of Paris, 1751." *Journal of Institutional and Theoretical Economics* 154 (September 1998): 499–530.

Hull, John. *Options. Futures and other Derivative Securities.* Englewood Cliffs, NJ: Prentice-Hall, 1989.

Luthy, Herbert. *La Banque Protestante en France.* Paris: SEVPEN, 1961.

Marion, Marcel. *Histoire financiere de la France depuis 1715.* New York: Burt Frankling, 1965. Ist published, 1914.

Martin, Marie Joseph Desire. *Etrennes financieres, ou Recueil des matures les plus importantes en Finance Banque Commerce etc.* Paris: by the author, 1789.

Murphy, Antoin. *Richard Cantillon: Entrepreneur and Economist.* Oxford: Clarendon Press, 1986.

Malpeyre, M., *Journal d'un agent de change*, a manuscript, 1775–1783.

Manuel des agents de change. Paris Compagnie des Agents de Change 1908.

Mirabeau, Honore Gabriel Riquetti comte de. *Denonciation de l'agiotage au roi.* Paris, 1788.

Mollien, Francois Nicholas. *Memoires d'un Ministre du Tresor Public.* Paris: Guillaumin, 1845.

Moniteur Universel. Paris.

Neal, Larry. *The Rise of Financial Capitalism: International Capital Markets in the Age of Reason.* New York: Cambridge University Press, 1990.

Riley, James C. "French Finances, 1727–1768." *Journal of Modern History* 58 (June 1987): 209–43.

Roll, Richard. "A Simple Implicit Measure of the Effective Bid-Ask Spread in an Efficient Market." *Journal of Finance* 39 (September 1984): 1127–39.

Saint-Germain, Jacques. *Les financiers sous Louis XIV*. Paris: P. Poisson de Bourvalais, 1950.

Schwartz, Robert A. *Equity Markets: Structure, Trading and Performance*. New York: Harper and Row, 1988.

Schwartz, Robert A., ed. *Global Equity Markets: Technological, Competitive and Regulatory Challenges*. New York: Irwin for New York University, 1995.

Taylor, George V. "The Paris Bourse on the Eve of the Revolution, 1781–1789." *American Historical Review* 67 (July 1962): 951–77.

Tedde, Pedro. *El Banco de San Carlos*. Madrid: Alianza Editorial/Banco de Espana, 1988.

Velde, Francois, and David R. Weir. "The Financial Market and Government Debt Policy in France, 1746–1793." *Journal of Economic History* 52 (March 1992): 1–39.

Vidal, E. *The History and Methods of the Paris Bourse*. Washington, DC: Government Printing Office, 1910.

Villain, Jean. "Heurs et malheurs de la speculation (1716–1722)." *Revue d'Histoire moderne et contemporaine* 4 (1957): 121–40.

Vuhrer, Alphonse. *Histoire de la dette Publique en France*. Paris: Berger-Leurault, 1886.

White, Eugene N. "Was There a Solution to the Ancien Regime's Financial Dilemma?" *Journal of Economic History* 49 (September 1989): 545–68.

White, Eugene N. "Experiments with Free Banking during the French Revolution," in *Unregulated Banking: Chaos or Order?* ed. Forrest Capie and Geoffrey E. Wood. London: Macmillan, 1991, 131–50.

White, Eugene N. "The French Revolution and the Politics of Government Finance, 1770–1815." *Journal of Economic History* 55 (June 1995): 227–55.

Zylberberg, Michel. "Capitalisme francais et banque espagnole a la fin de l'ancien regime: le canal de Saint-Denis." *Revue d'Histoire Moderne et Contemporaine* 27 (juillet-septembre 1980): 353–73.

3

No Exit: Notarial Bankruptcies and the Evolution of Financial Intermediation in Nineteenth Century Paris

Philip T. Hoffman, Gilles Postel-Vinay, and Jean-Laurent Rosenthal

Introduction

In early nineteenth-century Paris, notaries and bankers competed for the business of financial intermediation. They did so in an environment full of uncertainty and risk, for between 1808 and 1855, 143 bankers failed, and 26 notaries declared bankruptcy (Table 3.1). On average, nearly 12 percent of all banking houses and 3 percent of notarial businesses (études) went belly up in each five-year period between 1815 and 1855 – large figures in financial circles.

Surprisingly, it was the bankers who emerged victorious from this competition even though they were the ones who failed more often. Here, we study the notaries they vanquished, in order to learn more about the interaction between competition, asymmetric information, and financial regulation. To explain the initial institutional evolution of notaries and bankers, we stress the importance of clients' learning, at least up to 1843. Thereafter, we examine how government intervention eliminated notarial bankruptcies and produced a fundamentally different equilibrium.

Our interest in how financial intermediaries and clients interacted is inspired by Lance Davis's research on the role of competition and government regulation in financial markets. Davis, it is true, works on different topics, comparing distinct markets or analyzing financial flows from one location to another. Yet he, too, stresses clients' learning and savers' heterogeneity (in his words, "rubes and sophisticates"), and his approach has a direct echo in our model with two types of clients.[1] Furthermore, in his work shocks brought on by bankruptcies and liquidity crises shape the financial system and help favor the survival of robust firms, a theme that is important in our

---

[1] See Lance E. Davis and Robert Cull, *International Capital Markets and American Economic Growth 1820–1914.* (Cambridge: Cambridge University Press, 1994).

TABLE 3.1. Bankers and Notaries in Paris 1815–54 and Their Turnover

Numbers	1815	1820	1825	1830	1835	1840	1845	1850	1855
Notaries	114	114	114	114	114	114	114	114	114
Bankers	64	71	72	129	122	213	285	246	227
Bankruptcies	1815–19	1820–24	1825–29	1830–34	1835–39	1840–44	1845–49	1850–54	1815–54
Notaries	1	0	4	7	3	3	7	1	26
Bankers	7	11	18	23	13	23	23	25	143
Failure rate									
Notaries (percent)	1	0	4	6	3	3	6	1	2.9
Bankers (percent)	11	15	25	18	11	11	8	10	11.9
Entry									
Notaries	30	33	40	32	31	28	26	20	
Bankers	54	86	65	54	131	72	62	117	

Source: Archives de la Chambre des Notaires de Paris (henceforth ACNP), Archives Nationales (henceforth AN) BB10; Archives départementales de la Seine (henceforth AD Seine) D10/U3, Registers 1–30.

Note: There is no data for bankers for 1815, 1816, 1820, 1834, 1835, 1840.

own research.[2] Finally, like Davis we emphasize the interplay of private and public institutions, especially legal institutions and government regulation.[3]

The chapter opens with an introduction to the institutions of credit in early nineteenth-century Paris, then after a brief presentation of the data on financial failures, we proceed to a simple model of competition for clients. We then use the model to explain the evolution of financial intermediation by notaries with a focus on how bankruptcy affected the value of notarial firms. After a look at some illuminating failures, we turn to another factor influencing the value of notarial études: the transmission of a notary's intangible assets (such as human capital) to his successor. The final section recounts how government intervention finally brought the bankruptcies to an end.

Bankers and Notaries in Nineteenth Century Paris

After the Revolution, bankers and notaries competed against one another. They had both been important financial intermediaries in the eighteenth century, but each now faced a new and different institutional environment – new laws, new regulations, and new ways of doing business. Because the institutional environments were different – and so foreign to our eyes – we review them here.

Throughout the period, nearly all banks in Paris were partnerships and as such could open and close without any government authorization.[4] Although they could issue, endorse, and discount commercial paper, they could not issue bank notes – that privilege was reserved for the Bank of France. As far as one can ascertain, capital came in two forms: the personal wealth of the partners (which in the case of Mallet, Rothschild, and others would end up being vast), and the deposits that their clients entrusted to them. The dominant use of the capital was for short-run credit, either discounting bills or underwriting securities issues.

When a banker failed, he had recourse to the commercial code's bankruptcy provisions. These allowed him to submit to the commercial jurisdiction his books and a balance sheet that named all his creditors and debtors. The commercial jurisdiction encouraged the creditors to reach a settlement

---

[2] Lance E. Davis and Robert E. Gallman, *Evolving Financial Markets and International Capital Flows: Britain, the Americas, and Australia, 1865–1914* (Cambridge: Cambridge University Press, 2001).

[3] Lance E. Davis and Robert A. Huttenback, *Mammon and the Pursuit of Empire; The Political Economy of British Imperialism, 1860–1912* (Cambridge: Cambridge University Press, 1986); Lance Davis and Douglass C. North, *Institutional Change and American Economic Growth* (Cambridge: Cambridge University Press, 1971).

[4] Among the exceptions were the Bank of France, the Caisse des Dépôts, the Caisse d'Epargne, the Caisse Laffitte, and the Banque Hypothécaire, which were either joint stock banks or *sociétés en commandite par actions*.

with the banker that frequently allowed him considerable freedom to recover his assets. Most often, the business was liquidated, and the liabilities settled for a fraction of their par value. Once the bankruptcy process was over, the banker could start a new business, and even a new bank, without fear of his old creditors. Obviously, there were strategic bankruptcies. (The French in fact distinguished such a bankruptcy by calling it a *banqueroute frauduleuse* rather than a simple *faillite*.) It was the duty of the commercial tribunal to decide whether the failure really was a simple bankruptcy.

If bankers' first line of business was short-term commercial bills, notaries dealt with personal wealth and hence long-term credit. Notaries were origin-ally scriveners appointed by the court system to draft and record private contracts. Under the Old Regime, they had taken on important roles as loan and asset brokers. At the beginning of the nineteenth century, they continued to play two roles: drawing up legal contracts and financial intermediation. The intermediation they undertook was often limited to providing informa-tion, as when they served as brokers for loans or real estate sales. But they could move beyond this sort of simple brokerage and edge into what one might call deposit banking, by borrowing from some clients and then using the money to provide others with short- or medium-term loans. When a no-tary engaged in this sort of banking, he accumulated one of three types of liabilities toward the clients who provided him with funds. He either took their money on account, or he accepted it as a short-term deposit for which he signed notes that could not be discounted, or he indebted himself toward them in a long-term debt contract, such as a notarized obligation or an an-nuity. Whatever the form of the liability, it was the borrowing that caused notaries to fail.

While free entry applied to banking, the exact opposite was the case for the notarial business. Indeed, during the entire period, the number of notaries in Paris remained stable at 114 (Table 3.1).[5] Hence, becoming a Parisian notary required purchasing a position from a retiring incumbent. Moreover, save for rare exceptions, the only bidders for open positions were the senior clerks of Parisian notaries, so for the six to eight positions that opened every year there were at most 114 bidders. Though negotiations between buyer and seller were conducted in private, they were subject to extensive review by the corporation of notaries and, because the notaries were court officers, by the Ministry of Justice.

As a result, Parisian notaries meet the first criterion for a cartel – entry was limited. Competition, however, prevailed among the notaries themselves. Al-though the notaries were always organized as a corporation, their company did little to regulate their dealings with their clients – or most other aspects

---

[5] It was only in Paris that the number of notaries remained constant. Elsewhere in France, the state "adjusted" the number of notaries to meet "demand."

of their business – until the 1840s. Nonetheless, as we have shown in earlier work, the notaries had formed an effective information cartel in the eighteenth century by sharing among themselves their knowledge of their clients – knowledge that they kept from other financial intermediaries.[6] Neither the corporation nor an informal cartel fixed prices; the cost of service was negotiable. Although fees for the drafting of documents were controlled, the cost of brokerage and other services was unregulated. On the contrary, the notarial corporation of Paris rigidly defended the free negotiation of fees against the wishes of many provincial notaries who advocated setting a national fee schedule. Although it is clear fees varied both by type of contract and across notaries in Paris, for loans they averaged 1 percent of the capital when a notary brokered the transaction.[7]

When a notary failed, the legal proceedings were not governed by French commercial legislation. Rather, he was under the regulation of the Ministry of Justice, and in case of bankruptcy, his debts and assets were governed by the provisions of civil law. He would have to resign as notary, sell his business, and, unlike a merchant, face unlimited liability for his debts. In addition, he could be prosecuted in the criminal courts (and severely punished if convicted) for any wrongdoing in his role as a court official. But if there were no fraud or other serious wrongdoing as an official, the notary would usually avoid criminal charges, and his creditors would reach an agreement among themselves about how to settle his debts. Although the procedure would be slow, the notarial corporation would rarely get involved; neither would the state, apart from the rulings of civil court judges.

Bankruptcy proceedings of this sort – with little intervention by the corporation or the state – continued at least until 1843, when the government barred the notaries from engaging in deposit banking and threatened to prosecute those who did (Table 3.1 and Appendix 3.1). As for the notarial corporation, its major concern was protecting the notaries' information and the privacy of their clients, not preventing bankruptcies. To be sure, the corporation did monitor who became a notary. Indeed, it has preserved to this day records that detail the wealth, civic qualifications, and job experience of individuals who bought notarial businesses. But the most the corporation did was to reimburse wronged clients in egregious cases of notarial malfeasance (when notary Bauchau falsified debt contracts and went belly up in 1825, for example). Its only other concern was warding off government intervention. Not until the state outlawed deposit banking in 1843 did the corporation actually begin reviewing notaries' account books to ensure that

---

6 Philip T. Hoffman, Gilles Postel-Vinay, and Jean-Laurent Rosenthal, *Priceless Markets; The Political Economy of Credit in Paris; 1660–1870* (Chicago: University of Chicago Press, 2001).
7 Archives de la Chambre des Notaires de Paris (ACNP), dossiers 114 and 114b. The fee structure can also be inferred from the summary data in the individual files of notaries after 1860, and these suggest some variation around an average fee of 1 percent.

they complied with the government ban. Even then it dragged its feet. It took until 1858 for regular audits and for more intensive monitoring of notaries who were suspected of circumventing the rules.[8] By the mid-1850s, the combination of legislation and threats of further government intervention finally had an effect, for only one Parisian notary failed between 1852 and 1870, a bankruptcy rate lower than at any time since the early 1820s.

The notaries who moved into deposit banking were competing with bankers. Both were lending out funds that were by and large borrowed via short-term liabilities. The problem, for notaries and bankers alike, was that the loans they made often had much longer maturities than the short-term liabilities that funded the loans. That, in turn, was why so many bankers and notaries failed. The reason for the maturity mismatch can be traced back to the French Revolution. Between 1790 and 1796, the revolutionary governments had unleashed rapid inflation, which had done the greatest damage to investors holding long-term private bonds. The investors' losses were in fact in direct proportion to the maturity of the bonds in their portfolios, and the whole experience counseled them against making long-term loans, particularly in periods of political instability. The French Revolution had taught that instability brought in its wake a risk of governmental insolvency and a return of rapid inflation. After 1797, savers in France therefore preferred to lend short term so as to be able to withdraw their funds at the slightest hint of political uncertainty. Borrowers, however, continued to have projects that required long-term funding. Both the notaries and the bankers were trying to bridge the gap in maturities – an arbitrage opportunity that carried considerable risk.

The notaries and bankers each had certain strengths in trying to bridge the gap in maturities. A banker, for his part, had easy access to short-term funds, for rich, private individuals were accustomed to having some money on deposit with a banker. The notes he issued could also be discounted, which provided his lenders with some liquidity should they want to dispose of his notes before they matured. The problem for the banker was that although he had good information about borrowers seeking short-term loans, he knew much less about long-term borrowers, for information about them was held by notaries. Still, because he likely faced an excess supply of short-term funds, he would be tempted to cross the maturity gap and use his short-term funds to finance long-term loans such as mortgages.[9]

A notary had the reverse problem. He had much more information than bankers about long-term borrowers. But because the supply of long-term funds was limited, he would have to fund the long-term loans he made by borrowing short term, a realm in which he had much less experience. Worse

---

[8] The earliest general audit seems to have occurred in 1853 (ACNP, dossier 445).

[9] On the term maturity of debt see Bertrand Gille, *La banque et le crédit en France de 1815 à 1848* (Paris: Presses Universitaires de France, 1959), 57.

yet, the notes he might issue to borrow short term could not be discounted. His lenders would therefore be stuck with his notes until they matured, and that limited his access to capital. Both the notary and the banker faced yet another danger as well: There was no lender of last resort. Neither the Ministry of Finance nor the Bank of France had the resources to intervene to save banks from runs on their deposits, and a liquidity crisis could well stop the arbitrage between short-term lenders and long-term borrowers and segment the credit market.

If either the banker or the notary had had an overwhelming comparative advantage in making such loans, then we might not have observed both of them trying to bridge the maturity gap and going bankrupt as a result of the risks involved. Which one possessed the clear comparative advantage was simply not clear. The banker enjoyed the benefits of liquidity, and his depositors and other potential creditors knew that, if he happened to fail, then the resulting bankruptcy would be swiftly resolved. Their money would not be tied up for years. As for the notary, he knew more about long-term investments than the banker, and he had a greater incentive to be prudent in deposit banking because he faced an enormous penalty – being cast out of the notarial corporation forever – should he fail.

One might assume that the notaries and bankers would cooperate, but cooperation was nearly impossible to arrange. First, for legal reasons, it was difficult to write a contract that would govern cooperation between a notary and a banker. The notary could not commit to exclusive dealing with the banker, for the notary had to draft a contract whenever any two parties desired it, and he had to protect all his clients' privacy. He thus could not show the banker the contracts he had written, making it impossible for the banker to monitor his dealings. In addition, cooperation with the banker undermined the notary's private information about his clients. If he referred his best clients to the banker, the banker might draw nearly all of their deposit banking away and cease involving him at all. Finally, it was unclear how long any tacit agreement to cooperate could last because bankers were just too prone to failure. Cooperation was therefore out of the question so long as notaries engaged in deposit banking, and it only became possible after the notaries left banking aside.

Why then did the notaries give up on deposit banking? One might presume that it was because they and their clients learned that the risks of deposit banking were large and the costs high. It is even possible that the notaries found informal ways to restrict deposit banking – informal in the sense that there was no involvement by the government or by formal regulatory bodies like the notarial corporation. The alternative was that the government or the notarial corporation had to intervene to stop it.

To see why the notaries abandoned deposit banking, we analyze how formal and informal institutions influenced the choices that notaries made. In doing so, we combine theory and data. Although we would of course have preferred to study the bankers too, they have unfortunately left behind little historical data, in contrast to the notaries, who labored under the constant scrutiny of the notarial corporation and the Ministry of Justice. Thanks to the abundant archival records, we can examine the businesses of the notaries who failed and see whether their relationships with their clients went beyond brokerage and drafting of contracts. Admittedly, the notaries who went bankrupt were somewhat exceptional, and we must take care to compare them with colleagues who avoided failure. Here the fact that the number of notarial businesses was fixed actually turns out to be an advantage. Indeed, every exiting notary had to sell his position to a successor, so we can analyze the connection between the business strategies notaries pursued and the price of their études.

Strategies, Services, and Risk

Notarial bankruptcies increased after 1820 and then vanished after 1848; in the interim they affected only a minority of the études. In all likelihood then, the bankruptcies reflected decisions made by specific notaries at a specific point in time rather than the recurring financial crises of the early nineteenth century. The key strategic decision for a notary was whether or not to enter (or exit) the risky business of deposit banking. We focus on this decision and build a simple model of it.

Any such model must begin with the market for notarial services. On the supply side of this market lay the notaries, who possessed various technologies for serving their clients. Among the services they could offer were deposit banking and the more traditional services of brokerage and the drafting of contracts. The key issue on the supply side concerns the relationship between these traditional services on the one hand and deposit banking on the other: Were they complements or substitutes?

On the demand side, we have Parisian notaries' clients, many of whom will not use notarial services in equilibrium. At the risk of simplifying, let us suppose that the clients are divided into two types: those who require only the notary's traditional brokerage and drafting of contracts, and those who want him to offer deposit banking as well. This second group was potentially sizeable, for it would presumably include wealthy individuals with money to lend who were scared of commercial bankers because of their high failure rates. It would also include individuals who wanted to borrow short term but did not have access to a banker's services.

This market was characterized by asymmetric information of three kinds. First of all, the notary knew more about his own clients than the clients of his colleagues, and his knowledge of his colleagues' practices (whether they were dabbling in deposit banking, for example) was imperfect. Second, a client knew little about his notary's activities with other clients, and he knew even less about what other notaries were doing. It was therefore difficult for a client to tell whether his own notary was engaged in banking, and he would have even a harder time telling whether other notaries were doing so. Finally, a client also had limited information about the rest of his notary's clientele: He did not know whether they had money on deposit, nor how they would react in a liquidity crisis.

Let us start with a world where clients are ill-informed about what notaries are doing. They can make no inference about the specific behavior of a notary who goes belly up, but his failure does allow them to update their beliefs about the likelihood of future bankruptcies by notaries as a whole. The clients can compare that likelihood with the risk of failure by other types of financial intermediaries and select the combination of services and risks that suits them best. While maintaining their ties to a notary, they may choose to shift some assets or liabilities to other financial intermediaries and to redistribute their portfolio between real and financial assets. In that case, the costs of one notary's failure would be borne equally by all notaries, and there would be no client mobility after a notary's bankruptcy.

If we also assume that clients are homogenous, then all notaries will adopt the same business practices and offer identical services.[10] The outcome is likely both because clients will all move to the notaries who offer the most highly desired package of services and because such a package will maximize a notary's profits. In this simple world, notaries' business practices will converge. For instance, if it happens that banking and brokerage are complements, then all notaries will move into deposit banking.

Paris, however, was more complicated than that, for few notaries engaged in banking. Why did only a minority do so, while most of their colleagues hesitated? The explanation is both that clients were diverse and that banking and brokerage were only weak complements. Clients, after all, differed in their demand for various kinds of financial services and in their willingness to bear the risks that deposit banking entailed in an era before deposit insurance and lenders of last resort. Some clients were wealthy enough to shoulder

---

[10] One might wonder about the effects of notary heterogeneity in a world of homogeneous clients. Consider the case of two types of notaries – types 1 and 2 – with type 1 notaries having better financial connections than type 2 notaries. Since all clients are identical, they prefer one of the two types, and without loss of generality, let us assume that is type 1 they prefer. Three equilibria are possible. First, all type 2 notaries sell their positions to type 1 entrants, and all notaries are identical in equilibrium. Second, type 1 notaries are scarce, but there are no capacity constraints that limit a notary's ability to carry out transactions. In this case, the price of a notarial business falls to zero because all clients move to the type 1 notaries, leaving type 2 notaries with no business. In this equilibrium, all active notaries are identical. Finally, if type 1 notaries are scarce and there are capacity constraints, then, in equilibrium, type 1 notaries charge more for services in such a way that clients are indifferent between which type of notary they hire. Type 1 notaries will end up having higher revenue than type 2 notaries, and in general they will have more clients. Because we have no indication that there was scarcity in particular types of notarial practices, we prefer to derive the observed heterogeneity from clients' characteristics rather than from notaries'.

the risks and did not have ready access to commercial bankers. They would want their notary to offer deposit banking. But because they were far from the majority, the complementarities between banking and brokerage would remain weak. The other clients, who sought only brokerage services, would not want their notary to offer deposit banking to any of his clients because of the risks involved. If deposit banking caused him to fail, transactions that he was arranging as their broker would be interrupted, and funds they had placed on deposit while the transaction cleared might be lost or immobilized during lengthy bankruptcy proceedings. The question is to determine how the two sorts of clients (the traditional ones and the ones who wanted deposit banking) would respond to a notarial bankruptcy. In the nineteenth century, both the notarial corporation and the Minister of Justice noted that notarial bankruptcies (and other changes in notaries' services) caused clients to react and even to switch études. How can we model the clients' reactions?

A game theoretical model for the choice of service can answer this question. We study a game with T periods, in which the players are notaries and clients. During each period of the game, each notary makes a decision about the type of service that he will offer. He can offer two types of service: limited intermediation (brokerage only) at a fee f, or both brokerage and deposit banking at a fee r. The common discount rate is d. If the notary offers both brokerage and deposit banking, which we henceforth call extensive intermediation, he risks going bankrupt, with the probability of bankruptcy in any period being q. If he does fail, his position is confiscated and a successor appointed, but no further penalties are levied. If he does not fail, he continues to provide services.

At the beginning of play, we assume that all notaries have the same number of clients. This assumption is made both for simplicity and because we want to emphasize the endogenous changes in clientele size. Among the clients there are two types: L and E. Notary j has L_j clients of type L who demand only limited intermediation (brokerage alone), and E_j clients of type E who demand extensive intermediation (both brokerage and deposit banking). Thus, although the total number of clients will be the same initially for all notaries, each notary will have a different number of L and E clients. The notary knows each client's type.

For type L clients, the notary's failure interrupts transactions and is thus costly. For E clients, the value of extensive intermediation exceeds the expected risk of failure times the costs associated with failure. A client only observes what his notary does or does not do for him and not what the notary does for other clients. The client also observes whether notarial businesses have or have not experienced failures in the past.

For simplicity, we also assume prices (f and r) are exogenous. There are two reasons for this assumption. First, in a perfectly competitive market r

will be set to compensate for risk of failure, and f will reflect the marginal cost of brokerage. As long as risks and costs are similar across notaries (as would be the case, for example, if notaries could imitate one another) then taking r and f as fixed is reasonable. Second, there is no evidence of capacity constraints that would lead to rising marginal cost for notaries. The only weakness in the assumption is that notaries could have had market power as a group, which would make prices endogenous. Dealing with this issue would require an analysis of the competition between notaries and bankers, an unnecessary step at this stage.

In period 1, the game proceeds in six steps: (1) Clients make requests for services (L or E) to an incumbent notary. (2) The notary can serve those requests or not. (3) Clients who are denied the service they want can move to another notary. (4) The notary decides whether to serve these new clients. (5) The notary collects fees. (6) Each notary who offers extensive intermediation fails with probability q, while those who only offer limited intermediation never fail.

In periods 2 or greater, the game proceeds in eight steps: (1) A successor is appointed for each notary who failed at the end of the previous period. (2) Clients chose a notary. (3) Clients make requests for services to their notary. (4) The notary can serve those requests or not. (5) Clients who are denied the service they want can move to another notary. (6) The notary decides whether to serve these new clients. (7) The notary collects fees. (8) Each notary who offers extensive intermediation fails with probability q.

Proposition: A subgame of perfect Nash equilibrium exists for this game. In it, clients have the following strategy:

> If no notaries have failed, clients who get the service they want stay with their notary. Those clients of type E who are denied the service they want randomly switch in step 4.
>
> If at least one notary has failed in the past, clients who are denied extensive intermediation switch to a successor of a failed notary. Clients who only want brokerage leave the successors of failed notaries for notarial businesses where no failure has ever occurred. All other types of clients stay with their notary.

Notaries have the following strategy in the equilibrium:

> Notaries with homogenous clienteles (that is, either all E or all L) give them the service they want. If a notarial business has never experienced failure and has offered extensive intermediation in the past, then the notary who owns the business continues to provide extensive intermediation, and he only stops doing so if a period-specific function of the number of E clients and the number of L clients in his étude rises above zero. This period-specific function is increasing in L and decreasing in

E. In the last period, all notaries with heterogeneous clienteles (that is, both *E* and *L* clients) offer extensive intermediation.[11]

For a proof see Appendix 3.2. This equilibrium has a number of implications:

1. Bankruptcies allow clients to chose notaries who will offer the services they prefer, leading clients to sort themselves. After the first bankruptcy, *E* clients all get the extensive intermediation they want. In the periods prior to the first failure, an increasing number of *E* clients get extensive intermediation in each period, but the sorting process is inefficient because *E* clients have no way to find notaries who provide extensive intermediation. If the first bankruptcy is delayed long enough, nearly all of the *E* clients may already be getting extensive intermediation. In that case, the successors of notaries who fail will receive only a few *E* clients and will lose all of their *L* clients. As a result, they will experience a net loss of business.

2. Eventually, clients will sort themselves perfectly and complaints about bankruptcies will cease. Bankruptcies will tend to recur in the same études.

3. In this model, *L* clients caught in a failure are the ones who complain. Because they cannot sort themselves efficiently, they will continue to complain about bankruptcies, but their complaints will diminish over time, as fewer and fewer notaries with heterogeneous clienteles are left to fail. There are two reasons why the number of such notaries will diminish. First, notaries will voluntarily abandon extensive intermediation. Second, notaries who offer extensive intermediation are increasingly likely to be the successors of failed notaries and hence will be unattractive to the type *L* clients who are the source of complaints. Although the bankruptcies of notaries with heterogeneous clienteles will become less frequent, they will grow increasingly bitter, because the number of *L* clients in the études will have increased before the failure.

4. The sorting process will not completely eliminate bankruptcies, for as long as some clients want extensive intermediation, some notaries will offer it and consequently fail. Two things will stop the bankruptcies: first, a decline in the demand for extensive intermediation (so *E* clients become *L* clients); second, state intervention. An exogenous

---

[11] Because the notaries use a threshold rule for deciding what services to offer, clients must coordinate leaving open the possibility of multiple equilibria. There exists an alternative pure strategy Nash equilibrium where it is the *E* clients who move after a bankruptcy. It is then an optimal response for the *L* clients to stay and for successor notaries to offer *L* services. *E* clients who are denied service switch to non-failed notaries. This equilibrium has an awkward coordination process, and with it bankruptcies do not tend to repeat in the same études, as is the case with our data from Paris.

increase in the demand for limited intermediation (more L clients arrive, who want only brokerage) is unlikely to change the equilibrium as long as the increase in demand is small. The reason is that the L clients will shun notarial businesses that have experienced failure. One might, of course, assume that the notarial corporation could eliminate bankruptcies altogether by monitoring its members and forbidding deposit banking. Getting the notaries to agree on such measures would be difficult, however, for two reasons. First, notaries who offer extensive intermediation will obviously oppose such a move. Second, those who provide brokerage alone will be divided over the issue because they might lose L clients to other notaries. Monitoring would lead business practices to converge, in which case L clients of large notaries might switch to notaries with less business. In the absence of any changes in the financial system that would cut demand for intermediation by notaries, state intervention will be the only way to bring the failures to a halt.

Our model involves many simplifying assumptions, but it does not do violence to the reality of the interaction between notaries and their clients. First, we model the interaction between extensive intermediation and the risk of failure in a simple way. We could instead have complicated matters by including economies or diseconomies of scale in extensive intermediation. If we had assumed economies of scale (with the risk of failure falling as the number of E clients increased), our findings would have been different, for in that case there would be an equilibrium in which the first notary who failed would collect all the E clients, and only his L clients would move. Yet that seems unrealistic. Alternatively, if we had assumed diseconomies of scale (with the risk of bankruptcy increasing as the number of E clients grows), then the model would not have been changed substantially. Indeed, L clients would still behave in the fashion just described. E clients would still use past failures to infer the type of clients and service in each étude, that in turn might induce E clients to move after each failure. But a given notary might only serve some of his E clients, given the risks involved. In any case, the extra insights seem too minor to justify the added complication.

A second simplifying assumption is that we have neglected problems of moral hazard on the part of notaries themselves. In our model, if notaries do offer intermediation, then the probability q that they fail is independent of their subsequent actions. While this assumption may seem unreasonable, it is unlikely that clients could influence what their notaries did. In particular, it was difficult for them to impose additional sanctions on the notary. As a result, the essential decision for a notary was whether to offer deposit banking or not.

A third simplifying assumption is that our clients live forever. It might appear important to know what would happen if the clients had finite and overlapping lives. But intuitively there seems to be little gain in doing so. With finite and overlapping lives, E clients would continue to behave in similar ways, with new clients distributing themselves randomly among notaries and switching to failed notaries if they are denied extensive intermediation. New L clients would also continue to behave in the way our model predicts and avoid failed notaries. As long as the number of new clients is small, the equilibrium would not likely change substantially.

A fourth simplifying assumption is the restriction we placed on information. In our model, the clients know next to nothing about what their own notaries or other notaries are doing. If clients are better informed, they will move earlier, and less of their movement will be provoked by failures. For instance, if we allow L clients to find out what services their own notary has offered in the previous period, then the clients will sort themselves out much more rapidly, because L clients whose notary has offered extensive intermediation will immediately leave for a notary whose étude has never failed. After a few periods, most of the L clients will have found a notary who does not offer intermediation, and complaints will consequently diminish.

The justification for this fourth assumption is the confidentiality of the notarial business: It prevented clients from knowing what their notaries or other notaries were doing. It would not even help an L client if he made a false request for extensive intermediation in order to discover whether his notary was offering extensive intermediation. The reason is that notaries knew their clients well and thus knew their type, L or E. The notary could easily defeat this sort of testing by offering extensive intermediation only to clients who were real E types.[12] Furthermore, the notaries could deduce the types of all clients who switched (because only E clients would leave notaries who had not gone bankrupt and only L clients would leave bankrupt notaries). Hence, he could defeat testing by clients who arrived in his étude. All in all, the assumption that clients knew little about their notary while he knew a great deal about them seems reasonable.

A final simplifying assumption is that we rule out advertising. It is true that clients would sort more rapidly if notaries could advertise, but we must recall that information dispersal is a two-edged sword. Advertising only concerns études that have never failed because everyone knows about the notarial businesses that have gone bankrupt in the past. Notaries in the études unblemished by failure are already implicitly advertising for L clients; ought they advertise for E clients too? If they do so, L clients can immediately infer that they offer extensive intermediation, and they will therefore leave.

---

[12] The notary could easily raise the cost of such an unexpected E request by requiring more information from the client and not divulging what the ultimate source of funds to meet a short-term loan request would be. Similarly he might test a depositor by refusing to pay interest and asking why the client wanted to make only a short-term investment.

As a result, advertising could well harm a notary's business. And even if advertising were attractive, the government would certainly have taken a dim view of it, however informal it might have been.

In any case, this simple model proves to be quite useful in understanding how bankruptcies affected notaries. We can use it to analyze the effect of bankruptcies in three ways. We will begin by comparing the value of the études of notaries who went bankrupt and of notaries who did not. We will then examine notaries' businesses to determine how brokerage and extensive intermediation affected their incomes. Finally, we will check qualitative evidence for the sort of client mobility that is essential to our model.

Bankruptcy, Notaries' Revenues, and the Value of Their Businesses

Although we know a great deal about the regulations notaries faced, their actual business practices are shrouded in mystery, for few records of their day-to-day dealings have survived. Essentially, the only documents we do have are chronological indexes of the contracts they drafted and copies of the documents they preserved. For that reason, bankruptcy records are particularly precious, because they reveal what a notary's business was actually like at the moment he failed. We can in fact use these records to study how bankruptcy changed their business practices, how clients reacted to failures, and what the consequences were for the value of études. To do so we proceed in two steps. First, we investigate how notarial businesses were transmitted from one holder to the next. In particular we must understand how the businesses were priced. Second, we examine how failure affected the value of études and notaries' incomes and the taxes they paid.

Let us begin with the market for notarial businesses. Although retiring notaries had been selling their positions for centuries, sales were prohibited during the Revolution. The practice resumed, at first informally and after 1816 with the government's blessing. Soon the notarial corporation began to keep files on all its members.[13] By 1816, these files usually contained sales contracts when études changed hands, and by 1824 these documents were always included, yielding excellent information on prices. The same files reveal the state of a notary's business before the sale and the reasons why his étude was being put on the market. As a result, we know much about the causes of notary bankruptcies in the nineteenth century.

The information for the period 1815–1869 shows that prices of études were always dispersed: The ratio of the high price to the low price is most often more than two and at times even three. The price variation is derived from the differences in clienteles from étude to étude. We know that clienteles mattered that much because when a notary sold his business, he

---

[13] Law of Ventose an XI.

TABLE 3.2. *Sales of Notarial Études: Descriptive Statistics (1817–1869)*

	Not Failed				Failed			
	Mean	N	Std	Median	Mean	N	Std	Median
Price	403,750	248	113193	400,000	282,923	27	62,399	280,000
Tenure	17.99	246	10	17	11.42	27	6.28	11
Date	1840	248	15.44	1839	1839	27	12.35	1839
Inside buyer	0.42	186			0.055	18		
Revenue	54,938	123	22,685	52295	45317	20	19,045	42,762
Yield on government bonds	4.33	123	0.61	4.27	4.81	20	0.99	4.72
Price gain during tenure	74,548	125	107,688	80,000	−70318	22	107,688	−77,500
Annual Growth Rate of Price (%)	1.56	125	2.96	1.25	−2.88	22	5.66	−2.12

Source: ACNP, dossiers de notaires and AN BB10.
Note: Revenue is reported for each of the five years prior to the sale of the étude. We have the information for 123 non-failed notaries, or 615 observations. For failed notaries, we have 20 notaries and 100 observations. All monetary amounts are in francs, and "std" is the standard deviation.

used information about the important clients to justify its price. Clearly, clienteles really mattered to notaries.

The price data also make it clear that bankrupt notaries sold their businesses for much less than other notaries (Table 3.2). Furthermore, while the typical notarial étude increased in value between sales, after a bankruptcy the price fell. The contrast in the behavior of prices remains even if we take into account the difference in tenure between notaries who went bankrupt and their colleagues who did not: Études that had not experienced failure appreciated at 1.6 percent a year, while études where a notary had failed lost value at 2.9 percent a year. The effect of bankruptcy is born out by a simple regression of étude prices on a dummy variable for bankruptcy and on a time trend to take into account the effects of the growth of the French economy. The regression suggests that the failure cost the notary 118,000 francs, or nearly a third of the mean resale price of an étude (Table 3.3, regression 1). The regression does not change appreciably if we include other variables, such as étude characteristics or whether the sale had taken place during a political crisis (Table 3.3, regressions 2 and 3).

In all likelihood, the reason bankruptcy cut étude prices was that clients moved. As implication 1 of our model suggests, failures probably led clients who only wanted brokerage to desert a notarial business after a bankruptcy. Clients of other notaries who wanted to avoid deposit banking would not

TABLE 3.3. *Regression of the Étude Prices on Tenure, Bankruptcy, and a Time Trend (1817–69)*

Regression Number	Dependent Variable: Price of Étude		
	(1)	(2)	(3)
Constant	221,655	231,346	258,529
	(14,676)	(14,265)	(18,525)
Date	4,526	4,457	4,214
	(337)	(325)	(410)
Revoked	32,306	35,857	25,883
	(32,514)	(31,296)	(34,160)
Failed	−118,068	−85,195	−95,540
	(17,489)	(18,167)	(22,637)
Political Crisis		−73,934	−64,504
		(15,390)	(17,467)
Tenure			−622
			(647)
Inside buyer			−12,981
			(12,242)
R Square	0.45	0.50	0.46
Adjusted R Square	0.45	0.49	0.44
Standard Error	84,816	81,615	82,107
Mean of dependent variable (francs)	393,828		398,088
Observations	280	280	203

Source: ACNP, dossiers de notaires and AN BB10.

Note: Standard errors in parentheses. Political crisis is a dummy variable that takes on a 1 in 1830–31 and 1848–51. Inside buyer is a dummy variable that takes on a 1 when the buyer was either a relative of the seller or his senior clerk. Tenure is the number of years that the seller had been in the position. Revoked is a dummy variable that takes on a 1 if the seller was forced by the corporation to resign. Failed is a dummy variable that takes on a 1 if the seller had failed. Date is the number of years from 1800. The price of the études is in francs.

switch to the étude either. Nor would those who desired deposit banking, for in all likelihood they had already found notaries who provided banking before the first wave of failures in the 1820s. With old clients departing and no newcomers arriving, it is no wonder that étude prices dropped.

But to be sure that clients' movement cut the value of études after bankruptcy, we have to take a closer look at the economics of pricing in the market for notarial businesses. To begin with, we must consider the possibility that the state's own pricing rules for notarial études determined prices and drove them down after bankruptcy. The state – specifically the Ministry of Justice – reviewed the sales of notarial businesses. In principal it could force down the price that any étude fetched, whether the étude was bankrupt or not. In the ministry's view, a notary's net annual income R should fall between 12 percent and 18 percent of the price P that he paid for his position. (Here the ministry estimated future net income by averaging net income over the previous five years before the sale of an étude.) Were this rule binding, a specification of the form $P = \alpha + \beta R + \varepsilon$ would explain most of the variance in prices, where α and β are constants and ε is an error term. To assess the effect of bankruptcies, we would also include a dummy variable F for études sold after failure and run the regression $P = \alpha + \beta R + \delta F + \varepsilon$. If the ministry's rules determined prices, α would be 0, and β would be positive, with a value such that $1/\beta$ would lie between 0.12 and 0.18. We would also expect δ to be negative, but with the ministry setting prices a negative δ would not necessarily mean that clients were fleeing after bankruptcy. It could simply be that the ministry was driving the price down.

Regression 1 of Table 3.4 suggests that the ministry's simple rule did not determine the price of études. In the regression, the constant term was positive and significant while the reciprocal of the coefficient on revenue was 0.36, much larger than 0.18. Either the state used a more complicated rule, or – more likely – the market set prices.

If the ministry was unable to regulate prices, and credit to buy études was not rationed, then we would expect buyers to pay the present discounted value of notarial positions. In a world of unchanging demand for notarial services, the present value would be R/r, where r is the interest rate. We can estimate this model in one of two ways. We can use a log specification and estimate $\ln P = \alpha + \beta \ln R + \gamma \ln r + \varepsilon$, with a test for $\beta = -\gamma = 1$ and $\alpha = 0$. Alternatively, we can estimate a fuller model not in logs that takes into account bankruptcies, political crises, and a quadratic time trend (here t is time):

$$P = \alpha + \beta_1 R/r + \beta_2 F + \beta_3 F^* R/r + \beta_4 t + \beta_5 t^2 + \beta_6 crises + \varepsilon$$

These regressions lead to a number of conclusions (Table 3.4). Let us first take the logarithmic specification (Table 3.4, regressions 2 and 3). Both the interest rate and revenues have a pronounced effect on prices, as one would expect from a present value calculation, and both the coefficients have the expected sign. But neither of the coefficients is close to 1 in absolute value, as the simple present value calculation would imply. The coefficients in fact indicate that there was a considerable discount from the price that would have prevailed if present value calculations alone mattered. Furthermore, the revenue coefficient is in absolute value about half the interest rate coefficient, which suggests that the supply of credit to étude buyers shrank dramatically when the yield on government bonds increased. If we now turn to the linear specification (regression 4), it is clear here too that present value calculation mattered, but once again in a dampened way. The present value of a notarial étude was not the R/r that the simple calculation based on unchanging past revenues would suggest. Rather, it was greatly discounted, as with the logarithmic specification. Indeed, boosting P by 1 franc required more than a 9 franc jump in R/r.

TABLE 3.4. *Regressions of Étude Prices on Net Revenue and Interest rates (1820–69)*

Regression Number	1	2	3	4	5
Dependent variable	Price	Ln(Price)	Ln(Price)	Price	Price
Constant	297,373	10.45	9.98	208,364	263,865
	(16,811)	(0.37)	(0.36)	(26,068)	(16,898)
Ln Net Revenue (R)		0.32	0.28		
		(0.03)	(0.03)		
Ln Interest rate (r)		−0.68	−0.59		
		(0.10)	(0.17)		
Revenue (R)	2.74				
	(0.28)				
Revenue/ Interest rate (R/r)				0.11	0.14
				(0.01)	(0.01)
Bankruptcy	−87,268	−0.25	−0.27	−47388	−59,937
	(18,312)	(0.04)	(0.05)	(16,450)	(45,701)
Bankruptcy*R/r					−0.04
					(0.04)
Time (year-1800)			0.23	2,097	
			(0.05)	(523)	
Tenure			−0.01	−196	
			(0.02)	(791)	
Inside Buyer			−0.01	−776	
			(0.03)	(14,654)	
Political Crises	−74,382		−0.06	−53,005	
	(16,156)		(0.06)	(18,396)	
R Square	0.57	0.61	0.68	0.63	0.59
Adjusted R Square	0.56	0.60	0.67	0.61	0.58
Standard Error	73,297	0.17	0.16	69,293	71,661
Mean of dependent variable (francs)	416,601	12.93	12.95	424,250	
Observations	143	143	123	123	143

Source: ACNP, dossiers de notaires and AN BB10.

Note: Standard errors in parentheses. Political crises is a dummy variable that takes on a 1 in 1830–31 and 1848–51. Inside buyer is a dummy variable that takes on a 1 when the buyer was either a relative of the seller or his senior clerk. Tenure is the number of years that the seller had been in the position. Bankruptcy is a dummy variable that takes on a 1 if the seller had failed. Date is the number of years from 1800. The interest rate (r) is the yield on government bonds. Revenue is the average revenue for selling notaries. For those notaries who did not report revenue figures, we used estimates based on taxes paid to the government. All monetary amounts are in francs.

On the whole, the regressions are consistent with the view that the value of a notarial business could be broken down into two parts. The first part was the value of being a notary, independent of the clientele that came with an étude. We can evaluate this part of the étude's price via the constant term, which is always significant and roughly half the sample mean of the dependent variable. Its size suggests that in the early nineteenth century an étude was worth more than 200,000 francs, even without clients. The implication is that barriers to entry played an important role in maintaining notaries' rents, for according to the various regressions, a notary who purchased an étude that did no business would swiftly build up a practice by attracting clients. Furthermore, the value of being a notary, even without clients, was increasing at the rate of 2,000 francs a year (Table 3.4, regression 4).

The second part of an étude's value was the clientele and the revenue they generated. But only a fraction of the clients would remain with an étude when it was purchased. Expected revenues could therefore fall below R in the future, and that is why the regression showed the price of études to be discounted below the R/r of the simple present value calculation.

Finally – and more important for our purposes here – bankruptcy had a severe effect on prices. In fact it cut the value of a notarial business by a considerable amount: 11 percent in the linear specification (Table 3.4, regression 4) and 27 percent in the logarithmic specification (Table 3.4, regression 3). The drop in price here was over and above what we would expect from the lower revenues of notaries who failed, the high interest rates that typically prevailed when they went belly up, and the way political crises depressed what they could fetch for their études: All these other factors that depressed the price of études have been taken into account. In all the regressions, the coefficient for bankruptcy was large and statistically significant: Apparently, the clerks who bought the études after bankruptcies expected clients to leave and business to remain depressed for years.

To test the effect of bankruptcy on clienteles, we added an interaction term between bankruptcy and the present value of revenue R/r (Table 3.4, regression 5). We did so because R/r measured the value of the clientele transmitted by the outgoing notary at the time of sale. If bankruptcy costs an étude clients, then the interaction term should have a negative coefficient. It does, though it could well be a chance result. If it is not a statistical fluke, then the value of a notary's clientele diminished by about a third after failure.[14]

If true, that would fit the prediction of our model, which implied that not all clients would leave after bankruptcy. On the other hand, if the coefficient of the interaction term is a statistical fluke, then the number of clients leaving is largely independent of the size of the failed étude. That is not necessarily inconsistent with our model. Recall that in the model only L clients leave after a bankruptcy. It could well be that their business was far less lucrative than that of E clients, who in the model would stick with an étude after failure. With the lucrative clients staying in place, the effect of bankruptcy on revenue would be accentuated.

[14] It dropped from 0.14 R/r to (0.14 − 0.04) R/r = 0.10 R/r.

What other evidence is there for the effect bankruptcy had on an étude's business? One source of information is the taxes that the state levied on notarial documents. The taxes reveal much more than another piece of evidence – the income that the notaries reported for the years prior to sale – for the income reports were unavailable after bankruptcy and therefore cannot tell directly what the consequences of failure were, at least if we use the income reports alone.[15] But if we compare the income reports and the tax figures in the years when both are available for each notary, then we can establish a relationship between income and taxes and infer what happened to notarial income immediately after a bankruptcy.

The taxes paid were roughly a linear function of the value of a notary's transactions. Because the notaries assessed regressive fees, the taxes fluctuated more sharply than income. Nonetheless, both taxes and income point to a sharp decline in business after bankruptcy and a limited recovery thereafter. The shock of bankruptcy cut income by more than 25 percent in the year before failure and by an additional 5 percent the year after.[16] From this nadir, business eventually returned to a level some 10 percent below what the étude had known before bankruptcy.

Clearly, recovery after bankruptcy was difficult. The contrast between the études that suffered a bankruptcy and those that had never known failure is even more dramatic. Income for failed notaries was 15 percent less than for their colleagues, although the income they reported no doubt omitted earnings from deposit banking. And the 15 percent figure may well be an underestimate, for it ignores the effect bankruptcy had on future income growth. We can gauge the size of this effect by applying the long-term growth rate of average income for the notaries as a whole to those who went bankrupt. To do so, we take as a base the étude's income five years before the bankruptcy and then extrapolate to five years after via the assumed long-term growth rate. With this hypothetical growth rate, bankruptcy costs the étude a quarter of its value. Altogether, the étude would lose 40 percent of its value: 15 percent from a sudden but permanent drop in the level of income at the time of bankruptcy, and 25 percent from slower income growth rate in the future.

As our model predicts, bankruptcy cut the price of études by a large amount – indeed, as much as 40 percent depending on how we calculate its consequences. That was what we learned by analyzing the sale prices of notarial études, notaries' incomes, and the taxes they paid. Bankruptcy continued to depress prices even when we took into account the lower revenues that notaries could expect after failure and the factors (such as political crises

---

[15] Notaries reported income annually for the five years prior to a sale. They reported gross and income net of rental charges for their offices and payments to staff. We focus on net income because it is more often available.

[16] The discussion that follows does not apply to étude 48, which managed to capture a particularly large clientele shortly after bankruptcy.

and the higher interest rates during liquidity crunches) that drove notaries over the brink. It reduced both the level of an étude's income and the rate of income growth, and as our model predicts, it seemed to work by driving away L clients.

Evidence from Notaries' Bankruptcies

We can learn more about bankruptcy by studying individual notaries, for there was considerable variation from étude to étude. Some notaries went belly up because they were unable to develop their business. Their successors seem to have revitalized their clienteles, and these études experienced rapid growth after a failure. By contrast, the études of the two busiest notaries – Jacques Francois Lehon and Aristide Barbier – experienced the steepest and most persistent decline. We examine Lehon's case in detail and also that of Charles Marie Brun, one of the notaries who managed to revive an étude after a bankrutpcy.

When Lehon failed in 1841, it was the greatest scandal to tarnish the corporation since Antoine Pierre Laideguive had done so in 1744. Lehon left behind in excess of 4 million francs of debts, three times more than the next largest bankruptcy in the nineteenth century. Despite incomplete evidence (the asset side of his balance sheet is lacking) it is clear he was running a deposit bank. Many of his clients had left money on deposit, in some cases for at least ten years. Although they did not testify that Lehon was running a deposit bank, they knew that their funds would be invested in mortgage debt.

The striking thing about Lehon was that his liabilities were extraordinarily concentrated. He had taken on over half his debt from a mere 17 creditors, and two of them, André Henri Comte Du Hamel and Madeleine Piscatory, the widow of Claude Emmanuel Marquis de Pastoret, were each owed half a million francs or more. Clearly, Lehon was not trying to reduce the likelihood of a run on his bank by borrowing or taking deposits from a large number of small clients. On the contrary, he seems to have been trying to limit depositor access to his banking business.

Lehon had clearly been involved in deposit banking from the moment he bought his étude. His liabilities to Madeleine Piscatory reached back to 1826, when he first entered the notarial business, and another client had 200,000 francs on deposit with him since 1830. Typically, Lehon had 4 million francs on deposit, and if he earned 1 percent interest for managing it, he would have boosted his income from 60,000 to nearly 100,000 francs a year. No wonder deposit banking was tempting![17]

---

[17] Most mortgage loans yielded 5 percent, but deposits typically earned less than 4 percent. See Gille 1959, 57.

One of Lehon's two major creditors, the Count Du Hamel, claimed that he had been led to deposit half a million francs with Lehon because the extraordinary confidence that the notary inspired. According to Du Hamel, this sense of trust (which implicitly was conferred by the position) kept him from monitoring the notary's dealings. He and other clients also maintained that they had no idea of the state of Lehon's affairs.[18] Such statements are of course self-serving, but they are borne out by the information we gathered on bankrupt notaries' businesses (the number of notarial acts they drew up, their reported income, and the taxes they paid) in the five years proceeding their failure. Like the clients' statements, the quantitative evidence all suggest that the notaries' bankruptcies were unanticipated. According to all three indicators, an étude's business did decline the year before a bankruptcy, but the drop off was in all likelihood the cause of the bankruptcy, rather than an anticipation of trouble. The same story emerges from the files that were assembled when notaries collapsed, for the files contain little evidence that bankruptcies resulted from a slow erosion of client confidence. Rather, notaries failed when one or two clients called in loans or requested that deposits be returned. Interestingly, the bankrupt notaries' income fell more (28 percent) than did the number of contracts they drafted, which was down only 24 percent. The implication is that they were losing large transactions. Perhaps wealthy clients who wanted extensive financial intermediation were leaving their études for rival notaries with better financial or political connections, just as our model implies.[19]

Lehon practically ruined his étude by reckless banking, and his collapse helped bring on the 1843 ban on deposit banking by notaries. Charles Marie Brun, by contrast, managed to revive an étude by reassuring old clients and attracting new ones. Brun purchased étude 53 from Jean Ferrand after Ferrand failed in 1849. Although Brun paid 250,000 francs for the business, he sold it some 17 years later for a much larger sum, 440,000 francs. The increase in the étude's value was so large that Brun and the corporation drew up a report of how the étude had been resuscitated. According to the report,

---

[18] Archives départementales de la Seine (AD Seine), D4/U1/131.

[19] In the 1820s, the Ministry of Justice decided that notarial offices should remain open even after a notary failed. This decision complicates the analysis of the effects of bankruptcy because an interim notary would take over the étude temporarily after the failure. Because the interim notary already had a business of his own, he faced an obvious conflict of interest. At the very least, he in all likelihood did less business than the average notary because he had to watch over two études. Furthermore, because he had to present obvious signs of conservatism, he was probably older than average. What the effects on clients would be are not clear. On the one hand, clients who had had no financial dealings with the notary would have experienced little inconvenience and thus would have little reason to move. On the other hand, the interim notary would likely have made every effort to attach these clients to himself and transfer them to his own étude. Unraveling both effects must await a study of the mobility of clients.

the étude had been quite busy in the eighteenth century, when it had counted among its clients one of the king's brothers, the Count d'Artois. The étude recovered him in the early nineteenth-century, when he was heir to the throne and ultimately became King Charles X. After he abdicated in 1830, however, the étude began to decline, though it was sold for 440,000 francs in 1837. The next two notaries in the étude failed to maintain the business, but Brun then purchased it and rebuilt the clientele. The report found Brun's success easy to justify while stressing that Brun had never done anything untoward:

> Mr. Brun worked diligently to liquidate all the past business of mortgage lending and other litigious matters, and to salvage as many as possible. He then chose to avoid all business giving rise to investment of funds. In this manner the old clientele rediscovered its habits of the past and returned of its own ... It is interesting to note as a result of preceding events [the difficulties of his predecessors] that the success of Mr. Brun is due to the number and loyalty of the clients of his predecessors ... But one can confidently say that the étude still has not regained a clientele as important as the one it had enjoyed in the past. No one for instance replaces the Count of Artois, Hope [bankers] or the Caisse Hypothécaire or even the prince Pignatelli, so it is not as active as it had been in the past.[20]

It was all a matter of attracting and retaining clients.

Brun's report went on to list three types of clients. First came families who had remained loyal to the étude for three decades or more. Then came individuals who had deserted the business between 1835 and 1849. Finally, there were the new clients whom Brun had attracted during his tenure. Brun did not reveal how he lured these newcomers to his practice. Although he may have offered them deposit banking, it was now anathema, and Brun never discussed it and would in any case never have done so. Because he did rebuild the étude after the 1843 ban on banking by notaries, he probably did not engage in deposit banking himself. It is more likely that he linked clients up with bankers or other sources of short-term credit. The important thing to notice, though, is that retaining clients and adding new ones is what boosted the value of the étude.[21]

That is what our model predicts, and the Brun case fits the model well. Lehon's case, which we also examined, was not such a good fit. On the one hand, by taking extraordinary risks, he served many E clients, and after more than a decade of offering deposit banking, he failed. On the other, his bankruptcy was so severe that it alienated even E clients. Still, his case does bear out our contention that there was no way to stop notaries from offering

---

[20] ACNP, dossier Brun.

[21] Brun had married a Miss Gobin, daughter of an important banker in Epernay. He was a new notary, able to use his alliance with Gobin to offer short-term funds, and the CFF to secure long-term loans for his clients. ACNP, dossier Brun.

extensive intermediation – no way, that is, short of the sort of government ban enacted in 1843.

Failures and the Transmission of Intangible Assets

During the nineteenth century, the notarial corporation treated notarial bankruptcies as isolated events, which were the product of reckless behavior of wayward, atypical colleagues. The corporation's solution was more careful investigation of the candidates for notarial positions. The Ministry of Justice, however, came to view the problem differently. After 1830, it began to stress short-term credit as the root cause of bankruptcies, and it consequently threatened to monitor all the notaries and not just focus on wayward ones.

The difference between the ministry's attitude and the corporation's was not simply a question of self-interest, for it connects with one of the assumptions of our model – namely, that the difference in clienteles was what drove notaries to take risks. If differences in clienteles were the driving force behind the notaries' behavior, then we have to ask how a notary managed to pass along his clients' goodwill when he sold his étude. How did he transmit it to his successor? How did the successor acquire the skills and human capital needed to deal with the clients? How, in short, were these and other intangible assets conveyed when an étude was sold?

Let us begin to answer these questions by considering the Ministry of Justice's position on notarial bankruptcy. It is clear that the ministry's position fits our model, for like the model the ministry assumes that notaries are all alike. The ministry then explains which notaries are drawn to deposit banking not by differences among the notaries but by differences among clienteles. This assumption, which we made for simplicity, is of course worth testing. The question is whether the bankruptcies result from heterogeneity among the notaries themselves, or among their clients, as our model assumes.

If the heterogeneity of notaries caused the bankruptcies and if the notaries' behavior was not correlated with clienteles, then the failures should be random. By contrast, if different clienteles drove the notaries to take risks, then as implication 2 of our model states, bankruptcies should reoccur in the same études. In fact that is precisely what happened. Of the 114 études in Paris, a mere 6 accounted for over a third of the bankruptcies (12 of 32, to be precise) between 1810 and 1855.[22] And of the 12 études that experienced a failure before 1831, 4 saw a second notary go belly up after 1832. By contrast, the 102 études that had not witnessed a bankruptcy before 1831 had only a 13 percent failure rate over the next 24 years. The difference was too large to be a chance event. Quite simply, bankruptcy bred failure in the

---

[22] Études XLVII, LII, LIII, LXII, XVII, CXVI, CXIX. See Appendix 3.1 for details.

future, a result that is inconsistent with the existence of "bad" notaries who arrive randomly in études. The implication is that notaries were not heterogeneous. Rather, clients were, and it was their demands for service that drove the notaries to court disaster.[23]

The bankruptcies' recurrence points to the role of intangible assets in the Paris credit market, intangible assets such as human capital, clients' good will, or the reputation of the notarial corporation. These assets operated at two levels. First, within a particular étude, the intangible assets involved all of the informal knowledge that the notary had accumulated about his clients and all the trust that he had engendered. In this sense, the intangible assets comprise the transmissible part of the notary's human capital. The value of the position would certainly be enhanced if such intangible assets could be transmitted, but it is always difficult to sell the human capital. To be sure, in their étude sales contracts, the retiring notaries promised to introduce and to recommend their successor to their clients. They also agreed to tell the successor all that they knew. But it would be difficult to enforce such contract clauses and difficult to tell whether a retiring notary had carried out his part of the bargain. Furthermore, a bankruptcy could intervene and disrupt the transmission of the departing notary's human capital, even if he were intent on transmitting it to his successor. The end result – whether from problems conveying human capital or the disruptions of bankruptcy – would be a lower value for the étude.

On a second level, to the extent that clients used what they knew about notaries as a whole to make inferences about their own notary, the group possessed a collective reputation that was damaged by failures. That, in turn, was another intangible asset shared by notaries as a group. As we note in implication 4, notaries who offered deposit banking were no doubt opposed to any intervention by the government or by the corporation, for deposit banking maximized their profits and regulation could only hurt them. Although only a minority of the études were directly involved in deposit banking, they had allies among the other notaries, who might want the notarial corporation to limit bankruptcies but opposed any government intervention that might threaten their intangible assets. In particular, these other notaries would resist government audits that would make public the risks that individual notaries were taking and thereby harm the reputation of all notaries, even those who were not engaged in deposit banking. Although audits might be necessary to stop bankruptcies, nearly all notaries would oppose them.

When a notarial étude changed hands, there was clearly one purchaser who had an obvious advantage as far as all of these intangible assets were

---

[23] Not that all notaries were identical. Rather, prospective notaries selected études that fit their skills and their taste for risk. Without additional data, we can say little more, but it is clear that it was still the clienteles that drove the process.

TABLE 3.5. *Notaries' Successors, 1810–69*

| Type of Successor | Insider | | | | Fraction of |
Decade	Family	Senior Clerk	Outsider	Total	Outsiders
	Number of Successors for All Sales of Études				
1810	4	3	4	11	0.36
1820	7	22	42	71	0.59
1830	5	7	21	33	0.64
1840	2	10	31	43	0.72
1850	6	5	29	40	0.73
1860	6	8	18	32	0.56
	Successors of Notaries Who Did Not Fail				
1810	4	3	3	10	0.30
1820	7	22	40	69	0.58
1830	5	6	13	24	0.54
1840	2	9	23	34	0.68
1850	6	4	28	38	0.74
1860	6	8	17	31	0.55
	Totals, 1810–69				
Outgoing notaries who did not fail	30	52	124	206	0.60
Outgoing notaries who failed	0	3	21	24	0.88
All sales of études	30	55	145	230	0.63

Source: ACNP, dossiers de notaires and AN BB10.
Note: Insiders include both the outgoing notary's senior clerk and his relatives.

concerned. That was the old notary's senior clerk. He already had access to much of the étude's intangible capital, and if it was difficult to transmit this capital (difficult to enforce the appropriate contracts, for example), then we would expect senior clerks to buy the études where they had worked. We would also expect frequent sales to family members, for they had the same advantage.

Both types of sales were common. In 230 instances in which an étude changed hands, 24 percent involved a sale to the old notary's senior clerk, and 13 percent a sale to a family member (Table 3.5). True, 63 percent of the études passed to someone else, but that may have simply reflected the difficulties that senior clerks had in financing their purchases.

If it was difficult to transmit a notary's intangible assets, then our regressions for the price of an étude might be misspecified. If so, then an étude would fetch a significantly higher price when it was sold to a relative of the notary or to his senior clerk. But a regression indicates that the problem was not so severe, for the senior clerks or the relatives of the notary did not pay more than other buyers (Table 3.3, regression 3).

Apparently, the notaries had devised a way to pass along their intangible assets. One common way to do so was to have the outgoing notary personally finance the sale. In the 1850s, for example, notary Delagrevol sold his étude for 365,000 francs and financed 165,000 francs of the sale price in a note payable over the next six years. Having lent the buyer the money needed to purchase the étude, Delagrevol had every reason to see that the buyer prospered, for otherwise he might default on the loan. The outgoing notaries thus had an incentive to give the buyer access to all of the étude's intangible assets. They taught him about the clientele, and if the buyer was their senior clerk, the education no doubt began well before the étude changed hands.[24]

The sale of études was affected by the notarial corporation's efforts to screen prospective purchasers more carefully. As we know, the corporation began to investigate prospective buyers more stringently in the 1840s. It did so in order to reduce the number of bankruptcies, which threatened to bring on feared government intervention. What the corporation apparently did was to rule out many sales to the outgoing notary's senior clerk or to his relatives. This screening did not placate the government, however, and the notarial corporation had to begin the sort of auditing of notaries that it had long opposed. But once auditing was in place, in the 1860s, sales to the outgoing notary's senior clerk or to his relatives shot back up again (Table 3.5).

Although the notarial corporation blamed bankruptcies on wayward colleagues, the real cause lay elsewhere, with the intense demand, at least among certain clients, for deposit banking. It was this demand among a fraction of the clients that drove notaries to engage in deposit banking and thereby run the risk of failure, just as our model assumes. And because the clients who sought deposit banking were drawn to the same risky études, the bankruptcies tended to reoccur in the same notarial businesses.

Our assumption that differences among clienteles explained the bankruptcies is born out by qualitative evidence and by the repetition of bankruptcies in the same études. But if clienteles explain the bankruptcies, then we have to explain how a notary managed to transmit a number of intangible assets when he sold his étude: the clients' goodwill, information about what sort of financial intermediation they preferred, and the skills and human capital needed to meet their demands. Notaries managed to pass on these assets, in part because the outgoing notary had typically financed the sale and thus had an interest in seeing that his successor prospered. Evidence from the

[24] Archives Nationales (AN) BB10, 1326b.

sale prices suggests that this mechanism for transmitting intangible assets functioned well, for relatives and senior clerks of outgoing notaries who had easy access to the intangible assets did not pay more for études than other buyers. The mechanism continued to function well even after the notarial corporation began to screen prospective buyers of études, in an effort to cut bankruptcies.

Conclusion: Government Intervention, the End of Bankruptcies, and the Evolution of Financial Intermediation in Paris

Ultimately, the notarial corporation proved unable to stop the bankruptcies on its own. Despite repeated admonition by the Ministry of Justice, the corporation did little to control wayward members. It did screen prospective notaries, but the screening meant treating each bankruptcy as an individual crisis, rather than as a symptom of a deeper problem. It only took more effective steps, such as auditing notaries' dealings, when the government exerted pressure. At bottom, the corporation wanted to protect the notaries from government intervention. That is why the corporation's assemblies were practically silent about the problem of banking even though the government was deeply concerned. And that is also why it took government intervention to bring the bankruptcies to a halt.

Why was the government so concerned? In part, it was because the notaries were semi-public officials. In part too it was because they played a sensitive fiduciary role (as stewards of estates, for example) that could easily be compromised by bankruptcy. And then there was the scandal provoked by certain great bankruptcies, such as Lehon's in 1841. Two years after his crash, the government made deposit banking by notaries a crime. Although the ban did not stop the bankruptcies completely, it did spell the end of deposit banking.[25]

Thereafter, the notaries of Paris slowly reverted to the older practice of brokerage – of arranging loans rather than serving as bankers. To secure additional funds many formed loose alliances with bankers, but they generally prefered to match borrowers and lenders. And after 1852, they progressively lost even that role, as more and more clients turned to the new mortgage bank, the Crédit Foncier de France. They were left with the task – an important one, to be sure – of arranging real estate transactions and providing the rich with estate planning and financial advice. But they left financial intermediation to others.

Why then did it take so long for the state to intervene? In part it was the scarcity of long-term mortgage credit after the French Revolution. Because

---

[25] The reason some notaries continued to fail is that they found it difficult to refinance the loans used to purchase their offices, particularly in the credit crunch that occurred during the political crisis of 1848–49.

the notaries were one of the rare sources of funds for long-term loans, the government hesitated to intervene. Bankers could hardly replace the notaries, for they had an even higher rate of failure, particularly when they tried to delve into the world of mortgage credit.[26] Yet eventually, bankers managed to overcome the high rates of bankruptcy, and they began to thrive. The number of bankers in Paris grew nearly four-fold in Paris between 1815 and 1850, and the assets these banks held probably climbed even faster. With the banks finally thriving, it was even easier for the government to intervene.

The government did not act out of hostility to all forms of risk taking in the financial sector. Rather it made an important distinction between those organizations that it regulated (the Bank of France, the savings banks, or notaries) and those that functioned with little government oversight, such as commercial and investment banks. Although the state would tolerate high rates of bankruptcy in the second group (recall that bankers failed at nearly ten times the rate notaries did), it was much more conservative when it came to the notaries and the other organizations it supervised.

Both notaries and bankers had to contend with a terrible maturity mismatch, a mismatch brought on by the history of the French Revolution. To resolve the mismatch, notaries (and bankers too) were tempted to fund long-term loans with deposits and other short-term liabilities, a risky practice that caused many to fail. The failures, we argued in our model, were not the result of differences between the notaries themselves. Rather, they resulted from differences between clients. Some clients wanted notaries to take money on deposit and engage in banking. Others wanted notaries to steer clear of this sort of risky deposit banking and stick to their traditional safe role as financial brokers. If a notary had enough of the clients who wanted deposit banking, he would give it to them, even if it carried a risk of failure.

The movement of clients from étude to étude explains why some notaries were drawn into deposit banking and why bankruptcies struck the same notarial businesses repeatedly. It also fits the evidence from taxes and the sale prices of notarial études – in particular, the fact that études lost value after bankruptcies. Along with our model, the difference in clienteles sheds light on bankruptcies of individual notaries and on the problem all notaries had in passing along their human capital and the intangible assets of their études to their successors. And finally, our model of heterogeneous clients makes it clear why the bankruptcies lasted so long and why only the government could bring them to a halt.

---

[26] The Banque Territoriale, the Caisse Hypothécaire, and the Caisse Laffitte (not to mention the Crédit Mobilier in the 1860s). See, for instance, Gérard Jacquemet, *Belleville au xixe siècle: du faubourg à la ville* (Paris: Editions de l' École des hautes études en sciences sociales, 1984).

APPENDIX 3.1: PARISIAN NOTARIES WHO WENT BANKRUPT, 1817–69

Étude	Surname of Notary	First Name of Notary	Entered Notarial Business	Left Notarial Business	Problem
4	BARBIER	Aristide	1826	1831	Failed
6	GUERINET	Jean-Baptiste	1822	1831	Failed
21	DEHERAIN	Théophile	1813	1827	Revoked
22	NOEL	Alphonse	1831	1839	Failed
30	LOUVANCOURT	Justin	1832	1843	Revoked
39	LEBAUDY		1836	1847	Failed
41	MARECHAL	Charles	1834	1847	Revoked
45	HAILIG	Louis-Claude	1826	1848	Failed
47	BACQ	Louis-Jacques	1805	1819	Failed
47	DORIVAL	Alfred-Louis	1844	1848	Failed
48	CAHOUET		1825	1848	Failed
52	DUBOIS	François	1821	1831	Revoked
52	BERTIN	Jules-François	1831	1837	Failed
53	LINARD	Denis	1837	1841	Revoked
53	FERRAND	Jean	1841	1849	Failed
55	CHEVRIER	Antoine-Marie	1808	1825	Revoked
62	THIBERT	Antoine-Denis	1811	1814	Failed
62	BEAUDENOM DE LA MAZE	Jacques	1814	1836	Revoked
62	PETINEAU	Adolphe	1836	1852	Failed
77	ROUSSEAU	Eugène-Pierre	1827	1842	Revoked
79	COLIN DE SAINT-MENGE	Marc-Louis	1820	1831	Failed
81	ANDRY	Pierre-André	1830	1849	Failed
82	LEHON	Jacques-François	1826	1841	Failed
83	FORQUERAY	Jean-Baptiste	1819	1831	Failed
94	BOURSIER	Guy	1810	1828	Failed
95	GOUDECHAUX	Léon	1841	1857	Failed
101	BAUCHAU	Joseph-Marie	1817	1825	Failed
107	LEMAIRE	Alphonse-Jean	1827	1831	Failed
107	CADET DE CHAMBINE	Stanislas-Edmond	1835	1839	Failed
111	MARCQ	Pierre-Eugène	1860	1870	Failed
113	LAMBERT	Dominique	1826	1831	Failed
116	BERTINOT	Antoine-Jacques	1818	1841	Failed
116	GOSSART	Louis-Céleste	1841	1861	Revoked
119	DELAMOTTE	Alexandre-Marie	1826	1844	Failed
119	DAUTRIVE	Albert-Aimé	1844	1849	Failed

Source: Archives de la Chambre des Notaires de Paris (henceforth ACNP), Archives Nationales (henceforth AN) BB10.

Note: The table includes both notaries who actually went bankrupt (denoted by "failed" in the problem column) and those who were expelled from the notarial corporation for deposit banking (with "revoked" in the problem column). The revoked notaries were often teetering on the edge of bankruptcy. Note that several études experienced more than one failure or revocation.

APPENDIX 3.2: EQUILIBRIUM PROOF

Part A: Nash Equilibrium

It is easy to check that each client's strategy is the best response to the strategies of the notaries and the other clients. Notaries with homogeneous clienteles have dominant strategies. To check on the Nash equilibrium, we must examine notaries with heterogeneous clienteles. To simplify matters, we suppose that at least one notary has already failed – a historically reasonable assumption in Paris; doing away with this assumption simply requires more complicated notation. At time t, the only notaries with heterogeneous clienteles are those who have offered extensive intermediation at time $t-1$ but whose businesses have never gone bankrupt, either at time $t-1$ or before.

Consider such a notary and let Π_t^L be his profit from offering only brokerage in period t:

$$\Pi_t^L = L_t f + d V(L_{t+1}, 0),$$

where $V(L, E)$ is the continuation value of the game given that the notary expects to have L clients of type L and E clients of type E. Similarly, let Π_t^E be his profit from offering extensive services in period t:

$$\Pi_t^E = (L_t + E) f + E r + (1 - q) d V(L_{t+1}, E).$$

Note that we can neglect time subscripts for the number of E clients because of the assumption that at least one notary has already failed. E clients who are denied extensive services will move to the successors of the failed notaries, and as a result, our notary will acquire no additional E clients as long as he does not go bankrupt.

It is clear that $\Pi_t^L - \Pi_t^E$ is a function of L_t and E and the exogenous parameters q, d, f, and r. The sign of $\Pi_t^L - \Pi_t^E$ will determine whether our notary will choose to offer brokerage only (when $\Pi_t^L - \Pi_t^E \geq 0$) or extensive services (when $\Pi_t^L - \Pi_t^E < 0$). Our claim is that $\Pi_t^L - \Pi_t^E$ an increasing function of L_t and a decreasing function of E; $\Pi_t^L - \Pi_t^E$ will then be the period specific function of the proposition in the text.

To prove that $\Pi_t^L - \Pi_t^E$ is an increasing function of L_t and a decreasing function of E, we proceed by backward induction on t. We first check that the statement is true at the terminal period T, when $\Pi_T^L - \Pi_T^E = -E(f + r)$, which is obviously decreasing in E and increasing in L_t. Note that because $-E(f + r) < 0$, we have also established that our notary will always offer extensive services in the final period.

Now consider time t and assume that $\Pi_{t+1}^L - \Pi_{t+1}^E$ is decreasing in E and increasing in L_{t+1}. We must establish that $\Pi_t^L - \Pi_t^E$ is itself a decreasing function of E and an increasing function of L_t.

Let us first consider the case in which our notary offers only limited intermediation at t. Because all of his E clients will leave, $\Pi_t^L = L_t f + d V(L_{t+1}, 0)$ and $V(L_{t+1}, 0) = \Pi_{t+1}^L$. As a result, $\Pi_t^L = L_t f + d \Pi_{t+1}^L = \Sigma d^j L_{t+j} f$, where the sum is taken over all j from 0 to $T - t$. Now $L_{t+j} = L_{t+j-1} + L'_{t+j}$, where L'_{t+j} is the number of additional type L clients who arrive in our notary's étude at time $t + j$ after having left notaries who have gone bankrupt in the previous period. Because L'_{t+j} is independent of L_{t+j-1} and of our notary's actions, $\Sigma d^j L_{t+j} f$ is increasing in L_t; it is also obviously a decreasing function of E.

Consider now a notary who offers extensive intermediation at time t. He retains all his clients as long as he does not go bankrupt, where the probability of bankruptcy is q. For him,

$$\Pi_t^E = (L_t + E)f + Er + (\mathrm{1} - q)dV(L_{t+1},E).$$

The continuation value of the game at $t + \mathrm{1}$ will depend on whether the notary then chooses extensive or limited intermediation at $t + \mathrm{1}$

$$V(L_{t+1},E) = \mathrm{Max}\Big\{\Pi_{t+1}^L,\Pi_{t+1}^E\Big\}.$$

Hence Π_t^E takes on one of two possible values:

(a) $\Pi_t^E = (L_t + E)f + Er + (\mathrm{1} - q)d\Pi_{t+1}^L$ if he offers limited intermediation at $t + \mathrm{1}$, or

(b) $\Pi_t^E = (L_t + E)f + Er + (\mathrm{1} - q)d\Pi_{t+1}^E$ if he offers extensive intermediation at $t + \mathrm{1}$.

We consider each of the two cases (a) and (b) in turn, starting with (a). In that case,

$$\Pi_t^L - \Pi_t^E = -E(f + r) + dq\Pi_{t+1}^L = -E(f + r) + qd\Sigma d^j L_{t+j}f,$$

where the sum is taken over all j from o to $T - t$. The first term is decreasing in E and independent of L_t. As for the terms in the sum, once again $L_{t+j} = L_{t+j-1} + L'_{t+j}$, where L'_{t+j} is the number of additional type L clients who arrive in our notary's étude at time $t + j$. Because L'_{t+j} is independent of L_{t+j-1} and of our notary's actions, the sum is independent of E and increasing in L_t. As a result, $\Pi_t^L - \Pi_t^E$ is increasing in L and decreasing in E.

Now consider the second case: $\Pi_t^E = (L_t + E)f + Er + (\mathrm{1} - q)d\Pi_{t+1}^E$. Then

$$\Pi_t^L - \Pi_t^E = L_t f + d\Pi_{t+1}^L - (L_t + E)f - Er - (\mathrm{1} - q)d\Pi_{t+1}^E$$

$$= -E(f + r) + dq\Pi_{t+1}^L + (\mathrm{1} - q)d\Big(\Pi_{t+1}^L - \Pi_{t+1}^E\Big)$$

$$= -E(f + r) + dq\Sigma d^j L_{t+j}f + (\mathrm{1} - q)d\Big(\Pi_{t+1}^L - \Pi_{t+1}^E\Big),$$

where the sum is taken over all j from o to $T - t$. The term $-E(f + r)$ is independent of L_t and decreasing in E, and the second term (the sum) is independent of E and increasing in L_t. Finally by the recursive assumption $\Pi_{t+1}^L - \Pi_{t+1}^E$ is increasing in L_{t+1} and decreasing in E. Because $L_{t+1} = L_t + L'_{t+1}$, $\Pi_{t+1}^L - \Pi_{t+1}^E$ must be increasing in L_t and decreasing in E. As a result, in this instance too, $\Pi_t^L - \Pi_t^E$ is increasing in L_t and decreasing in E.

Part B: Subgame Perfection

We need to check what happens if a client fails to move and also what happens if a notary switches strategies. Begin with the client. As long as clienteles are large, his deviation will not affect a notary's payoff. Hence, the notary will not have reason to change his strategy; nor will other clients. Next consider a notary who switches strategies. If he replaces a notary who has failed, then his deviation will involve refusing to offer anything more than brokerage after the étude's L clients have left. But then his E clients will abandon the étude too, leaving the notary with only migrant E clients. He will therefore want to offer intermediation again, implying that the equilibrium will be undisturbed. The same argument applies if he denies service to the migrants. Now consider a notary who switches to offering intermediation after his E clients have left. Because none of his clients will want the extra service, the equilibrium will remain the same.

Further, the equilibrium is robust to two types of coalitional deviations. First, if L clients do not leave after a bankruptcy, the new notary will still offer intermediation because he will attract even more E clients. Similarly, if E clients do not leave a notary who offers only brokerage, he will still want to offer only limited services because he will have even more L clients joining his étude.

However, because this is a coordination game and notaries are homogeneous, the equilibrium is not robust to other kinds of coalitional deviations. For instance, if brokerage and intermediation clients jointly reverse their strategies, then a completely different equilibrium will arise.

II

FINANCIAL INTERMEDIARIES IN THE AMERICAS

4

The Mortgage Market in Upper Canada: Window on a Pioneer Economy

Angela Redish

Introduction

It is commonly accepted that well-functioning capital markets are a key to economic development and growth, yet our knowledge of capital markets in historical times is very limited. Recent research has begun to characterize the nature and evolution of stock markets in England, France, and the United States and, to a lesser extent, the markets and institutions that had a direct impact on large numbers of people such as credit cooperatives and mortgage markets.[1] This chapter contributes to the latter literature by examining the mortgage market in the Niagara District of Upper Canada (now Ontario) in the first half of the nineteenth century.

Through this period banks were the only financial intermediaries, and their lending was restricted to "real bills," and their clientele therefore limited to the commercial sector. In the large agricultural and smaller industrial sectors, credit was limited to direct transactions between borrowers and lenders, and the resulting decentralization has made it difficult to collect data to determine the nature and extent of the credit market. However, Upper Canada had a land registration system that required registration of mortgages, providing a rich source of information on one piece of the credit market. This chapter summarizes the evidence on three aspects of the mortgage market: the extent of mortgage indebtedness; the characteristics of the market – who lent how much to whom and, in particular, the extent to which borrowing was internal (lenders came from the Niagara District) or external (lenders came from elsewhere in Upper Canada, Lower Canada,

[1] This is a growing literature; examples include Neal (1990), Hoffman, Postel-Vinay, and Rosenthal (1992), Guinnnane (1994), Hollis and Sweetman (1998), Rothenberg (1998), and Snowden (1987, 1995, and 1997).

The author would like to thank Ken Snowden for his comments, Doug McCalla and Gillian Hamilton for comments on an earlier draft, and the SSHRCC for funding.

the United States, or the United Kingdom); and the rationale for mortgage borrowing.

It is estimated that between 1815 and 1850 mortgage indebtedness was of the same order of magnitude as indebtedness to banks (there was virtually no overlap), and that the land of about one in ten landowners was mortgaged. Because Niagara District was a newly settled region through this period, we might expect that there would be an inflow of funds into the region. On the other hand, problems of moral hazard might raise the costs of lending from afar, perhaps prohibitively. The majority of loans were from "local" lenders, giving support to this second effect. However, if moral hazard was costly, we would expect that there would be significant differences in loan characteristics as lenders attempt to mitigate those costs. There is little evidence of such differences. Finally, motives for borrowing such as consumption-smoothing over harvest and business cycles, and the need to finance the purchase of farms are considered, however the conclusion is that, whereas mortgages were often used to finance the purchase of land, the majority of borrowing was to finance major improvements both to farms and small industry, and to finance inventory.

Historical Context

The data for this study are taken from the Niagara District in Ontario – essentially the peninsula south of Lake Ontario and north of Lake Erie – for the years between 1800 and 1850. The first major influx of European settlers in the District were Loyalists who arrived in 1784, and a considerable part of the land in the District was granted to Loyalists, Late Loyalists, and their descendants, in 200-acre lots. In 1824, the Census counted 17,552 residents in the Niagara District (half in Lincoln County), while the population of Ontario was 150,000. By 1850, mainly as a result of immigration and extensive settlement, the population of Upper Canada had risen to 950,000, while that of Niagara District had risen only to 49,747 (with Lincoln County at 15,777). Lewis and Urquhart (1999) report that Upper Canada was the fastest growing region of North America between 1826 and 1851.

The early settlers had been attracted by the possibility of supplying the military posts in the District, but the posts became unimportant, and the growth in the province passed the District by. In common with the rest of the province, the major economic activities were forwarding (i.e. transportation and trade) and agriculture. The two urban areas in the District were Niagara and St. Catherines.[2] Although Niagara was settled earlier, by the end of the period St. Catherines had surpassed it. Informative descriptions of the two towns in 1846 are given in Smith's *Gazetteer* for that year, and suggest busy,

---

[2] Niagara was originally named Newark, and is now Niagara on the Lake.

small towns of a few thousand people serving an agricultural hinterland. In addition, to the service sector, Niagara had a major shipbuilding facility that had been building steamboats (for Great Lake shipping) since 1832, and employed between 150 and 350 people in the 1830s and 1840s.[3]

There were agencies and branches of the chartered banks within the District, but banks were prohibited from lending directly on the security of land, although they could take a mortgage as additional security for a loan and in the case of a loan default had the usual right to seize land under a writ of *fieri facias* (seizure of chattels by a creditor if a debtor is in default). In the sample, only twelve mortgages were granted by banks: the Montreal Bank, the Bank of Upper Canada, the Gore Bank, and the Commercial Bank. Until 1847 the banks were the only formal financial intermediary in Upper Canada, but in that year the Niagara District Building Society and the St. Catherines Building Society began operations. By 1850 they had made thirty mortgage loans.

Legal Context

The data used in this study are drawn from the mortgages registered in the Niagara District before 1850. A clear understanding about the legal processes, both the mortgage contract and the registration process, that generated the data is essential to its interpretation.

The basic land law system was established in 1792, when Upper Canada adopted the land law of England. Indeed, the introduction of British land law had been part of the *raison d'etre* of the division of Quebec into Upper and Lower Canada. Yet this adoption of English law was ambiguous in that one of the key institutions of English land law – the Chancery Court – was not implemented until 1837.

---

[3] The description of Niagara lists as professions and trades: "three physicians and surgeons, nine lawyers, one foundry, 12 stores, some taverns, two chemists and druggists, three booksellers and stationers, two saddlers, four wagonmakers, two watchmakers, one gunsmith, two tallow-chandlers, marble works, two printers, two cabinet makers, one hatter, four bakers, two livery stables, two tinsmiths, three blacksmiths, six tailors, seven shoemakers, one tobacconist, and an agency of the Bank of Upper Canada." Smith (1970), 130.

For St. Catherines, the list included: "6 physicians and surgeons, five lawyers, four grist mills (containing 20 run of stones), one trip hammer, one brewery, three distilleries, one tannery, one foundry, one ashery, one machine and pump factory, two surveyors, one pottery, 14 stores, two auctioneers, 24 groceries, one stove store, one printer, one pail factory, one broom factory, one tallow chandler, 8 taverns, 3 saddlers, three cabinet makers, two booksellers and stationers, three druggists, one gunsmith, two watchmakers, three carriage makers, three bakers, two hatters, two livery stables, 7 blacksmiths, one veterinary surgeon, three tinsmiths, one tobacconist, 7 tailors, 9 shoemakers, one grammar school, 4 schools for young ladies, and agencies of the Bank of Montreal, Bank of Upper Canada, and the Commercial Bank." Smith (1970), 178.

Under English law, a mortgage was a conveyance of land in fee simple to the creditor/grantee with a covenant that required return of the land (i.e., from creditor to debtor) if repayment of the loan were done as prescribed in the mortgage. In England the harshness of mortgages (and consequently their lack of appeal as security for a loan) had been modified by the creation of an equity of redemption. That is, a borrower could be in default of his loan, and lose his land, but if he subsequently repaid the loan and interest outstanding, he could reclaim his land. This right in turn was modified by the ability of lenders to foreclose the equity of redemption, by going to the Chancery Court and serving notice that if the borrower did not repay within six months, the equity of redemption would be gone. (The right to foreclose the equity of redemption required appearance at court, and if the property were worth more than the outstanding debt, the Court could order the property sold, and the proceeds in excess of the debt returned to the borrower.) The effect of these laws was to make the stated term of a mortgage unimportant, and "it became customary to fix the initial legal redemption date very early, commonly at six months' distance."[4]

The existence of the equity of redemption in Upper Canada before 1834 was unclear. While some lawyers argued that equity had "come over in the pockets of the settlers" (i.e., was an established legal right), an alternative interpretation held that because there was no Chancery Court, the equity of redemption could not be foreclosed and therefore did not exist. While this ambiguity clouded the rights of lenders, Weaver (1990) argues that by 1809 case law had evolved to the benefit of the mortgagee. The mechanism was the right of fieri facias (or fi fa). This legislation provided for the seizure of chattels by a creditor if a debtor were in default. In England the legislation explicitly excluded the right to seize land. In 1732 English legislation ("An Act for the more easy recovery of debts") modified the application of fi fa in the colonies to permit the seizure of land. Despite the assumption of English law in 1792, the courts permitted the continuation of this modification in Upper Canada. Indeed (to protect themselves against the possible existence of an equity of redemption) lenders seized both the land and the borrower's equity of redemption under fi fa. A borrower in default would forfeit his land if the lender acquired a judgment in ejection and a writ of possession.

The situation by which the lender held the upper hand was altered in 1834 by the unambiguous establishment of the equity of redemption by legislation (1834 UC c1, c16) and subsequently by the introduction of the Court of Chancery in 1837.[5] Yet, the implications of these changes, in the absence of rules prohibiting the use of fi fa for land and the equity of redemption, is unclear.

---

[4] Megarry and Wade (1975), 890; Allen (1992), 102.
[5] Weaver (1990) and Pearlston (1999) examine the politics of these legal changes.

While land registration was not implemented generally in Britain until 1925 (Middlesex and Yorkshire being counterexamples), registration was introduced into Upper Canada in 1795 (35 Geo. III c5).[6] Registers were established in each county for the registration of title (patents, deeds, grants, and mortgages). The Act did not make registration mandatory, and it did not change the legality of any document. However, a registered document had priority over an unregistered document, and "every deed and conveyance that shall at any time after any memorial is so registered . . . . shall be adjudged fraudulent and void [with respect to subsequent mortgagees only]." Lenders thus had a strong incentive to register a mortgage, because otherwise the borrower could take out a second mortgage and if that deed were registered it would have priority over the first mortgage.[7] Although the evidence is thin, Youdan (1986) argues that after 1795 registration of mortgages was "in fact rarely omitted."[8] The discharge of a mortgage could also be registered, but the incentive (for either party) to do so was considerably less.

Two other aspects of the legal environment affected mortgages. The first is the married woman's right of dower. The right of dower assigned a married woman the right to one-third of the property of her husband, or the income thereof. Particularly, the husband's sale (or mortgage) of the land did not affect this right, and so the grantee of a mortgage in default would not acquire clear title to the land if subsequently the husband died, for his widow might have a valid claim to the land. To avoid this possibility, the mortgagee could ask the wife to extinguish her right of dower, and typical mortgages noted that the wife had done so in consideration for a nominal fee (often 6 pence, 6d.).

Finally, mortgage loans were subject to usury laws. These laws stated that all contracts where the interest rate was greater than 6 percent were "utterly void" and that if such a contract could be proved, the lender would lose three times the amount lent.[9] There were no cases in the data where the explicit interest rate was greater than 6 percent, but whether the actual transaction occurred at 6 percent is impossible to determine.[10] Neufeld (1972, 544) argues that the legislation was typically circumvented by selling mortgages at a discount, and he quotes from a letter to the Canadian Merchant Magazine

---

[6] The motives for introducing the Registry are not known, although some historians attribute it to the traditions of Loyalists from New England, while others (e.g., Neave 1977) focus on the similarity between the Upper Canadian system and that of Middlesex.

[7] The costs of registering a mortgage were set in the Act at 2.6 pence for the first 100 words, plus 1 shilling for each subsequent 100 words.

[8] Armour (1925) similarly states that registration was "rarely omitted."

[9] This is from legislation in 1811 (51 Geo III c9); prior to 1811 lenders were bound by usury laws with similar provisions in Quebec. The legislation was not significantly altered until 1853, although Building Societies were granted an exemption in 1846. Neufeld (1972), 188.

[10] A total of seven cases named specific interest rates less than 6 percent.

and Commercial Review in October 1857: "On private notes, and on private mortgages does not every one know, the rate of interest brought by money, is in every case regulated by mutual conditions, in utter indifference to all attempts at Parliamentary restraint."

The Extent of Indebtedness

The data for this study come from the 1,368 mortgages registered in the Niagara District between 1795 and 1849. The data set was compiled by matching mortgages in the Abstract Index of Deeds with the Copybook of Deeds. The Abstract Indexes were kept on a geographical basis. There was essentially a book for each township with a page for each lot on each concession. The information recorded included the type of transaction (sale, mortgage, discharge of mortgage, or probated will being the typical transactions), the names of the parties, the date of the transaction, as well as the date of registration, and (usually) the amount. The Copybook of Deeds, recorded chronologically, had a copy of the entire document and included information on the addresses and occupations of the parties, as well as the details of the repayment scheme: term, interest rate, and whether it would be amortised or paid in full at the end of the term.

Figure 4.1 shows the number of new mortgages registered each year. Prior to the end of the War of 1812 (in 1815) there were very few mortgages, but the number of new mortgages rose fairly steadily after that so that in 1847 and 1848 there were over 100 new mortgages registered each year. The distribution of the value of mortgages remained remarkably stable with the mean loan being about £400 and the median close to £200 throughout

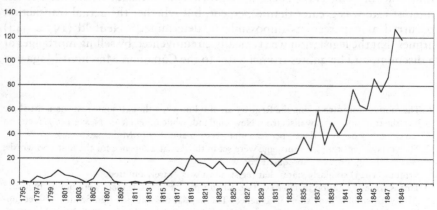

FIGURE 4.1. New Mortgages per Annum
Source: See text.

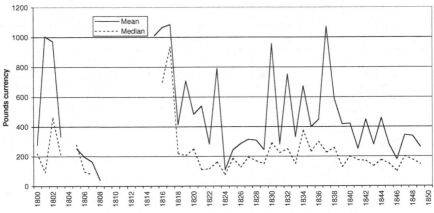

FIGURE 4.2. Mean and Median Loan Value
Source: See text.

the period (see Figure 4.2).[11] To put these numbers into perspective, note that the majority of loans were to farmers and Lewis and Urquhart (1999) estimate that the annual output of a (fully developed) farm in 1851 to have been $297 or £74. They also estimate that the cost of purchasing a farm (land and animals) would be about £105. The amounts being borrowed were significant.

The stock of outstanding mortgage debt is harder to estimate than the amount of new debt because it requires information on the "ex post" term of the debt and the schedule of principal repayment. Data on one or both of those variables was omitted in about 50 percent of the cases, typically because the mortgage was used to provide additional security for a bonded debt, and the details of the repayment schedule were only recorded in the bond. Of those that did state a repayment plan, 40 percent planned to repay the principal in equal annual installments, 40 percent planned to repay it in a lump sum, and the other 20 percent stated other plans, such as half-yearly installments or, after 1847, a building society plan.

Analysis of the mortgages that state a repayment schedule does not suggest an easy way to determine the probable plans for those for which there is no data. Specifically, there is no significant correlation between repayment plans and the amount borrowed, the occupation of the lender or borrower, or the location of the lender (within the Niagara District or from outside the District, or a finer breakdown). There *is* a significant correlation between the term of the mortgage and the repayment plan, with longer mortgages being

[11] Throughout the period, the unit of account was the pound Halifax currency, which equated £1 to $4(U.S.) The high variability in the averages before 1821 should be seen in the context of the low sample size (see Figure 4.1).

Angela Redish

TABLE 4.1. *Comparison of Stated and Actual Terms of Mortgages*

Actual Term		Stated Term				
		0–2 Years	3–5 Years	6–10 Years	More Than 10 Years	TOTAL
0–2 years	Count	56	33	2		91
	% of column	30.9%	17.7%	3.2%		20.7%
3–5 years	Count	55	76	16	1	148
	% of column	30.4%	40.9%	25.4%	11.1%	33.7%
6–10 years	Count	41	51	30	3	125
	% of column	22.7%	27.4%	47.6%	33.3%	28.5%
More than 10 years	Count	29	26	15	5	75
	% of column	16.0%	14.0%	23.8%	55.6%	17.1%
TOTAL	Count	181	186	63	9	439
	% of column	100.0%	100.0%	100.0%	100.0%	100.0%

Source: Computed from data, see text.

more likely to be repaid in installments. However, the R^2 of a probit regression of repayment plans on the term of the mortgage is only 22 percent. The nature of the correlation can be simply modelled by assuming that all mortgages whose term was two years or less will be repaid by lump sum, and all those of longer term will be repaid in equal annual installments. Such a model predicts the repayment schedule accurately 67 percent of the time. The probit model yielded the correct prediction 68 percent of the time but without incorporating the integer constraints implicit in a plan for annual installments.

The second necessity for calculating the amount of mortgage debt outstanding is to determine the *actual* term of the mortgages, which may have differed from the *ex ante* planned term. Ideally, the date that mortgages were discharged would provide evidence on the *ex post* term, however, data on discharges are incomplete with only a third of mortgages discharged (up to 1860). It is unclear how to interpret the status of mortgages for which no discharge was registered. Were they discharged without registration? Were they in default? Or were they rolled over without a new mortgage being registered? High default rates are not consistent with evidence from the Sheriff's courts so the choice is between assuming that the mortgages were rolled over and assuming they were paid off. The information on mortgages that were discharged can provide some guide.

For the set of 439 mortgages that were discharged and that provided data on the ex ante repayment schedule, Table 4.1 compares the term as stated in

TABLE 4.2. *Stated Term for Discharged and Undischarged Mortgages*

Stated Term		Discharged	No Discharge Recorded	TOTAL
0–2 years	Count	179	334	513
	% of row	34.9%	65.1%	100.0%
3–5 years	Count	162	279	441
	% of row	36.7%	63.3%	100.0%
6–10 years	Count	50	91	141
	% of row	35.5%	64.5%	100.0%
More than 10 years	Count	8	16	24
	% of row	33.3%	66.7%	100.0%
TOTAL	Count	399	720	1119
	% of row	35.7%	64.3%	100.0%

Source: Computed from data, see text.

the mortgage and the term as computed by comparing the date of discharge (not the date the discharged was registered[12]) with the starting date of the mortgage. The ex post term of the mortgages was far longer than the ex ante term: 84 percent of mortgages were written with terms of five years or less, however, only 54 percent had been discharged within that period.[13]

Although mortgages were not repaid as quickly as the deed stated, there was a significant correlation between ex ante and ex post terms. The data in Table 4.2 indicate that the term structure of mortgages that were discharged was similar to that of the whole set of mortgages. Therefore I estimate the stock of outstanding mortgage debt on the assumption that the mortgages for which no discharge was registered were in fact discharged at the same rate as those for which a discharge was registered. More specifically, I model the relationship between planned and actual mortgage term of mortgages that are discharged. This is given by the equation (1):

$$(1) \text{ Actual term} = 2.78 + 0.502 \text{ planned term} - 0.154 \text{ year}$$
$$(5.12) \quad (4.70) \quad\quad\quad (-5.9)$$
$$R^2 = .13 \quad n = 381,$$

where terms are measured in years, year is measured as (year of mortgage − 1850) and *t*-statistics are in parentheses.[14] Although the variables are significant, the explanatory power of the regression is low.

[12] There was frequently a considerable lag between the registration of a discharge and the actual discharge.

[13] Rothenberg (1998) found that, for mortgages with a stated term of one year and for which discharges were registered, the ex post term averaged 8.75 years.

[14] The time trend does not seem to be a result of censoring (i.e., lack of data on discharges after fifteen years for mortgages taken out after 1845, after twelve years if taken out after 1848, etc.).

TABLE 4.3. *Stock of Outstanding
Mortgages*

Year	Number of Mortgages Outstanding
1799	15
1809	57
1819	56
1829	126
1839	248
1849	505

Source: Computed from data, see text.

The second step involves using the estimated coefficients to compute an "actual" term for all mortgages, and then computing the stock of outstanding debt each year. This is shown as the "stock" variable in Figure 4.3. The impact of the War of 1812 is clear, as is the expansion of activity following the War. The downturn in the late 1820s is steeper than one might expect – it reflects the "assumed" expiry of the spate of mortgages issued after the War of 1812. In 1837 there were many new mortgages issued, yet these occurred prior to the passage of the legislation introducing Chancery Courts. The dramatic increase in the mortgage debt outstanding in 1837 reflects the ten large mortgages totaling £45,500 issued to finance the construction of the Erie and Ontario Railroad. To highlight the effect of this small set of mortgages, the data are also presented net of these ten mortgages. The stable mean value (especially after 1820) implies that the number of outstanding mortgages shows roughly the same trend as the value of mortgages (see Table 4.3).

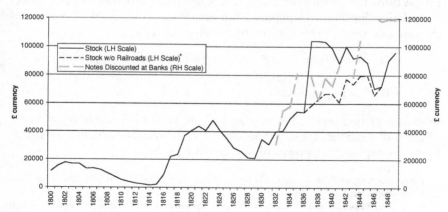

FIGURE 4.3. Value of Outstanding Mortgages
*Without railroads omits ten mortgages to finance the Erie and Ontario Railroad.
Source: See text.

The data are roughly consistent with earlier work. In his study of Toronto Gore Township, David Gagan linked mortgage data with the manuscript census and found that in 1841, 16 percent of proprietors had mortgage debts. The manuscript census for very few townships in the Niagara District has survived, but those that do suggest that the number of households is approximately one-sixth of the population and that half of those were proprietors.[15] The population of Niagara District in 1824 was about 17,552 and in 1841, 34,577 implying about 1,462 and 2,881 proprietors respectively. The stock of outstanding mortgages in those years is estimated at 128 and 285 or about 9 percent of proprietors in each year.

To put the data on the extent of indebtedness in context, Figure 4.3 also shows data on the amount of bank loans (discounts) in Upper Canada. Because the population of the Niagara District was about 10 percent of that of Upper Canada, the right hand side scale is ten times that of the left hand side scale. (That is, if bank loans were proportionally distributed across the province, bank loans in the Niagara District could be read off the same scale as the stock of mortgage debt.) The data suggest that until the late 1840s the mortgage market was of a similar order of magnitude to the scale of bank lending, although both debtors and creditors were likely very different – an aspect to which we now turn.

Characteristics of Mortgages

With every loan the lender faces the prospect of not being repaid, and that prospect has led to a variety of institutions to encourage repayment, and thereby encourage lending. Recent historical analysis has shown that in the absence of formal institutions, social sanctions may be an effective enforcement mechanism in small communities. These sanctions work best in an environment where geographical mobility (and therefore the ability to evade sanctions) is limited. In a frontier environment their effectiveness would be limited. The development of the system for registering and enforcing mortgages was an alternative method to enforce loan contracts. Yet enforcement would still be incomplete and costly, and a lender would still be influenced

[15] For example:

Year	Twp	Population	Hh heads	% Pop'n	Proprietors	% Pop'n
1828	Clinton	1,513	253	17%		
1828	Gainsboro	814	164	20%		
1842	Stamford	2,636	457	17%	269	10%
1842	Thorold	2,284			197	9%
1842	Willoughby	979			207	21%

TABLE 4.4. *Number of Mortgages Granted by Decade and Residence of Lender*

| | | | Residence of Lender | | | |
Decade		Niagara District	Other Upper Canada	Lower Canada	United States	United Kingdom	TOTAL
1790	Count	8	2	5	1		16
	% of row	50.0%	12.5%	31.3%	6.3%		100.0%
1800	Count	38	4	5		1	48
	% of row	79.2%	8.3%	10.4%		2.1%	100.0%
1810	Count	38	8	9		1	56
	% of row	67.9%	14.3%	16.1%		1.8%	100.0%
1820	Count	114	14	14	1		143
	% of row	79.7%	9.8%	9.8%	.7%		100.0%
1830	Count	229	47	24	1	7	308
	% of row	74.4%	15.3%	7.8%	.3%	2.3%	100.0%
1840	Count	561	148	34	22	19	784
	% of row	71.6%	18.9%	4.3%	2.8%	2.4%	100.0%
TOTAL	Count	988	223	91	25	28	1,355
	% of row	72.9%	16.5%	6.7%	1.8%	2.1%	100.0%

Source: Computed from data, see text.

by the probability of repayment.[16] The ability to determine that probability would have varied by geographical proximity; lenders in the Niagara District would have more information about the quality of land being mortgaged and the reputation of borrowers.

Table 4.4 shows the extent of lending broken down by the residence of the lender, and how it changed over time. Column 1 includes mortgages where the lender lived in the Niagara District; column 2 mortgages where the lender lived in Upper Canada but outside the Niagara District – typically in Toronto but sometimes Kingston (especially prior to 1820) or Gore District adjacent to Niagara District; column 3 includes lenders from Lower Canada, typically Montreal, and Columns 4 and 5 show lenders resident in the United States and United Kingdom respectively.

Table 4.4 shows that mortgages very largely supported local lending, especially after 1820. The sixteen mortgages granted in the 1790s included five (31 percent) from Montreal merchants to Niagara District merchants. After 1800, although there are more such mortgages in absolute numbers, their relative share fell to less than 10 percent after 1820, and less than 5 percent in the 1840s. In part, this reflected the rise of Toronto as the metropolitan center for the Niagara District, and in part the rise of lending to nonmerchants who

---

[16] If usury laws were effective and binding, then we would expect that loans would not be made to groups that were unlikely to repay.

TABLE 4.5. *Number of Mortgages Granted by Class of Borrower and Residence of Lender*

Borrower Class		Niagara District	Other Upper Canada	Lower Canada	United States	United Kingdom	TOTAL
				Residence of Lender			
Yeoman	Count	445	64	4	7	3	523
	% of row	85.1%	12.2%	.8%	1.3%	.6%	100.0%
Elite	Count	264	80	70	11	25	450
	% of row	58.7%	17.8%	15.6%	2.4%	5.6%	100.0%
Other	Count	216	32	10	6	4	268
	% of row	80.6%	11.9%	3.7%	2.2%	1.5%	100.0%
TOTAL	Count	925	176	84	24	32	1,241
	% of row	74.5%	14.2%	6.8%	1.9%	2.6%	100.0%

Source: Computed from data, see text.

tended to borrow locally. The other message from Table 4.4 is the very small proportion of mortgages from lenders outside of the Canadas. Inspection of the mortgages by those lenders whose residence was in the United Kingdom shows that the majority had close family connections with the borrower or had previously resided in the Niagara District.

Not shown in Table 4.4 is the frequency with which specific lenders made loans. There were very few cases where a grantor (be it an individual, partnership, or couple) made more than one loan; with one exception no grantors made more than twenty loans. That exception was the partnership of Thomas Clark and Samuel Street who, as partners or individuals, made a total of 198 loans, accounting for 20 percent of the loans made by residents of the Niagara District.

Remarkably little is known about Clark and Street. Samuel Street, Sr. had been a Loyalist immigrant from Conneticut, and Clark had immigrated from Scotland to work for his cousin, Robert Hamilton, one of the wealthiest men in Upper Canada at the time.[17] The partners became well known for their milling operations and land speculation and finance. They borrowed money on mortgages nine times over the period with an average loan size of £1,650, most of which was borrowed in the first ten years of the sample period, to finance acquisition of land and their mill. There is no evidence that the partners acted as an intermediary either by brokering or by taking deposits for lending.

Table 4.5 presents a summary of the type of borrowers, again broken down by the residence of the lender. Occupations were almost always stated

---

[17] See Nelles (1966) and the *Dictionary of Canadian Biography*, Vols. VI and VII.

in the mortgage; however, they were self-defined. The occupations most frequently listed were yeoman (41 percent), esquire (16 percent), merchant (8 percent), gentleman (8 percent), and innkeeper (5 percent). The difficulty lies in knowing how people defined themselves, particularly as some people defined themselves differently on different mortgages; e.g., as a gentleman on one mortgage and as an esquire on another, or as a gentleman and as a merchant. Therefore, these categories were combined into an elite category, and all those who weren't yeomen or the elite were aggregated into an 'other' category, primarily comprising a wide variety of artisans and also women who defined themselves as widows or spinsters (1 percent of borrowers). Overwhelmingly, yeomen and others borrowed locally (85 percent and 80 percent of loans respectively) while the elite borrowed much more heavily outside the Niagara District (41 percent).

I examined the disaggregated data for evidence of occupational segmentation within the other group, but found no evidence of such a bias. Of the 268 loans in this group, there were only seven cases where people borrowed within an occupation: one each of carpenters, blacksmiths, shoemakers, joiners and saddlers, and two innkeepers.

The amount of money lent varied significantly with the residence of the lender (see Table 4.6): the mean loan by a resident of the Niagara District was £308 and by a nonresident, £740 (the medians were £150 and £269 respectively). However, this difference reflects the difference in mean loan to yeomen and elite borrowers – yeomen averaged £224 per mortgage, and elite £747. (The mean loan to other borrowers was £288, but the standard deviation in this category is much higher because the category is so heterogeneous.) Finally, while the scale of lending to yeomen was not dependent on the source of the funds, lending to elite borrowers typically increased the farther away the lender.

The loans by Clark and Street were on average smaller than those by Niagara District lenders, with a median loan size of £148, and a third of loans being for less than £90. Clark and Street were also more likely than the average Niagara District lender to lend to yeomen, with 62 percent of their loans being made to yeomen. There is some evidence that geographical proximity increased the probability of a loan from the partnership as mortgages to residents of the township of Stamford (where Clark and Street resided) made up 13 percent of loans, whereas the township had only 8 percent of the population of Niagara District in 1841. More broadly, geographical segmentation is suggested by the fact that 35 percent of all mortgages were between borrowers and lenders residing in the same township (there were twenty-two townships in the District).

Having established that out-of-District lenders tended to lend more frequently to the elite and to lend larger sums, the question becomes whether there were differences in the contract terms, especially whether there were differences that might serve to enforce the contract or differentially compensate

TABLE 4.6. *Average Size of Mortgage by Class of Borrower and Residence of Lender (pounds currency)*

	Mean	Std. Deviation	Median	Count
Borrower: Yeomen				
Niagara District	223	259	137	445
Other Upper C.	241	396	141	64
Lower Canada	250	206	178	4
United States	211	98	150	7
United Kingdom	94	106	33	3
Total	224	276	*138*	*531*
Borrower: Elite				
Niagara District	530	1,009	250	264
Other Upper C.	627	834	350	80
Lower Canada	1,004	1,244	500	70
United States	2,267	3,260	763	11
United Kingdom	2,044	2,047	1,000	25
Total	747	1,262	*307*	*441*
Borrower: Other				
Niagara District	228	443	112	216
Other Upper C.	265	369	106	32
Lower Canada	1,230	2,400	470	10
United States	122	96	119	6
United Kingdom	1,583	2,329	615	4
Total	288	704	*120*	*264*

Source: Computed from data, see text.

the lender for risk. As noted earlier, when an interest rate was explicitly stated in the mortgages it was either 'the legal rate' (83 percent of mortgages), or '6 percent' (16 percent of mortgages) so that little variation is observable in this dimension.

There is also little difference in the ex ante term of mortgages by residence of lender: Niagara District lenders averaged ex ante terms of 2.9 years, whereas out-of-district lenders averaged 3.25 years, a difference that is not quite significant at the 5 percent level (p value 5.7 percent). The difference between the two groups in ex post term – 6.3 years for the in-district lenders, and 5.1 years for out-of-district lenders – is statistically significant. There is no difference in the rate at which discharges were registered: with 34 percent of the mortgages with in-district lenders and 31 percent of those with out-of-district lenders having discharges registered.

Finally the amount of collateral offered by borrowers is examined by comparing the amount borrowed with the value of the property being pledged. Data on the value of the property is only available for half of the mortgages, for most of the other cases the property was not acquired by purchase but

TABLE 4.7. *Regression of Loan Size on Collateral*

Variable	Model 1			Model 2		
	Coefficient	Std. Error	T Stat.	Coefficient	Std. Error	T Stat.
Constant	47.9	38.2	1.2			
Elite	268.4*	63.8	4.2	320*	48	6.6
Not ND.	250.5*	67.7	3.7	241*	50.6	4.8
Price Paid	.45*	.08	5.6	.515*	.04	12.7
PP* Not ND	−6.4 E-02	.1	−.64			
PP*Elite	8.6 E-02	.095	.90			

*significant at 1 percent level.

by inheritance or patenting. Where the data are available, they refer to the most recent land transaction, which was frequently many years before the mortgage was granted, and so the value of the land is undoubtedly biased downward. On the positive side, the sample of mortgages for which the value of the land is available seems to be a roughly random sample.

The results of regressions run to examine the determinants of collateral are shown in Table 4.7. The first model regressed the amount borrowed on a constant, a dummy variable equal to 1 if the borrower belonged to the elite group (elite), a dummy variable equal to 1 if the lender lived outside the Niagara District (not ND), the price paid for the property used as collateral (price paid), and interactive dummies capturing the effect of out-of-district lenders (PP* Not ND) and elite borrowers (PP*Elite) on the coefficient on price paid. The results suggested that the constant and the two interactive dummy variables were insignificant so a second regression was estimated omitting those variables.

The value of the property being mortgaged has a direct effect on the amount of the loan, and for the majority of borrowers (who were yeomen or others who borrowed from a local lender) the amount they could borrow was about 50 percent of the value of their land (coefficient on land of ϕ.515). The insignificance of the constant term suggests that this proportion did not vary with the amount of the loan. For borrowers who were in the elite group or who borrowed from someone living outside the Niagara District, the insignificance of the two interactive dummy variables implies that the effect of an extra £100 collateral was to increase the loan by about £50, as it was for the yeomen. However, the dummy variables for nonresident and elite were both statistically and economically significant and imply that for those two groups effective collateral requirements were much less. For example, the median borrower from a nonresident of the Niagara District borrowed £269 and his or her collateral would have been property estimated at £56 [(269 − 241)/.515].[18]

---

[18] Similar analysis of loans made by Clark and Street showed that the "best fit" regression estimated loan size as £81 plus 38 percent of the price paid, with both coefficients being

In summary, the most common type of mortgage was used by a yeoman to borrow a sum of less than £200 from another resident of the Niagara District. But there were also significant numbers of the elite who borrowed much larger sums, with lower rates of collateral and with a greater probability of borrowing from outside the District. Most mortgages were for terms of one to five years, but borrowers took longer than planned to pay back their debts. Borrowers typically promised to repay the principal in equal annual installments if the loan was for more than two years, but as a lump sum if the term were shorter. In almost all cases interest payments were, at a minimum, to be made annually.

The Motivation for Borrowing

A few mortgages included the reason that the funds were being borrowed, but the majority did not, leaving us to attempt to draw inferences from the data that do exist. When a mortgage was used to secure a previously created bonded debt, the mortgage typically stated that the lender gave the borrower 5/- "in consideration" for the mortgage: 35 percent of the mortgages included such a clause, suggesting that mortgages were fairly widely used to secure preexisting debts.[19] The frequency of such a clause does not vary by borrower class or loan size.

A primary reason for borrowing against a mortgage was to purchase a farm. Where it existed (689 cases or 50 percent of the total) data were collected on the land purchase that most nearly preceded each mortgage; in the other cases the borrower acquired the land by inheritance or grant. From this sample, for 343 mortgages the land was purchased in the same year as the mortgage was granted, leading to the conclusion that these mortgages (25 percent of the total) were for the objective of purchasing the land. The amount borrowed varied with 75 percent borrowing more than 50 percent of the purchase price.[20] However, it must be remembered that the vast majority of land purchases were accomplished without borrowing money. There may well have been 10,000 land purchases in Niagara District, suggesting that about 4 percent were financed by a mortgage.

The proportion of borrowers who took a mortgage to purchase land varied across borrower type: 28 percent of yeoman mortgages, 21 percent of elite mortgages, and 30 percent of other mortgages were within the same

---

statistically significant. When the constant term was forced to zero, the coefficient on the price paid was 54 percent, not significantly different from that in the full sample.

[19] The rationale here is that for a valid contract both parties must give up something; because the debt preexisted, the mortgage cannot be given in exchange for the debt, so the mortgage is given "in consideration" of the 5/- paid to the borrower.

[20] 15 percent borrowed more than the value of the land, but whether this was because other lands were included or because the lender was willing to make a less than fully secured loan cannot be determined.

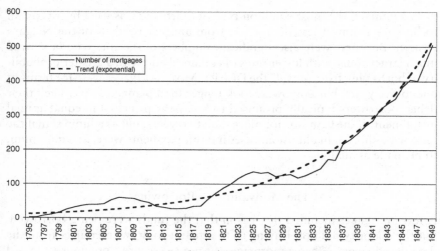

FIGURE 4.4. Number of Mortgages Outstanding
Source: See text.

year that the land was purchased. The most reasonable interpretation of this difference (given a lack of data on the total number of land purchases of each group) is that the elite were far more likely to borrow for other reasons than the other borrower classes.

The theoretical effect of business cycles and financial crises on the amount of mortgage debt is ambiguous. During a financial crisis, some borrowers would be cash-strapped and increase their demand for loans, while the supply of loanable funds might decrease. If usury laws were binding, we would expect to see a decline in the number of mortgages; while if they were unenforceable, the stock of mortgages might rise with an increase in interest rates.

We see evidence of both effects in the data. Figure 4.4 shows that during the financial crises of 1837 and 1847 the number of mortgages outstanding fell absolutely and was significantly below trend (the trend is based on the estimated growth rate of 7 percent per annum). But there is qualitative evidence of increased mortgaging to deal with a liquidity shortage caused by the crisis of 1847. In that year, the Ball family, a prominent merchant and milling family in St. Catherines, found themselves with a serious cash flow problem. In 1847 and 1848 Frederick Ball and his cousin, George P. M. Ball, granted eleven mortgages as they (successfully) staved off their (unsecured) creditors. They borrowed from family members, from the new local Building Society, the Commercial Bank, and even a local surgeon.[21]

---

[21] Although banks were not permitted to lend against mortgages, they could take mortgages as additional credit, which is apparently what they did here. The story behind the mortgage data is told in Millar (1974).

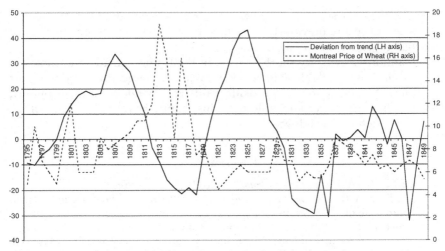

FIGURE 4.5. Montreal Wheat Price and Number of Outstanding Mortgages
Source: See text.

Finally, we can examine the extent to which mortgage activity was related to the performance of grain prices. There is an ongoing debate in Upper Canadian historiography about the significance of export markets for grain for the performance of the Upper Canadian economy.[22] Figure 4.5 shows the relationship between the price of wheat in Montreal and the deviation of the number of mortgages from trend. It shows little relationship between the two, a conclusion supported by correlation coefficients between the two series. This finding provides support for the McCalla and McInnis position that the diversification of the economy muted the influence of wheat export markets.

Conclusions

This chapter examined the characteristics of the mortgage market in one of the earliest regions of Upper Canada to be settled, the Niagara District. The data show that, while mortgages were not used by the majority of inhabitants, they played as large a role in the economy as bank lending – albeit a different role. As a financial intermediary, Upper Canadian banks primarily moved funds between members of the commercial elite, and between the landed class and the commercial class. In contrast, two-thirds of mortgage borrowers were yeomen farmers and artisans and a third of lenders were yeomen farmers. Mortgage loans were long term, with the mean stated term

---

[22] See for example McCallum (1980) who argues that such markets were central, and McCalla (1993) and McInnis (1992) who argue that they were not.

being 3.2 years, the median 2.7 years. Mortgages were used for a variety of purposes: to secure previously-unsecured debts, and perhaps one quarter of mortgages were used to buy land.

Quantitative evidence on the nature of the Upper Canadian economy is limited and the available evidence is very much biased toward the export economy. Mortgage markets provide a different window on the economy, one that has largely been unexploited. This chapter has sketched some of the views through that window.

Bibliography

Allen, R. C. *Enclosure and the Yeoman*. Oxford: Claredon Press, 1992.

Armour, E. D. *A Treatise on the Investigation of Titles to Real Property in Ontario*. Toronto: Canada Law Book Company, 1925.

Dictionary of Canadian Biography, various volumes.

Gagan, D. "The Security of Land: Mortgaging in Toronto Gore Township 1835–95," in *Aspects of Nineteenth-Century Ontario*, eds. F. Armstrong, H. Stevenson, J. Wilson. Toronto: University of Toronto Press, 1974.

Guinnane, T. "A failed institutional transplant: Raiffeisen's credit cooperatives in Ireland, 1894–1914," *Explorations in Economic History* 31 (1994): 38–61.

Hoffman, P., G. Postel-Vinay, and J-L. Rosenthal. "Private Credit Markets in Paris," *Journal of Economic History* 52 (1992): 293–406.

Hollis, A., and A. Sweetman, "Microcredit in Prefamine Ireland," *Explorations in Economic History* 35 (1998): 347–80.

Lewis, F., and M. Urquhart. "Growth and the Standard of Living in a Pioneer Economy," *William and Mary Quarterly* 56 (1999): 151–81.

McCalla, D. *Planting the Province: The Economic History of Upper Canada 1784–1870*. Toronto: University of Toronto Press, 1993.

McCallum, J. *Unequal Beginnings: Agriculture and Economic Development in Quebec and Ontario until 1870*. Toronto: University of Toronto Press, 1980.

McInnis, M. *Perspectives on Ontario Agriculture, 1815–1930*. Gananoque: Langdale Press, 1992.

Megarry, R. E., and H. W. R. Wade. *The Law of Real Property*. London: Stevens and Sons, 1975.

Millar, W. D. J. "George P. M. Ball: A Rural Businessman in Upper Canada," *Ontario History* 66 (1974): 65–78.

Neal, L. *The Rise of Financial Capitalism: International Capital Markets in the Age of Reason*. New York: Cambridge University Press, 1990.

Neave, M. "Conveyancing," *Canadian Bar Review* 55, (1977).

Nelles, H. V. "Loyalism and Local Power: The District of Niagara, 1792–1837," *Ontario History* 58 (1966): 99–114.

Neufeld, E. P. *The Financial System of Canada*. Toronto: Macmillan, 1972.

Pearlston, K. "For the More Easy Recovery of Debts in His Majesty's Plantations: Credit and Conflict in Upper Canada, 1788–1809," LL.M. thesis, University of British Columbia, 1999.

Rayner W. B., and R. H. McLaren. *Falconbridge on Mortgages*. Fourth Edition: Agincourt, Ont., Canada Law Book, 1977.

Rothenberg, W. "Mortgage Credit at the Origins of a Capital Market: Middlesex County, Massachusetts, 1642–1770." Paper presented at the Economic History Association Conference, Durham, NC, September 1998.

Smith, W. H. *Smith's Canadian Gazeteer*. Toronto: Coles, 1970, first published 1846.

Snowden, K. "Mortgage Rates and American Capital Market Development in the Late Nineteenth Century," *Journal of Economic History* 47 (1987): 771–91.

Snowden, K. "The Evolution of Interregional Mortgage Lending Channels, 1870–1940: The Life Insurance–Mortgage Company Connection," in *Coordination and Information: Historical Perspectives on the Organization of Enterprise*, eds. Naomi L. Lamoreaux and Daniel M. G. Raff. Chicago: University of Chicago Press, 1995, 209–47.

Snowden, K. "Building and Loan Associations in the U.S., 1880–1893: The Origins of Localization in the Residential Mortgage Market," *Research in Economics* 51, (1997): 227–50.

Weaver, J. "While Equity Slumbered: Creditor Advantage, a Capitalist Land Market, and Upper Canada's Missing Court," *Osgoode Hall Law Journal* 28 (1990): 871–914.

Wilson, B. G. *The Enterprises of Robert Hamilton: A Study of Wealth and Influence in Early Upper Canada, 1776–1812*. Ottawa: Carleton University Press, 1983.

Youdan, T. G. "The Length of a Title Search in Ontario," *Canadian Bar Review* 64 (1986): 507–33.

5

Integration of U.S. Capital Markets: Southern Stock Markets and the Case of New Orleans, 1871–1913

John B. Legler and Richard Sylla

Introduction

As the twenty-first century begins, capital flows across regional and national boundaries in search of the best return available, commensurate with the risks involved. It is a new era of financial globalization. As capital flows into less developed regions and countries, emerging markets arise and development occurs. When capital flows out, however, financial crises erupt and development is stopped in its tracks and sometimes reversed. Capital market integration is a two-edged sword.

Among economic historians, no one has done more than Lance Davis to demonstrate the importance of capital markets and capital mobility for economic progress. This has been a grand theme of his five decades of scholarly work. Where capital markets are more innovative, efficient, and integrated, more rapid economic growth should result. Conversely, growth would likely be less rapid than it might have been if capital markets suffered from persistent "imperfections" as evidenced by lasting regional and national differentials, sometimes wide, in interest rates on loans and in returns on other financial assets. These are simple predictions of economic theory that guided Davis's work. The important lessons he taught others who followed in his footsteps had to do with data and their interpretation. He showed by example that there were available in historical records abundant datasets to be assembled for examining the predictions of theory. In addition, Davis demonstrated how to use such datasets to frame and address historical questions such as why some places had more efficient and integrated capital markets than others, what differences resulted, and how capital markets themselves changed – for better or for worse – over time.

In this study, we attempt to apply the lessons Lance Davis taught us to a relatively neglected area of research, the capital market institutions – in particular, the stock markets – of the U.S. South during the nineteenth century. Historians of the nineteenth century United States often treat the South as a separate, "peculiar," and different region from the rest of the country. Before the Civil War, slavery became more entrenched in the South while it was phased out, or never developed in, other regions. After the Civil War, the South for decades seemed in many ways a separate economy. It was a region mired in agricultural poverty and limited socioeconomic mobility; in other regions industrialization and economic modernization proceeded rapidly. There are elements of truth in these characterizations. But they should not be exaggerated. Apart from the Civil War years, the South was always a part of the U.S. economy, and it shared in the institutional and other developments of the United States.

That was certainly the case, we hope to demonstrate, with respect to capital market institutions, a distinctive feature of U.S. economic development. What one of us (Sylla 1998) has termed "the Federalist financial revolution" of the 1790s did not bypass the South. That revolution encompassed at the national level the restructuring of public finances and debts, the creation of a national bank with branches, and the introduction of the new U.S. dollar as a specie-based monetary unit. These changes simultaneously provoked a rapid growth of state-chartered banking corporations and the appearance of securities markets in leading U.S. cities. Others have documented banking development in the antebellum South (e.g., Green 1972 and Schweikart 1987) and the integration of southern banks and short-term capital markets with those elsewhere in the United States (Bodenhorn 2000). But historians have given little attention to the securities markets that emerged in the early United States, in both the Northeast and the South.

The next section of the study will present some of the evidence on antebellum southern securities markets. It is a preliminary survey of the terrain, one that is intended to encourage others to explore the subject in more depth.

Then we turn to the "meat" of the study, a detailed look at the New Orleans stock market in the half-century after the Civil War. Based on newspaper accounts of market activity, we construct indexes of New Orleans stock prices and compare them with an existing index for the market in New York, the nation's financial center. The comparison provides grounds for some preliminary speculations on the integration of stock markets in the post–Civil War era of U.S. history.

Securities Markets in the Antebellum South

The Federalist financial revolution of the 1790s would have its greatest impacts on the northeastern United States. It was there that the preponderance of banking and securities market development took place (Sylla 1998). But the South, and later the emerging West, were not left out of the new financial system. As War of Independence accounts were settled and the federal government assumed most debts of the states in the early 1790s, state governments, including some in the South, became owners of federal securities (Perkins 1994). Moreover, merchants in southern port cities, like their northern counterparts, became accustomed to investing in federal bonds, in stock of the new Bank of the United States, and in local securities – mostly new banking and insurance companies.

Nowhere was this more the case than in Charleston, the leading port of the South in the early decades of U.S. history. The recently opened Arthur H. Cole papers at Harvard's Baker Library record sporadic price quotations for "Continental stock" and "indents" from Charleston newspapers of the 1780s, before the Federalist financial revolution. Once that revolution was underway, other securities appeared. In the Cole papers, some quotes of South Carolina bank shares are given for 1796–97, and after 1803 they are recorded more or less continuously each month down to 1860. Following Arthur Cole's lead, we discovered that in 1803, Charleston newspapers began to publish weekly quotations of prices in the Charleston stock market. The earliest quotation lists included the following federal, state, and private-sector securities:

US 8s	South Carolina Bank shares
US 6s	State Bank shares
US 3s	SC 6s
US Navy 6s	SC 3s
US 5 1/2s	SC deferreds
Bank of United States shares	

Also quoted were domestic and foreign exchange prices, and – with some lag – prices of U.S. bonds and U.S. Bank stock in other cities, both North (New York and Philadelphia) and South (Norfolk).

As Charleston's business activity and stock market expanded, the Cole papers contain monthly quotations for a growing list of securities, with the following corporate shares appearing in the years indicated:

Mutual Insurance Co., 1804	Commercial Bank of Columbia, 1835
South Carolina Insurance Co., 1805	Camden Bank, 1837
Union Insurance Co., 1809	Charleston Insurance and Trust Co., 1839
Union Bank, 1810	Gas Light Co., 1839
Fire Insurance Co., 1810	Bank of Georgetown, 1841
Planters and Mechanics Bank, 1815	Hamburg Bank, 1842
Santee Canal, 1815	Merchants Bank, 1849
Fire and Marine Insurance Co., 1820	Farmers and Exchange Bank, 1853
SC Canal and Railroad Co., 1833	Fireman's Insurance Co., 1853
Charleston Bank, 1835	Peoples Bank, 1854

These are the companies for which Arthur Cole and his collaborators, who were interested mainly in financial and transportation company securities (see Smith and Cole 1935), gathered quotations seven decades ago, and it is likely that further investigations of the original newspaper sources they used will uncover other securities. The antebellum Charleston stock market had many characteristics of the contemporary markets in Boston, New York, Philadelphia, and Baltimore. It traded the "national market securities" (United States debt securities and United States Bank stock) as well as a steadily expanding list of state debt securities and the shares of local private companies (see Sylla 1998).

Further evidence of antebellum southern stock market development and U.S. market integration comes from a Philadelphia newspaper, the *Commercial List*, and was brought to our attention by Warren Weber of the Federal Reserve Bank of Minneapolis. From that paper, Weber gathered (and shared with us) semiannual bank stock quotations in the Philadelphia market starting in 1835. Among others, the Philadelphia quotations include three banks in Tennessee, six in Mississippi, six in Louisiana, three in Kentucky, along with twenty-four Pennsylvania and three Ohio banks, and the Bank of the United States. We think it likely that southern and midwestern bank stocks that traded in Philadelphia probably also had markets – perhaps not highly developed or formal markets – in the home states. The fact that they were traded in Philadelphia is evidence capital did flow from the developed markets of the northeast to other regions of the country.

For the 1850s, the Cole papers record monthly price quotations for the stocks of several railroads in the South. From the *Richmond Enquirer* come quotations for the Virginia Central (starting in 1850), the Richmond and Petersburg (1850), the Richmond and Fredericksburg (1850), and the Richmond and Danville (1853). From the *New Orleans Price Current*, there are quotations for the Pontchartrain RR (starting 1853) and the Carrollton RR (1854).

The lists presented here, and even the monthly price quotations that can be found along with them in the Cole papers, are admittedly sketchy information. Much more work needs to be done before we will fully understand the extent of antebellum securities market development in the South (and elsewhere in the United States, for that matter), and market integration. But we hope that the sketches made here will convey an impression that something interesting (and possibly important) is out there to be investigated, and encourage others to join us in the investigations. The antebellum South, despite its peculiar features related to the persistence of slavery, from the 1790s onward, participated in the banking and securities market developments that distinguished the northeastern United States from most of the rest of the world.

Before turning to our comparative study of the New Orleans and New York stock markets during the period 1871–1913, we briefly note, to focus on continuities, what the Charleston and New Orleans stock markets looked like shortly after the war. We have located monthly price quotations for the following list of equity securities from Charleston:

Banks	*Railroads*
People's National Bank of Charleston	Atlantic and Gulf
First National Bank of Charleston	Central Georgia
South Carolina Loan & Trust Co.	Charlotte, Columbia, and Augusta
Carolina National Bank of Charleston	Georgia
Central National Bank of Charleston	Greenville and Columbia
National Bank of Chester	Macon and Augusta
South Carolina Bank & Trust Co.	Macon and Western
Bank of Charleston	Memphis and Charleston
Union Bank	Northeastern
People's Bank	Northeastern pfd.
Planters and Mechanics Bank	Savannah and Charleston
Bank of Newberry	South Carolina RR Co.
Bank of Camden	South Carolina RR & Bank
	Southwestern Georgia

Miscellaneous
Charleston Mining & Manufacturing
Wando Mining & Manufacturing
Sulphuric Acid and Super Phosphate
Marine and River Mining Co.
Atlantic Mining & Manufacturing
Charleston Gas Light Co.
Charleston City Railway
Graniteville Manufacturing Co.

There is some overlap with the antebellum quotation lists. Not all antebellum southern companies disappeared in the upheavals of 1861–65, and neither did the markets that earlier had emerged to trade their securities. That is interesting in itself, and it has a bearing on issues related to the pace of the South's recovery from the Civil War. Whatever else might have been involved in the slow pace and often disappointing results of that recovery, it does not appear to have derived from an absence of institutions for raising capital and giving liquidity to capital market instruments.

For New Orleans at war's end, we present in Table 5.1 more detail than we now have for Charleston. Nearly all of the stocks quoted sold at prices well below their par values in September 1865. A year later, all of them had posted substantial price gains from the depressed levels reached shortly after the war.

TABLE 5.1. *New Orleans Stock Prices, 1865–1866*

Stock	Par Value	September 1, 1865 Price	Percent of Par Value	September 1, 1866 Price	Percent of Par Value	Percent Change 1865–1866
Banks						
Bank of America	$100	$67.00	67.00%	$137.00	137.00%	104.5%
Bank of New Orleans	100	16.00	16.00	40.00	40.00	150.0
Canal Bank	50	42.00	84.00	58.50	117.00	39.3
Citizens' Bank	100	76.00	76.00	156.00	156.00	105.3
Crescent City Bank	100	19.00	19.00	42.00	42.00	121.1
First National Bank	100	99.00	99.00	125.00	125.00	26.3
Louisiana State Bank	100	15.00	15.00	28.50	28.50	90.0
Mechanics & Traders' Bank	100	29.00	29.00	59.50	59.50	105.2
Merchants' Bank	100	8.00	8.00	26.00	26.00	225.0
Southern Bank	100	63.00	63.00	94.00	94.00	49.2
Union Bank	100	19.00	19.00	53.00	53.00	178.9
Average	**$95**	**$38.60**	**42.80%**	**$68.25**	**74.10%**	**109.0%**
Insurance						
Hope Insurance Company	$100	$35.00	35.00%	$92.50	92.50%	164.3%
Union Insurance Company	100	17.50	17.50	73.00	73.00	317.1
Average	**$100**	**$26.25**	**26.25%**	**$82.75**	**82.75%**	**240.7%**
Railroads						
City Railroad	$100	$130.00	130.00%	$197.00	197.00%	51.5%
Jackson Railroad	25	2.75	11.00	8.75	35.00	218.2
Pontchartrain Railroad	100	50.00	50.00	102.00	102.00	104.0
Average	**$75**	**$60.92**	**63.67%**	**$102.58**	**111.33%**	**124.6%**
Miscellaneous						
Gas Light	$100	$132.00	132.00%	$161.00	161.00%	22.0%
Water Works	100	40.00	40.00	55.00	55.00	37.5
Average	**$100**	**$86.00**	**86.00%**	**$108.00**	**108.00%**	**29.7**
Overall Average	**$93**	**$47.79**	**50.58%**	**$83.82**	**88.53%**	**117.2%**

Source: Bankers' Magazine, "The Money Market of New Orleans and the Southwest," November 1866.
Note: The Opelousas Railroad traded at $2.25 at the close of 1865 and at $6.50 at the close of 1866, but we have been unable to obtain a par value for this stock. The par values for all stocks except the banks were taken from *The Daily Picayune.*

Postbellum Southern Securities Market Developments: New Orleans, 1879–1913

In assessing the existence of a national market in the postbellum period, Davis (1965) based his now famous conclusion that interest rates varied across regions by as much as 4 or 5 percentage points on data pertaining to short-term interest rates. The short-term instruments Davis relied on, in modern parlance, would be classified as bank loans or money market securities, those with a maturity of one year or less. The short-term loans and bills tracked by Davis were used to finance trade and smooth the flow of agricultural products.

We would distinguish the money-market focus of Davis's 1965 study from one focusing on capital or securities markets. The capital market can have a very general meaning (analogously, the labor market), but is also used to connote the market based on securities with maturities of greater than a year. Regardless of Davis's findings about the money market after the Civil War, the question remains, Was there a national capital market? Was there a national market for securities of longer maturity and different in character than the short-term instruments analyzed by Davis? In particular, were there regional differences in returns on common equity? And if so, were they justified by considerations of risk and transactions costs?

A number of researchers have investigated segments of the long-term market. Among them, Snowden (1987) investigated the market for home and farm mortgages, and he too found pronounced interregional differences in interest rates. Carty (1994) investigated the market for railroad bonds, and found that the bonds of railroads in the West and South commanded a premium over those of the Northeast, although the premium was less than Davis found in the short-term market and Snowden discovered in the mortgage market.

In general terms that contrast with the postbellum findings of Davis and others, Bodenhorn (1992, 2000) characterizes the antebellum market for short-term capital as integrated, and he attributes the postbellum interest rate differentials between North and South to the South's different standing before and after the Civil War. Before the Civil War, Bodenhorn's evidence, drawn from a detailed study of United States antebellum banking data, indicates that capital flowed fairly freely among United States regions. But after the war, capital flows were impeded as a result of the failure of Southern intermediaries, the decline in importance of the cotton factors and other changes in the crop marketing, and provisions of the federal banking legislation that were adverse to the reestablishment of banking in the South.

Some anecdotal evidence suggests that southerners in the antebellum period invested funds in the North and in Europe (Kettell 1860). Such an outflow of capital might have been a contributing factor to the slower accumulation of capital in the South than the North. The institution of slavery is said by some to have had the same effect. On the other hand, it might be considered as evidence of how well integrated were antebellum capital markets.

To further explore these issues, we study the returns investors achieved on equity investments in New Orleans stocks after the Civil War and contrast those returns with those on New York-listed stocks. During the same period, Davis showed, short-term lenders financing the South's trade extracted a premium over and above northeastern lending rates. Could it be that holders of southern equities also extracted a premium compared to what they could have earned by investing in the more developed northern capital markets? And if so, what were the reasons?

THE NEW ORLEANS STOCK EXCHANGE. Our primary reason for studying the New Orleans Stock Exchange (rather than another market such as Charleston) is the convenient availability and usability of data provided by *The Daily Picayune* newspaper of New Orleans. Each year beginning in the late 1870s, this newspaper published a review of the commercial activities of the city for the year ending in August, along with stock prices for listed securities at the end of August and the same information for the end of August in the prior year. It also provided information on dividends paid during the year along with dividends of the prior year. Frequently, dividends paid by companies not in the group of listed securities were also published. Prior to 1879, dividends were not stated in the annual report or were limited to dividends paid by banks.

The New Orleans Stock Exchange was similar to other regional exchanges including Charleston during the period. These regional exchanges traded the stocks of local banks, insurance companies, railroads, and miscellaneous companies tied to the local economies. The Charleston exchange traded the stocks of its local manufacturing companies (e.g., the textile companies and phosphates); the New Orleans Stock Exchange traded the securities of its local manufacturing companies (e.g., refineries and brewing). A detailed study comparing the performance and returns on various regional exchanges is a topic for future research, after more evidence such as that presented here is extracted from historical records. At this point we have no reason to believe that the New Orleans Exchange was atypical compared to the other southern regional exchanges. It traded a broad range of stocks tied to the local economy.

The question we explore is: How did rates of return on New Orleans "local" stocks compare with returns available in New York? Is there any evidence that northerners might have been reluctant to invest in the South, or that southerners were reluctant to invest in the North? Thus, the focus of this part of our paper is on regional differences in rates of return on equity investments.

RATES OF RETURNS AND STOCK PRICE INDEXES. Shareholders receive their returns in the form of dividends and capital gains, or appreciation in the market value of their shares. Accordingly, we collected data on dividends and share prices, and calculated holding-period returns. Annual holding-period returns for stocks listed on the New Orleans Stock Exchange are compared with annual holding-period returns of New York stocks calculated from data contained in Cowles (1939) volume on common stock indexes.

For consistency, we report both stock price indexes and returns from 1879 to 1913 for the period from September 1 to August 31 of the following year for each year. The study ends with 1913, in part because both the New York and New Orleans exchanges were closed (for stock trading) in August 1914, after the outbreak of World War I. For purposes of comparing New Orleans and New York returns, we adopt the New Orleans commercial year (September 1 to the following August 31) and apply it in analyzing the New York data.

In addition to calculating annual rates of return, we calculate two stock price indexes for the New Orleans Stock Exchange. One index is what we call a Dow-type index, meaning an unweighted index that is a simple average of the prices of the stocks making up the index. Because the Cowles stock price series is value weighted, we also construct an index for the New Orleans Stock Exchange that is value-weighted. Such an index gives more weight to those stocks with greater market value in comparison to a Dow-type index.

DATA SOURCES AND THE CALCULATION OF INDEXES. Stock prices and dividend data for the New Orleans Stock Exchange were taken from *The Daily Picayune* newspaper. Our first index is based on the simple average of the prices of the stocks included in the index. Because it is the same type index as the Dow Jones Industrial Average, equivalent percentage changes in share prices of companies with higher priced shares have a greater effect on the index than will companies with lower priced shares. The second index is a value-weighted index similar to the indexes reported by Cowles. For the value-weighted stock price index and value-weighted rate of return calculations, the weights are based on the number of shares we estimate to have been outstanding multiplied by the price of a company's stock at the beginning of the period or when a company entered the index. We estimated the number of shares outstanding by dividing the capital stock (book value) by the par value per share. The capital stock (book value) and par values of shares were obtained from *The Daily Picayune* and *Listed and Non-listed Securities: New Orleans Stock Exchange and Bankers and Brokers Directory* (Huntington 1897). It appears that some of the companies were recapitalized during the period we studied. In calculating the value-weighted indexes, we used the first reported (or first we found) amount of capital stock.

Par value was a more meaningful concept during the period we studied than it is now (Frankfurter and Wood, Jr. 1997). Dividends were usually based on a percentage of par value, and par values were reported frequently in *The Daily Picayune*. Adjustments were made for the few changes in par values that were found. The capital stock figures were harder to obtain. The capital stock of banks and insurance companies was generally reported in *The Daily Picayune*, at least on an occasional basis, but the capitalization of the other types of companies (railways, utilities, and miscellaneous stocks) was more difficult to find. We were able to find the capital values for most of the stocks. The number of companies in the value-weighted index is only a few less than the unweighted (Dow-type) index.

In constructing a stock price index, ideally the number and list of companies would remain constant. For the period studied, the number and list of companies traded on the New Orleans Stock Exchange varied from year to year. Obviously, selection bias could be a problem. An example of selection bias would be if we had selected only companies that survived for the entire study period. Few companies survived the entire period. Also, there was considerable change in the composition of the listed companies during the early 1900s. Recognizing these realities, we selected for inclusion in our analysis companies with a trading history of at least ten years. We believe that this selection criterion is broadly consistent with modern practice in making changes in major stock price indexes.

In principle, the entry or exit of a company from an index should not be a factor influencing the index in the year of entry or exit. Companies leave the modern Dow indexes, and new ones are added. In constructing the indexes, we have followed the practice of not allowing the entry or exit of a company from the list of companies to influence the index in the year of entry or exit.

The performance of the New Orleans stock price indexes depends on the weighting of the individual securities. The value-weighted index is heavily influenced by the importance of bank stocks because of their relatively large capitalizations relative to other companies. All three indexes, the two for New Orleans and that for New York, are set at the level of the New York index, 32.8 for 1879. The New Orleans indexes are presented along with the Cowles index for the New York Stock Exchange in Tables 5.2 and 5.3, and New Orleans – New York index comparisons are charted in Figures 5.1 and 5.2. Although we do not present it here, the New Orleans value-weighted index during the 1870s was lower than the New York index much of the time because of difficulties New Orleans' banks encountered in recovering from the financial dislocations of the Civil War. These difficulties lasted into the early 1880s, despite strong rallies in markets elsewhere in the country after the resumption of dollar convertibility in 1879. At the end of 1882, the New Orleans value-weighted index stood at 35.5, about 71 percent of the New York's 49.7.

From 1882 to 1888 the New Orleans value-weighted index traded in a fairly narrow range, with a low of 34.1 in 1885 and a high of 38.7 in 1883. During this period, the New York index declined from 49.7 in 1882 to 42.2 in 1888.

During the 1890s, the New Orleans value-weighted index again was quite stable, ranging from 53.3 in 1897 to 60.3 in 1900. In contrast to the stability of the New Orleans index, the New York index declined for most of the decade, closing at 38.3 in 1897, well below its level in 1882. At the end of the century, in 1900, the New Orleans value-weighted index was somewhat above the New York index (60.3 vs. 47.8). The unweighted New Orleans index (not strictly comparable with New York) at 56.9 was not quite as high.

In the first years of the new century, both New Orleans indexes advanced sharply. The value-weighted index more than doubled from 1900 to 1906, peaking (on an annual basis) at 145.5 in the latter year. The unweighted index also more than doubled, peaking at 131.6 in 1906. The New York

TABLE 5.2. *New Orleans and New York Stock Exchange Price Indexes, 1879–1913 (New Orleans: Dow-Type Index)*

Year	New Orleans Stock Exchange Index	Legler–Sylla New Orleans Stock Exchange Index	Cowles New York Stock Exchange Index
1879	70.066	32.8	32.8
1880	80.376	37.6	41.8
1881	95.521	44.7	49.9
1882	96.362	45.1	49.7
1883	99.123	46.4	44.0
1884	95.852	44.9	38.2
1885	91.514	42.8	37.9
1886	92.046	43.1	43.2
1887	95.512	44.7	43.8
1888	104.940	49.1	42.2
1889	119.362	55.9	43.2
1890	130.474	61.1	43.6
1891	138.356	64.8	39.7
1892	132.832	62.2	45.3
1893	133.305	62.4	32.9
1894	129.924	60.8	35.5
1895	123.114	57.6	38.5
1896	114.103	53.4	30.7
1897	111.595	52.2	38.3
1898	110.852	51.9	42.4
1899	118.553	55.5	51.8
1900	121.524	56.9	47.8
1901	144.050	67.4	64.7
1902	188.382	88.2	71.0
1903	203.171	95.1	53.3
1904	224.897	105.3	56.4
1905	257.706	120.6	74.1
1906	281.191	131.6	78.3
1907	254.485	119.1	60.6
1908	228.169	106.8	66.5
1909	250.753	117.4	81.9
1910	252.386	118.1	71.2
1911	254.471	119.1	73.8
1912	236.522	110.7	79.0
1913	220.500	103.2	68.0

Source: New Orleans Stock Exchange, Legler and Sylla; New York Exchange, Alfred Cowles and Associates, *Common Stock Indexes* (Bloomington, IN: Principia Press, Inc., 1939): Series P-1.

TABLE 5.3. *New Orleans and New York Stock Exchange Price Indexes, 1879–1913 (New Orleans: Value-Weighted Index)*

Year	New Orleans Stock Exchange Index	Legler–Sylla New Orleans Stock Exchange Index	Cowles New York Stock Exchange Index
1879	85.861	32.8	32.8
1880	88.235	33.7	41.8
1881	97.266	37.2	49.9
1882	92.955	35.5	49.7
1883	101.237	38.7	44.0
1884	94.924	36.3	38.2
1885	89.286	34.1	37.9
1886	94.883	36.2	43.2
1887	94.951	36.3	43.8
1888	108.829	41.6	42.2
1889	129.176	49.3	43.2
1890	142.882	54.6	43.6
1891	152.015	58.1	39.7
1892	150.851	57.6	45.3
1893	156.506	59.8	32.9
1894	157.149	60.0	35.5
1895	152.318	58.2	38.5
1896	144.928	55.4	30.7
1897	139.505	53.3	38.3
1898	145.195	55.5	42.4
1899	150.898	57.6	51.8
1900	157.776	60.3	47.8
1901	189.253	72.3	64.7
1902	228.471	87.3	71.0
1903	270.837	103.5	53.3
1904	298.232	113.9	56.4
1905	380.190	145.2	74.1
1906	380.751	145.5	78.3
1907	337.877	129.1	60.6
1908	277.974	106.2	66.5
1909	315.030	120.3	81.9
1910	318.449	121.7	71.2
1911	323.123	123.4	73.8
1912	263.206	100.5	79.0
1913	221.597	84.7	68.0

Source: New Orleans Stock Exchange, Legler and Sylla; New York Exchange, Alfred Cowles and Associates, *Common Stock Indexes* (Bloomington, IN: Principia Press, Inc., 1939): Series P-1.

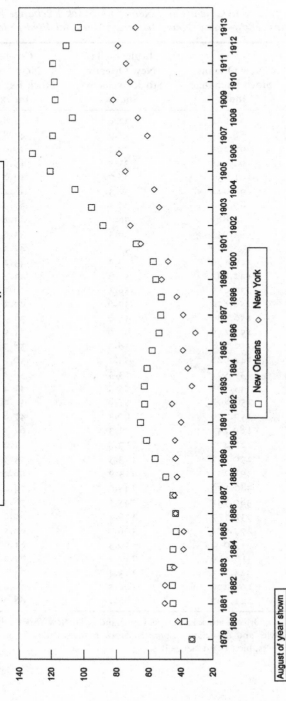

New Orleans vs. New York Stock Exchange
New Orleans: Dow Type

August of year shown

☐ New Orleans   ◇ New York

FIGURE 5.1. New Orleans (Dow-type) and New York Stock Price Indexes, 1879–1913

Sources: See Table 5.2 and text. The two indexes are set equal to one another in 1879. The "squares" index is New Orleans, and the "diamonds" index is New York. The data are for the end of August each year.

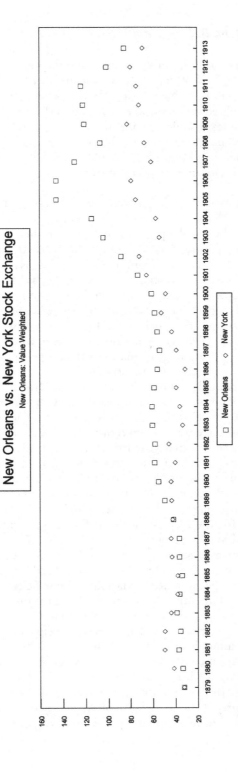

FIGURE 5.2. New Orleans (value-weighted) and New York Stock Price Indexes, 1879–1913

Sources: See Table 5.3 and text. The two indexes are set equal to one another in 1879. The "squares" index is New Orleans, and the "diamonds" index is New York. The data are for the end of August each year.

index also rose, to a level of 78.3 in 1906, although the percentage increase after 1900 was less than half of that in New Orleans over the same period.

After peaking in 1906, both New Orleans indexes generally declined to 1913, when the unweighted index stood at 103.2, and the weighted index at 84.7. The New York index also declined from 1906 to 1913, but the decline was much less in percentage terms than that in New Orleans, just as its increase had been much less between 1900 and 1906. By 1913, the value-weighted index of each city market was just over 40 percent higher than it had been in 1900.

RATES OF RETURN. We have calculated annual rates of return for stocks listed on the New Orleans Stock Exchange. Annual rates of return are the sum of the dividend yield and the percentage change in the price of a stock over a one-year-holding period. A company's dividend yield was computed by dividing the dividend paid by the beginning stock price, assumed to be the closing price of the prior year. Dividends were generally paid as a percentage of par value. For example, an 8 percent dividend on a $100 par value stock is $8. Most, but not all, stocks had a par value of $100. We note that stocks that were selling for several times their par value, often had what appeared to be outrageously high dividends on par value. However, when the dividend yield was calculated as a percentage of market value, it generally fell in line with the typical dividend yield of its industry.

We have calculated annual rates of return for all New Orleans-listed stocks for which we could obtain price data, not just those with ten or more years of trading history that we selected for our two indexes. The first series in Table 5.4 presents simple average annual returns for this all-stocks concept. The series begins in 1879, the first year for which dividends were reported on a consolidated basis in *The Daily Picayune*. Comparing the New Orleans results with the rates of return for New York stocks calculated from data in the Cowles study, we find that over the 1879–1913 period both the average dividend yield and the average rate of return were higher for the New Orleans Stock Exchange than for the New York Stock Exchange. The unweighted average dividend yield was 1.32 percent higher in New Orleans, and the average rate of return was 2.84 percent higher. We also find that not only was the rate of return on the New Orleans Exchange higher, it was also less volatile as measured by the standard deviation and coefficient of variation over the period studied. The standard deviation of returns on the New York Exchange was 15.43 compared to 11.47 on the New Orleans Exchange. Coefficients of variation were 1.87 and 1.03, respectively.

We also calculated annual rates of return for the stocks with extensive trading histories that are included in our two New Orleans stock price indexes, as previously described. Although the number of stocks in these indexes varied somewhat from year to year, the average number of stocks in this index is about thirty. (The actual list of stocks included in the price indexes and their periods of inclusion are provided in Appendix 5.1.)

TABLE 5.4. *Rates of Return and Dividend Yields: New Orleans Stock & New York Stock Exchanges, 1879–1913 (New Orleans Stock Exchange: All Listed Stocks Unweighted)*

Year	New Orleans Stock Exchange		New York Stock Exchange	
	Rate of Return	Dividend Yield	Rate of Return	Dividend Yield
1879	18.68%	9.88%	22.95%	4.54%
1880	41.01	12.01	32.27	4.83
1881	34.10	9.32	23.68	4.30
1882	10.86	7.95	4.49	4.89
1883	12.55	9.04	−5.47	6.00
1884	0.58	6.08	−6.65	6.53
1885	−1.40	5.64	4.06	4.85
1886	7.61	6.15	17.69	3.71
1887	14.03	5.68	5.63	4.24
1888	6.03	5.41	0.60	4.25
1889	17.36	5.65	6.41	4.04
1890	12.24	5.03	4.80	3.87
1891	18.90	5.27	−4.60	4.34
1892	−1.34	4.36	18.01	3.90
1893	7.75	4.74	−21.78	5.59
1894	9.86	5.38	12.47	4.57
1895	4.07	5.54	12.14	3.69
1896	−4.42	5.39	−15.64	4.62
1897	5.66	6.20	28.26	3.50
1898	11.53	6.55	14.10	3.40
1899	16.81	5.30	25.25	3.08
1900	10.31	6.16	−3.71	4.01
1901	24.89	5.27	38.71	3.35
1902	22.44	5.51	13.21	3.47
1903	14.22	5.39	−20.02	4.91
1904	13.44	4.16	10.01	4.19
1905	36.53	4.91	34.73	3.35
1906	3.90	2.88	9.03	3.36
1907	−5.57	3.39	−17.17	5.44
1908	−10.23	3.06	14.36	4.62
1909	20.69	3.90	27.19	4.03
1910	8.58	4.26	−8.05	5.01
1911	9.26	5.29	8.59	4.94
1912	−0.02	4.39	11.68	4.63
1913	−2.91	4.61	−8.49	5.43
Average	11.09%	5.71%	8.25%	4.39%
Std. Deviation	11.47	1.88	15.43	0.80
Coefficient of Variation	1.03	0.33	1.87	0.18

Source: New Orleans Stock Exchange, Legler and Sylla; New York Stock Exchange, Alfred Cowles and Associates, *Common Stock Indexes* (Bloomington, IN: Principia Press, Inc., 1939): Series P-1 and Y-1.

In comparison with the all-stock New Orleans series, the average annual return for the index stocks is lower, and also less volatile. The average return is 10.14 percent with a standard deviation of 9.65 for the unweighted stock index (see Table 5.5), and 8.33 percent with a standard deviation of 10.80 for the value-weighted index. The average dividend yield for the Dow-type unweighted stock series is higher than it was for the all-stock series (6.46 percent vs. 5.71 percent), but the average dividend on the value-weighted series in Table 5.6 is lower (5.31 percent vs. 5.71 percent). This suggests that the capital appreciation component of return was lower for the larger, "seasoned" companies in our indexes than it was for the broader range of companies in the all-stock series.

Again, although the New Orleans return and risk for the index stocks are not strictly comparable to those for New York (the value-weighted return is reasonably comparable), we see from Tables 5.4, 5.5, and 5.6 a consistent pattern. For the whole period 1879–1913, the average stock return was higher in New Orleans than New York, while the standard deviations of returns were considerably lower than for the New York stock index. This suggests that there were barriers to the flow of long-term capital to the postbellum South, just as Davis (1965) found for the short-term loan market, Snowden (1987) found in the mortgage market, and Carty (1994) found in the railroad bond market.

Contemporary Comments on New Orleans Business and the Stock Price Indexes

Our New Orleans stock price indexes based on the *Picayune's* annual market summaries provide one reflection of the course of business activity in New Orleans. Although data availability led us to select 1879 as the initial year of our study (the Cowles price indexes began in 1871), our period was not long after the end of the Civil War and Reconstruction. Financially, New Orleans was still recovering from these upheavals. What follows is a short summary of how the *Picayune* itself analyzed New Orleans business and stock market activity. We are interested in such contemporary discussions for what they might reveal about the relative importance of local versus national and international influences. This could bear on the issue of market integration.

THE CIVIL WAR. On the eve of the Civil War, New Orleans was one of the country's most prosperous cities. The War took a tremendous toll on the city and its banks. The banks suffered not only from forced participation in Confederate finance, but also from the harsh rule of Union generals who occupied the city beginning in May 1862. Prior to the Union occupation, the Confederacy removed $4 million in specie that it had placed with the banks, to prevent it from falling into Union hands. Union General Butler then forced the banks to turn over Confederate government deposits that had been made

TABLE 5.5. *Rates of Return and Dividend Yields: New Orleans Stock & New York Stock Exchanges, 1879–1913 (New Orleans Stock Exchange: Dow Type Unweighted Index)*

| Year | New Orleans Stock Exchange | | New York Stock Exchange | |
	Rate of Return	Dividend Yield	Rate of Return	Dividend Yield
1879	9.68%	10.77%	22.95%	4.54%
1880	24.78	10.07	32.27	4.83
1881	29.21	10.37	23.68	4.30
1882	8.27	7.39	4.49	4.89
1883	11.01	8.14	−5.47	6.00
1884	3.26	6.56	−6.65	6.53
1885	1.54	6.07	4.06	4.85
1886	6.72	6.14	17.69	3.71
1887	9.86	6.09	5.63	4.24
1888	15.92	6.05	0.60	4.25
1889	19.96	6.22	6.41	4.04
1890	14.47	5.16	4.80	3.87
1891	11.89	5.85	−4.60	4.34
1892	1.14	5.13	18.01	3.90
1893	5.89	5.53	−21.78	5.59
1894	3.76	6.30	12.47	4.57
1895	1.34	6.58	12.14	3.69
1896	−0.78	6.54	−15.64	4.62
1897	5.38	7.58	28.26	3.50
1898	7.27	7.94	14.10	3.40
1899	13.19	6.24	25.25	3.08
1900	9.90	7.39	−3.71	4.01
1901	25.25	6.71	38.71	3.35
1902	38.26	7.48	13.21	3.47
1903	14.93	7.08	−20.02	4.91
1904	15.49	4.80	10.01	4.19
1905	21.38	6.79	34.73	3.35
1906	11.64	2.53	9.03	3.36
1907	−5.15	4.35	−17.17	5.44
1908	−6.16	4.18	14.36	4.62
1909	14.91	5.01	27.19	4.03
1910	5.92	5.27	−8.05	5.01
1911	7.46	6.63	8.59	4.94
1912	−1.50	5.55	11.68	4.63
1913	−1.30	5.47	−8.49	5.43
Average	10.14%	6.46%	8.25%	4.39%
Std. Deviation	9.65	1.65	15.43	0.80
Coefficient of Variation	0.95	0.26	1.87	0.18

Source: New Orleans Stock Exchange, Legler and Sylla; New York Stock Exchange, Alfred Cowles and Associates, *Common Stock Indexes* (Bloomington, IN: Principia Press, Inc., 1939): Series P-1 and Y-1.

TABLE 5.6. *Rates of Return and Dividend Yields: New Orleans Stock & New York Stock Exchanges, 1879–1913 (New Orleans Stock Exchange: Value Weighted Index)*

| Year | New Orleans Stock Exchange | | New York Stock Exchange | |
	Rate of Return	Dividend Yield	Rate of Return	Dividend Yield
1879	−1.32%	8.57%	22.95%	4.54%
1880	11.56	8.82	32.27	4.83
1881	19.28	8.89	23.68	4.30
1882	2.46	7.03	4.49	4.89
1883	17.49	8.48	−5.47	6.00
1884	−0.88	5.32	−6.65	6.53
1885	−0.28	5.78	4.06	4.85
1886	12.48	6.32	17.69	3.71
1887	5.86	5.58	5.63	4.24
1888	20.14	5.54	0.60	4.25
1889	23.65	5.14	6.41	4.04
1890	15.53	4.78	4.80	3.87
1891	10.87	4.46	−4.60	4.34
1892	3.20	4.06	18.01	3.90
1893	7.77	3.95	−21.78	5.59
1894	4.94	4.61	12.47	4.57
1895	1.57	4.57	12.14	3.69
1896	0.12	4.93	−15.64	4.62
1897	1.27	5.06	28.26	3.50
1898	9.12	4.99	14.10	3.40
1899	8.32	4.54	25.25	3.08
1900	9.64	4.95	−3.71	4.01
1901	25.00	5.10	38.71	3.35
1902	25.38	4.63	13.21	3.47
1903	21.83	3.27	−20.02	4.91
1904	13.14	3.09	10.01	4.19
1905	32.28	4.80	34.73	3.35
1906	3.51	3.30	9.03	3.36
1907	−6.85	4.42	−17.17	5.44
1908	−12.77	4.97	14.36	4.62
1909	17.98	4.70	27.19	4.03
1910	4.73	3.57	−8.05	5.01
1911	7.20	5.80	8.59	4.94
1912	−12.65	5.91	11.68	4.63
1913	−9.88	5.84	−8.49	5.43
Average	8.33%	5.31%	8.25%	4.39%
Std. Deviation	10.80	1.47	15.43	0.80
Coefficient of Variation	1.30	0.28	1.87	0.18

Source: New Orleans Stock Exchange, Legler and Sylla; New York Stock Exchange, Alfred Cowles and Associates, *Common Stock Indexes* (Bloomington, IN: Principia Press, Inc., 1939): Series P-1 and Y-1.

in Confederate notes, but in the form of gold, silver, or U.S. notes, not in Confederate notes. The banks also were forced to pay Confederate currency depositors in their own notes or specie. In short, the Union authorities forced the banks to honor their liabilities with assets acceptable to the northern occupiers. These Draconian measures took their toll. By the end of the War, the New Orleans banking system was but a shadow of what it had been before the Union occupation.

The depressed condition of New Orleans banks and commerce at the end of the war was reflected in stock prices. Prices of New Orleans stocks at September 1, 1865, and one year later, September 1, 1866, were given in Table 5.1. Excepting the City Railroad and Gas Light issues, all of the stocks traded below par value in 1865, with an average of about 50 percent of par for all stocks. A year later, there were signs of recovery. Investors bid up the stock prices of stronger banks, partly in anticipation of the legislature forcing the liquidation of the weaker banks. Four banks (Bank of America, Canal Bank, Citizens' Bank, and the First National Bank) were traded above par value. Stock prices on average increased more than 100 percent during the year, led by a 240 percent average increase in the prices of two insurance stocks.

THE 1870s. By the 1870s, New Orleans banking was well on the way to recovery, but the city was experiencing a decline in trade. Even before the Civil War, New Orleans had experienced a decline in its trading territory, but this decline was offset by increased trade within the smaller territory. After 1870, the volume of trade in the remaining territory also began to decrease. New Orleans was, therefore, ill prepared to meet the nationwide (and worldwide) financial panic of 1873.

The year 1874 was a turning point for New Orleans. Congress provided funding for the improvement of Mississippi River navigation, and by the end of the decade New Orleans had reestablished its antebellum position as a major trading center. Reflecting these vicissitudes, stock prices generally declined early in the decade, and then experienced modest recovery, almost the opposite of New York stock price trends as shown in Cowles (1939).

"Carpetbagger" rule ended in 1877, and by 1879, the year of a State constitutional convention, there was strong sentiment favoring repudiation of State debts incurred by the carpetbagger regime. Fear of repudiation led to runs on the banks, which were forced to suspend. Three banks were liquidated, their depositors receiving 15 to 50 percent of their funds. Despite the financial problems of the 1870s, the New Orleans stock index had not fallen to the extent that the New York index had fallen. The 1870s, a decade of deflation and labor unrest, were not favorable for stock prices in U.S. most markets.

THE 1880s. In 1880, sales of stock on the New Orleans Stock Exchange reached a reported total of $7,891,300, and 52,609 shares changed hands. With an influx of $1 million of new capital in the manufacturing sector, the

New Orleans stock price index in 1882 finally rose above its 1871 level. The overall stock index remained around its 1882 level for several years, although there was movement in some individual securities and among sectors. In 1884, *The Daily Picayune* reported that the local economy was not prosperous, and the "principal cause of the [stock market] disturbance, depression and shrinkage [in values] was the panic in New York and the loss of confidence engendered thereby" [*The Daily Picayune*, September 1, 1884]. Major market events elsewhere apparently had some effect in New Orleans.

In 1886, two reasons given for relatively sluggish stock prices. First, lower interest rates reduced bank profits and the prices of bank stocks. Second, a great Galveston fire had saddled New Orleans insurance companies with losses that adversely affected insurance stock prices.

In 1887, increased trading volumes led the Exchange to extend its hours to 4 P.M. The *Picayune* noted demand from eastern capitalists and orders from London. The observation suggests that at times at least some capital from outside the South flowed into southern equities. Bank shares advanced on higher rates for loans and discounts, reflecting a general improvement in local trade. Insurance stocks, however, continued to suffer from heavy fire losses and increased competition. Several insurance companies passed their customary dividends, leading to shrinkage in the value of their shares. Also noted was that increasing competition from electricity caused a depreciation in the price of gas stocks. Yet overall, 1888 and 1889 witnessed solid advances in the New Orleans stock index.

THE 1890S. In 1890, bank shares continued to advance, there was a recovery in insurance stocks, and miscellaneous (speculative) stocks were quite active. A notable feature of the year was the consolidation of all the city breweries into one association with the issuance of new shares to replace the old shares.

After closing the 1891 commercial year at what were all time highs, the New Orleans index generally trended down from then to 1898. Nonetheless, monetary controversies over silver versus gold and the financial panic of 1893 barely affected the New Orleans stock market, lending credence to the notion that it was isolated. The *Picayune* referred to the panic as a "financial flurry" in the summer of 1893. Prevailing high interest rates actually contributed to increased earnings for banks. The dull trading of previous years continued in 1894, when financial pressures forced the liquidation of some companies. Little change occurred in the indexes, however. Stock prices declined from 1894 to 1898. In the latter year the newspaper attributed lower prices to a yellow fever scare and the war with Spain.

THE EARLY 1900S. The year 1899 marked a turning point in the New Orleans stock indexes, which more than doubled between then and 1906. In the early 1900s, mergers and consolidations impacted the securities market of New Orleans, much as they did in the rest of the country (Smith and

Sylla 1993). Consolidations of street railroads in New Orleans were such that by 1900 only four operating companies remained. In 1902, these four combined into the New Orleans Railways Company. In 1905, that company went into receivership and was reorganized as the New Orleans Railway & Light Company. It later became part of the reorganization of all street railways and power companies in New Orleans as the New Orleans Public Service Company. The merger mania was good for stock prices, and perhaps rising stock prices were good for it.

In 1906, the New Orleans Stock Exchange celebrated its increased business and maturing as an institution by moving into a new grand building. The building was described as the most artistic and most expensive structure of its size in the city. A marble and mahogany palace, it was modest in size, built on a lot of only twenty-nine-and-a-half feet wide by ninety-one-and-a-half feet deep. But the Exchange was taking on new life because of the commercial progress of the city. The value of its membership share had grown from an initial worth of $100 to over $6,000. Membership was limited to seventy members, but there were provisions for "visiting members," who numbered sixty-one in 1906.

THE YEARS 1906–1913. After 1906, our indexes generally trend lower to 1913, although there were some year-over-year gains. As in 1893, the nationwide financial panic of 1907 affected New York far more than New Orleans. The New York stock index declined by a greater percentage than did either of the New Orleans indexes. By 1912, however, the *Picayune* noted in its annual review that activity on the New Orleans Exchange increasingly was influenced by that on Wall Street.

Our summary of the *Picayune's* annual reports on New Orleans stock market activity indicates that in most years local factors specific to New Orleans and its region, not national or international events, were judged by observers at the time to have been the main influences on local stock prices. This is broadly consistent with our finding that New Orleans returns were higher and risks seemingly lower than in New York. Thus, contemporary observations and our comparative analysis tend toward a conclusion that the New Orleans market was not well integrated with other U.S. securities markets during the late nineteenth and early twentieth centuries.

Conclusion

New Orleans in the half century after the Civil War, judging by our evidence, was slow to become an emerging market within the United States, in the sense of attracting outside capital and integrating its financial markets with markets elsewhere. Our findings are consistent with others pointing to a lack of capital market integration in the postbellum United States, with the South in particular standing out for its "separateness." Of course, we would not jump too quickly to a sweeping conclusion. More studies like the one we present here should be made; the materials for them, as our discussion of Charleston indicated, exist and are waiting to be used. And the data gathered for such studies, including this one, should be subjected to more sophisticated modeling and hypothesis testing.

Pending such further work, our findings here indicate that the United States may have retrogressed financially from the pre– to post–Civil War eras. Based on his studies of short-term credit markets, Bodenhorn (2000, 228) makes this case forcefully:

Southern interest rates before the Civil War were, within narrow bounds, equal to northern rates and capital flowed freely between the two regions. After the war, southern rates generally exceeded northern rates and at times were twice as high as rates in New York City. Capital flowed into the South after the war, but apparently not in sufficient quantities to eliminate short-term interest rate differentials. The Civil War, then, marks a sharp discontinuity in the history of American credit markets.

Although our securities market evidence for the two eras is less extensive than Bodenhorn's banking and credit market evidence, in a tentative way it points to the same conclusion. It appears that southern capital markets may have been more integrated with those elsewhere in the country in the era of Nicholas Biddle and Andrew Jackson than in the era of J. P. Morgan and Grover Cleveland six-to-seven decades later. But the causes of such regression in the efficiency and integration of capital markets, if indeed it occurred, would seem less clearly traceable to Civil War events and federal legislation than it was in Bodenhorn's (2000) study of banking and short-term credit markets. As is often the case, research raises as many questions as it answers.

Bibliography

Anonymous, "The Money Market of New Orleans and the Southwest." *Bankers' Magazine*, Vol. XXI, (November 1866): 373–5.

Bodenhorn, Howard. "Capital Mobility and Financial Integration in Antebellum America." *Journal of Economic History* 52 (September 1992): 585–610.

———. *A History of Banking in Antebellum America: Financial Markets and Economic Development in an Era of Nation-Building.* Cambridge: Cambridge University Press, 2000.

Carty, Lea. *"Regional Interest Premia and the American Railroad Bond Market From 1876 to 1890."* Unpublished Master's thesis, Columbia University, 1994.

Cowles, Alfred and Associates. *Common-Stock Indexes.* Bloomington, IN: Principia Press, Inc., 1939.

The Daily Picayune, New Orleans, 1870–1913.

Davis, Lance. "The Investment Market, 1870–1914: The Evolution of a National Market." *Journal of Economic History* 25 (September 1965): 355–399.

Frankfurter, George M., and Bob G. Wood, Jr. "The Evolution of Corporate Dividend Policy." *Journal of Financial Education* 23 (Spring 1997): 16–33.

Green, George D. *Finance and Economic Development in the Old South.* Stanford: Stanford University Press, 1972.

Huntington, H. L. *Listed and Non-listed Securities: New Orleans Stock Exchange and Bankers and Brokers Directory.* New Orleans: Hopkins' Printing Office, 1897.

Kettell, Thomas Prentice. *Southern Wealth and Northern Profits.* New York: George W. & John A. Wood, 1860.

Perkins, Edwin J. *American Public Finance and Financial Services, 1700–1815.* Columbus: Ohio State University Press, 1994.

Schweikart, Larry. *Banking in the American South from the Age of Jackson to Reconstruction.* Baton Rouge: Louisiana State University Press, 1987.

Smith, George David, and Richard Sylla. *The Transformation of Financial Capitalism: An Essay on the History of American Capital Markets,* Vol. 2, No. 2. Cambridge, MA: Blackwell Publishers, 1993.

Smith, Walter B., and Arthur H. Cole. *Fluctuations in American Business, 1790–1860.* Cambridge, MA: Harvard University Press, 1935.

Snowden, Kenneth A. "Mortgage Rates and American Capital Market Development in the Late Nineteenth Century." *Journal of Economic History* 47 (September 1987): 671–691.

Sylla, Richard. "U.S. Securities Markets and the Banking System, 1790–1840." *Federal Reserve Bank of St. Louis Review* 80 (May/June 1998): 83–98.

APPENDIX 5.1. STOCKS IN THE NEW ORLEANS STOCK PRICE INDEX

Banks		
	Canal	All Years
	Citizens	All Years
	Germania National	All Years
	Hibernia National	All Years
	Louisiana National	All Years
	New Oreans National	1873–1909
	Peoples	1871–1906
	State National	1871–1906
	Whitney National	1884–1913
Insurance Companies		
	Crescent	1872–1898
	Factors & Traders	1871–1889
	Germania	1871–1907
	Hibernia	1871–1902
	Home	1875–1902
	Hope	1871–1887
	Lafayette	1878–1908
	Mechanics & Traders	1872–1905

(continued)

Merchants	1872–1903
New Orleans Insurance Association	1872–1908
Southern	1883–1908
Sun	1873–1910
Teutonia	1878–1913

Railroads

Birmingham R., Lt., & Pwr. Co.	1906–1913
Carrolton	1871–1901
Crescent	1872–1898
Canal & Claiborne	1871–1898
Little Rock R., and E. Co.	1906–1913
Nashville R. and Lt. Co. Com.	1906–1913
N. O. City	1871–1902
New Orleans Rail. and Lt., Pref.	1906–1913
Orleans	1871–1901
St. Charles	1872–1902

Miscellaneous

Crescent City Slaughterhouse	1871–1913
Equitable Real Estate	1906–1913
Importers' Bonded Warehouse	1877–1899
Jefferson City Gas	1871–1897
N. O. Gaslight	1871–1904
N. O. Land Co.	1906–1913
N. O. Water Works	1877–1902
Sugar Shed	1871–1894

6

The Transition from Building and Loan to Savings and Loan, 1890–1940

Kenneth A. Snowden

> Building and loan management will meet its responsibilities to the twelve million owners of the building and loan business in America, and so conduct its affairs that the second century of building and loan will be one of unequalled progress, maximum service, and untarnished financial reputation.
>
> Morton Bodfish, *History of Building and Loan in the U.S.*, 1931

Bodfish was a vice president of the United States Building and Loan League, the national trade organization of the Building and Loan (B&L) industry, when he penned his prediction – probably in 1930 before the Depression gained real momentum. One year after his book was published, he was appointed by President Hoover as one of the five original members of the new Federal Home Loan Bank Board. During the next two years a system of federally chartered Savings and Loans Associations and the Federal Savings and Loan Insurance Corporation were created. In three short years, and at breakneck speed, the federal government put in place the entire institutional and regulatory structure of the modern Savings and Loan (S&L) industry. Despite these efforts the B&L/S&L industry suffered even greater losses in their number, assets, and membership after 1934 than before. Bodfish proved to be dead wrong – what lay ahead in 1930 was not a second century of unequalled progress for building and loan, but a decade of demise.

This chapter connects the development of the building and loan industry before 1930 to the transformation of the industry that occurred during the following decade, and in doing so, reverses the temporal focus of most academic discussion of the Depression-era initiatives that molded the modern S&L industry. A consensus view of this structure began to take shape in the late 1960s – the S&L industry then looked to be increasingly fettered

The author is indebted to Margaret Levenstein, Carol Heim, and the participants of the 1998 conference honoring Lance Davis for comments on a preliminary draft of this paper.

by regulation that was deemed to be anachronistic and debilitating. Federal S&Ls were still required to invest almost exclusively in fixed-rate mortgages written on local residential property, just as they had in 1933. The industry also suffered, the thinking went, from rigid and inefficient management that was protected from competition and external threats to their control by provisions that had been enacted when the industry was struggling to survive the Depression. These criticisms led to a program of deregulation that progressed gradually during the early 1970s and accelerated later in the decade. At the time most observers believed that the industry would become more adaptable and competitive as the worst elements of fifty-year-old regulation were dismantled – instead the modern S&L industry imploded in the 1980s and then virtually disappeared.

Far too much of the criticism that was leveled at the Depression-era regulatory structure simply ignored its connection to earlier developments (for notable exceptions see Barth and Regalia 1988 and Brumbaugh 1988, 2–12). The modern S&L industry was not made out of regulatory whole cloth – it grew out of an intermediary that had been in continuous operation for a century by 1930 and had spread to every corner of the nation by 1890 before even state regulators took notice. Moreover, Depression-era legislation was not imposed on B&Ls: Leaders of the industry helped to create the modern "savings and loan" by transmitting their own understanding of "building and loan principles" into the new federal structure. And while it may be difficult to recall after the events of the last fifteen years, B&Ls and S&Ls were the dominant provider of residential mortgage finance during the 1880s, 1920s, and the 1950s – the three episodes in the last century when the nonfarm housing stock expanded dramatically and rates of homeownership surged. A more complete understanding of these historical roots – how the building and loan originally emerged and why it flourished – will help us better understand the forces that were set loose when the transition that had been accomplished in the 1930s was dismantled in the 1980s.

The first two sections of the chapter briefly survey trends in residential construction, homeownership, and building and loan growth over the 1890–1940 period. The point of the discussion is to show that the pre-Depression B&L industry was affected by and responded to the same secular trends that the S&L industry faced in the post–WWII period – a regional shift in the housing stock and a growing reliance on mortgage debt by homeowners. It also turns out that B&Ls had by 1930 reached the same position of dominance in the single-family mortgage market that their S&L descendants would achieve thirty years later. The third and fourth sections of the chapter examine the initial development of B&L regulation in the 1890s and the progress that had been made in the regulatory structure by the 1920s. These discussions lay out the specific purposes that industry leaders hoped that state regulation would perform, and explain why they remained dissatisfied with the results right before the Depression.

The last two sections examine the transition from B&L to S&L during the 1930s in detail. The failure of the traditional B&L is explained first by examining how its unique contractual structure rendered it more vulnerable to Depression-era shocks than other institutional mortgage lenders. Widespread failures among these institutions persisted throughout the 1930s and led to the development of a new set of "savings" and "loan" contracts that were used throughout the industry after 1940. With all of this background in place, the last section of the chapter examines the connection between the rise of the modern S&L industry and federal legislation. It is shown that the transition from B&L to S&L was designed and directed by industry leaders under the mantle of the Federal Home Loan Bank System. Political leaders handed off these reins because they needed to revive the homebuilding industry; industry leaders accepted them because it provided an opportunity to mold the traditional B&L sector into the modern S&L industry that they had long favored.

Nonfarm Housing and Residential Mortgage Debt, 1890–1940

Between 1880 and 1890 the share of U.S. population living in urban areas increased from 28 to 35 percent while nonfarm residential construction reached 8 percent of GNP and 40 percent of aggregate net investment. The U.S. Census took note of the burst in urban homebuilding activity by conducting its first enumeration of nonfarm housing in 1890 and counted just under 8 million units. Five decades later, in 1940, the number had increased to 28 million. The rapid long-run growth of the nation's urban housing stock over the period was accompanied by violent, short-term changes in annual production levels and markedly different trends in ownership patterns and production levels across regions. A brief survey of these housing facts are offered in Figure 6.1 to highlight several important features of the environment within which the B&L industry grew, flourished, and was ultimately transformed into its modern S&L form.

The volatile growth of the nonfarm housing stock between 1890 and 1940 is revealed by the course of housing starts shown in Figure 6.1. The 1880s burst in housing production persisted until the Depression of 1893, but then housing starts trailed off to reach just under 200,000 units in 1900. From this low-point, homebuilding activity increased sharply until 1905, then remained at a plateau of just over 400,000 units each year until wartime dislocations cut production in half. The postwar expansion that began in 1921 was impressive – total housing starts exceeded 700,000 units for the next seven years and exceeded 900,000 units in 1925. At their peaks in the mid-1920s the shares of residential construction in aggregate investment and national output once again regained the levels they had reached in the 1880s. But the subsequent contraction was equally dramatic: Only 93,000 new housing units were started in 1933, a level of production not seen since

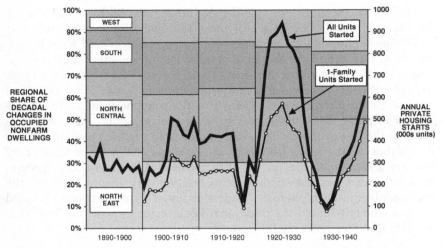

FIGURE 6.1. Private Housing Starts and Changes in Nonfarm Households by Region 1890–1940
Source: Nonfarm Households by Region, 1890–1940, Grebler et al. (1956), Table H-2, 398–99. Privately-financed Housing Starts, 1890–1940, *Historical Statistics* (1975), Series N156, N159.

the 1870s. It took the remainder of the decade for housing starts to once again reach 600,000 units. By 1940, production levels still remained below peak levels of the 1920s.

During the 1920s other institutional mortgage lenders, notably life insurance companies and mutual savings banks, were active financing both single- and multi-family housing production. Building and loans, meanwhile, specialized exclusively on single-family homes. The vertical distances between total and single-family housing starts in Figure 6.1 represent multi-family production, which clearly accounts for a disproportionate share of the extreme swings in housing production after 1920. Single-family starts certainly peaked and collapsed over the period, but neither was as dramatic as the swings in multi-family building. More importantly, the production of single-family homes actually returned to mid-1920 levels by 1940. We need to look closely, therefore, at how and how well the recently transformed S&L industry performed during the relatively robust recovery in single-family housing production that occurred during the late 1930s.

Accompanying the short-run volatility of housing production over the 1890–1940 period was a persistent long-term shift in the regional composition of the homebuilding industry. Seventy-two percent of the nation's nonfarm families resided in the Northeast and North Central regions in 1890, but by 1940 this share had fallen to 63 percent. Underlying the relatively modest relocation of the housing stock was a more dramatic change over time in the regional composition of additions to the stock. These are shown in Figure 6.1 as shaded blocks for each decade. The Northeast and North Central regions, for example, accounted for 70 percent of the increase in occupied nonfarm dwelling units between 1890 and 1900, but 60 percent in the 1920s and only 50 percent in the 1930s.

These shares of total changes in the housing stock include conversions of farm structures and demolitions as well as new production, but for this period variation in housing starts appears to have been the dominant force reshaping the regional distribution of the housing stock. This was certainly the case after 1920 when regional breakdowns of the aggregate housing start series become available – the Northeast and North Central regions claimed 58 percent of all housing starts during the 1920s, but only 47 percent in the 1930s (Grebler, Blank, and Winnick 1956, Table H-1, 396–7). Evidence collected in the 1940 Census of Housing suggests that the same pattern was at work before 1920. Households were asked in that year to report the year in which their dwelling had been built and 71 percent of those who reported a "year built" between 1890 and 1909 lived in either the Northeast or North Central regions. The share declined to 58 percent for dwellings built between 1910 and 1929, and to only 44 percent for those built after 1929 (U.S. National Housing Agency 1948, Tables 44, 53). We shall see that the B&L industry accommodated this early "sunbelt" phenomenon in housing markets by growing in a similarly unbalanced regional pattern and opening itself up to new and different kinds of institutional arrangements. The tensions that arose because of this increased heterogeneity among B&Ls were resolved, in large part, by the transformation from building and loan to savings and loan.

B&Ls financed homeownership as well as homebuilding. At first glance it appears that B&Ls and other financial intermediaries made only modest headway in this area before WWII because the share of all households owning homes in the U.S. increased only from 52 percent in 1890 to 56 percent in 1940. But the national average misleads for two reasons. First, it combines the markedly different experiences of farm and nonfarm households – between 1890 and 1940 rates of owner-occupancy declined steadily among farmers (from 66 to 53 percent) while they increased for nonfarm families (from 37 to 46 percent). Second, one-half of the increase in homeownership that was made before 1930 was reversed during the Depression – only 41 percent of nonfarm families owned their own homes by 1940 (U.S. National Housing Agency 1948, 60).

Complicating the difference in sectoral trends was a marked convergence in regional rates of homeownership that are shown in Figure 6.2. The total homeownership rate for each region and census date is indicated by bars in the figure while the shaded areas within the bars divide the total rate into the proportions of homes owned free and those owned with a mortgage. (Information on mortgage status was not collected in the 1930 Census.) The rate shown for the Northeast region at all census dates has been calculated excluding New York City because the city's size and unusually low rate of

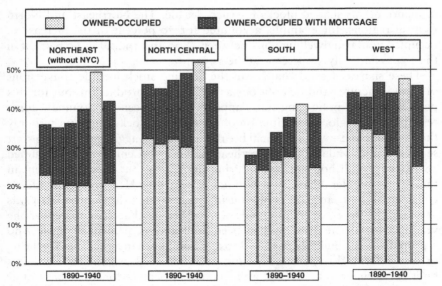

FIGURE 6.2. Percentage of Owner-occupied Nonfarm Homes by Census Date, 1890–
1940
Source: 1890–1920: U.S. Census, *Mortgages on Homes* (1923), Table 23, 130–33,
1930: U.S. Census of Population, Vol. VI, Table 42, 35.
1940: U.S. Census, Housing, Vol. II, Pt. 1, Tables G-1, H-1, I-1, J-1, 43–58.

homeownership (especially in Manhattan and the Bronx) distort the experience of the remainder of the region.

Total owner occupancy among nonfarm families in the North Central and
West regions averaged around 45 percent in 1890, well above the rate for
the Northeast (36 percent) and far higher than the average for the South (28
percent). A combination of three developments worked to close these gaps
by 1940. First, nonfarm homeownership increased steadily and rapidly in
the South from 1890 to 1930, and surged in the Northeast during the 1920s.
Second, gains in homeownership were relatively modest between 1890 and
1940 in the North Central and West regions. Finally, owner occupancy fell
during the Depression in all regions, but most dramatically in the Northeast
and North Central regions. Reverses in the Northeast undid nearly all of
the spectacular increase in homeownership that had occurred in the region
during the 1920s, while rates of owner-occupancy fell all the way back to
1900 levels in the North Central region. By 1940 the combined effect of
these different regional trends left between 38 and 45 percent of nonfarm
families owning their homes in all four regions of the country. A convergence
in rates of homeownership across regions, therefore, is an important piece
of the historical background within which the building and loan industry
developed and then was transformed.

The convergence of regional rates of ownership over the period was accompanied by an increased reliance on mortgage finance. As national nonfarm homeownership rates (including New York City) increased from 36 to 41 percent between 1890 and 1940, the proportion of homeowners that were free of mortgage debt declined from 72 to 55 percent. This deepening of the residential mortgage market occurred in all regions over the period, but once again in a pattern of regional convergence. Thirty-six percent of homeowners in the Northeast and 30 percent in the North Central regions had encumbered their home in 1890. The share in both regions increased by 15 points over the next fifty years. In the South and West, on the other hand, only 8 and 18 percent of owned nonfarm homes were mortgaged in 1890. By 1940, however, mortgage finance was used just as frequently by homeowners in the West as in the North Central region, and 36 percent of owned homes were encumbered even in the South.

To place the accomplishment in homeownership and mortgage finance before 1940 within a longer-run context, consider that by 1960 the national rate of nonfarm home ownership had increased to 61 percent with 57 percent of these homes under mortgage (*Historical Statistics* 1975, Series N243 and N305). Stated differently, 26 percent of all nonfarm dwelling units (including those rented) were owned without a mortgage in 1960. The share was exactly the same in 1890. The entire increase in homeownership rates between the two dates, therefore, was attributable to increases in the proportion of nonfarm dwellings that were owned with mortgage – from 10 percent in 1890 to 35 percent in 1960. The share in 1940 was 19 percent, which indicates that one-third of the secular increase in mortgage-financed homeownership had been accomplished by this date. This is surely an understatement of the progress that had been made in residential mortgage finance up to that time because rates of both homeownership and mortgage-financed homeownership fell during the Depression. Had the Census collected information on home mortgages in 1930, in fact, those data would have almost certainly shown that at least one-half of the secular increase in the reliance on mortgage debt between 1890 and 1960 had already been accomplished by 1930.[1] Building and loans were a central player in this development.

This brief summary of homebuilding and residential finance before 1940 establishes several important generalizations that serve as a backdrop for the rest of this chapter. To begin with, the Great Depression should not be treated as a watershed that permanently altered trends in housing production or residential finance. The 1930s is better viewed as a temporary, dramatic interruption of several long-run developments that took shape early in the twentieth century and continued well into the post–World War II era. Most important among these were a shift of housing production and housing stock

---

[1] During the 1920s the rate of nonfarm ownership increased sharply from 41 to 46 percent, while total residential mortgage debt tripled in volume (from $9.1 to $27.6 billion).

to the South and West, a secular increase in rates of mortgage-financed non-farm homeownership, and a convergence in rates of homeownership and mortgage encumbrance across regions. The first of these developments actually intensified during the Depression, while the second suffered a setback of unknown magnitude. The building and loan industry made important contributions to all three long-run developments before it was transformed into the modern savings and loan industry.

The Growth of Building and Loans, 1880–1930

The American residential mortgage market was relatively immature in 1880. The most important institutional home mortgage lender, mutual savings banks, were concentrated along the northern half of the Atlantic seaboard beyond which they never spread in large number. Outside of this area state-chartered commercial banks made loans on real estate, but they were more involved in lending on farm and commercial properties than on homes. Meanwhile, two important twentieth-century residential mortgage lenders, national banks and life insurance companies, had yet to enter the market in a serious way. National banks were discouraged by custom and prohibited by regulation from lending on real estate of any kind before 1900, while life insurance companies concentrated their mortgage lending on western farm property and urban commercial property. In most of the nation, therefore, prospective homeowners in 1880 either saved to buy their homes, or financed their home purchases with mortgages written and held by individual lenders.

Although building and loans had been specializing in home mortgage lending for nearly fifty years, by 1880 they remained a relatively small and idiosyncratic corner of the nation's financial structure. The next decade witnessed a "Building and Loan Movement" of striking proportion, however. The growth and spread of B&Ls became so pronounced during the decade that the U.S. Commissioner of Labor, Carroll Wright, commissioned a special enumeration of every association that was open for business on January 1, 1893. The Commissioner expressed confidence that the enumeration was relatively complete and accurate, and its results are summarized in the top panel of Table 6.1 (Wright 1893, 7–15).

The 5,597 building associations that were operating in the United States in 1893 are divided into three groups in the table. Shown in the second column are 528 associations that had opened for business prior to 1880 and were still operating in 1893.[2] Two-thirds of these associations (338) were located in the

---

[2] The survey provides no information about B&Ls that were established before 1893, but had ceased operation by then. Fortunately, very few associations that were established after 1880 would have fallen into this category – closures of B&Ls were rare during the expansion of the 1880s, and the survey was conducted just before the 1893 Depression. Because of fortuitous timing, therefore, the Labor Bureau's enumeration captured the overwhelming majority of associations that were established between 1880 and 1893, and not only those that remained in operation at the later date.

TABLE 6.1. *Spread of Building and Loans, 1880–93: by City Size and Region*

City Size Population in 1890	Cities with B&Ls in 1880			First B&L after 1881		All Cities
	Number of Cities	Number of B&Ls: 1880	New B&Ls 1880–93	Number of Cities	New B&Ls 1880–93	B&Ls in 1893
UNITED STATES						
ALL CITIES	176	528	1,755	1,829	3,314	5,597
>100,000	15	302	1,503	13	548	2,353
25-100,000	26	67	110	63	360	537
<25,000	135	159	142	1,753	2,406	2,707
NORTHEAST						
>100,000	7	202	637	4	166	1,005
25-100,000	16	40	70	26	130	240
<25,000	81	96	60	422	552	708
NORTH CENTRAL						
>100,000	4	52	612	7	360	1,024
25-100,000	5	13	18	20	117	148
<25,000	35	42	48	934	1,295	1,385
SOUTH						
>100,000	2	46	170	2	22	238
25-100,000	3	7	17	17	97	121
<25,000	18	20	32	300	449	501
WEST						
25-100,000	2	7	5	4	16	28
<25,000	1	1	2	97	110	113

Year	Number, Members, and Assets of B&Ls by Region, 1920–1930					
	Number of B&Ls	% Change 1920–30	Members (000s)	% Change 1920–30	Assets ($000,000)	% Change (1920–30)
NORTHEAST						
1920	4,305		2,071		$1,034	
		32%		92%		257%
1930	5,670		3,985		$3,688	
NORTH CENTRAL						
1920	2,507		2,002		$999	
		22%		169%		209%
1930	3,052		5,393		$3,083	
SOUTH[a]						
1920	1,655		664		$370	
		54%		257%		235%
1930	2,555		1,703		$1,240	
WEST[a]						
1920	269		204		$114	
		81%		516%		615%
1930	486		1,256		$814	

Sources: 1880–1893: Wright (1893), Building and Loan Associations.
1920–30: Bodfish (1931), Statistical Appendix, 627–56.
Notes: [a]Data for Florida, Georgia, Mississippi, Virginia, Idaho, Nevada, and Wyoming begin between 1924 and 1926. For these states, and especially for the South, the growth rates are understated.

Northeast with most of them (285) located in just four cities – Philadelphia (191), Baltimore (44), Cincinnati (38) and Minneapolis–St. Paul (12). The remaining large-city associations in 1880 (17 in number) were sprinkled among Boston, Buffalo, Pittsburgh, Washington, DC, Chicago, Denver, and San Francisco. There appears to have been no building and loan activity at all in 1880 in major urban centers such as New York City, Rochester, Detroit, Cleveland, Indianapolis, Louisville, New Orleans, St. Louis, or Omaha.

Building and loans remained so unevenly dispersed across major urban areas in 1880 because before then they had often failed soon after being introduced (Dexter 1889, 322–5). In New York City, for example, seventy-two associations were organized in the early 1850s, but most of these were forced to close during a mid-decade break in the local real estate market. The state legislature passed remedial legislation after investigating these failures in 1856, but building associations disappeared from the city altogether until 1883. Similar episodes occurred in Rochester and Buffalo, where the revival of building associations also occurred during the 1880s. Building and loans experienced early problems in Connecticut and Massachusetts as well, but at least a few associations continued to operate in the latter state throughout the nineteenth century (Smith 1852).

Building and loans had not been widely integrated into the nation's financial infrastructure by 1880, but the foundation for a remarkable expansion had been laid. The rapid expansion in nonfarm mortgage debt that occurred between 1880 and 1890 affected cities of all sizes and in all regions, but was especially rapid in the smaller and mid-sized cities of the South and West (Snowden 1988). The Commissioner's enumeration reveals that B&Ls were integral to the process. More than five thousand new associations were established between 1880 and 1893, or some 90 percent of all B&Ls that were operating at the time of the Labor Bureau's study.

About one-third of the new associations (1,755) were located in a city in which a B&L had been established before 1880 (Table 6.1, col. 3), the overwhelming majority in large cities. But more than three thousand B&Ls were open for business in 1893 in cities that did not claim a single association in 1880. Ninety-five percent of these 1,829 new B&L cities (Table 6.1, cols. 4 and 5) had populations less than 25,000, and most were located in the Northeast and East North Central regions. The B&L movement also reached more than 100 small cities in both the South Atlantic and East South Central regions by 1893, nearly 300 in the West North Central states, and 136 that were spread among the West South Central, Mountain, and Pacific regions. The diffusion was equally impressive across mid-sized markets. Ninety-six cities had populations between 25,000 and 100,000 in 1890. Ten years earlier B&Ls had been established in only 26 of these communities, but by 1893 associations were operating in all but seven, and four of these were in New England. Finally, B&Ls were established in all thirteen large cities that had not been served in 1880. By 1893, in fact, two of these had become major B&L centers (Indianapolis with 117 associations and St. Louis with 197).

By 1893 building associations were operating in every region of the country and in cities of all sizes. They claimed nearly 1.4 million members and held $473 million of assets. Three-fourths of the associations answered the Commissioner's question about numbers of mortgage loans held, and together they reported having financed 291,000 home purchases, or nearly 14 percent of the 2.1 million owner-occupied homes in the counties that contained an association.[3] By 1896, in fact, it has been estimated that B&Ls held nearly one-third of all outstanding institutionally held residential debt, and trailed only mutual savings banks as a provider of home mortgage funds[4] (see Figure 6.3). Over the next decade B&Ls lost ground to other institutional lenders as their share of the institutional mortgage market fell to only 24 percent in 1905. This was attributable to a cessation of growth in absolute terms in the decade following the "Building and Loan Movement." Between 1897 and 1905 the number of associations operating in the country fell by nearly 9 percent while the number of B&L members and total B&L assets did not return to 1897 levels until 1905. The reasons for this period of absolute and relative decline are examined at length in the next section.

B&L growth resumed at a modest pace after 1905 and through World War I so that these institutions claimed 35 percent of the institutionally held mortgage debt by 1920 and had replaced mutual savings banks as the nation's single largest provider of mortgage finance. It is hardly surprising, therefore, that B&L growth was spectacular by all absolute measures during the building boom of the 1920s. The number of operating associations increased by 67 percent between 1918 and 1928, while B&L membership tripled and

---

[3] Three years before the Commissioner of Labor enumerated the building associations, Congress directed the Census Office to investigate the extent of home ownership and indebtedness for the entire country. According to this report, 2.1 million families owned a home in 1890 in counties in which a building and loan had been established by 1893. These counties contained 75 percent of the nation's total population, and 85 percent of all nonfarm families. The Commissioner of Labor asked these building associations three years later to report the number of homes their members had purchased through them. Three-fourths responded, and they reported having financed 291,000 homes during their lives, or nearly 14 percent of the owner-occupied housing stock in these areas. If the responding associations were representative of those that did not, the contribution of building associations would have been 364,000 or 7 percent of the owned homes in these areas. This was a remarkable accomplishment for institutions that had been so narrowly concentrated, and so few in number, little more than a decade earlier.

[4] Mortgages held by individual investors are not accounted for in Figure 6.3. Individual investors held just about one-half of the outstanding residential mortgage debt in the late 1890s after which their share decreased gradually to 40 percent by 1920, and to 30 percent during the 1930s. These are shares of all outstanding residential debt, including mortgages written on multifamily structures. The shares in the figure understate the contribution of building and loans, therefore, because they specialized in the single-family mortgage market.

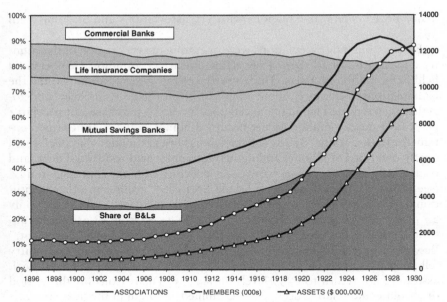

FIGURE 6.3. Building and Loan Growth, 1896–1930. (Number, Members and Total Assets) With Shares of Residential Mortgage Holdings by Institutional Lenders *Sources:* Bodfish 1931, 136; Grebler et al. 1956, Table N-2.

the total assets of the industry grew by a factor of four. Nonetheless, the B&L share of institutionally held residential mortgage debt held remarkably steady at around 36 percent throughout the 1920s because of equally rapid growth in the mortgage portfolios of other institutional lenders, especially life insurance companies and commercial banks. Unlike these other institutions, however, B&Ls lent almost exclusively on single-family homes and had become the dominant institutional mortgage lender serving that market by the end of the 1920s. Between 1925 and 1930, in fact, B&Ls held just under 50 percent of the nation's institutionally held mortgage debt on one- to four-family houses – a far larger share than any other type of lender.

Building and loans rose to such dominance in the single-family mortgage market by 1930 because they proved to be remarkably adaptable to the shift of homebuilding activity to the South and West that was described in the last section. In the lower panel of Table 6.1 the best available estimates of B&L growth for the 1920s are summarized by region. These data clearly show that the growth of B&Ls in the West far outpaced increases in the Northeast and North Central regions. B&Ls appear to have grown no faster in the South than in the two northern regions, but the growth rates for this region are unambiguously understated because of peculiarities in the data.[5] Crude

[5] The only comprehensive state-level data on building and loan activities for the period between 1893 and the early 1930s was assembled by the industry's own trade group, the U.S. Building

1930 estimates of the proportion of all owner-occupied homes in each region that were financed by B&Ls also point to a southern and western shift in the industry during the 1920s.[6] Measured in this way, in fact, the industry played a remarkably similar role across regions on the eve of the Depression – B&Ls financed 17 percent of the owner-occupied housing stock in the Northeast, 16 percent in both the North Central and South, and 15 percent in the West.

Between 1900 and 1930 B&L associations grew in pace with the single-family homebuilding industry and came to dominate the financing of its output. This is why Richard Ely, in the Foreword to the 1923 Census volume "Mortgages on Homes" observed that, "[t]he American method of acquiring a home is to buy the site, gradually pay for it, *then to mortgage it through a building and loan association or otherwise*, to construct the home with the aid of the mortgage and gradually to extinguish the mortgage" (Italics added, p. 12). In the 1920s prospective homeowners throughout the United States thought first of the building and loan industry when they sought mortgage financing.

Regulatory Beginnings: The 1890s and Aftermath

Intrinsic risk and informational asymmetries inhibit the development of financial intermediaries unless outsiders are convinced that the managers of the institution will select loan recipients with care and enforce loan contracts diligently. Regulation can mitigate the problem by imposing incentive mechanisms such as capital requirements on manager–owners or by specifying that institutions accept only appropriate loan risks. Building and loans, in contrast, were essentially self-regulating during the 1880s and unlike commercial or mutual savings banks were organized under general incorporation laws whenever and wherever a small group found it in their interest to do so. State legislatures began to catch up in the late 1880s by passing special incorporation laws for B&L associations, but regulatory supervision remained

and Loan League (USBLL). For each year during this period, the USBLL assembled reports of state supervisory agencies, but there were often significant time lags between the introduction of building associations in a given state and the creation of a regulatory agency to supervise them. Annual data for several southern and western states were not collected by state agencies until the mid-1920s. For these cases the earliest year available (normally between 1924 and 1926) has been used as the 1920 observation. As a result, the growth rates for these two regions over the period are certainly understated because the regional totals capture the expansion of the industry for only the second half of the decade in such large and important states as Florida, Georgia, and Virginia.

[6] To derive these estimates total B&L assets in each region had to be converted into estimates of number of loans outstanding. To do so I applied the national average of the ratio of B&L loans outstanding to assets held (ϕ.70) to the total B&L assets in each regions. I then estimated the average loan size by taking the average value of single-family homes in each region from the 1930 Census of Housing, and multiplying that value by ϕ.6, which was the normal initial debt-to-value ratio used by B&Ls during the period.

rudimentary before 1900 even in the most progressive states and virtually nonexistent in the rest. Although few of them were subject to meaningful regulation, B&Ls attracted the savings of more than one million members by 1893 into associations that usually had been in operation for less than a decade. This impressive accomplishment immediately raises several intriguing questions: How were these institutions managed and controlled? How was their safety and soundness assured? Why and how was regulation imposed on an industry that seemed to be flourishing in its absence?

To explain the success of B&Ls as self-regulated intermediaries we must look to one or more of the industry's defining characteristics: (1) B&Ls were mutually owned so that their members had incentives to monitor their operations; (2) B&Ls were usually small in size and local in orientation so that information asymmetries were minimized; and (3) B&Ls were promoted with missionary zeal by a vocal group of "building and loan men" who extolled homeownership as the means by which workers could better themselves and their communities.[7] In all but the third characteristic, B&Ls were structured similarly to the cooperative credit circles that are used extensively in modern developing economies.[8] Membership in these informal organizations is restricted within the boundaries of existing social and familial networks. Because it is small in size and local in character, the members of a credit circle can acquire information about each other at low cost and use nonpecuniary social sanctions to induce borrowing members to honor their contracts. Moreover, because all members own a share of the cooperative's loan portfolio, each has incentive to monitor borrowing members and to impose sanctions if necessary. Because of its small size and personal character the cooperative credit circle functions effectively in the absence of regulation.

In a previous paper (Snowden 1997) I examined whether the building and loans of the 1880s worked in a similar fashion. Many B&Ls had all the trappings of fraternal organizations – they were often organized among members of a church or an ethnic club, or sometimes at the workplace. Organizers and proponents also emphasized the cooperative character of B&Ls and the importance they placed on holding frequent membership meetings. It was reasonable, therefore, to conjecture that variations in the relative importance of B&L's across urban markets in 1893 could be explained by variations in the importance of immigrants, church members, and industrial workers in the population. It turns out that they were not, and I concluded that the B&Ls of the 1880s were not organized or managed like modern cooperative credit circles.

---

[7] For an extensive discussion of the historical development of building and loan literature see Bodfish 1931, Chapter XV.

[8] See Besley, Coate, and Loury 1993, and Stiglitz 1990 for a discussion of modern cooperative credit circles.

The explanation of the institutional structure of the building and loan that I favored in 1997 was directly tied to the "building and loan men." Their role is most easily understood by considering the mortgage loan transaction that represented the underlying rationale for these organizations. Then, as now, a mortgage was the culmination of a multifaceted and complex set of transactions. When an existing home was purchased, buyer and seller had to locate each other and then negotiate; the property had to be surveyed and appraised; the title had to be cleared and the deed registered; and, if the lender required, hazard insurance on the property had to be written. Additional steps were required if the mortgage financed the construction of a new home – building plans had to be approved and the builder's reputation investigated; materials had to be purchased and paid for before construction was completed; all mechanic's liens had to be identified and extinguished to preserve the seniority of the lender's claim. For either new or existing construction more was required after the loan was closed – payments had to be collected and accounts updated; borrowers or foreclosure had to be pursued in cases of delinquency; and property had to be managed, rented, or sold if it were ultimately taken. The important point is that a mortgage loan creates demand for the services of an entire network of real estate and building professionals – surveyors, title specialists, attorneys, real estate and insurance agents, homebuilders, and building material suppliers. These were the "building and loan men" of the nineteenth century who organized and operated associations on a part-time, voluntary basis to provide a local supply of home mortgage credit and, thereby, to increase the demand for the services they offered in their mainline occupations.

The building and loan men brought specialized skills into their associations, but they also introduced conflicts of interest that posed a threat to their associations' safety and soundness. I argued in Snowden (1997), in fact, that the local and mutual character of the nineteenth century building and loan is best interpreted as institutional features designed to control the actions of its organizers, and not its members. Mutual ownership provided organizers with only a small direct claim, or sometimes no claim at all, on the profits of the association. As a result, these insiders had a collective self-interest in protecting the safety and soundness of the credit channel that increased the income they earned in their ancillary occupations. Localization, on the other hand, allowed the organizers of a B&L to monitor each other so that no one of them could misuse its lending facilities to improperly augment his own income.[9] Moreover, the small scale of operation fit the character of the

---

[9] The appraisal committee was key to the safety and soundness of a B&L. The directors that served on this committee were generally builders or in a building-related occupation. The loan papers, on the other hand, were drawn up by the association's secretary who was normally a real estate or property insurance agent. The association was set up so the appraisal committee members and the secretary could observe each other's performance on every loan.

homebuilding and real estate industries at this time – the average builder produced only two or three homes each year, while real estate transactions and mortgage lending required intimate knowledge of local lending conditions and property values. So B&Ls remained small in size and local in character in order to minimize the coordination and information costs among their organizers.

We know that the building and loan men emphasized the mutual and local character of their associations because they said so when forming the U.S. Building and Loan League in 1893. The impetus was to take collective action against the new "national" building and loan associations.[10] These institutions appeared during the late 1880s to extend the operations of the building and loan mechanism over much wider geographic areas than had previously been attempted. Organizers of the national associations argued that the innovation provided several benefits – greater safety (because the loan portfolio was geographically diverse), higher earnings (because the association could penetrate markets with high mortgage rates), and lower expenses (because of the efficiencies of large scale). Leaders of the local associations bridled at these arguments and the fact that these large, bureaucratic organizations could appropriate their name and methods while at the same time violating their basic principles. They opposed the nationals, they said, because they feared the impact these organizations would have on the reputation of all B&Ls as safe and sound, albeit self-regulated, financial institutions.

Brumbaugh (1988, 20–7) argues that the USBLL's opposition to the nationals, despite their rhetoric, was simply the attempt of a trade group to bar entry of a competitor. This was exactly the remedy that the local B&L men sought as they lobbied state legislators throughout the nation to prohibit "foreign" building associations from operating within their own states' borders. Two other generalizations support Brumbaugh's interpretation. First, we have seen that the organizers of local B&Ls were not altruistic, mutual "cranks" as they were characterized by the leaders of the national movement, but local real estate professionals and builders who had a clear self-interest in protecting the value of the local mortgage credit facilities they had organized and were controlling. In addition, Brumbaugh's argument squares with the record of success the nationals were enjoying at the time. In 1893 some 240 national associations were open for business and together they claimed nearly 400,000 members or about 30 percent of the membership of all local B&Ls. By then national building associations had been established in all regions of the country and in thirty-two states including seven in which they controlled more than one-quarter of all building and loan assets.[11] In

---

[10] Coggeshall 1927 is the best secondary source on the nationals of Minnesota. The Minnesota Public Examiners Report (various years) is also recommended. For broader treatments of the movement see Clark and Chase 1925 and Bodfish 1931.

[11] The market share of the nationals was smallest in the traditional local association strongholds such as Ohio, Pennsylvania, New Jersey, and Maryland, and in states where

1893 local B&L men knew that the nationals were committed to growing large and saw evidence that they were doing so.

To understand why regulation was introduced into the B&L industry we must disentangle the USBLL's rhetoric regarding the reputational consequences of the national movement from Brumbaugh's observation that they represented a competitive threat. I do so here in two steps. The probit regression model that is reported in the top panel of Table 6.2 is designed to identify the characteristics of local markets in which a national building association was most likely to appear before 1893. The sample for the regression is the 117 largest cities in the United States in 1890. National building associations had been established in 45 of these cities by 1893, and together these localities claimed 70 percent of total national association membership. The explanatory variables in the model include the 1890 population of each city and the growth in its population over the 1880s (all drawn from the 1890 Census of Population). In addition, the dollar volume of urban mortgage debt made in the county that contained each city was secured for each year between 1880 and 1889 (these were drawn from the 1890 U.S. Census Special Report on Mortgage Encumbrance). These annual mortgage lending figures were used to construct two other explanatory variables for each city: the average annual growth rate of total mortgage lending in each market over the 1880s and the volatility of the growth in lending.[12] Finally, two variables are included as measures of the competitive strength of local associations in each city – the year in which the first local was established and the average year of establishment for all local associations in the city.

The model correctly predicts (using the sample proportion as the cut-off probability) 27 of the 45 national association cities, and 67 out the 72 non-national cities. Interestingly, local building and loan activity (as measured by the year established variables) does not appear to have affected the probability that a national association appeared in a city. Instead, the model indicates that national building associations were more likely to appear in cities that experienced slower population or mortgage lending growth during the 1880s or those which had high levels of mortgage lending volatility. As can be seen in the last two columns of the table, each of these variables have large impacts on the predicted probabilities.

---

the numbers of locals had grown rapidly during the 1880s (such as New York, Illinois, Indiana, Iowa, and Missouri). They were most prominent in Georgia, Virginia, Michigan, Alabama, Tennessee, South Dakota, and Minnesota – the last is particularly noteworthy because Minnesota had been a hotbed of local association activity until it became the birthplace of the national movement.

[12] The dataset assembled for this study combines information from the 1890 Census of Population and the 1890 Census of Mortgages with the January 1, 1893, enumeration of building and loans. The maintained assumption, therefore, is that demographic characteristics like these move slowly enough through time so that the situation had not changed too much in two years. Mortgage volatility is measured as the standard deviations of differences from the logarithmic time trend between 1880 and 1889 in mortgage lending volume for each county.

TABLE 6.2. *The Appearance and Impact of National Building Associations: 1893 and Beyond*

Probit Model Predicting Cities in Which National Associations Located in 1893
117 Cities/ 45 Cities with Nationals

| | Model | | | Predicted Change in Probability | |
Variable	Coefficient	Standard Error	P-Value	Partial Derivative	From + 1 S.D. Change
Constant	−7.48	4.81	.12		
Log of City Population, 1890	1.62	.34	.00	.55	.49
Year First Local B&L Est.	−.03	.04	.42	−.01	−.08
Avg. Year All Local B&L Est.	.09	.08	.29	.04	.15
Annual Growth in Mortgage Debt for County, 1880–89	−.72	.25	.01	−.2	−.26
Volatility of Mortgage Growth in County, 1880–89	12.72	4.44	.01	4.29	.21
Percentage Change in City Population, 1880–89	−.002	.001	.07	−.001	−.38

Log Likelihood	−46.57			Predicted versus Actual (Cutoff = .615)	

Pred/Actual	D = 0	D = 1
D = 0	67	18
D = 1	5	27

Source: See text.

Percentage Growth in B&L Members per Capita in 46 States, 1893–1920[a]

| | Model 1: Base of All Members in 1893 (National + Local Members in 1893) | | | Model 2: Base of Local Members in 1893 (Local Members Only in 1893) | | |
Variable	Coefficient	Standard Error	P-Value	Coefficient	Standard Error	P-Value
Constant	3.38	1.36	.02	3.78	1.75	.04
Members Per Capita in 1893	−.015	.006	.02	−.0001	.00003	.07
Assets Per Local B&L Member in 1893	−.0017	.0007	.03	−.0014	.001	.16
Real Estate Loans to Dues Paid for Local B&Ls in 1893	−1.35	1.37	.33	−1.28	1.75	.47
Share of National Assn. in Total B&Ls in 1893	−3.63	.68	.00	−1.91	.89	.04
1920 B&L Membership from Unofficial Sources	−.05	.34	.89	.11	.42	.79
F-Statistic		11.08			2.47	
Adjusted R²		.53			.14	

Sources: See text and (for 1920 data) Bodfish (1931), Appendix Tables, 627–56.

Notes: [a] The percentage change measured as the logarithm of the ratio of membership per capita in 1920 to membership per capita in 1893.

The results indicate that national associations tended to locate in markets where conditions were inhospitable for the growth of local B&Ls, whether or not one had already been established. In particular, national associations were likely to appear where local mortgage demand was weak in the 1880s (population and mortgage lending growth were slow) or where the undiversified mortgage loan portfolio of a local B&L was very risky (mortgage lending volatility was high). This pattern would have emerged if the nationals, as they claimed, were primarily engaged in arbitrage between markets, where mortgage lending and local association growth had stalled and faster growing but more volatile markets in which local associations had yet to penetrate.

These results suggest that local and national building associations were not the close substitutes that Brumbaugh's argument suggests – they were different types of intermediaries designed for different environments. It is important to point out, in fact, the limited extent of head-to-head competition between the two types of associations. Thirty percent of the local members in these 117 cities lived in markets in which no nationals had been established, and another 25 percent lived in markets where nationals claimed less than 10 percent of all building and loan participants. These patterns, along with the probit model, suggest that the USBLL and its leaders may well have opposed the national movement to protect the reputation of all local building and loans and not simply to exclude a competitor.

The USBLL was quite specific, in fact, about the institutional features of the national associations that they believed threatened the good B&L name.[13] Because of their large size, national associations had to maintain centralized full-time staff and a field organization of agents to enlist members and to set up local loan boards. The local loan boards, in turn, accepted loan applications, appraised property, and enforced the mortgage in case of default. The national association's local loan board was typically comprised of builders, developers, lawyers, and financiers who were already engaged in local real estate markets. The recruiting agents and loan boards of the nationals were compensated with commissions based on the number of new members recruited and mortgage loans made. To offset the expense, new members paid an entrance fee and a fixed portion of their regular monthly dues to an expense fund.

These institutional features represented substantial departures from the practices of the local B&Ls. The directors and officers of these associations were directly responsible for recruiting members, keeping the books, and making and enforcing mortgage loans. Moreover, these organizers generally volunteered their time or accepted a nominal salary as compensation because

---

[13] The five part series in the 1923 *American Building Association News* recounts the arguments made in the 1890s regarding specific practices of the leadership of the nationals.

they already received remuneration through their ancillary businesses. The difference was important. *The Minnesota Public Examiner* reported in 1889 that the operating expenses of the national associations in the state ran to 6 percent of total receipts, whereas those of its local associations generally ran under 1 percent.[14] Local leaders argued that the national associations promised rates of return to their members that they could not possibly earn given the level of their expenses. The locals were also concerned that many national associations were vulnerable to failure because their field agents and local loan boards were not closely supervised. Either outcome, they maintained, would injure the reputation of all building and loans in the public's mind.

Their worst fears were realized in the 1890s when the national building association movement ended quickly and spectacularly. Minnesota's fifteen national associations held $6.8 million dollars of mortgage debt in 1893, but within two years that amount had fallen to $5.9 million while $2.3 million of real estate had been acquired through foreclosure.[15] Several of the state's associations were declared bankrupt at this point, six went into receivership, and eight were eventually liquidated under the supervision of the state. The sole remaining national in Minnesota converted to a trust company in 1903. Outside Minnesota the end of the movement is generally dated at 1896 when the largest national association in the country (located in Tennessee) failed. A wave of closings followed, and by the early 1900s only six national associations remained in active operation out of the 240 institutions that had been so popular a decade earlier. The failures of the 1890s seem to confirm the local B&L leaders' argument that national associations were poorly structured financial intermediaries. Legislators in nearly every state responded quickly by enacting strict prohibitions on the formation and spread of new national associations.

We are most interested here, however, in assessing whether the "national fiasco" caused the reputational damage that the USBLL professed to fear. A test of their claims is reported in the bottom panel of Table 6.2. The dependent variable in each regression is the percentage growth between 1893 and 1920 in per capita building and loan membership across forty-six states.[16] The explanatory variable of principal interest in the regressions is the share

---

[14] Minnesota, *Fourth Biennial Report of the Public Examiner*, 1889.

[15] Data drawn from Minnesota, *Reports of the Public Examiner*, various years.

[16] I have excluded Washington and New Hampshire from these regressions. For the former case it appears that the labor commissioner misclassified one of the few, and a very large, local association as a national. Bodfish (1931, 602) notes that "the word 'national' in its title was purely incidental and had nothing to do with the plan or scope of operation." The case of New Hampshire remains more of a mystery. Again, there was a very large institution in operation there that was denoted a national, but I have seen no other reference to the national movement in this state, and this institution clearly does not show up in other data on New Hampshire.

of each state's total building and loan assets that was held by national associations in 1893. If the reputation of the local B&Ls was threatened by the nationals, as the USBLL claimed, the damage to membership growth after the 1890s should have been most severe in states where the national associations had been most active. This is, fortunately, very different from the impact that the variable would have on membership growth rates if, as Brumbaugh argues, the USBLL was primarily interested in excluding a competitor. In that case we would expect local associations to have grown most rapidly in those states where a large pool of prospective new, local members had been "freed up" after the nationals disappeared. To isolate the impact of the national association variable, three control variables are included in the regression – the level of B&L members per capita in 1893 (to control for regression to the mean), and two characteristics of each state's local building associations in 1893 that should have affected the public's willingness to join them afterwards. The first, building association assets per capita, controls for differences in state-level characteristics that favored the acceptance of the traditional B&L model. The second, the ratio of mortgage loans to paid-in installment dues (the association's equity), measures the lending risk that local associations in each state carried into the Depression of 1893.

The growth in per capita membership is measured differently in the two regressions – in the first as growth from an 1893 base that includes both national and local association members and in the second from a base of local association members only. If, as Brumbaugh argues, local associations succeeded in excluding a competitor, then the national association variable should have a large positive impact on membership growth as it is measured in the second regression but no impact on growth in the first. This is because anti-national regulation would have merely shifted members from national to local associations but not affected total building and loan membership. The regression results are clearly not consistent with this story.

The regressions show, instead, that B&L membership grew significantly more slowly over the next thirty years in states where national associations had made the greatest inroads in 1893. The large, negative impact in the first regression indicates that total building and loan membership growth (including both national and local members in 1893) was slowest in states where national associations had been most important. Even more revealing, however, is the negative impact the national association variable had on local-only membership growth rates in the second regression – instead of benefiting from the demise of national associations, local B&Ls grew most slowly over the next three decades in states where national associations had been most prominent. The regression offers strong evidence that the concerns voiced by local leaders and the USBLL in their battle with the nationals were more than just rhetoric – the national building association movement appropriated their name, violated their principles, and injured their reputation.

Thirty years after the demise of the nationals the USBLL continued to remind its members that "it appears to have taken twenty years (1893–1913) for the associations to find their way back to public favor, after the disastrous effect of the national associations" (Clark and Chase 1925, 470). None of the foregoing suggests that the USBLL did not seek or favor regulation that bestowed special privilege on its members. The point, instead, is that the building and loan industry understood in the 1890s that regulation could be used to impose standards of safety and soundness on itself. The lesson was not soon forgotten.

Regulatory and Industrial Structure During the 1920s

The traditional, pre-Depression building and loan can be thought of as a small, undiversified mutual fund into which all members made weekly or monthly dues payments. The pooled dues were invested in mortgage loans that the association made to the subset of members who chose to purchase a new or existing home. The management of the fund was entrusted to a small group of officers and directors who were specialists in the real estate industry and who had ancillary interests in either the real estate transaction or the home itself. To establish and maintain the public's confidence in this form of intermediation, the B&L movement cultivated an ideology of cooperation, emphasized that it existed to improve its members' well-being, and trumpeted its external benefits to the community. But the battle with the national associations had shown industry leaders that sometimes external regulation was required to maintain a reputation for safety and soundness. This is why, in the decades following the national fiasco, "[a]lmost without exception, the demand for specific legislation, including that providing for supervision of thrift and home-financing institutions, has come from the business itself" (Bodfish and Theobald 1938, 509). We cannot fully understand the institutional transformation of the industry during the 1930s without first exploring what industry leaders hoped to gain from regulation before then.

The work of securing regulation fell primarily to individual state building and loan leagues. In assessing the overall condition of state regulation in the mid-1920s, the definitive pre-Depression text on building and loans noted that "[t]he lack of uniformity is at once apparent" and that "an outstanding feature of all the [state] laws is their lack of completeness" (Clark and Chase 1925, 385, 391). This conclusion was drawn on the basis on a comprehensive compilation of building and loan statutes across the states (Clark and Chase 1925, Chapter XX). By 1925 a specialized building and loan supervisory agency had been established in only three states (California, Ohio, and Pennsylvania), while in most others supervision of B&Ls was assigned to a commissioner of banking, a commissioner of insurance, or even the state auditor. Two states (Maryland and Wyoming) had still not established a supervisory authority over building and loans by the mid-1920s, while in three others (Florida, Texas, and Virginia) the state legislature had not yet funded the regulatory authority created by building and loan legislation.

Building and loans were corporations and so were free to specify their own structure and rules of operation unless these were prescribed by special building and loan statutes. Only 23 states, however, required that the supervising regulatory agency approve an association's by-laws. Even where special statutes applied, the restrictions were less stringent than for other regulated financial intermediaries. Take, for example, restrictions and obligations imposed on the organizers of a B&L. Twenty-five states set no minimum for the amount of capital that the organizers of a B&L were required to subscribe or even to pay in. Where minimum capital requirements were specified, moreover, they were most often stated in numbers of shares and not in dollar amounts. In the four cases where dollar amounts of capital were specified (Louisiana, New Jersey, New York, and Washington), the minimum applied to subscribed, and not paid-in, capital. In eighteen states an association's directors were not required to own any shares, whereas no minimum amount of investment was specified in most others. In the dozen states where directors were required to invest a specified amount in the association, the norm was only one or two shares. As a general rule, interested parties could organize and operate a building and loan with only a nominal contribution of capital.

Flexible regulation and nominal capital requirements served what had been a central mission of the industry since its inception – to encourage the entry of new building and loans within a variety of market settings. By the end of the 1920s, however, the ease of entry had created a building and loan industry that was increasingly heterogeneous in structure, purpose, and function. The distribution of average association size across states is a particularly revealing indicator of the institutional variation within the industry in 1929 (see Figure 6.4). In twelve states and the District of Columbia the average association held more than $1.25 million in assets – or about 400 mortgage loans. At the other end of the distribution were seventeen states in which the average B&L held under $∅.5 million of assets, or fewer than about 167 mortgage loans.

To emphasize the absence of any obvious relationship between average association size and state characteristics, the positions of the ten largest B&L states are indicated in the size distribution shown in Figure 6.4. Five of these states had large-sized average associations (above $1.25 million), while the average B&L in the other five held less than $∅.75 million in assets. These latter five states together claimed 40 percent of all B&L assets and two-thirds of the nation's 12,000 operating associations – most of them very small associations holding fewer than 100 mortgage loans. There was no clear connection, therefore, between association size and size of market. Differences

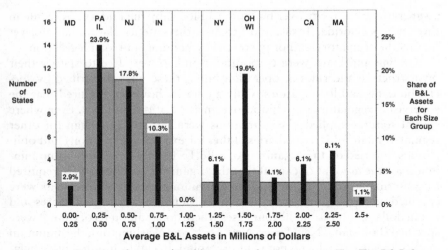

FIGURE 6.4. Size Distribution of Building Loans by State: 1929. Top Ten B&L States in Each Size Group
Source: Monthly Labor Review, November 1930, 114–5.

among neighboring states in average size were similarly striking. The average association in New York and Massachusetts was more than three times larger than in nearby Pennsylvania, and three times smaller in Illinois than in Ohio and Wisconsin. Moreover, B&Ls located in states as disparate in location, size, and economic structure as Utah, Nebraska, Louisiana, Oklahoma, and Rhode Island all had average association size greater than $1.25 million – among the largest in the nation.

Underlying these differences in average association size in 1929 was wide variation across states in the organizational structure and management of B&Ls. Three different types of B&Ls operated in the United States by the end of the 1920s.[17] The smallest in size were the traditional, "serial" associations that had been the workhorses of the building and loan movement of the 1880s. The name of this plan came from the practice of organizing groups of new members into separate series that were opened for subscription on a quarterly, semiannual, or annual basis. The small, serial association was frequently organized and managed on a part-time basis by a lawyer, a real estate agent, or a property insurance agent, and often shared offices with the manager's mainline business. These small, serial associations were particularly important in Illinois, New Jersey, and Pennsylvania. Together these

---

[17] The discussion concentrates on the three plans that dominated the industry. Also in use, but in small numbers, were the original terminating association plan that had been introduced in Pennsylvania in the 1830s, and a guaranty stock plan in Kansas. See Clark and Chase 1925, Chapter III for a discussion of the various plans in use during the 1920s.

three states claimed 52 percent of the nation's associations (or about 6,400 B&Ls), but only 35 percent of industry's assets.

Not all serial associations were small institutions, however. Some (such as those in Massachusetts and New York) built a home office, opened for daily business hours, and issued new series frequently enough to attract large numbers of members. A second type of B&L, called the permanent association, arose as a modification of the serial plan by treating each member's account as if it were a separate series. Members still purchased shares in installments in a permanent association, but an individual "series account" could be issued on any day that the association was open for business. Serial and permanent associations grew large in states like Massachusetts (where average association assets were $2.25 million), or Nebraska (where the average permanent association held just under $2 million of assets).

Nearly 90 percent of all associations in the 1920s were organized under the serial or permanent plans. The others adopted a plan of operation that would become widely implemented in the industry after 1930. Nearly all of the 810 associations in Ohio, for example, were organized under the Dayton Permanent Plan, which had originally appeared in that state during the 1880s. Members joined a Dayton permanent association by paying "dues" into individual share accounts at any time and in any amount they desired – there were no mandatory installment payments as in the serial and permanent associations. By the mid-1920s Dayton plan associations were also being used extensively in Minnesota, Louisiana, Oklahoma, Colorado, and California. There was criticism among some B&L traditionalists that the Dayton's "optional" payment feature made these associations no different than a savings bank, but Ohio was the only state that allowed its B&Ls to issue deposits as well as share accounts. Despite the criticism in the 1920s, the optional share account feature of the Dayton plan would become a central feature of the modern savings and loan that made its appearance in the 1930s.

Heterogeneity in state regulation and differences in plans of operation led to the use of a myriad of corporate titles within the industry so that B&Ls were known by no fewer than 143 appellations in the mid-1920s (Clark and Chase 1925, 518).[18] Less cosmetically, and of much more concern to industry observers and regulators, was the range of motivations organizers brought to their B&Ls. Particularly frowned upon were associations set up by subdividers and developers who would make loans to themselves and their associates to finance the development of their own residential building projects (Clark and Chase 1925, 90; Riegel and Doubman 1927, 36;

---

[18] The most common were "Building and Loan Association" (used in forty-seven states) and "Savings and Loan Association" (recognized in twenty-nine), along with variants and combinations of the two, but keywords such as Cooperative, Homestead, Investment, and Mutual were also liberally used.

Herman 1969, 820).[19] Regulators from Pennsylvania, Ohio, and Wisconsin documented specific cases of abuse in builder-dominated B&Ls during the homebuilding boom of the 1920s, but they generally had little success convincing legislatures to prohibit or even curtail the practice of making loans to an association's officers or directors (Herman 1969, 820). By 1928, 14 percent of the directors and 12 percent of the presidents of New Jersey's B&Ls were builders (Piquet 1931, 248). This was hardly a new development, or even a closely guarded secret because "such contacts are neither illegal nor unethical, although that they could come on occasion to be a source of corruption cannot be gainsaid" (249). After all, "[f]rom the very nature and plan of a building and loan association, its money must be loaned to . . . its own members, including its directors."[20] Builders, owners of building material supply houses, and real estate developers organized many B&Ls in the 1920s, but so did lawyers, real estate agents, and property insurance agents who typically ran the smallest serial associations. As a result, thousands of B&Ls conducted day-to-day business on a part-time basis out of the business offices of their organizers.

By the 1920s building and loan leaders had worked for three decades to fashion state legislation and regulation that embodied traditional B&L principles while controlling the inherent conflicts of interest so many B&L directors and officers brought with them. Harmonizing the two had proven to be difficult:

> Exploitation is the one serious menace to the building and loan movement today, as it has been in the past. Probably it is under better control today than ever before, but exploitation will always be present when the opportunity for large profit arises. One of the best ways to combat the tendency to exploitation is to adequately compensate efficient men for the service that they actually perform in making the affairs of the association safe and conducting them along equitable lines. No one should be permitted to pervert the movement for his private advantage (Clark and Chase 1925, 494).

This somber passage closes the Clark and Chase text, and some background is required to interpret its meaning and importance. The USBLL endorsed the creation of an affiliated educational organization at its 1922 annual convention and the American Savings, Building and Loan Institute was incorporated later that year. A first task taken on by the Institute was to produce a text (Clark and Chase 1925) that could be used to teach building and loan practices to untrained building and loan officers or to students who were interested in establishing careers within the industry. The industry's

---

[19] The builder could have the high profile of Harry Culver (creator of Culver City in Los Angeles) who served as president of the Pacific Building and Loan Association while maintaining interests in a savings bank and a mortgage company (Weiss 1987, 43–4).

[20] Taken from Herman 1969, 820 who quotes from J. H. Sundheim 1933, *Law of Building and Loans*, 73.

educational initiative was not unusual given that realtors, city planners, developers, builders, and property insurance agents were all sponsoring similar programs during the 1920s (Weiss 1987, Chap. 2–3). At the time all real estate and building professions were attempting to professionalize their occupations and to develop and lobby for state and local legislation that encouraged "best practices."

The building and loan case was unusual, however, because by the 1920s the USBLL had been in operation for thirty years promulgating the B&L ideology and constantly encouraging the formation of new associations. Taken in this light, the most interesting feature of the Clark and Chase passage is not its frank admission concerning the threat of exploitation, but its proposed solution. In 1925, when this passage was written, thousands of B&Ls were operating at low cost out of the offices of realtors, lawyers, insurance agents, and developers. This structure had developed over decades and had previously been strenuously defended by the USBLL. Clark and Chase suggest, however, that it was no longer an appropriate model for the industry. Large associations had begun to take on the trappings of a savings bank – by building home offices, opening for regular hours on a daily basis, and employing full-time, departmentalized staffs. This type of B&L came to dominate the USBLL and became increasingly disenchanted with sharing the stage with traditional, part-time building and loans.

During the 1920s the USBLL clearly favored professional managers who did not rely on ancillary income for their livelihood. The Clark and Chase passage is drawn from their chapter on "Trained Leadership as a Safeguard for the Movement" in which they outline an extensive college-level business degree program for aspiring managers. During the 1920s the USBLL also began to outline and endorse "model" legislation for B&Ls that drew heavily on the Ohio and New York precedents, states in which large, professionally managed building and loans dominated.[21] It is not surprising, therefore, that a USBLL executive could look back in 1938 with more candor than Clark and Chase to observe that "it is not necessary that every lawyer, real estate man, insurance agent or individual with a special interest have a personally sponsored and controlled savings and loan" (Bodfish and Theobald 1938, 514).

Transformation I: The Demise of Building and Loan

The transformation from B&L to S&L involved more than just a name change. By the end of the 1920s the building and loan industry had become bifurcated into small institutions that adhered to the traditional B&L model and larger, bureaucratic and professionally managed associations that

---

[21] For discussions of "best practices" and model legislation at the time see Bodfish 1931, 124–30; Clark and Chase 1925, Chapter XIX; and Riegel and Doubman 1927, Chapter XI.

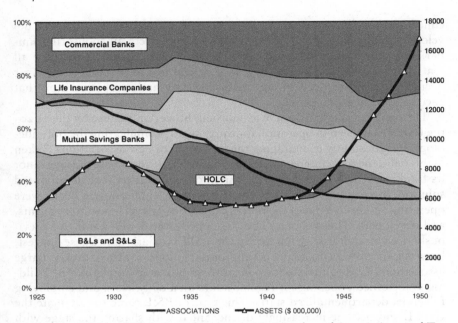

FIGURE 6.5. B&L and S&L Growth: 1925–1950. (Number of Associations and To-
tal Assets) With Shares of Mortgage Holdings on 1-4 Family Nonfarm Homes by
Institutional Lenders
Source: Savings and Home Financing Source Book, 1953, Table 11; 1960, Table 3.

controlled the USBLL and were favored by it. This tension was resolved by
the difficulties the industry faced during the Great Depression – the traditional B&L model virtually disappeared and a new S&L industry arose made
up of institutions that adopted the USBLL's preferred principles and practices. The second part of the transformation, the rise of the modern S&L, is
discussed in the last section of the chapter. First we examine how and why
the traditional B&L industry all but disappeared during the 1930s.

All financial intermediaries experienced dislocations during the 1930s, but
B&Ls were particularly hard hit. The market shares of the major institutional
residential mortgage lenders over the 1925–50 period (shown in Figure 6.5)
tell the story. In 1929 building and loans held 50 percent of the nation's
institutionally held, single-family mortgage debt – as much as life insurance companies, commercial banks, and mutual savings banks combined.
The volume of single-family mortgage debt held by all lenders decreased
substantially between 1929 and 1933, but the initial contraction was most
severe for B&Ls. More than 2,000 associations were forced to close in this
four-year period, the aggregate B&L mortgage portfolio decreased by nearly
one-third, and the industry's share of the single-family mortgage market fell
to 43 percent. Over the next two years the Home Owners' Loan Corporation

(HOLC) refinanced $2.9 billion of home mortgage debt – most of it to take slow-performing loans off the books of the four groups of intermediaries shown in Figure 6.5. The market shares of all these lenders fell as a result of HOLC refinancing activity, but, once again, none more than the building and loans. By 1935 the B&L industry held only 29 percent of the intermediated single-family residential debt (including HOLC) while over the entire 1929–35 period, the combined share of the other three lenders fell only 5 percentage points (from 50 to 45 percent).

The troubles were not over for the building and loans, however, as another 2,500 associations were forced to close between 1935 and 1940 and the industry's total assets decreased by another $150 million. By the end of the decade the S&L component of the industry had begun to recover so that the combined B&L/S&L mortgage loan portfolio (shown in Figure 6.5) actually increased by $800 million and their combined share of the home mortgage market rose to 33 percent. But even by 1950 the new S&L industry still held only 37 percent of institutionally held, single-family mortgage debt. It was not until 1960 that the new S&L industry regained the 50 percent market share that B&Ls had held in 1929.

The B&L industry performed so poorly during the 1930s because of the unique contractual structure it employed. The share installment plan had been the foundation of the building and loan movement for more than a century and was specifically designed to facilitate all of the essential functions of a traditional B&L. An association using this contract could offer amortized mortgage loans to borrowing members and compulsory savings plans with high returns to nonborrowing members; it also could refrain from holding costly reserves to maintain liquidity and adopt a simple accounting system that could be easily administered by a part-time officer. The traditional B&L contract also provided a long window of time within which flexibility was afforded in managing losses from loan delinquency or foreclosure. These features of the share installment plan had served the industry well for a century, but the contract proved to be particularly vulnerable to the macroeconomic forces that fueled the Great Depression. We must take a close look at how the share installment contract failed and why it was abandoned, therefore, to understand the demise of the traditional B&L sector during the 1930s.

Under the share installment plan B&L members agreed to purchase equity in an association by paying a series of regular weekly or monthly dues (often $1 each month for each $200 share). The contract was fulfilled when the accumulated dues plus the member's share of association profits reached the specified maturity value. At that point the member could (and was sometimes required to) withdraw from the association by taking a cash payment for his or her share. The contract typically ran for eleven or twelve years when the dividend rate was 6 percent, and changed in duration by seven or eight months for every percentage point change in average earnings. Under the share installment contract, building and loans were mutually owned corporations in both law and fact because each member directly participated in the profits and losses earned on the association's mortgage loan portfolio.

Several other features of the share installment plan made B&L membership far different from holding a deposit contract from a bank. B&L members were stockholders who purchased their shares over time and held this risky equity until they withdrew. They were also subject to fines if a dues payment was missed or made late, a compulsory feature that B&Ls used to promote the share installment contract as a savings program with built-in discipline. A member paid an early withdrawal penalty if he or she withdrew from the association before the installment share contract had matured. From early on, the courts ruled that a B&L member had a clear right to withdraw accumulated dues without penalty, but substantial withdrawal charges could be, and were, assessed against the member's accumulated profits. Early withdrawal penalties preserved the mutual character of the association (to earn higher returns the member must share risks) and also relieved the association from the costs of maintaining the liquidity needed to support a more liberal withdrawal policy. For this reason, building and loans prided themselves on holding small amounts of reserves before the 1930s, and regulation permitted them to do so.[22] Furthermore, under the share accumulation plan, an association had to maintain only one account for each series issued regardless of the number of investors in that series. With small reserves and modest administrative and operational expenses, building associations were able to offer members dividend rates two or three percentage points higher than the interest rate banks paid on savings deposits.

B&Ls introduced amortization to the American residential mortgage market in the mid-nineteenth century by combining the share installment contract with the ordinary straight loan that was used by nearly all mortgage lenders in the United States before 1930 (Clark and Chase 1925, 134–7). When a member applied for a loan, he or she was required to subscribe for shares that were equal in maturity value to the principal of the loan. The borrower paid interest on the entire loan amount throughout the life of the loan (normally 6 percent per annum), with the entire principal repaid in a lump sum at the end. Loans from B&Ls also carried premia (paid either as an initial discount or an addition to monthly interest payments) that adjusted

---

[22] Twenty states imposed no reserve requirements on their associations in 1925, seven were silent on the issue, and most of the twenty-two with a reserve requirement stipulated that the fund could not grow to more than 5 percent of total assets (Clark and Chase 1925, 404–5). Standard industry practice was to loan out available funds quickly so that members' dividends were maintained at a high level. As a result, building and loans entered the 1930s holding only 3.2 percent of their total assets in liquid investments compared to the 8.7 percent held by mutual savings banks (Teck 1968, 121).

the 6-percent contract rate to its equilibrium market level (Clark and Chase 1925, 407). After the loan was closed, therefore, the borrowing member made monthly payments of dues on his installment shares, and interest and premia payments on the loan. If the member missed or was late in making any of these payments, fines were levied against his or her shareholdings.

Amortization was accomplished in the pre-Depression building and loan, therefore, by using the share installment contract as a sinking fund. The borrower was at the same time a debtor to the association and a stockholder in it with full voting rights and a proportional claim on the profits and losses on its entire mortgage portfolio. When his or her shares matured, the borrower's equity was just equal to the loan balance, and the debt was cancelled. The essential problem with the contract was that the risks that the borrowing member bore as an equity holder "fed back" to affect his or her behavior as a debtor. If, for example, the association suffered a large loss because of a costly foreclosure, the equity of all members had to be written down. For borrowing members this loss in equity effectively increased the balance due on their loans and made them more likely to default.

It should now be clear why B&Ls fared so poorly during the 1930s relative to other residential mortgage lenders. When borrowers in these association stopped making monthly interest and premium payments because of a loss of employment or income, all remaining borrowing members had to pay dues and interest for a longer horizon than expected in order to extinguish their loans. The situation became much worse, however, when some borrowers defaulted and the association foreclosed on the home. Foreclosure proceedings were costly to the association, and it was then left with property that could generate additional losses if it could not readily be sold or rented – a common situation as residential property values fell during the 1930s. Under the share accumulation contract, the remaining borrowing members in the association had to share in these losses by suffering an unscheduled increase in the balance due, time to maturity, or interest rate on their mortgage loan. These shocks, and fears of similar shocks in the future, led some B&L borrowers to default, who would not have done so under a different contractual arrangement.

Between 1930 and 1933 the real estate holdings of B&Ls increased from $238 to $828 million, or from nearly 3 to 17 percent of total assets. But even worse lay ahead. The industry's real estate holdings peaked at $1.2 billion in 1935 (fully 20 percent of assets), and then began a slow protracted decline for the rest of the decade. By 1939 B&L real estate holdings (shown in the left-hand panel of Table 6.3) still represented 12 percent of assets for the industry as a whole, a staggering 22 percent in the Mid-Atlantic region, and between 9 and 12 percent in New England and the East North and South Central regions. Even more sobering, these figures apply only to B&Ls that were still operating in 1939; an unknown amount of real estate was owned

TABLE 6.3. *The Transformation from B&L to S&L in the United States: 1929–1940*

| | | The Collapse | | | | The New Savings & Loan Industry — Share of Associations and Assets | | | | | |
| | | Number of Associations / Assets ($000,000) | | Percentage Change | % Assets Held in Real Estate | Associations Assets | Federal S&L | | FHLB Members | | State-Chartered B&L |
Region		1929	1939	1929–39	1939	1941	New Charter	Converted State	Insured	Uninsured	Non-Members
U.S.	Assoc.	12,342	8,318	−33%		6,895	9%	12%	12%	22%	45%
	Assets	$8,695	$5,666	−35%	12%	$5,755	11%	24%	20%	26%	20%
New England	Assoc.	358	354	−1%		353	5%	9%	3%	43%	40%
	Assets	$637	$621	−2%	9%	$624	3%	22%	1%	57%	16%
Mid-Atlantic	Assoc.	5,772	3,100	−46%		2,423	2%	5%	7%	21%	65%
	Assets	$2,974	$1,448	−51%	22%	$1,192	6%	19%	13%	23%	39%
E. North Central	Assoc.	2,395	1,867	−22%		1,779	6%	14%	19%	24%	37%
	Assets	$2,488	$1,634	−34%	12%	$1,767	8%	25%	29%	25%	14%
W. North Central	Assoc.	671	629	−6%		577	13%	14%	15%	23%	35%
	Assets	$599	$413	−31%	8%	$442	11%	29%	15%	18%	27%
South Atlantic	Assoc.	1,911	1,300	−32%		749	17%	12%	7%	19%	45%
	Assets	$547	$645	18%	2%	$662	21%	18%	11%	30%	19%
E. South Central	Assoc.	279	297	6%		276	28%	20%	3%	14%	36%
	Assets	$176	$163	−7%	12%	$176	22%	46%	2%	18%	12%
W. South Central	Assoc.	444	337	−24%		326	33%	20%	29%	6%	12%
	Assets	$511	$268	−48%	6%	$308	13%	34%	45%	3%	4%
Mountain	Assoc.	178	154	−13%		137	23%	20%	17%	12%	28%
	Assets	$152	$99	−35%	8%	$112	15%	34%	27%	7%	17%
Pacific	Assoc.	334	280	−16%		275	23%	26%	26%	17%	8%
	Assets	$611	$376	−38%	5%	$472	25%	25%	29%	15%	6%

Sources: Monthly Labor Review November 1930, 114–5; January 1941, 126–7; May 1943, 937.
Federal Home Loan Bank Board, *Eighth Annual Report*, 1940, 175–6.
Federal Home Loan Bank Board, *Ninth Annual Report*, 1941, 242–5.

by closed B&Ls who were in the process of liquidating. Throughout the 1930s, therefore, the overhang of real estate on the B&L industry's balance sheet made it more costly for borrowing members to successfully repay their loans and, as a result, they were less likely to do so.

As the Depression worsened it became painfully clear to B&L members that their shareholdings were very different from bank deposits. Like mutual savings banks, building associations were entitled to a 30- to 90-day grace period before honoring a member's request to withdraw. But savings banks had to close and begin liquidation if they could not honor the withdrawal after the grace period was over – building associations faced no such obligation. By 1925 building and loans in nearly all states were protected from involuntary liquidation by statutes that prohibited total withdrawals during any month or year in excess of 50 percent of current earnings (Clark and Chase 1925, 400–1). An association facing large demands for withdrawals did not have to close, nor was it considered to be insolvent. In building and loan parlance, the association became "frozen." Thousands of associations found themselves in this condition during the 1930s.

The term "frozen" was apt (Ewalt 1962, 13–28). A building and loan in this situation remained open, but experienced a precipitous drop in installment payments as nonborrowing members rushed to withdraw. Dues and interest payments from borrowing members also slowed down either because some could not pay or, as previously explained, because others chose to default rather than to throw good money after bad into their "sinking fund." During the early 1930s a frozen building association had only one source of current receipts – the dues, interest, and premium payments made by a shrinking subset of its borrowing members. These resources first had to be allocated to current expenses that rose to unusual heights because of foreclosure proceedings and related property management activities. Only after these expenses had been met could the association pay off members who had requested to withdraw. A frozen building association was, in essence, gradually liquidating, and it took some associations until the early 1940s to complete the process.

Several responses were implemented during the 1930s to make this liquidation process more orderly. The first was quite natural for owners of stock: They sold off their association shares at large discounts in a secondary market that was usually brokered by a local investment house.[23] State legislatures fashioned a second response in the early 1930s by suspending the "order of filing method" for paying out withdrawals (Bodfish and Theobald 1938,

---

[23] See Kendall (1962, 144) for a reproduction of the quotation sheet of a Milwaukee dealer on May 1, 1936, nearly a full year after the Federal Savings and Loan Insurance Corporation (FSLIC) began operations. Prices for shares in nearly 100 associations range from $15 to $86 for each $100 "par" share, which Kendall estimates as an average discount of 20 to 30 percent off book value.

161). This familiar "first come, first served" sequential service rule created problems when a member with large shareholdings was first in line so that no other member could be paid until this first claim was satisfied. As soon as states allowed it, therefore, some associations began to pay each member a proportional share of the association's withdrawals each month. The rotation principle gained wide favor at the time and ultimately became the standard emergency withdrawal policy in the industry during the post–World War II era (Kendall 1962, 76–7). Under this procedure the association set a fixed dollar limit for withdrawals each month, and members queued up to receive it. They were then placed at the back of the line to wait for their next fixed payment. It took some members several years to withdraw all of their investment under the rotation system.

The most constructive response a frozen association could take was to reorganize by a segregation of assets (Ewalt 1962, 116–8). Under this arrangement the association, on approval of the membership, segregated its nonperforming loans from its good loans and placed the latter in a new association in which each member was given a proportional share. At the same time, the members accepted a write-down in the value of their shares in the original association – the loss they acknowledged on nonperforming loans. The new "healthy" association, however, could immediately begin to pay withdrawals on demand, attract new members, and make new mortgage loans. The members' certificates of participation in the "bad loan corporation," on the other hand, were paid off in dividends as its real estate holdings were liquidated.

The rotation principle, segregation of assets, and secondary market activity in shares establish clearly that the contract between a B&L and its member was fundamentally different than the relationship between a depositor and a commercial or mutual savings bank. It was equally clear by the early 1930s that it would be difficult for building and loans to reestablish public acceptance so long as they continued to rely on the traditional share installment contract. Industry leaders advocated replacing it with an investment vehicle that was as safe and liquid as a deposit in a mutual savings bank, and the "savings share account" became the workhorse of the new savings and loan associations (Bodfish and Theobald 1938, 618; Ewalt 1962, 171).[24] This

---

[24] Discussions within the industry during the 1920s regarding alternatives to the share installment contract were designed to provide members with more attractive and liquid financial arrangements. For nonborrowers the goal was to offer more liquid investment vehicles through one of three different approaches (Clark and Chase 1925, Chapter 8; Riegel and Doubman 1927, 93–5). Some associations eliminated the withdrawal charges members faced when they removed their investments from an association before their share installment contract had been fulfilled. Other B&Ls introduced greater liquidity by introducing prepaid and full-paid shares. Under these contracts, members could purchase shares at or close to their maturity value, so that the time they were subject to the early withdrawal fee was shortened or altogether eliminated.

contract was identical in structure to the optional payment account that was used in the 1920s by Dayton Permanent Plan building associations (see the previous section) – it eliminated the compulsory features of the installment share plan so that members could invest in the association in any amount and at any time they chose. Members were also allowed to withdraw without charges under the new contract, subject only to a 60- to 90-day grace period (if needed) and the limitations of the rotation principle (if the association came under severe stress). The similarities between the new savings account plan and a deposit in a mutual savings bank were striking. Building and loans had determined to compete with savings banks by offering nearly identical services (Teck 1968, 40–2).

Mimicking the withdrawal policy of savings banks implied adopting a similar approach to liquidity. Rather than following the pre-Depression practice of holding minimal reserves, savings and loan associations built them up to 8.7 percent of total assets by 1945 – just below the amounts held by mutual savings banks (Teck 1968, 128). To increase liquidity, moreover, dividend policy also had to fall in line. Gone were the days when B&Ls offered dividends of 7 percent, while mutual savings banks paid only 4 to 4.5 percent on their savings accounts (Piquet 1931, 101; Lintner 1948, 498). Both rates were much lower in the postwar era, but so was the differential – to an average of about ϕ.75 percentage points between 1945 and 1949, and to only ϕ.3 percentage points during the 1950s (Teck 1968, 95). The industry had attracted members with the promise of high profits right up to 1930, but by 1937 it had accepted that members "looking for 100% safety with reasonable availability are not so concerned about a *high* rate of return" (Bodfish and Theobald 1938, 621).

There had also been extensive discussion within B&L circles during the 1920s concerning the strengths and weaknesses of the loans written under the share installment plan. The traditional system previously described, nonetheless, was still being used by 80 percent of building and loans on the eve of the Depression. A small minority (around 10 percent of associations) had adopted what was called the direct reduction loan – the modern amortized mortgage loan contract under which the borrower paid principal and interest each month and continuously reduced the loan balance (Riegel and Doubman 1927, 148). The actual maturity and effective interest rate on this type of contract is fixed so long as the borrower makes all payments on schedule; as a result it carries none of the additional risks associated with the traditional share installment loan. Associations that used the direct reduction plan typically required the borrowing "member" to purchase only a nominal amount of equity when the loan was made and to pay no installment dues thereafter.

The building and loan literature treated the direct reduction plan favorably during the 1920s, but it was slow to be adopted (Riegel and Doubman 1927, 152–3). Some associations resisted the direct reduction loan because it undermined the principle of mutuality – it reduced the borrower's risk by virtually writing down his equity in the association as soon it was paid in. Others were concerned that the courts would question whether such borrowing members were "bona fide" and take away the industry's exemption from the federal corporate tax it had argued for on the basis of the mutual character of the traditional B&L (Bodfish 1931, 203–5). Finally, associations in 25 states could not adopt the direct reduction loan before 1930 because the law required building and loan members to subscribe to a sufficient number of shares to cover the full principal of the loan. So, ideological, legal, and regulatory barriers prevented the great majority of building and loans from adopting the direct reduction loan plan before the Depression.

All of the resistance to the adoption of the direct reduction loan was swept aside in the 1930s. Thousands of associations that operated under the share installment loan plan were forced to close, and the survivors reorganized under revised state law or joined the new federal chartering system, both of which permitted and then mandated the use of direct reduction loans. The Home Owners' Loan Corporation wrote only direct reduction loans when it refinanced one-tenth of all outstanding residential mortgage debt and a slightly higher proportion of building and loan mortgages. FHA mortgage insurance also required the modern contract. Perhaps most important, the U.S. League of Building and Loans encouraged its members to adopt the direct reduction loan, and three-quarters of all associations had done so by 1937.

In a few short years during the Depression the share installment contract, the core of the traditional B&L, had become a thing of the past. Along with it were lost thousands of associations that never adopted the share savings accounts or direct loan contracts. These traditional building and loans became frozen in the early- to mid-1930s and then often took several years to complete liquidation. But thousands of other building and loans adopted the new contracts, survived the 1930s, and became the new savings and loan industry. Most of these associations retained their state charters and worked to revise state law where necessary before adopting the new contracts (Ewalt 1962, 110–1). Others converted into federally chartered associations that at first had the option of retaining the share installment contract, but by 1936 were required to adopt both the direct reduction loan and the savings share account (Ewalt 1962, 84–7). We now turn to their story.

Transformation II: The Rise of Savings and Loan

Federal regulation of the savings and loan industry was implemented during the 1930s at breakneck speed: The Federal Home Loan Bank system and its discounting facility began operations in 1932, followed quickly by the Federal Savings & Loan chartering system (1933) and the Federal Savings

& Loan Insurance Corporation program (1934). To appreciate the pace of change consider the timing of similar developments within the commercial banking system: a federal chartering system in 1862, the Federal Reserve discounting facility in 1913, and the FDIC deposit insurance program twenty years later. The B&L/S&L industry had but three years to adapt to a set of institutional developments that had been introduced into the commercial banking system over a seventy-year period. The transformation of the thrifts, moreover, occurred during the worst depression in the nation's history.

The federalization of the thrift industry – and the rise of savings and loan – was accomplished with such speed and under such circumstances because it was an industry-driven process. By the end of the 1920s USBLL leaders were advocating a professionalized, bureaucratic, institutional model that was fundamentally different in structure than the thousands of small, part-time B&Ls that had just entered the industry. During the 1930s, with so many traditional B&Ls frozen and liquidating, industry leaders had an opportunity to fashion a modern S&L industry that they could only have imagined a few years earlier. Means were added to opportunity by political leaders who were desperate to revive a moribund homebuilding industry. Every major piece of Depression-era S&L legislation was designed by the USBLL and implemented under the supervision of its leaders. The remainder of this chapter explains how the modern S&L industry was shaped by USBLL leaders during the 1930s and how their actions determined the industrial structure and regional character of the industry for decades to come.

The USBLL had such influence during the 1930s because before then there had been a near complete lack of experience with or expertise about B&Ls within the federal government. The League had tried to raise the visibility of the building and loan industry on the national stage before the Depression, but it remained a relatively unknown and idiosyncratic corner of the financial market despite the importance of B&Ls as residential mortgage lenders. The only pre-1930 federal legislation that directly touched building and loans was an exemption the USBLL had won in 1894 from the corporate income tax that was authorized in the Wilson Tariff Act (Bodfish 1931, 186–7). Over the next three decades B&L energy and attention in Washington were spent defending the exemption no fewer than ten times. The only other high-profile federal initiative before 1930 was the League's unsuccessful attempt to establish a system of home loan discount banks for the exclusive use of B&Ls (Bodfish 1931, 207–14). Opponents offered alternatives that would have opened either the Federal Reserve or the Federal Farm Loan Bank Systems to building and loans, but these were rejected by the USBLL on the grounds that the industry's unique share installment loans would not easily fit into the practices of either institution. They stuck to their guns, prevailed upon congressional advocates to push for a separate home loan bank, and lost. The homebuilding industry and B&Ls were soon in the midst of the 1920s boom, and the home land bank proposal was shelved.

Hoover revived the idea of a home loan discount bank during his 1928 campaign but did not take action until he convened a special conference on home building and ownership in 1931. At the conference the proposed bank was opposed by commercial banks, life insurance companies, and mortgage banking interests, but the recommendation for establishment was passed over their objections. With the housing market suffering severely, moreover, there was no time for the type of prolonged investigation and discussion that had preceded the passage of both the Federal Reserve Act and the Federal Farm Loan Act. None was needed. The USBLL had drafted legislation for a discount bank years earlier and a special task force of the League was assigned to revisit and update these proposals in preparation for Hoover's conference (Ewalt 1962, 87). When the proposal for the establishment of a home loan discount bank was passed, therefore, two senior officers of the USBLL were able and willing to help Representative Luce of Massachusetts draft the Federal Home Loan Bank Act (Bodfish and Theobald 1938, 290). Commercial banks, life insurance companies, and their mortgage company affiliates once again fought hard to defeat the bill in Congress, but managed only to delay its passage until July 16 – the very last day of the 1932 congressional session.[25]

In his 1932 presidential address to the USBLL, William Best presented the good news for the membership:

On July 22, 1932, when President Hoover affixed his signature to the Federal Home Loan Bank Act, I believe that the most important era in the history of building and loan began (Bodfish 1931, 287).

One can only wonder at his audience's reaction – by that time the industry had lost 2,000 associations, two million members, and a billion dollars of assets, and greater losses in each loomed ahead. The discounting facility the industry had coveted for more than a decade had been established, but just as the industry was facing its greatest cataclysm. Time was of the essence in setting up and implementing the new federal structure, and League industry leaders took the lead in doing so (Ewalt 1962, 58–66). The first order of business was to appoint the five members of the governing Federal Home Loan Bank (FHLB) Board; included were two USBLL executives (William Best and Morton Bodfish). The Board was also charged with determining the number of regional banks to include in the system (twelve), choosing the location of the banks (each in a city that was not home to a Federal Reserve Bank), and appointing the board of directors for each regional bank (ninety-one of a total of 132 represented building and loan associations).

---

[25] Life insurance companies opposed the Federal Home Loan Bank (FHLB) Act even though they and savings banks were eligible to become members. A few actually did join, but never played a significant role in the system.

With the system's structure in place, the Board then devised the application process for membership (the law stipulated any building and loan, life insurance company, or savings bank was eligible) (Ewalt 1962, 61). The USBLL's original WWI proposal had called for a federal home loan discount bank that would have served all B&Ls, and only one year before being appointed to the FHLB Board, Morton Bodfish of the USBLL appeared to hold the same view:

[B]uilding and loan shares will emerge from the present business situation as among the soundest and most valuable intact investments, with the possible exception of the securities of our own Federal Government (Bodfish 1931, 298).

Bodfish's endorsement suggests that as a FHLB Board member he would favor broad access to FHLB's discounting facilities because most B&Ls could offer sound collateral for the liquidity that would help them avoid becoming frozen. It was another member of the original FHLB Board, however, who insisted that eligibility requirements be chosen to "broaden the function of the institution to the widest possible degree to take care of building and loan associations"; surprisingly, Bodfish and Best argued in opposition for "a little discretion in handling particular situations" on the basis of their own "knowledge of some of the sore spots in the picture" (Fort 1933, 7). Bodfish clarified his contribution to the discussion of eligibility:

I said that I did not believe that the Federal Reserve System had taken in any pawn shops and as far as I was concerned, the Home Loan Bank System was going to take in only honest-to-goodness sound institutions that were really serving their communities in living up to the best ideals of building and loan (Bodfish 1931, 16).

Bodfish went on to quote a passage of the FHLB Act that excluded any institution from the system if "the character of its management or its home-financing policy is inconsistent with sound and economical home financing" (Bodfish 1931, 19). He declared the passage to be the "Magna Carta of the building and loan industry for the next 100 years."

USBLL leaders who were in a position to facilitate assistance for the entire B&L industry in 1932 argued instead for selective eligibility criteria based on the Board's own judgment of an association's managerial character and financing practices. Given criticisms that the League had voiced in the 1920s of the small, traditional B&L, it is reasonable to conclude that its leaders were determined to use their influence to rid the industry of what they viewed as its weakest elements. At the same time the League provided encouragement and help in the application process to associations that it considered to be qualified for the system (Ewalt 1962, 65–8). State and local affiliates shepherded enabling legislation through state legislatures so that associations would be allowed to borrow from their regional FHLB after they became members. USBLL bulletins, meanwhile, explained in detail how the application for membership should be completed and how it would be evaluated.

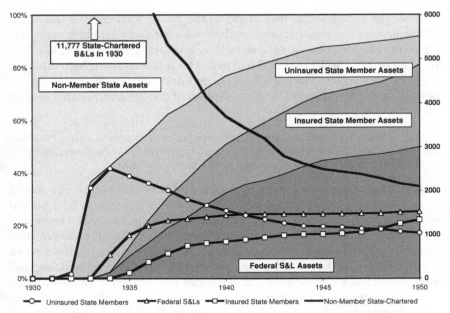

FIGURE 6.6. The Transformation from B&L to S&L: 1930–1950. (Number of Federal
S&Ls and State-Chartered Associations by FHLB and FSLIC Status) With Shares of
Total S&L and B&L Assets Held by Each Group of Associations
Source: Savings and Home Financing Source Book, 1960, Tables 3–4.

The FHLB membership patterns that emerged in the system's first five
years reshaped the old B&L industry into its modern S&L counterpart. By
the end of 1933 some 2,000 associations, with a combined share of one-
third of the industry's assets, had joined the FHLB system (see Figure 6.6).[26]
FHLB membership grew slowly from this point to reach a plateau of 3,900
institutions in 1937 and then fluctuated between 3,600 and 3,900 right up
until 1950. Although their numbers held steady, FHLB member institutions
grew to dominate the savings and loan industry over this period as their
share of total industry assets climbed from 60 percent in 1937, to 77 percent
in 1940, and 92 percent by 1950. Left behind were the great majority of the

---

[26] Events surrounding the Bank Holiday of March 1933 helped elicit the large initial response
for FHLB membership. B&Ls were initially closed under Roosevelt's initial emergency
directive, but the FHLB Board quickly informed administration officials that these organizations were member-owned corporations that did not issued deposit contracts, and that
they were protected by state legislation against a sudden rush of requests for withdrawals.
B&Ls were excused from the holiday in a matter of days (Ewalt 1962, 66–7). Somewhat
fortuitously, the Federal Home Loan Banks had together accumulated $40 million of cur-
rency by this time, and they made it all available to member associations. For a few short
but memorable days, local B&Ls that were first to join the new FHLB system were the only
institutions in the nation offering their members ready cash.

10,600 B&Ls that were in operation when the FHLB opened for business. Only 3,300 of these institutions joined the FHLB – they, along with more than 600 newly chartered Federal Savings and Loan Associations became the savings and loan industry. The remaining 7,300 B&Ls that were operating in 1933 never joined the FHLB system. Two thousand of them survived until 1950 to represent one-third of all associations but to hold only 8 percent of the industry's assets. The remaining 5,200 associations either failed or were merged into other associations after that date. The FHLB system, which USBLL leaders helped to design and implement, sorted the B&L industry into two camps – those that they considered to be "well-managed, safe and sound" became members and dominated the modern S&L industry. The rest languished at the periphery or simply disappeared.

Along with FHLB membership came benefits that were intended to promote the survival and growth of FHLB members. The discounting facilities at the regional banks made loans (called "advances") to member institutions that averaged $160 million between 1935 and 1940, or about 4 percent of their combined assets. In addition, the FHLB Board was given supervisory authority over the Home Owner's Loan Corporation (HOLC) – the New Deal agency designed to revive residential mortgage lending and homebuilding. One measure undertaken by the HOLC was to continue the Reconstruction Finance Corporation's program of investing directly in share accounts at selected federal- and state-chartered associations, nearly all of them FHLB members (Ewalt 1962, 46). At their peak in 1937, the combination of FHLB advances and direct government investments represented more than 12 percent of the total liabilities and capital of FHLB member institutions (Federal Home Loan Bank Board, Seventh Annual Report 1939, 195). Those B&L associations that remained outside the FHLB system, therefore, were cut off from important benefits that would have improved their chances of survival and renewed expansion.

HOLC also provided assistance to FHLB members, and all other financial intermediaries, when it undertook the largest refinancing of private debt in the nation's history. Between 1933 and 1936 the agency wrote more than 1 million long-term, amortized (direct reduction) mortgage loans to homeowners who were deemed to be in danger of defaulting on their original loans. The building and loan industry "sold off" more mortgage debt to HOLC than any other type of lender ($770 million out of a total of $3 billion), which helped surviving institutions to resume new lending and facilitated the liquidation of those that were frozen. But it was a third provision of the Home Owners' Loan Act that provided the FHLB Board, and the USBLL, with an additional opportunity to shape the new Savings and Loan industry.

Section 5 of HOLA authorized the FHLB Board to charter and regulate new entrants into the B&L industry – Federal Savings and Loan Associations. The Act provided no specific detail concerning how these institutions should be organized or operated; only that they should follow "the best practices of local mutual thrift and home financing institutions in the United States." We have seen earlier that the USBLL had begun to identify, combine, and codify "best practices" in the 1920s from the existing body of heterogeneous state building and loan statutes then in use. The work culminated in a single comprehensive "Uniform Code" that the League recommended to legislatures at the onset of the Depression so that B&Ls in their states could adopt share savings accounts, direct reduction loans, and the rotation principle. When the HOLC passed Congress, the USBLL naturally recommended its own code to the FHLB Board as a blueprint for setting up the regulatory structure for the new federal system (Bodfish and Theobald 1938, 516–7, 556–7; Ewalt 1962, 80–81). The similarity between the League's document and federal S&L charters was striking–so too was the appointment of a long-time USBLL official as the first chief of the FHLB Board's Federal Savings and Loan Division (Ewalt 1962, 80). By 1941 more than 20 percent of B&Ls and S&Ls (1,450 in number) operated under federal charters and together they held 35 percent of the industry's assets (see the right-hand panel of Table 6.3). More than 800 of these institutions had entered the federal system by converting from their original state charters, the remaining 639 were new associations that were originally organized as federal S&Ls.

After a brief transition period, the new federal charter required savings share accounts, direct reduction loans, and higher reserve holdings. The most lasting impact of the federal S&L system, however, may have been the barriers it erected to control entry into the new S&L industry (Bodfish and Theobald 1938, 515–9). Despite prohibitions against national associations, the B&L industry remained open to new local associations, and more than 4,000 were organized during the 1920s. Entry during that decade had been so rapid, in fact, that the USBLL began to discuss adding limitations on new associations to its model code. Two ideas were prominent: (a) new charters should be granted only if the applicant could demonstrate that an additional association was needed and that it would not injure an existing association and (b) a "50-mile rule" that restricted the lending activities of a chartered association to its local market. Both restrictions were incorporated into federal S&L chartering provisions. Taken together these provisions effectively carved out many regulatorily protected local S&L monopolies – a feature of the modern industry that critics often noted in the 1970s and 1980s when arguing for deregulation. These monopolies were no regulatory accident – the USBLL began to argue for restrictions on entry during the 1920s and successfully introduced them in the federal S&L system during the 1930s.

In a few short years USBLL leaders had used their access to and influence over the FHLB and the federal S&L systems to mold a new S&L industry – one with fewer and larger institutions, limited entry, and contracts similar to those offered by savings banks. The League was less successful, however, in distancing the managers and officers of S&Ls from the ancillary real estate activities that had led to pervasive conflicts of interest within the traditional B&L industry. The reason was Section 6 of the HOLA that appropriated $700,000 so that the FHLB Board could promote and charter new federal S&Ls. The Board assigned a group of building and loan veterans to solicit applications for new associations, and these individuals knew exactly who would be most interested in their appeal – the same types of building and real estate professionals that had dominated the B&L industry (Herman 1969, 804). These recruiting activities were remembered decades later when the FHLB Board proposed a new set of stringent disclosure rules in 1970 that were designed to control self-dealing behavior within the industry. S&L opposition to the proposed rules was "massive by usual standards" and came from "every sector of the industry and every part of the country" (Clarke 1970, 9). In arguing that it should delay implementation of the proposal, the Board's own general counsel noted that:

Many of the alleged conflicts of interest that are criticized today were encouraged in the 1930s by representatives of the Federal Government who were imploring people to charter Federal savings and loan associations. Thus, the realtor, the insurance agent, and the lawyer were advised that their occupations could be assisted and their incomes increased if they organized a savings and loan association (Liebold 1970, 16).

More than 600 new federal S&Ls were "recruited" between 1933 and 1936, while nearly all other federal charters granted between 1933 and 1950 were for conversions of state associations (refer to Figure 6.6). The Depression era rush to enlist so many new institutions transmitted the same conflicts of interest into the modern S&L industry that were endemic in traditional B&Ls.

The final element of the industry's transformation, the Federal Savings and Loan Insurance Corporation (FSLIC) insurance program, was neither anticipated nor favored by the USBLL. The irony, of course, is that FSLIC proved to be the weak regulatory link that destroyed the industry five decades later. League leaders expressed opposition to the proposed Federal Deposit Insurance Corporation (FDIC) system for banks even before FSLIC was considered on a variety of ideological and practical grounds. They were also concerned, of course, that S&Ls would suffer a competitive disadvantage in the market for savings once bank deposits were insured (Ewalt 1962, 91–6). After the FDIC system had been approved, however, the USBLL prevailed on the FHLB Board to propose a separate insurance program for the S&L industry, and it was authorized in the National Housing Act (1934). Federal S&Ls were required to join the new FSLIC system, although state-chartered associations could join if they met the system's requirements. Nearly all that chose to do so were FHLB members. Figure 6.6 reveals that insurance for savings accounts was one dimension of the transformation of the industry that was slow to be achieved. Relatively few state-chartered FHLB members chose to participate in the insurance program in its first two years. The number of insured FHLB members began to increase gradually after 1936, but it was not until 1950 that one-half of the eligible institutions had joined the FSLIC. The modern S&L industry was ultimately undone by an insurance program that its leaders proposed for purely defensive reasons and that it member institutions were slow to embrace.

During the late 1930s the FSLIC's "Community Programs" had a particularly interesting regional influence on the transformation of the industry. These programs were "designed to bring about comprehensive rehabilitation of the savings and loan industry in certain localities where general weaknesses in ... structure have been apparent" (Federal Home Loan Bank Board, *Eighth Annual Report*, 1940, 107–10, 227–31). The Bank Board and the USBLL had stood by as thousands of small associations failed during the 1930s but took action toward the end of the decade in several cities in which nearly all of the traditional institutions had either failed or were "frozen." Prominent among these were New Orleans, Milwaukee, Philadelphia, and several areas in New Jersey. In each case the FSLIC worked with state authorities to reestablish general real estate activity in the local area by supervising the reorganization of failed associations through a segregation of assets; by arranging for other "frozen" associations to disappear through merger; and by setting up city-wide property appraisal and sales bureaus to facilitate the disposal of real estate held by troubled B&Ls.

This brief summary of the FSLIC community programs helps to make sense of the unbalanced regional pattern that marked the regulatory transition from B&L to S&L. The right panel of Table 6.3 reveals that the development of the new S&L industry was as unbalanced across space between 1929 and 1939 as the simultaneous collapse of the traditional B&L industry. All of the new federal programs had their smallest impacts in the Mid-Atlantic region, which had suffered so badly during the 1930s, and New England, which had hardly suffered at all. More than 80 percent of operating associations in both areas remained state-chartered in 1941 and most of these had not even joined the FHLB. Before 1930 the regulatory frameworks in Massachusetts and New York were held up by B&L leaders as models for the nation. The 1941 data suggest that institutions in these states preferred to remain within their familiar regulatory system even in the presence of the new federal institutions. In New Jersey and Pennsylvania, on the other hand, many institutions had not taken advantage of the new federal structures by 1941 because they remained frozen and had yet to be rehabilitated by the FSLIC's community programs.

The West South Central, Mountain, and Pacific regions lie at the other extreme – by 1941 their traditional state-chartered B&L associations had been marginalized, and even uninsured FHLB members played a small role.

More than 60 percent of the associations in all three regions had become insured, and they held at least 70 percent of industry assets in these regions. The new federal associations also had their largest impact in the West. The distribution of associations and assets across charter types was most balanced in the South Atlantic and East South Central regions, but state-chartered institutions in these markets were very slow to adopt FSLIC insurance. In the two North Central regions, finally, the bulk of the industry chose to remain state-chartered although there was substantial participation in both the FHLB system and the federal insurance program.

The general pattern revealed by these data is that the transition from B&L to S&L was a difficult process in areas that had been early strongholds of the traditional B&L structure and was accomplished more easily and quickly where this structure had less time to root. There is much left to explore concerning the causes of the marked regional variations in the transformation from B&L to S&L, but the discussion here must be confined to examining one of its impacts. We found earlier in the chapter that the secular shift in the location of the homebuilding industry – from north and east to south and west – accelerated during the 1930s. Two measures of changes in the regional distribution of B&L/S&L mortgage lending activity over the 1930s are presented in Table 6.4 to examine whether the locational shift in housing production was connected to the institutional developments within the thrift industry.

The left-hand panel of the table reports the regional shares of outstanding mortgage debt held by all operating B&Ls and S&Ls in 1929 and 1939. These shares show little change over the decade, save for a pronounced decrease in the Mid-Atlantic region and a corresponding increase in the South Atlantic. This pattern provides some evidence that the industry's lending activities were following changes in the location of housing production, but hardly its speed or national character. These measures of total outstanding mortgage debt reflect lending activity on existing as well as new homes, however, and would have responded slowly to a locational shift in new lending activity because B&L mortgages were long-term loans.

A clearer picture of changes in the regional profile of B&L/S&L lending activity that occurred during the late 1930s is shown in the right-hand panel of Table 6.4. There we consider the regional shares of B&L/S&L mortgage lending in 1940 broken down by the age of the encumbered structure – separately for homes that were built after 1935 and those that were built in earlier years. Nearly 77 percent of the industry's loans in the latter category were written by associations in the Northeast and North Central regions, but these same institutions held only 44 percent of B&L/S&L loans that were written on the most recently built homes. The pattern is clearly reversed for associations in both the South and West that were relatively much more active after 1935 than before. This evidence indicates that the institutional

TABLE 6.4. *Regional Distribution of Mortgage Lending by Building (then Savings) & Loans: 1929–1940*

| Region | Outstanding B&L Loans ($000,000) | | | | 1-Family Homes Mortgaged to B&Ls in 1940 (000s of Homes) | | | |
| | 1929 | | 1939 | | Built Before 1936 | | Built 1936–39 | |
	Amount	% US	Amount	% US	Number	% US	Number	% US
U.S.	$7,787		$4,105		615.0		140.8	
Northeast		41.5%		35.1%		29.1%		14.8%
New England	$589	7.6%	$486	11.8%	37.4	6.1%	6.7	4.5%
Middle Atlantic	$2,642	33.9%	$953	23.2%	141.4	23.0%	14.4	10.3%
North Central		35.7%		34.9%		47.4%		29.0%
E. N. Central	$2,262	29.0%	$1,119	27.3%	224.7	36.5%	28.6	20.3%
W. N. Central	$520	6.7%	$311	7.6%	67.3	10.9%	12.2	8.7%
South		14.4%		21.0%		22.6%		37.3%
South Atlantic	$493	6.3%	$520	12.7%	71.4	11.6%	28.7	20.4%
E. S. Central	$166	2.1%	$127	3.1%	25.3	4.1%	6.1	4.3%
W. S. Central	$462	5.9%	$216	5.3%	42.6	6.9%	18.4	13.0%
West		8.3%		9.1%		9.4%		18.6%
Mountain	$128	1.6%	$70	1.7%	13.1	2.1%	5.1	3.6%
Pacific	$523	6.7%	$301	7.3%	44.9	7.3%	21.1	15.0%

Sources: Monthly Labor Review November 1930, 114–5; January 1941, 126–7.
Census of Housing, 1940, Vol. IV, *Mortgages on Owner-Occupied Nonfarm Homes, Pt. 1, Supp. A.*

transformation from B&L to S&L both accommodated to and was conditioned by the underlying regional shift in homebuilding activity.

Conclusion

The goal of this chapter has been to connect the modern S&L industry to its pre-1930 building and loan ancestor. The former has often been characterized as a creature of Depression-era federal intervention – this mischaracterization can now be laid to rest. The pre-Depression B&L and post–World War II S&L industries both responded to secular trends that dominated the residential housing industry over the entire twentieth century – an increase in the rate of mortgage-financed homeownership and a shift of homebuilding and the housing stock to the South and West. Furthermore, by the 1920s, the B&L industry had divided into two different types of intermediaries – small associations that employed traditional nineteenth-century methods, and larger, bureaucratic institutions that were operated by professional, full-time managers. Before 1930, building and loan leaders were drawn from and sympathetic to the second group of building associations, and by 1930 they had already anticipated and attempted to implement nearly all of the institutional modifications that were finally realized in Depression-era legislation. Finally, this same group of leaders supported, devised, wrote, and helped implement every piece of federal legislation that was S&L-related. By doing so they helped to create a modern S&L industry that they could only envision years before.

The broader goal of this chapter is to understand why the B&L/S&L industry that had experienced three periods of rapid and successful growth between 1880 and 1970, suddenly collapsed and disappeared in the 1980s. In order to complete this project, the analysis that has been presented here must be extended in two ways. Both involve the conflicts of interests that arise when real estate and building professionals organize and control the institutions that provide residential mortgage credit to their local markets. This pattern first appeared in the traditional building and loan industry and was then transmitted to the new savings and loan industry when the new federal savings and loan system was implemented during the 1930s. We first need to better understand how these conflicts of interest were, for the most part, successfully controlled in the new S&L industry during its successful postwar expansion (1945–1970). Central to this story, I believe, is the professionally managed, regulatorily protected S&L "model" that the USBLL worked so hard to implement in the 1930s in order to mitigate the ever-present threat of internal "exploitation," which they associated with the traditional B&L structure. With a better understanding of how the USBLL's "solution" succeeded for a quarter-century, we will be prepared to take a fresh look at the 1970–1985 deregulatory episode that dismantled much of what the USBLL had accomplished during the Depression, and the role these policies played in the demise of the modern S&L industry.

Bibliography

American Building Association News. "National Installment Loan Companies." Cincinnati, *American Building Association News,* 1923: 167–71, 210–2, 254–7, 311–3, 416–9, 460–3.

Barth, James, and Martin Regalia. "The Evolving Role of Regulation in the Savings and Loan Industry," in *The Financial Services Revolution,* eds. C. England and T. Huertas, Norwell, MA: Kluwer Academic Publishers, 1988, 131–61.

Besley, Timothy, Stephen Coate, and Glenn Loury. "The Economics of Rotating Savings and Credit Associations," *American Economic Review* 83 (September 1993): 792–810.

Bodfish, H. Morton. *History of Building and Loan in the United States.* Chicago: United States Building and Loan League, 1931.

Bodfish, H. Morton, and A. D. Theobald. *Savings and Loan Principles.* New York: Prentice Hall, 1938.

Brumbaugh, R. Dan. *Thrifts Under Siege.* Cambridge, MA: Ballinger, 1988.

Clark, Horace, and Frank A. Chase. *Elements of the Modern Building and Loan Associations.* New York: Macmillan, 1925.

Clarke, Thomas Hal. "Board Weighs Heavy Comment on Conflict Proposals," *The Journal of the Federal Home Loan Bank Board* (October 1970): 9–19.

Coggeshall, Ralph. *The Development of Building and Loan Associations in Minnesota.* Unpublished Thesis. Minneapolis: University of Minnesota, 1927.

Colean, Miles. *American Housing: Problems and Prospects.* New York: Twentieth Century Fund, 1944.

Colean, Miles, and R. Newcomb. *Stabilizing Construction: The Record and Potential.* New York: McGraw-Hill, 1952.

Dexter, Seymour. "Co-operative Savings and Loan Associations," *Quarterly Journal of Economics* 3 (1889): 315–35.

Ewalt, Josephine H. *A Business Reborn.* Chicago: American Savings and Loan Institute Press, 1962.

Federal Home Loan Bank Board. *Annual Report.* Washington, DC: Government Printing Office, Various years.

Federal Home Loan Bank Board. *Savings and Home Financing Source Book.* Washington, DC: Government Printing Office, Various years.

Fort, Franklin. "Federal Home Loan Bank System." *Building and Loan Annals 1933.* Chicago, United States Building and Loan League, 1933: 1–12.

Friend, Irwin, ed. *Study of the Saving and Loan Industry.* (4 Vols.). Washington, DC: Government Printing Office, 1969.

Grebler, Leo, David Blank, and Louis Winnick. *Capital Formation in Residential Real Estate.* Princeton: Princeton University Press, 1956.

Herman, Edward, S. "Conflicts in the Savings and Loan Industry," in *Study of the Saving and Loan Industry.* Vol. 2, ed. Irwin Friend. Washington, DC: Government Printing Office, 1969.

Kendall, Leon T. *The Savings and Loan Business.* Englewood Cliffs, NJ: Prentice-Hall, 1962.

Liebold, Arthur W. "Conflicts of Interest," *The Journal of the Federal Home Loan Bank Board* (June 1970): 17–24.

Lintner, John. *Mutual Savings Banks in the Savings and Mortgage Markets*. Boston: Harvard University, 1948.

Marvell, Thomas B. *The Federal Home Loan Bank Board*. New York: Praeger, 1969.

Minnesota. *Biennial Reports of the Public Examiner and Superintendent of Banks*. Fourth-Eleventh Reports. St. Paul, Public Examiner and Superintendent of Banks of the State of Minnesota, 1889–1904.

Piquet, Howard. *Building and Loan Associations in New Jersey*. Princeton, NJ: Princeton University Press, 1931.

President's Conference on Home Building and Home Ownership. *Slums, Large-Scale Housing and Decentralization*. Edited by J. M. Gries and J. Ford. Washington, DC: National Capital Press, 1932.

Riegel, Robert, and J. Russell Doubman. *The Building and Loan Association*. New York: John Wiley & Sons, 1927.

Smith, W. P. *Building and Loan Association: their Character, Operations and Advantages*. Boston: Moore and Crosby, 1852.

Snowden, Kenneth. "Mortgage Lending and American Urbanization, 1880–1890." *Journal of Economic History* 48 (1988): 273–285.

Snowden, Kenneth. "Building and Loan Associations in the U.S., 1880–1913: The Origins of Localization in the Residential Mortgage Market," *Research in Economics* 51 (1997): 227–50.

Stiglitz, Joseph. "Peer Monitoring and Credit Markets," *The World Bank Economic Review* 4 (1990): 351–66.

Teck, Alan. *Mutual Savings Banks and Savings and Loan Associations: Aspects of Growth*. New York: Columbia University Press, 1968.

U.S. Bureau of the Census. *Historical Statistics of the United States: Colonial Times to 1970: Part 2*. Washington, DC: Government Printing Office, 1975.

U.S. Bureau of the Census. *Mortgages on Homes*. Washington, DC: Government Printing Office, 1923.

U.S. Census Office. *The Report on Real Estate Mortgages in the United States*. Washington, DC: U.S. Census Office, 1895.

U.S. Census Office. *The Report on Farm and Home Proprietorship and Indebtedness*. Washington, DC: U.S. Census Office, 1895a.

U.S. Bureau of the Census. *Census of Housing 1930*. Washington, DC: Government Printing Office, 1930.

U.S. Bureau of the Census. *Census of Housing 1940: Vol. I & III*. Washington, DC: Government Printing Office, 1940.

U.S. Bureau of Labor Statistics. *Monthly Labor Review*. Washington, DC: U.S. Bureau of Labor Statistics, Various years.

U.S. Department of the Treasury. *1997 Office of Thrift Supervision Fact Book*. Washington, DC: Office of Thrift Supervision Dissemination Branch, 1997.

U.S. Department of the Treasury, Office of Thrift Supervision. "Historical Framework for Regulation of Activities of Unitary Savings and Loan Holding Companies." On website [online]. Washington, DC: 1997. Available at *www.ots.treas.gov*.

U.S. National Housing Agency. *Housing Statistics Handbook*. Washington, DC: Government Printing Office, 1948.

U.S. Savings and Loan League. *Fact Books*. Chicago, IL: U.S. Savings and Loan League, Various years.

Weiss, Marc. *The Rise of the Community Builders*. New York: Columbia University Press, 1987.

White, Lawrence. *The S&L Debacle*. New York: Oxford University Press, 1991.

Wright, Carroll. *Ninth Annual Report of the Commissioner of Labor: Building and Loan Associations*. Washington, DC: Government Printing Office, 1893.

III

OTHER FORMS OF INTERMEDIATION

7

Intermediaries in the U.S. Market for Technology, 1870–1920

Naomi R. Lamoreaux and Kenneth L. Sokoloff

The critical role played by intermediaries in the operation of financial markets is well known. Because entrepreneurs often lack sufficient savings to finance their ventures on their own and people with savings often do not have projects that will put their funds to profitable use, there are significant benefits to be derived from trades in which savers transfer funds to entrepreneurs in return for income in the form of interest or dividend payments. The problem, however, is that high transaction costs may prevent such mutually advantageous exchanges from occurring. Because it is costly for savers to assess the prospects of each entrepreneurial project, or conversely for entrepreneurs to convince savers individually of the merits of their ventures, many good (if risky) projects may be starved for support, while savings get channeled to more conventional, easier to evaluate, investments. Intermediaries can

We would like to express our appreciation to our research assistants Marigee Bacolod, Young-Nahn Baek, Dalit Baranoff, Lisa Boehmer, Nancy Cole, Yael Elad, Svjetlana Gacinovic, Anna Maria Lagiss, Huagang Li, Catherine Truong Ly, Homan Dayani, Gina Franco, Charles Kaljian, David Madero Suarez, John Majewski, Yolanda McDonough, Dhanoos Sutthiphisal, and Matthew Wiswall. We are also indebted to Marjorie Ciarlante and Carolyn Cooper for their assistance in accessing the Patent Office's assignment records at the National Archives, and to the many helpful archivists and librarians we encountered at the Rutgers University Library, the AT&T Archives, and the Harvard Business School's Baker Library. We have also benefited from the suggestions of Ann Carlos, Yongmin Chen, Lance Davis, Stanley Engerman, Louis Galambos, Laura Giuiliano, Stuart Graham, Rose Marie Ham, David Hounshell, Adam Jaffe, Zorina Khan, Margaret Levenstein, Kyle J. Mayer, Terra McKinnish, Richard Nelson, Ariel Pakes, Daniel Raff, Roger Ransom, Jean-Laurent Rosenthal, Bhaven Sampat, Deepak Somaya, William Summerhill, Peter Temin, Steven Usselman, David Weiman, Oliver Williamson, Mary Yeager, and participants in seminar presentations at Columbia University, Harvard University, McGill University, Queen's University, the University of California, Berkeley, the University of Colorado, the University of Toronto, the All-UC Group in Economic History, and at a conference held at the California Institute of Technology in honor of Lance Davis. We gratefully acknowledge the financial support we have received for this research from the National Science Foundation, as well as from the Collins Endowment and the Academic Senate at the University of California, Los Angeles.

significantly reduce this problem by mobilizing and pooling resources from savers and investigating the creditworthiness of alternative investment opportunities on their behalf. By thus economizing on information costs, intermediaries increase the efficiency with which existing savings are employed to support economic development. Moreover, because their activities raise the return to saving in the economy as a whole, they also have a positive effect on the pool of available investment funds.[1]

Similar kinds of transaction costs can impede both the generation and exploitation of technological knowledge. In the first place, the individuals who come up with ideas for new products or processes often need capital from outside investors in order to transform their visions into workable inventions. They thus face financing problems analogous to those of traditional entrepreneurs. In addition, because the comparative advantage of inventors typically stems from their creativity or specific knowledge, any time and resources they are compelled to devote to developing and commercializing their inventions may be relatively unproductively spent; indeed, they may, in fact, be poorly suited for these tasks. As a consequence, there are potential advantages to exchanges in which inventors sell or license the rights to the new technologies they have created to others better able to exploit their commercial potential. The problem, however, is that it is extremely costly for would-be buyers or lessors to assess the worth of the many and varied ideas that inventors devise. As in the case of financial markets, therefore, one might reasonably expect specialized intermediaries to emerge to economize on assessment costs and improve allocative efficiency.[2]

During the early twentieth century, large firms as diverse as General Electric, DuPont, and General Motors began to build in-house R&D laboratories. The apparent success of these investments, and the spread of this model to other important firms throughout the economy, led scholars to posit that vertical integration was a solution to the information problems associated with the market exchange of technological information. Indeed, some went so far as to argue that the development of complex technologies depended on the movement of R&D inside large, managerially coordinated enterprises.[3] Recent events, however, have brought this view increasingly

---

[1] Lance Davis and Robert Gallman, "Capital Formation in the United States During the Nineteenth Century," in *The Cambridge Economic History of Europe*, Vol. 7, part II, eds. P. Mathias and M. M. Postan (Cambridge: Cambridge University Press, 1978), 1–69.

[2] Although they do not discuss the technology sector, Ariel Rubinstein and Asher Wolinsky and Gary Biglaiser have provided theoretical rationales for the emergence of middlemen in industries with similar types of matching and assessment problems. See Rubinstein and Wolinsky, "Middlemen," *Quarterly Journal of Economics*, 102 (Aug. 1987), 581–94; and Biglaiser, "Middlemen as Experts," *Rand Journal of Economics*, 24 (Summer 1993), 212–23.

[3] See David J. Teece, "Technological Change and the Nature of the Firm," in *Technical Change and Economic Theory*, ed. Giovanni Dosi et al. (London: Pinter, 1988), 256–81; David C. Mowery, "The Relationship Between Intrafirm and Contractual Forms of Industrial Research

into doubt. Many large firms have reduced or even eliminated their research operations, and venture capital has flowed to smaller enterprises that focus on inventive activity and sell or license the resulting intellectual property – not infrequently to the same firms that earlier had built their own in-house labs.[4] These developments, which intriguingly have been most prominent in the "high-tech" sectors of the economy, mark a return, we argue, to an earlier pattern that scholars have neglected, perhaps because of their preoccupation with the rise of big business. As we show, over the course of the nineteenth century there was a tremendous expansion of market trade in technology that facilitated a division of labor across (rather than within) organizations between those who generated and those who exploited new technological knowledge. By enabling, indeed encouraging, creative but ambitious inventors to focus on what they did best, this division of labor gave rise to the most technologically fertile period in American history, at least as measured by patents issued on a per capita basis (see Figure 7.1).

In this chapter we examine some of the mechanisms through which this market for technology operated. We show that the U.S. patent system created a framework that supported trade in technology, and that the patent agents and lawyers who serviced this system often took on the functions of intermediaries, matching inventors seeking capital with investors seeking profitable outlets for their funds and also inventors seeking to sell new technological ideas with buyers eager to develop and commercialize them. Through systematic analysis of samples drawn from the Patent Office's manuscript records of patent sales and from other official sources, we explore the effect of these intermediaries on patentees' access to, and use of, the market for

in American Manufacturing, 1900–1940," *Explorations in Economic History*, 20 (October 1983), 351–74; and "The Boundaries of the U.S. Firm in R&D," in *Coordination and Information: Historical Perspectives on the Organization of Enterprise*, eds. Naomi R. Lamoreaux and Daniel M. G. Raff (Chicago: University of Chicago Press, 1995), 147–76; and Richard Zeckhauser, "The Challenge of Contracting for Technological Information," *Proceedings of the National Academy of Sciences*, 93 (Nov. 1996), 12743–48. Earlier scholars were more likely to attribute the success of these labs to the benefits of putting together teams of researchers to work systematically on technological problems. See, for example, Joseph A. Schumpeter, *Capitalism, Socialism, and Democracy* (New York: Harper, 1942); Alfred P. Sloan, *My Years at General Motors*, eds. John McDonald and Catharine Stevens (Garden City: Doubleday, 1964); and John Kenneth Galbraith, *The New Industrial State* (Boston: Houghton Mifflin, 1975).

[4] The principal explanations offered thus far for this change have focused on the effects of increases in the security of intellectual property rights and of expanded access to venture capital. For examples, see Josh Lerner and Robert Merges, "The Control of Strategic Alliances: An Empirical Analysis of the Biotechnology Industry," *Journal of Industrial Economics*, 46 (March 1998), 125–156; and Joshua S. Gans and Scott Stern, "Incumbency and R&D Incentives: Licensing the Gale of Creative Destruction," *Journal of Economics and Management Strategy*, 9 (Winter 2000), 485–511. For a general theoretical treatment, see Philippe Aghion and Jean Tirole, "The Management of Innovation," *Quarterly Journal of Economics*, 109 (Nov. 1994), 1185–1210.

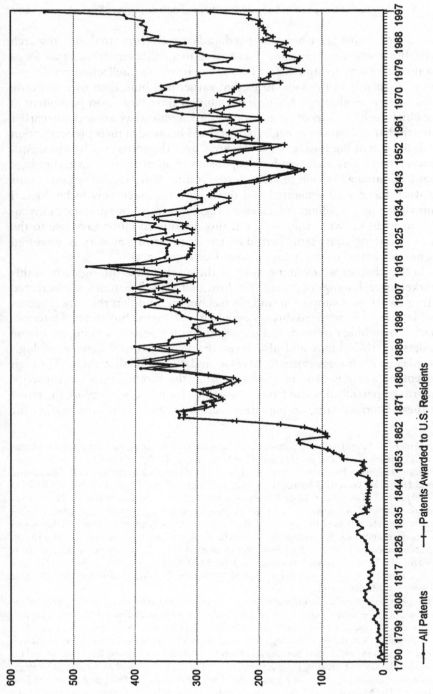

FIGURE 7.1. Rate of Patenting Per Million Residents in the United States, 1790–1998

— All Patents   —+— Patents Awarded to U.S. Residents

1790 1799 1808 1817 1826 1835 1844 1853 1862 1871 1880 1889 1898 1907 1916 1925 1934 1943 1952 1961 1970 1979 1988 1997

technology. Our findings suggest that intermediaries appear to have lowered transactions costs and improved the efficiency of exchange and that, as one might expect, inventors who were most specialized in patenting and most likely to sell off the rights to their intellectual property were the ones who made the most intensive use of intermediaries. We also provide evidence in support of the idea that the increased ability to extract returns from invention by selling off patent rights was in fact associated with a growing division of labor that enabled talented inventors to devote a greater proportion of their time and resources to creative work. In the final section of the chapter, we draw on a particularly rich set of papers for one patent attorney, Edward Van Winkle, to develop a more complete picture of what services these intermediaries provided to support the market for technology. Although Van Winkle's activities may not have been representative of patent attorneys in general, his papers open a window on a world that hitherto had been largely unknown – a world in which at least some patent attorneys played key informational roles at the center of overlapping groups of businessmen who were in effect operating much like modern-day venture capitalists, investing in new technologies and financing high-tech startups.

The U.S. Patent System and the Sale of Patent Rights

The patent system provided the institutional framework within which trade in technology evolved over the course of the nineteenth century. Consciously designed with the aim of encouraging inventive activity – and thus technological progress – the U.S. system provided the inventor of a device with an exclusive property right for a fixed term of years. Because patent rights were transferable assets, inventors who did not wish to exploit their inventions themselves could sell (assign) or lease (license) the rights to others.[5] Moreover, because a patent could be awarded only to the "first and true" inventor of a device, sellers of new technologies could reveal information to potential buyers at an early stage and still be protected against the possibility that someone else would patent their ideas.

Of course, this protection and, more generally, the ability of inventors to find buyers or licensees for their patents depended on the security of these property rights. From the beginning the law left responsibility for enforcing patents to the federal courts, and as Zorina Khan has shown, judges quickly evolved an effective set of principles for protecting the rights of patentees and also of those who purchased or licensed patented technologies. Subsequent legislation in 1836 instituted an examination system under which, before granting patents, technical experts scrutinized applications for novelty

---

[5] One important feature of the law was the requirement that patentees be individual men or women. Firms could not be awarded patents for ideas developed in their shops but could obtain the rights by assignment.

and for the appropriateness of claims about invention. This procedure made patent rights more secure by increasing the likelihood that a grant for a specified technology would survive a court challenge, and may also have provided some signal about the significance of the new technology. Thereafter, both patenting and sales of patent rights boomed.[6]

Although the main purpose of the patent system was to stimulate invention by granting creative individuals secure rights to their intellectual property, another important goal was to promote the diffusion of technological knowledge. The law required patentees to provide the Patent Office with detailed specifications for their inventions (including, where appropriate, working models), and the result was a central storehouse of information that was open to all. Anyone could journey to Washington and research others' inventions in the Patent Office files. In addition, more convenient means of tapping this rich source of information soon developed. The Patent Office itself opened branch offices around the country and published on a regular basis lists (some with descriptions of specifications and drawings) of the patents it granted. By the middle of the century, moreover, a number of private journals had emerged to improve upon these official services. One of the most important was *Scientific American*, published by Munn and Company, the largest patent agency of the nineteenth century. Others included the *American Artisan*, published by the patent agency Brown, Coombs & Company; the *American Inventor*, by the American Patent Agency; and the *Patent Right Gazette*, by the United States Patent Right Association (which, despite its name, functioned as a general patent agency). Covering the full spectrum of technologies, these journals featured articles about important new inventions, printed complete lists of patents issued, and offered to provide readers with copies of patent specifications for a small fee. Over time, the scope and number of these periodicals increased, reflecting an expanding and ever more articulated demand for information about new technologies. Moreover, specialized trade journals also appeared to report on developments in particular industries. The *Journal of the Society of Glass Technology*, for example, provided detailed descriptions of all patents taken out in the United States and Britain that were relevant to the manufacture of glass.

In addition to disseminating information about new technologies, these periodicals provided a forum for those seeking to sell rights in patents. *The Patent Record and Monthly Review*, for example, featured lists of "Inventions and Patents for Sale" and of "Partners Wanted: Capital Wanted to Develop these Inventions." The inventions described in these columns ranged

---

[6] See B. Zorina Khan and Kenneth L. Sokoloff, "Patent Institutions, Industrial Organization, and Early Technological Change: Britain and the United States, 1790–1850," in *Technological Revolutions in Europe: Historical Perspectives*, eds. Maxine Berg and Kristine Bruland (Cheltenham, UK: Edward Elgar, 1997), 292–313; and Khan, "Property Rights and Patent Litigation in Early Nineteenth-Century America," *Journal of Economic History*, 55 (March 1995), 58–97.

from the simple (curtain fastener, clothes line reel, can opener) to the complex (automatic street railway switch, rotary engine, flying machine).[7] Moreover, the texts of these brief advertisements suggest that inventors felt secure enough in their intellectual property to seek buyers actively for their inventions before they secured the protection of patents. The very titles of these lists (for example, "Inventions *and* Patents for Sale") provide evidence for this claim, as do the many advertisements that did not include patent numbers.[8] Because, all other things being equal, having a patent already in hand should have raised the value of the invention in the eyes of prospective buyers, it is reasonable to conclude that most of the inventions listed without patent numbers had not yet been protected in this manner.

It is, of course, difficult to know how effective any of these advertisements were, but the advice manuals that targeted audiences of inventors at this time generally agreed that such methods could work if they were coupled with other efforts. The best option "if the inventor [could] afford it" was to have the invention "illustrated and described in one or more of the scientific and mechanical publications of the day," like *Scientific American* or the *American Artisan*. But if the inventor did not have sufficient resources, it was still effective, the manuals claimed, to put a notice in the "regular advertising columns," especially if one took care to choose specialized publications that would "meet the eye of the class or classes of persons to whom the invention is of special interest."[9] In addition, however, the patentee was advised to prepare a circular describing his invention and its potential market, to procure a list of businesses most likely to be interested in the invention, and to mail the circular to these firms. He should then follow up these circulars with personal solicitations.[10]

Marketing a patent in this way was not only expensive but time consuming, and it distracted an inventor from more creative tasks. Not surprisingly, therefore, these publications also contained advertisements from individuals and companies offering to handle the sale of patent rights for inventors. For example, one issue of *The Patent Record* included advertisements from

---

[7] This particular journal claimed that its mission was "to bring the capitalist and inventor together for mutual benefit." It earned revenues from advertisements placed by both buyers and sellers of inventions. See *The Patent Record and Monthly Review*, New Series, 3 (Jan.–Feb. 1902), 47.

[8] See, for example, the lists in *The Patent Record and Monthly Review*, New Series, 3 (May 1902), 32.

[9] William Edgar Simonds, *Practical Suggestions on the Sale of Patents* (Hartford, CT: privately printed, 1871), 24–5; F. A. Cresee, *Practical Pointers for Patentees, Containing Valuable Information and Advice on the Sale of Patents* (New York: Munn & Co., 1907), 46–52.

[10] The quotes are from Simonds, *Practical Suggestions on the Sale of Patents*, 19–28; but for additional examples, see W. B. Hutchinson and J. A. E. Criswell, *Patents and How to Make Money Out of Them* (New York: D. Van Nostrand, 1899); An Experienced and Successful Inventor, *Inventor's Manual: How to Work a Patent To Make It Pay* (Rev. ed.; New York: Norman W. Henly & Co., 1901); and Cresee, *Practical Pointers for Patentees*.

Dr. J. O. White of Philadelphia asserting that he had "excellent facilities for placing a valuable patent, suited to that market, in Europe"; from Messrs. Comere & Co. announcing, "We have several customers wanting to purchase patented articles suited to the mail-order trade"; from the International Patent Promotion Company of Cleveland claiming, "We have a large number of good patents for sale and would be pleased to have you call your attention to this fact in your paper"; and from the Wouther Patent Promoting Co. of Roswell, Georgia declaring that "We promote patents, and if there are any inventors desiring their inventions promoted, would be glad to hear from them."[11]

More important, the patent agencies that published these kinds of journals were themselves in the business of buying and selling patents and, indeed, often saw their publications as a means to solicit inventions. Hence, the U.S. Patent Right Association used the pages of its *Patent Right Gazette* to tell inventors that it was the best agent to choose "if you wish to dispose of a Patent with the greatest possible certainty, in the shortest time and at its full value."[12] Similarly, the American Patent Agency heavily advertised the patent selling arm of its business in the *American Inventor*, crowing that it was "the only Agency for the sale of patents in America that has two PRINCIPAL OFFICES and permanent branch offices in all the prominent cities of the Union."[13] Although Munn and Company and Brown, Coombs and Company, the publishers respectively of *Scientific American* and the *American Artisan* (the two leading journals in the field), may not have so explicitly advertised such services, they too were functioning as intermediaries. An examination of manuscript assignment records for the years preceding and following the Civil War suggests that Munn and Company alone served as correspondent for roughly 15 percent of all of the contracts for the sale of patents recorded by the Patent Office in 1866, though by the mid 1870s its share had dropped to less than 5 percent.[14]

Beginning around this same time, advice manuals increasingly warned inventors to stay away from intermediaries who advertised in trade publications or mailed out circulars soliciting their business. Such agents, the writers of the manuals claimed, "are unreliable and seek only to get what money they can from the patentee. It is seldom indeed that most of them effect a sale." Although agents typically advertised that they sold patents on commission, they often charged up-front fees ranging from $25 to $250 to cover

[11] *The Patent Record and Monthly Review*, New Series, 3 (May 1902), 33.

[12] See, for example, the cover pages of *The Patent Right Gazette*, 3 (July 1872).

[13] See, for example, *American Inventor*, 6 (Jan. 1883), 23.

[14] These figures are based on an examination (for patentees whose surnames began with the letter "B") of the manuscript digests of assignments kept by the Patent Office. For a more complete description of these records, see footnote 29 and the accompanying text. The share for Munn and Co. appears to have increased from the 1840s and 1850s to the period just after the Civil War, and then dropped off rather substantially.

advertising costs. Patentees, therefore, bore relatively high costs with little assurance of return. Indeed, one writer went so far as to claim, "from long experience and observation," that he had "never known where a patentee was ever materially benefited by placing his interests in the hands of these concerns." He went on to assert that "very few of these concerns have any facilities whatever for selling patents," all of their time being taken up in "working inventors up to the remitting point which usually ends the matter so far as they are concerned."[15]

Rather than work through these kinds of agencies, inventors who needed help selling their patents were advised to seek the assistance of business people whom they knew they could trust. Some of the men to whom inventors thus turned were local manufacturers or merchants whose enterprises were completely unrelated to the purpose of the invention. Thus, when James Edward Smith, a machinist and professional inventor, designed a cigar machine, he approached George E. Molleson, owner of a granite quarry and agent for marble producers, for help in getting "a practical moneyed man who understood the manufacture of cigars to take an interest in Mr. Smith's cigar machine."[16] Molleson had previously advanced Smith money to help him develop a patent letter box. How the initial contact was made is unclear, but this previous association encouraged Smith to entrust the marketing of his cigar patent to Molleson. It may be that similar connections account for other cases where businessmen handled the sale of patents unconnected to their main areas of expertise. For example, intermediaries whose businesses were as diverse as textile manufacturing and engineering consulting submitted telephone inventions for sale to AT&T on behalf of inventors.[17]

More commonly, however, inventors turned for marketing assistance to the local attorneys and agents who processed their patent applications. After the 1836 law increased the security of patent rights and both patenting

---

[15] It is not entirely clear whether or not these advice manuals were including firms such as Munn and Co. among the agencies they were encouraging inventors to avoid. Probably not, given that these last quotes came from a pamphlet published by Munn and Co. It seems likely that, although their overall market share declined, firms like Munn and Co. were able to establish themselves as reputable enterprises, both because the journals they published were so prestigious and because they eschewed such questionable practices. For example, in response to an inquiry from an agent offering a patent for sale, Brown, Coombs, & Co, haughtily replied, "We [do] not interest ourselves in patents as a matter of speculation." Letter of 3 Dec. 1870 to Lemuel Jenks, Box 2, Folder 45, Mss. 867, Lemuel Jenks, 1844–1879, Baker Library, Harvard Graduate School of Business Administration. For the warnings, see Cresee, *Practical Pointers for Patentees*, 42–3; Hutchinson and Criswell, *Patents and How to Make Money Out of Them*, 161–2; An Experienced and Successful Inventor, *Inventor's Manual*, 61; and Simonds, *Practical Suggestions on the Sale of Patents*, 7–9.

[16] "Testimony Taken on Behalf of James Edward Smith," *Hammerstein v. Smith* (1890), 62–8, Case 13,618, Box 1868, Interference Case Files, 1836–1905, Records of the Patent Office, Record Group 241, National Archives.

[17] T. D. Lockwood, Reports of Inventions (Not Approved), 1904–8, Box 1383, AT&T Corporate Archives.

activity and trade in patented inventions took off, the numbers of these practitioners began to grow – first in the vicinity of Washington, D.C. (where, of course, the Patent Office was located), and then in other urban centers, especially in the Northeast (where the overwhelming majority of patented inventions were generated). By the early 1880s there were about 550 such agents registered to practice before the Patent Office. Slightly more than half of these were located in New England and the Middle Atlantic states, a quarter in the District of Columbia, another fifth in the Midwest, and the rest were scattered through a few southern and western locations.[18]

The ostensible function of these specialists was to shepherd inventions through the Patent Office's application process and, in the case of lawyers, to defend their clients' patents in interference and infringement proceedings. In the regular course of their business, however, patent agents and lawyers obtained a great deal of information about participants on both sides of the market for technology. They were used, for example, by buyers of new technology to evaluate the merits of inventions in advance of purchase, and, in this manner, gained knowledge about the kinds of patents buyers were interested in purchasing, as well as personal insight into the character of the people involved. Inventors, of course, used them to file patent applications, in the process providing them with advance information about technologies soon to come on the market. Moreover, inventors frequently developed close relationships with their patent agents, which encouraged them to try out new ideas on these specialists. For example, when Joseph Arbes, a fur manufacturer in New York City who also invented sewing machines, came up with an idea for a blind stitching machine that would use a flat-sided needle, he immediately dispatched a sketch of the needle to his attorney, William E. Knight, for a judgment as to its potential patentability. He had not even experimented with the needle on a sewing machine at that point, and both the casualness with which he made the request and the primitive state of his invention at that time suggest that he had an ongoing relationship with his attorney, who acted in part as a sounding board for his ideas.[19]

---

[18] U.S. Patent Office, *Roster of Registered Attorneys Entitled to Practice Before the United States Patent Office* (1883). The practice of inventors extracting income from their inventions by selling off or licensing the rights to their patents began early. Among a sample of "great inventors" active during the first half of the nineteenth century, roughly two-thirds derived some income from either the sale or licensing of their patent rights. It is also relevant to note that these great inventors were disproportionately located in those areas where patent agents and lawyers were concentrated. See B. Zorina Khan and Kenneth L. Sokoloff, "'Schemes of Practical Utility': Entrepreneurship and Innovation Among 'Great Inventors' in the United States, 1790–1865," *Journal of Economic History*, 53 (June 1993), 289–307. Around the turn of the twentieth century, Cresee estimated that only about one-fifth of inventors wanted to manufacture their devices themselves, whereas about four-fifths wanted to sell off the rights to others. See *Practical Pointer for Patentees*, 15.

[19] Knight apparently thought that the invention was not promising, so Arbes experimented with it for a few months before approaching Knight again. See "Testimony on Behalf of

Patent agents and solicitors were advantageously placed to function as intermediaries in another way as well: They often had links with colleagues in different cities who could be sources of information about new inventions originating elsewhere and about potential buyers for patents developed locally. Some of these links were formal. For example, Boston patent lawyer Frederick Fish took on a partner, Charles Neave, in 1893. Two years later Fish sent Neave to New York City to open a branch office.[20] Similarly, after Samuel S. Fisher, U.S. Commissioner of Patents during the Grant administration, returned to private practice in Cincinnati, he took in Samuel A. Duncan as a partner and almost immediately packed him off to New York to open an office for the firm there.[21] Other links derived from familial connections. For example, the Boston firm of Wright, Brown, Quinby, & May had ties with a Chicago firm established by the brother of one of the partners. Still other links were built up through letters of introduction and repeat business. Thus, Wright, Brown, Quinby, & May funneled their Philadelphia business through a firm with which the partners had no apparent personal connection but with which they had long done business. Virtually all patent agents, moreover, had regular dealings with at least one attorney in Washington, who assumed responsibility for conducting searches of patent records and also represented them in preliminary interviews with examiners in the Patent Office.[22] That these links to agents in other parts of the country could be used to market patents is suggested by a letter from one intermediary to "friend Jenks" (Lemuel Jenks, a patent lawyer), asking for Jenks's assistance in marketing the device: "We have offered said Patent so far to the B&O and NCRR Comps.... We intend to sell it to one person for the six New England States and I therefore wish you would give me your opinion in that matter: to viz what price you think we should ask; what would we have to pay you for your assistence [sic] in carrying and effecting a sale."[23]

Just as advice manuals cautioned inventors not to trust intermediaries who advertised in trade publications, there were warnings to be wary of unscrupulous patent agents and attorneys. Indeed, some practitioners themselves took

---

Joseph Arbes," 10, 22–3, 26, *Arbes v. Lewis* (1900), Case 20,049, Box 2,715, Interference Case Files, 1836–1905.

[20] John E. Nathan, *Fish & Neave: Leaders in the Law of Ideas* (New York: Newcomen Society, 1997), 13, 19.

[21] *In Memoriam: Samuel S. Fisher* (Cincinnati: Robert Clarke & Co., 1874), 23–4. It was common for individuals who worked in the patent office, even as simple examiners, to move on to become private patent agents later in their careers.

[22] For insight into such correspondent relations, see Wright, Brown, Quinby, & May Correspondence Files, Waltham Watch Company, 1854–1929, Mss. 598, Case 2, Baker Library, Harvard Graduate School of Business Administration.

[23] Letter of 30 April 1870 from Aug. H. Fick [last name not completely legible] to Jenks, Box 3, Folder 59, MSS 867, Lemuel Jenks, 1844–1879, Baker Library, Harvard Graduate School of Business Administration.

the extreme position that it was improper for members of their profession to function as intermediaries. Thus, H. W. Boardman & Company announced in a pamphlet promoting the firm's services that it was "a rule rigidly adhered to in this establishment, never to take contingent interests in applications for Patents, nor to negotiate sales of Patent rights, or become the owners in whole or in part of them." As the pamphlet explained, such activity potentially put the interests of the patentee in conflict with those of his attorney: "If an attorney become a dabbler in Patents (as many do), how is it possible for an Investor to be assured that he is not disclosing his secret to the very party who will be the most interested in defeating his application?"[24]

Certainly, when patent solicitors functioned as intermediaries, all kinds of conflicts of interest were possible. Although some patentees may have hesitated to reveal information about their inventions to agents who "dabbled" in patents in this way, the more likely problem was that agents interested in seeing transactions concluded may have put their own interests before those of either the patentee or the assignee. In this respect the market for technology can be thought of as much like the real estate market, where an agent's primary goal is a sale, and where buyers and sellers alike face a great deal of uncertainty about whose interest the agent is truly representing. Although these kinds of conflicts of interest have been mitigated in the case of real estate by a combination of regulation and self-policing, during the late nineteenth and early twentieth centuries the market for technology was largely unregulated, and professional organizations like the bar association were extremely weak. In such a context, one would expect to see reputational mechanisms playing an increasingly important role and to observe that successful patent agents and lawyers were those who made substantial investments in cultivating reputations for fair, as well as insightful, dealing.[25]

As we will show in the next two sections of this chapter, there is evidence that successful intermediaries did indeed make such investments and that, as a result, they were able to improve the efficiency of the market for patented technology. Before proceeding to this analysis, however, it is

---

[24] H. W. Boardman & Co., Solicitors of American & European Patents for Inventions, *Hints to Inventors and Others Interested in Patent Matters* (Boston: privately printed, 1869), 13. Practitioners in this wing of the profession also warned inventors that if they entrusted their inventions to agents who were primarily intermediaries rather than legal specialists, they risked obtaining patents that would not withstand scrutiny by the courts. "The result is, that out of the numerous patents which have been litigated since the foundation of our Patent System, not one in ten has been sustained by the courts without being reissued to cure defects." See the brochure of A. H. Evans & Co., Solicitors of American and Foreign Patents (Rev. ed.; Washington, DC: privately printed, n.d.), 1.

[25] For a more formal analysis of an analogous case, see Asher Wolinsky, "Competition in a Market for Informed Experts' Services," *Rand Journal of Economics*, 24 (Autumn 1993), 380–98.

important to note that the willingness of patent agents and lawyers to function as intermediaries sometimes made it possible for inventors without funds to gain access to patent protection in the first place. Although the cost of filing a patent application in the United States was modest by British standards, the $35 filing fee was still a substantial barrier for many wage earners. Moreover, even in routine cases, the additional charges associated with securing drawings, models, searches of patent office records, and legal assistance might add another $50 to $100 to total costs. Patent agents and lawyers who functioned as intermediaries might reduce or even waive many of these charges in the case of patents they thought were valuable, or they might find purchasers for the inventions who would bear the costs of applying for the patents. For example, Lansing Onderdonk, an inventor of sewing machines, testified that he did not have the funds to patent his lock-stitch invention. When he secured employment with the Union Special Sewing Machine Company, he tried to interest his new employers in the invention without success (the firm specialized in a different type of stitch). He was only able to patent the device when lawyer Charles L. Sturtevant took an interest in the invention and "said he would take the case and that I could pay him as I could."[26]

Quantitative Evidence on the Role of Intermediaries

It seems likely that, when patent agents and lawyers functioned as intermediaries in the market for technology, they improved the efficiency with which patents were traded. The sheer number of patents offered for sale by the late nineteenth century suggests that the knowledge these specialists were well positioned to acquire, both about inventions still on the drawing boards and also about the needs of potential purchasers of new technologies, would have helped them match sellers with appropriate buyers in an expeditious way.[27] It

[26] See "Deposition of witnesses examined on behalf of Lansing Onderdonk," 36–8, 47–8, *Onderdonk v. Mack* (1897), Case 18,194, Box 2,521, Interference Case Files, 1836–1905. The interference records are filled with statements by patentees that lack of funds had prevented them from patenting inventions or from filing applications in a timely fashion.

[27] Moreover, the personal knowledge that they were also able to acquire about parties on both sides of the market helped them solve information problems that were unique to these kinds of transactions. To give one example, suppose that a firm bought a patent from an independent inventor and the patent was subsequently challenged in an infringement or interference proceeding. Although an assignee could seek redress against an assignor who conveyed a patent later declared invalid, there were many instances in which the assignee's position vis à vis competitors depended on the successful defense of the patent – which in turn often depended on the cooperation of the patentee. For example, in an interference case (a proceeding set in motion when two inventors applied for or received patents for the same device), the outcome usually hinged on the inventors' relative ability to demonstrate priority by documenting the dates on which they conceived of the invention and reduced it to practice. Hence, when a firm bought an invention, it needed to know more than technical details. It needed personal knowledge of the patentee – the assurance that, if necessary, the

also seems likely that such intermediation would have had positive effects on the pace of technological change in general. By facilitating a division of labor that enabled inventors to spin off the distracting and time-consuming work of commercialization to others, intermediaries should have made it possible for creative people to focus their attention more exclusively on coming up with new technological ideas.

In this section, we explore these possibilities systematically, using the rich trove of data that the Patent Office has left to historians. These sources include published lists of patent grants that contain the names and places of residence of the patentees and of any assignees to whom the patentees transferred rights in advance of issue.[28] More important for the purposes of this chapter are the manuscript copies of contracts for the assignment of patent rights now stored in the National Archives. In order to be legally valid, a complete copy of any contract selling or transferring the right to a patent had to be deposited with the Patent Office within three months. Patent Office clerks maintained a chronological registry of these documents and, in addition, summarized their basic details into a separate digest that was organized chronologically but also divided into volumes according to the first letter of the patentee's surname.[29]

Our first step was to document the changes that occurred over the course of the nineteenth century in the way that rights to patents were most commonly sold. Although intermediaries potentially increased the efficiency with which patents could be marketed, their role was shaped in turn by the kinds of rights that purchasers most wanted to buy and patentees to sell. Inspection of the Patent Office's assignment records for the 1840s and 1850s – that is, for the period when the sale of patent rights first exploded after passage of the 1836 patent law – reveals that most of the contracts entailed geographically specific assignments to producers in different parts of the country. Such assignments, which constituted the vast majority of the total until well into the 1850s and as much as 90 percent during the 1840s, made a great deal of sense in a context where high transportation costs led to geographically segmented markets protected against competition from other regions. Even inventors engaged in exploiting their ideas themselves could increase their returns by selling geographically limited rights to their inventions in other parts of the country.[30] Once, however, the expansion of railroads and other

---

patentee would assist in a patent office or court proceeding and, further, that the patentee would be an articulate witness who would be able to document the priority and substance of his claim.

[28] See the *Annual Report of the Commissioner of Patents*, published by the Government Printing Office in Washington.

[29] See Record Group 241, Records of the Patent and Trademark Office.

[30] For an excellent example, see Carolyn Cooper's account of the assiduousness with which Thomas Blanchard, inventor of the gunstocking lathe and other wood-shaping inventions, assigned geographically limited patent rights to producers in distant areas. See *Shaping*

improvements in transportation and distribution made it possible for manufacturers in a single location to market their products nationally, producers increasingly wanted to purchase full national rights to technologies important in their businesses. Not surprisingly, the proportion of assignments that involved geographically limited rights began to decline rapidly. Table 7.1 reports descriptive statistics for all of the approximately 4,600 contracts filed with the Patent Office during the months of January 1871, January 1891, and January 1911. Already by 1871 geographic assignments accounted for less than a quarter of the total for the nation as a whole, though they retained greater importance in the Middle West, particularly in the West North Central states. By 1911, they had almost completely disappeared in all regions of the country.[31]

Table 7.1 also provides suggestive indications that the efficiency of the market for technology was increasing at the same time as the nature of the rights being sold was changing. In the first place, there was a drop in the proportion of secondary assignments (sales of patents where the assignor was neither the patentee nor a relative of the patentee). That there was less reselling of patents as time went on may be an indication that the market was doing a better job of matching patentees who wanted to sell patents with buyers who were well placed to exploit them. In any event, an increasingly large proportion of sales were being made directly by patentees to assignees who would hold on to the property rights for the duration of the grants.[32] Second, the table records a dramatic fall in the proportion of assignments that occurred after the date the patent was issued – from 72.3 percent of the total in 1870–71 to 36.5 percent in 1910–11. That patentees were able to sell their inventions earlier and earlier – increasingly before their patents were actually issued – may also be an important indication that the efficiency of trade in patents was improving.[33]

Invention: Thomas Blanchard's Machinery and Patent Management in Nineteenth-Century America (New York: Columbia University Press, 1991).

[31] Because of this shift away from multiple geographic assignments, the reported ratio of assignments in our sample to the total number of patents should not be interpreted as a measure of the proportion of patents that were ever assigned. Nor should trends in this ratio be taken to indicate trends in the proportion of patents assigned.

[32] The assignor might, however, license the right to use the invention to others. Although assignment contracts had to be filed with the Patent Office in order to be legally binding, there was no similar legal requirement to file licensing agreements. Our sample of assignment contracts does contain some licensing agreements, but they are very few in number, and anecdotal evidence suggests that those recorded in this manner were a declining proportion of the total of such agreements over time.

[33] At least part of the rise in the fraction of assignments that occurred before issue resulted from an increase in the length of time consumed by the application process. In order to get a rough idea of the extent of the increase, we compared two samples of 125 patents each drawn from the October 1874 and October 1911 issues of the *Official Gazette of the United States Patent Office*. In 1874 the median time between application and issue was 4 months and the mean 5.8 months. In 1911 the median was 12 months and the mean 18.2 months.

	1870–71	1890–91	1910–11
New England			
Assignment to Patenting Index	115.1	109.5	132.4
% Assigned After Issue	70.4	31.2	30.1
% Secondary Assignments	26.6	14.8	12.0
% Geographic Assignments	17.1	0.8	0.0
Middle Atlantic			
Assignment to Patenting Index	100.7	94.8	116.3
% Assigned After Issue	70.9	44.4	37.9
% Secondary Assignments	33.3	16.4	11.0
% Geographic Assignments	19.1	1.9	0.7
East North Central			
Assignment to Patenting Index	96.3	118.1	104.9
% Assigned After Issue	77.7	48.5	32.8
% Secondary Assignments	18.1	18.4	11.8
% Geographic Assignments	34.3	5.7	1.8
West North Central			
Assignment to Patenting Index	90.7	110.1	73.5
% Assigned After Issue	77.4	48.6	42.6
% Secondary Assignments	32.3	19.2	11.0
% Geographic Assignments	41.9	13.0	2.6
South			
Assignment to Patenting Index	60.0	68.9	68.0
% Assigned After Issue	74.4	42.3	48.2
% Secondary Assignments	27.9	11.3	19.1
% Geographic Assignments	20.9	6.2	2.5
West			
Assignment to Patenting Index	150.0	67.2	81.5
% Assigned After Issue	59.1	57.4	36.0
% Secondary Assignments	22.7	11.4	10.4
% Geographic Assignments	18.2	7.4	1.2
Total Domestic			
Assignment to Patenting Index	100.0	100.0	100.0
% Assigned After Issue	72.3	44.1	36.5
% Secondary Assignments	27.8	16.4	12.0
% Geographic Assignments	22.8	4.6	1.2
Assignments to Patents Ratio	0.83	0.71	0.71
Number of Contracts	794	1,373	1,869

Sources and Notes: Our sample consists of all assignment contracts filed with the Patent Office during the months of January 1871, January 1891, and January 1911. These contracts are recorded in "Liber" volumes stored at the National Archives. There are a total of about 4,600 contracts in our sample. Only those involving assignors that resided in the United States are included in this table. The assignment to patenting index is based on the ratio of assignments originating in the respective regions (given by the residence of the assignor) to the number of patents filed from that region in 1870, 1890, and 1910 respectively. In each year the index has been set so that the national average equals 100. The percentage of secondary assignments refers to the proportion of assignments where the assignor was neither the patentee nor a relative of the patentee. The percentage of geographic patent assignments refers to the proportion of assignments where the right transferred was for a geographic unit smaller than the nation.

Whether these changes signaled real advances in the operation of the market for technology and, if so, whether intermediaries were responsible for a significant proportion of the gains are issues that remain to be explored. We tackle these questions by exploiting an intriguing feature of the Patent Office's digests of assignment contracts – their inclusion of the names and addresses of the persons to whom all correspondence concerning assignments was to be addressed. Although some of these correspondents may simply have handled the paperwork associated with drawing up and recording contracts for the sale of patent rights, others likely functioned as deal makers. We investigate this possibility by testing whether change in the identity of these correspondents was systematically related to other developments in the market for technology – for example, increases in the speed with which patent rights were sold.

Examination of the digests of the assignment contracts for the 1840s and 1850s, when the great majority of assignments entailed geographically limited rights, suggests that there was wide variety in the identity of the correspondents. Many, of course, were principals in the transactions. Some of these were assignors who previously had received shares of the patents and who may have been taken on as partners with responsibility for marketing the rights. Many others were located near assignees who purchased rights limited to the geographic areas in which they resided. These correspondents may simply have been local attorneys with diverse practices. Assignees may have learned about the patents through other channels and have come to them to process the paperwork.[34]

Over time, however, the identity of the correspondents changed in important ways. As already mentioned, for a brief period around the Civil War, a substantial fraction of assignments was handled by the large patent agencies (such as Munn and Company) that published respected periodicals on technological developments. By the 1870s, however, the market share of these firms had begun to decline as patentees increasingly turned to specialized patent agents and lawyers to handle their assignments. In order to gauge the role that this new category of correspondents played in the market for technology, we collected information from the assignment digests on all of the contracts filed with the Patent Office during the first three months of 1871, 1891, and 1911 for patents whose inventors had surnames beginning with the letter "B."[35] We then classified each assignment contract (and the patents

---

34 This interpretation is supported by the observation that it was not uncommon for multiple geographically limited assignments of the same patent to be handled by different correspondents. That some of the correspondents during this period were merely processing paperwork is also implied by the identification of quite a few of them as congressmen.

35 We chose "B" because more surnames began with this letter than with any other. The sample included 286 contracts (involving 437 patents) from 1871, 423 contracts (858 patents) from 1891, and 614 contracts (880 patents) from 1911.

it included) by the identity of the correspondent. Working with lists of patent agents and lawyers from 1883 and 1905, we distinguished correspondents who were formally registered with the Patent Office in at least one of these two years as a separate class of intermediaries. Correspondents who were principals to the contract (either the patentee, the assignor, or the assignee of one of the patents involved) were grouped together in a second category of intermediaries. A third category consisted of third parties who did not appear on either of the two lists of registered agents. It seems likely, however, that we would have been able to identify some of these correspondents as registered agents if we had rosters for additional years. Finally, we include in an "unknown" category cases where no correspondent was reported in the digest. Because some of these contracts in the sample covered more than one patent, we present the data with the unit of analysis defined in two different ways: the individual patent assigned and the complete assignment contract (with the descriptive statistics calculated on the basis of the first patent described in the contract).

In Table 7.2 we report descriptive statistics (across both patents and contracts) for each of the correspondent classes for 1871, 1891, and 1911. As is immediately evident, the relative prominence of registered patent agents in this trade increased over time. Registered agents served as correspondents for 26.1 (29.7) percent of the patents (contracts) assigned in 1871, with their shares increasing to 42.7 (51.8) percent in 1891, and 55.7 (58.1) percent in 1911. The rise in importance of these registered agents was paralleled by a decline in the proportion of patent assignments handled by one of the principals (patentees, assignors, or assignees) – from 33.0 (33.9) percent of patents (contracts) in 1871 to 11.2 (9.5) percent in 1911. There was also a drop in the fraction handled by third parties, indicating that not only was there a shift over time toward the use of intermediaries, but there was a shift toward more specialized ones as well. That registered agents were indeed relatively more specialized in this activity is indicated by the higher average numbers of contracts they handled, compared to correspondents in the other categories. For example, in 1871 the average registered agent served as correspondent for 2.36 contracts, whereas the averages for principals and unregistered third parties were 1.05 and 1.26 respectively. These figures, moreover, undoubtedly underestimate the total number of contracts handled by specialized intermediaries, as they are based on only a small subset of all assignment contracts (3 months of assignments for patents whose patentees had surnames beginning with the letter "B").

The use of specialized intermediaries seems to have been particularly important for the types of assignments that, as we saw from Table 7.1, were growing in relative importance by the end of the century – that is, primary assignments that were geographically unrestricted. Although all types of correspondents handled roughly similar proportions of secondary assignments in 1871, by 1911 only 9 percent of the contracts mediated by registered

TABLE 7.2. *Descriptive Statistics on Patent Assignments, by Correspondent Type, 1871–1911*

		Registered Patent Agent	Patentee, Assignor, or Assignee	Third Party but not Registered	Unknown
1871					
Number	Patents	114	144	126	53
	Contracts	85	98	82	21
% of Total Number	Patents	26.1	33.0	28.8	12.1
	Contracts	29.7	33.9	29.4	7.0
Proportion Assigned	Patents	0.47	0.09	0.18	–
Before Issue	Contracts	0.61	0.08	0.23	–
Proportion Secondary	Patents	0.35	0.33	0.32	0.85
Assignments	Contracts	0.20	0.31	0.30	0.80
Proportion National	Patents	0.89	0.53	0.71	–
Assignments	Contracts	0.89	0.51	0.70	–
Proportion Assigned	Patents	0.28	0.24	0.20	0.66
to Company	Contracts	0.25	0.16	0.20	0.48
Prop. Where Patentee	Patents	0.46	0.28	0.40	0.32
in County With	Contracts	0.39	0.31	0.35	0.38
City of >100,000					
Patentees' Avg. 5-Yr.	Patents	3.90	3.73	3.35	4.69
Total of Patents	Contracts	2.45	3.10	3.27	3.05
Patentees' Avg. 5-Yr.	Patents	1.47	0.88	0.80	0.88
Total of Patents	Contracts	1.08	0.64	0.88	0.70
Assigned at Issue					
Avg. No. of Contracts					
Assigned by	Contracts	2.36	1.05	1.26	–
Correspondent					
1891					
Number	Patents	336	188	235	69
	Contracts	219	89	88	27
% of Total Number	Patents	42.7	21.9	27.4	8.0
	Contracts	51.8	21.0	20.8	6.4
Proportion Assigned	Patents	0.44	0.15	0.32	0.24
Before Issue	Contracts	0.52	0.18	0.40	0.37
Proportion Secondary	Patents	0.20	0.31	0.37	0.81
Assignments	Contracts	0.13	0.25	0.23	0.78
Proportion National	Patents	0.91	0.78	0.86	–
Assignments	Contracts	0.94	0.72	0.78	–
Proportion Assigned	Patents	0.39	0.28	0.48	0.68
to Company	Contracts	0.41	0.27	0.45	0.52
Prop. Where Patentee	Patents	0.51	0.45	0.55	0.58
in County With	Contracts	0.46	0.45	0.48	0.52
City of >100,000					
Patentees' Avg. 5-Yr.	Patents	6.61	3.65	5.80	5.45
Total of Patents	Contracts	4.90	3.43	5.17	3.00
Patentees' Avg. 5-Yr.	Patents	4.29	1.10	3.50	3.65
Total of Patents	Contracts	3.39	1.27	3.43	1.74
Assigned at Issue					

(continued)

TABLE 7.2. *(continued)*

		Registered Patent Agent	Patentee, Assignor, or Assignee	Third Party but not Registered	Unknown
Avg. No. of Contracts Assigned by Correspondent	Contracts	1.77	1.07	1.24	–
1911					
Number	Patents	467	94	189	89
	Contracts	337	55	112	77
% of Total Number	Patents	55.7	11.2	22.5	10.6
	Contracts	58.1	9.5	19.2	13.2
Proportion Assigned	Patents	0.70	0.15	0.31	–
Before Issue	Contracts	0.72	0.18	0.41	–
Proportion Secondary	Patents	0.15	0.28	0.31	–
Assignments	Contracts	0.09	0.24	0.21	–
Proportion National	Patents	0.97	0.69	0.89	–
Assignments	Contracts	0.97	0.69	0.92	–
Proportion Assigned	Patents	0.61	0.55	0.46	–
to Company	Contracts	0.57	0.47	0.51	–
Prop. Where Patentee	Patents	0.51	0.32	0.49	0.37
in County With City of >100,000	Contracts	0.50	0.40	0.43	0.39
Patentees' Avg. 5-Yr.	Patents	6.92	2.28	3.76	2.96
Total of Patents	Contracts	4.99	2.45	4.04	3.13
Patentees' Avg. 5-Yr.	Patents	5.97	0.69	2.66	2.49
Total of Patents Assigned at Issue	Contracts	4.21	0.84	3.11	2.64
Avg. No. of Contracts Assigned by Correspondent	Contracts	1.72	1.04	1.24	–

Sources and Notes: The data were collected from the Patent Office Digests of assignment contracts for patentees whose family names began with the letter "B." Our data set includes information on all such patent assignments filed with the Patent Office during the months of January through March for 1871, 1891, and 1911. Because some contracts involved the sale or transfer of more than one patent, and some encompassed multiple transfers of the same patent (such as the sale of a patent from A to B, and then another transfer of the patent from B to C), we report one set of figures computed over all patents assigned and another set computed over all contracts. For every patent in our sample of assignments, we compiled a five-year record of all of the patents received by the patentee, using the year of the assigned patent as the central year. From this record, we computed the total number of patents the patentee received over the five years and the total number of these patents that he assigned at issue. We categorized each assignment contract (and the patents it included) by the identity of the person to whom all correspondence about the assignments was to be addressed. Working with lists of patent agents and lawyers from 1883 and 1905, we distinguished correspondents who were formally registered with the Patent Office in at least one of these two years as a separate class of intermediaries. Correspondents who were principals to the contract (either the patentee, the assignor, or the assignee of one of the patents involved) were grouped together in a second category of intermediaries. A third category consisted of third parties who did not appear on either of the two lists of registered agents that we relied upon. It seems likely, however, that we would have been able to identify some of these correspondents as registered agents if we had rosters for additional years. Finally, we include an "unknown" category that is primarily comprised of cases where multiple patents were assigned together and where the details of the contract were summarized in the record of another patentee whose family name began with a letter other than "B," and was thus in another Digest volume.

agents (15 percent of patents) involved secondary assignments, as opposed to 24 (28) percent for principals and 21 (31) percent for unregistered third parties. As early as 1871, moreover, assignments handled by intermediaries (especially registered agents) were much more likely to be national in scope than those handled by principals. Fully 89 percent of the contracts for which the correspondent was a registered patent agent were national, as opposed to 70 percent for unregistered third parties and 51 percent for principals. Despite the general shift toward national assignments, the differences were still evident in 1911, when 97 percent of the contracts mediated by specialized agents were for national assignments but only 69 percent of the contracts handled by principals.

Although skeptics might object that the increased use of patent agents might simply reflect a growing tendency for employees to transfer patent rights to their employers, rather than a true professionalization of inter-mediation in arms-length trading of technology, the evidence in the table suggests otherwise. The reported percentages of patent assignments going to companies (as opposed to individuals), show that the trend over time to-ward assigning patents to companies accounts for very little of the change in the composition of correspondents. If we look at patents, for example, the proportion of the assignments handled by registered agents that went to companies (28, 39, and 61 percent in 1871, 1891, and 1911 respectively) was in general only slightly greater than the fraction in the category handled by principals (24, 28, and 55 percent in the respective years) and that handled by unregistered third parties (20, 48, and 46 percent). It seems, therefore, that the growth of trade in patented technologies over the late nineteenth and early twentieth centuries was indeed accompanied by the emergence and in-creased importance of agents who were specialized at working in that market.

If patent agents offered efficiency advantages in trading patents, we would expect to find that patentees who employed them were able to dispose of their rights more quickly than those who used less specialized intermediaries and than those who handled the sale of their patents themselves. Table 7.2 shows that this expectation is borne out by the data. In 1871, for example, 47 percent of the patent assignments (61 percent of the assignment contracts) handled by registered patent agents occurred before issue, as opposed to only 18 (23) percent for those handled by unregistered third parties and 9 (8) percent of those handled by principals. At this time, the average interval between application for and grant of a patent was very short – less than half a year. The high proportion of assignments handled by registered agents that nonetheless occurred before issue suggests that these specialists were indeed performing an important matching function – that, perhaps by cultivating long-term relationships with inventors, they were able to obtain advance information about new technologies coming on the market, and that they also had a sufficient range of contacts within the business community to enable them sell patents very quickly.

Table 7.3 provides additional evidence that the use of registered agents enabled inventors to dispose of their property rights more quickly than they could on their own. The table reports for different classes of correspondents the distributions of both primary and secondary assignments, broken down by the speed of assignment (measured relative to the date the patent in question was granted by the Patent Office). Once again, assignments handled by registered agents were much more likely to occur before the patent was actually issued than those handled by others. Conversely, registered agents were less likely to handle assignments that occurred more than five years after issue. These patterns, moreover, held in general for secondary as well as for primary assignments.

We can get a better sense of the importance of the role played by these specialized intermediaries by comparing the characteristics of patentees whose assignments were handled by registered agents to patentees who either negotiated their assignments themselves or relied on other principals (assignors or assignees) to do so. If intermediaries did indeed offer some advantage in trading patent rights, such as lower transactions costs, one would expect that the inventors who sought out relationships with them would be those who were both more specialized at inventive activity and more inclined to extract the returns to their efforts by selling off the rights to their inventions. In order to test this proposition, we retrieved, for each of the assigned patents in our sample, a five-year history of all patents received by the respective patentees (including information on whether the patent was assigned at issue), using the year the assigned patent was granted as the mid-year (thus, we looked two years back and two years forward from the base year). The results, which are reported in Table 7.2, indicate that the predicted pattern did develop over time.

In 1871, the average five-year total of patents awarded to patentees whose contracts were handled by registered agents was roughly similar to the numbers for patentees whose assignments were handled by the other categories of correspondents (although patentees whose contracts were handled by registered agents were somewhat more likely to assign their patents at issue). By 1891, however, a clear difference had emerged between patentees whose assignments were mediated by third parties and those who used principals as correspondents – both in terms of the average number of patents obtained over the five-year period and the proportion of those patents assigned at issue. As time went on, moreover, the use of the two types of intermediaries grew even more differentiated, such that by 1911 the tendency for patentees who were both most productive and most involved in the market to turn to registered agents to handle their contracts was even more pronounced. In that year, patentees who used registered agents averaged five-year totals of 6.92 patents weighting over patents (4.99 over contracts), compared to 3.76 (4.04) patents for those who used unregistered third parties and 2.28 (2.45)

TABLE 7.3. *Distribution of Assignments by Date and Type of Assignment and by Correspondent Class*

		Assignment Before Issue of Patent		After Issue, but Within 5 Years		Assignment More Than 5 Years After Issue		Total	
		No.	%	No.	%	No.	%	No.	%
1871									
Registered	Prim.	40	69.0	17	29.3	1	1.7	58	24.3
Patent Agent	Sec.	5	13.2	26	68.4	7	18.4	38	23.3
Principal	Prim.	12	12.8	77	81.9	5	5.3	94	39.3
	Sec.	0	–	39	86.7	6	13.3	45	27.6
Unregistered	Prim.	21	26.6	53	67.1	5	6.3	79	33.1
Third Party	Sec.	0	–	31	81.6	7	18.4	38	23.3
Unknown	Prim.	0	–	6	75.0	2	25.0	8	3.4
	Sec.	1	2.4	38	90.5	3	7.1	42	25.8
Total	Prim.	73	30.5	153	64.0	13	5.4	239	
	Sec.	6	3.7	134	82.2	23	14.1	163	
1891									
Registered	Prim.	141	48.3	127	43.5	24	8.2	292	50.3
Patent Agent	Sec.	20	27.0	40	54.1	14	18.9	74	27.1
Principal	Prim.	25	19.4	82	63.6	22	17.1	129	22.2
	Sec.	4	6.8	27	45.8	28	47.5	59	21.6
Unregistered	Prim.	60	40.8	59	40.1	28	19.1	147	25.3
Third Party	Sec.	14	16.1	47	54.0	26	29.9	87	31.9
Unknown	Prim.	7	53.9	2	15.4	4	30.8	13	2.2
	Sec.	9	17.0	28	52.8	16	30.2	53	19.4
Total	Prim.	233	40.1	270	46.5	78	13.4	581	
	Sec.	47	17.2	142	52.0	84	30.8	273	
1911									
Registered	Prim.	231	76.5	57	18.9	14	4.6	303	63.7
Patent Agent	Sec.	19	33.9	25	44.6	12	21.4	56	43.4
Principal	Prim.	12	18.8	40	62.5	12	18.8	64	13.5
	Sec.	1	4.6	17	77.3	4	18.2	22	17.1
Unregistered	Prim.	46	42.6	45	41.7	17	15.7	108	22.8
Third Party	Sec.	4	7.8	36	70.6	11	21.6	51	39.5
Total	Prim.	289	61.0	142	30.0	43	9.1	474	
	Sec.	24	18.6	78	60.5	27	20.9	129	

Sources: See Table 7.2.

Notes: The unit of analysis in this table is the patent. For 1911, we omit the unknown category because we have no information on the assignments as well as on the correspondents for those cases.

patents for those who used principals. Patentees who used registered agents also, on average, assigned markedly higher proportions of their patents at issue: 5.97 (4.21) of the patents they received during the five-year period, as opposed to 2.66 (3.11) for those who used unregistered third parties and 0.69 (0.84) for those who relied on principals.

The increased association between specialized inventors and specialized intermediaries is explored in another way in Table 7.4. Here the total number of contracts (appearing in our sample) that were handled by each correspondent is employed as an indicator, albeit perhaps a weak one, of his degree of specialization in this function. Although the choices of productive (or specialized) inventors appear to have been little different from those of other patentees in 1871, over time a stronger relationship between specialized inventors and specialized intermediaries emerged. For example, in 1911, 67 percent of the contracts involving the least productive patentees (those with only one patent over five years) were handled by correspondents with only one contract, and a mere 4 percent by correspondents with six or more contracts to their credit. By contrast, patentees with four or more patents over the five-year period were relatively more likely to have turned to correspondents with six or more contracts in our sample (who handled 16 percent of their contracts), and relatively less likely to use correspondents with only one (who handled 35 percent of their contracts). Although not strong evidence, this pattern is remarkably striking, given that our measure of a correspondent's degree of specialization includes only three months of assignments for patentees with surnames beginning with the letter "B" and, therefore, provides only a crude means of distinguishing between specialized and unspecialized correspondents.

The tendency for patentees with the greatest market involvement to turn to professional intermediaries is also evident in Table 7.5, which shows that as early as 1871, 80 percent of the patentees who assigned at issue more than 60 percent of their five-year total of patents (not including the patent involved in the assignment originally sampled from the Digest) made use of an intermediary (that is, a correspondent that was not a principal to the contract) for the recorded transaction, and that fully 50 percent employed a registered agent. Over time, moreover, the table reveals a general shift toward both higher rates of assignment and the use of registered agents. Indeed, by 1911 the modal cell in the entire distribution was patentees who assigned more than 60 percent of their five-year total of patents and who also used a registered agent. Two-thirds of the patentees who assigned more than 60 percent of their patents employed registered agents for the transaction sampled. These results provide intriguing support for the idea that because registered agents were more efficient at intermediation in the market for technology than other types of correspondents, inventors who wanted to make extensive use of the market sought them out.

TABLE 7.4. *Distribution of Contracts by the Five-Year Total of Patents Received by the Inventor and by the Number of Contracts Handled by the Correspondent*

		Number of Contracts Handled by Correspondent				
		1	2–3	4–5	6+	Total
1871 Patentees with						
1 Patent	Number	64	18	5	12	99
	Row %	65	18	5	12	
	Col. %	36	37	29	52	37
2–3 Patents	Number	73	17	6	10	106
	Row %	69	16	6	9	
	Col. %	41	35	35	43	39
4+ Patents	Number	43	14	6	1	64
	Row %	67	22	9	2	
	Col. %	24	29	35	4	24
Total	Number	180	49	17	23	269
	Row %	67	18	6	9	
1891 Patentees with						
1 Patent	Number	79	24	3	10	116
	Row %	68	21	3	9	
	Col. %	35	23	10	26	29
2–3 Patents	Number	66	31	14	19	130
	Row %	51	24	11	15	
	Col. %	30	30	48	50	33
4+ Patents	Number	78	50	12	9	149
	Row %	52	34	8	6	
	Col. %	35	48	41	24	38
Total	Number	223	105	29	38	395
	Row %	56	27	7	10	
1911 Patentees with						
1 Patent	Number	137	35	23	9	204
	Row %	67	17	11	4	
	Col. %	48	27	37	21	39
2–3 Patents	Number	83	32	13	3	131
	Row %	63	24	10	2	
	Col. %	29	25	21	7	25
4+ Patents	Number	64	61	27	30	182
	Row %	35	34	15	16	
	Col. %	23	48	43	71	35
Total	Number	284	128	63	42	517
	Row %	55	25	12	8	

Source: See Table 7.2.

TABLE 7.5. *Distribution of Assigned Patents by Correspondent Type and by Proportion of Patentee's Five-Year Patents that were Assigned at Issue*

Proportion of Five-Year Patents Assigned at Issue	Registered Patent Agent		Inventor, Assignor, or Assignee		Unregistered Third Party		Unknown		Total	
	No.	Row %	No.	Row %	No.	Row %	No.	Row %	No.	Col. %
1871										
0	10	13.7	17	23.3	20	27.4	26	35.6	73	46.5
0+ to 0.2	0	–	3	30.0	4	40.0	3	30.0	10	6.4
0.2+ to 0.4	11	29.7	19	51.4	6	16.2	1	2.7	37	23.6
0.4+ to 0.6	5	29.4	5	29.4	7	41.2	0	–	17	10.8
>0.6	10	50.0	4	20.0	6	30.0	0	–	20	12.7
Total	36	22.9	48	30.6	43	27.4	30	19.1	157	
1891										
0	40	28.4	57	40.4	33	23.4	11	7.8	141	27.6
0+ to 0.2	9	25.7	4	11.4	16	45.7	6	17.1	35	6.9
0.2+ to 0.4	14	28.6	12	24.5	19	38.8	4	8.2	49	9.6
0.4+ to 0.6	20	37.7	8	15.1	15	28.3	10	18.9	53	10.4
>0.6	134	57.5	21	9.0	56	24.0	22	9.4	233	45.6
Total	217	42.5	102	20.0	139	27.2	53	10.4	511	
1911										
0	26	44.8	10	17.2	20	34.5	2	3.5	58	9.3
0+ to 0.2	4	33.3	4	33.3	4	33.3	0	–	12	1.9
0.2+ to 0.4	8	57.1	0	–	4	28.6	2	14.3	14	2.2
0.4+ to 0.6	17	73.9	2	8.7	3	13.0	1	4.4	23	3.7
>0.6	275	66.6	19	4.6	66	16.0	53	12.8	520	82.9
Total	330	52.6	35	5.6	97	15.5	58	9.3	627	

Sources: See Table 7.2.

Notes: The unit of analysis in this table is the patent. For each patent, the proportion of five-year patents assigned at issue was calculated by subtracting from the patentees' five-year total the patent originally sampled from the digest of assignment contracts and then computing for the remaining patents the proportion assigned at issue.

The literature on financial markets, to which we alluded in our introduction, makes the case that intermediaries not only improved the efficiency with which funds were transferred from savers to investors, but also raised the level of savings in the economy. One might expect that the appearance of intermediaries between buyers and sellers of patented technology might have had a similar effect on the pace of technological change by encouraging creative people to specialize in invention. Unfortunately, we cannot test this proposition directly, but the evidence that we can present is highly suggestive. For example, the effect of the growth of the market

TABLE 7.6. *Assignment of Patents at Issue, 1870–1911*

	1870–71	1890–91	1910–11
Number of Patents	1,563	2,031	2,512
% of Patents Assigned	18.4	29.3	31.1
% of Assignments to Group Including Patentee	52.1	41.5	25.4
% of Assignments in Which Patentee Assigned Away All Rights to Unrelated Individuals	24.7	11.1	10.4
% of Assignments in Which Patentee Assigned Away All Rights to a Company	23.6	47.1	64.2
% of Assignments in Which Patentee Assigned Away All Rights to a Company with the Same Name as the Patentee	5.6	11.8	9.2

Sources and Notes: The table is based on three random cross-sectional samples of patents drawn from the *Annual Report of the Commissioner of Patents* for the years 1870–71, 1890–91, 1910–11. The three samples total slightly under 6,600 patents, including those granted to foreigners. The table includes only patents awarded to residents of the United States. The category "% of Assignments to Group Including Patentee" consists of patents assigned to one or more individuals including the patentee, an individual with the same family name as the patentee, or an individual specifically designated as an agent for the patentee. Patents assigned to companies with the same last name as the patentee were included in the general category of patents assigned to companies, as well as in the particular category of companies with the same name as the patentee. It is, of course, also possible that patentees had an ownership stake in companies that did not bear their name.

for patented technology on the assignment behavior of inventors can be traced in Table 7.6, which reports descriptive statistics for three random cross-sectional samples of patents drawn from the *Annual Report of the Commissioner of Patents* for the years 1870–71, 1890–91, and 1910–11. It is important to note that the table only includes assignments that were arranged in advance of the grant of the patent. Nonetheless, we can see from the table that there was a sharp increase over time in the proportion of patents thus assigned – from 18.4 to 31.1 percent. There was also a pronounced shift toward assignments in which patentees transferred all rights to their intellectual property to buyers with whom they had no formal connection. In 1870–71, for example, more than half of the assignments (52.1 percent) went to groups that included the patentee. By 1910–11 this proportion had fallen to 25.4 percent. At the same time, the share of assignments going to companies increased sharply from 23.6 percent in 1870–71 to 64.2 percent in 1910–11. Although some of these transfers involved companies in which the patentee had an ownership interest (for example, the proportion made to companies bearing the patentee's name increased from 5.6 percent in 1870–71 to 9.2 percent in 1910–11), the vast majority were arms-length sales. As we have shown in other work, assignments by employees to the firms that employed them were not a major determinant of the increased frequency of assignments at issue or the trend toward assignments to companies.[36]

That this increased ability to sell off patent rights did indeed make it possible for creative individuals to specialize in inventive activity is supported by the evidence in Table 7.7, which we constructed first by selecting from our three random cross-sectional samples patentees whose surnames began with the letter "B" and then by collecting data on all the patents awarded to these individuals over the twenty-five years before and after they appeared in one of our samples. We analyze the patenting and assignment behavior of these individuals in two ways: by including in our calculations each patent they obtained and by selecting for analysis only one patent per patentee (the patent included in the original cross-sectional sample). The table reports descriptive statistics for four categories of patentees: those who did not assign their patent before issue; those who assigned the patent but also maintained an ownership interest in it; those who assigned away all of their rights to the patent to an individual; and those who assigned full rights to a company.

As Table 7.7 shows, in each of the three time periods patentees who assigned all their rights to companies by the time of issue had very different careers of inventive activity than other groups of patentees. They received many more patents over time, were active at inventive activity for a longer period, and assigned away a much higher proportion of the patents they were awarded. The contrasts are evident as early as the 1870–71 cohort, but they are much starker by 1910–11. For example, the means computed over patentees (patents) drawn in the 1910–11 cross-section indicate that those who assigned their patents at issue to companies received 32.6 (135.6) patents over their careers on average, whereas those who did not assign, those who made only partial assignments, and those who made full assignments to individuals were granted 6.4 (38.2), 2.6 (24.4), and 3.0 (39.2) patents on average.

In general, Table 7.7 highlights the emergence over time of two rather sharply differentiated classes of inventors. The first was comprised primarily of individuals who tended to retain control of the relatively few patents they received over rather short careers at invention. These occasional inventors had little involvement with the market for technology. The other class of inventors, by contrast, had careers that were largely shaped by the market.

---

[36] See Naomi R. Lamoreaux and Kenneth L. Sokoloff, "Inventors, Firms, and the Market for Technology in the Late Nineteenth and Early Twentieth Centuries," in *Learning by Doing in Firms, Markets, and Countries*, eds. Naomi R. Lamoreaux, Daniel M. G. Raff, and Peter Temin, eds. (Chicago: University of Chicago Press, 1999), 31–40.

TABLE 7.7. *Descriptive Statistics on the Careers of Patentees in the "B" Sample*

	1870–71	1890–91	1910–11	Total
	Means Computed Over Patentees			
Not Assigned at Issue				
Avg. No. of Patents	8.0	10.0	6.4	7.9
Length of Career (Yrs.)	13.2	14.7	11.1	12.7
Career Assign. Rate (%)	8.3	11.5	9.2	9.6
Number of Patentees	121	117	178	416
Percent of All Patentees	84.6	63.9	75.7	74.2
Share Assignment				
Avg. No. of Patents	5.4	11.1	2.6	6.9
Length of Career (Yrs.)	10.6	13.5	8.1	11.0
Career Assign. Rate (%)	67.1	75.3	87.5	76.7
Number of Patentees	13	19	14	46
Percent of All Patentees	9.1	10.4	6.0	8.2
Full Assign. to Individual				
Avg. No. of Patents	5.3	29.0	3.0	12.1
Length of Career (Yrs.)	12.0	18.3	5.3	11.9
Career Assign. Rate (%)	52.1	74.1	76.4	66.7
Number of Patentees	7	6	6	19
Percent of All Patentees	4.9	3.3	2.6	3.4
Full Assign. to Company				
Avg. No. of Patents	30.0	23.7	32.6	28.0
Length of Career (Yrs.)	25.5	21.7	23.5	22.6
Career Assign. Rate (%)	62.1	70.7	80.9	75.2
Number of Patentees	2	41	37	80
Percent of All Patentees	1.4	22.4	15.7	14.3
	Means Computed Over Patents			
Not Assigned at Issue				
Avg. No. of Patents	20.0	39.7	38.2	33.7
Length of Career (Yrs.)	21.5	28.2	26.0	25.6
Career Assign. Rate (%)	14.2	23.5	22.0	20.4
Number of Patents	900	1264	1053	3217
Percent of All Patents	80.0	50.1	43.8	53.1
Share Assignment				
Avg. No. of Patents	19.3	40.5	24.4	30.7
Length of Career (Yrs.)	20.7	27.5	25.6	25.4
Career Assign. Rate (%)	39.9	66.5	62.8	59.4
Number of Patents	75	156	108	339
Percent of All Patents	6.6	6.2	4.5	5.6
Full Assign. to Individual				
Avg. No. of Patents	27.3	76.5	39.2	58.6
Length of Career (Yrs.)	26.1	30.6	28.3	29.2

(continued)

TABLE 7.7. *(continued)*

	1870–71	1890–91	1910–11	Total
Career Assign. Rate (%)	40.3	77.0	70.9	67.9
Number of Patents	82	224	74	381
Percent of All Patents	7.3	8.9	3.1	6.2
Full Assign. to Company				
Avg. No. of Patents	35.9	62.5	135.6	101.8
Length of Career (Yrs.)	26.6	32.9	35.1	33.9
Career Assign. Rate (%)	53.3	78.0	85.5	81.3
Number of Patents	73	880	1168	2121
Percent of All Patents	6.5	34.9	48.6	35.0

Sources and Notes: The table is based on a longitudinal dataset constructed by select-ing all of the patentees in the cross-sectional samples (see Table 7.6 for a description) whose family names began with the letter "B" and collecting information from the *An-nual Report of the Commissioner of Patents* on the patents they received during the twenty-five years before and after they appeared in the samples. This data set contains information on 6,057 patents granted to 561 "B" inventors. The top panel treats each patentee as a single case, based on the patent that appeared in the cross-section. The bottom panel analyzes each patent obtained by the patentee separately. Patentees are divided into categories depending on whether the patent in the original cross-section was assigned at issue or not and how that assignment was made. The career assignment rate includes only assignments at issue.

They assigned away a high proportion of their inventions (especially to companies) and were quite focused on generating patented inventions, re-ceiving many patents over careers that extended over several decades. Most prolific patentees fell into this second category, and it would seem reasonable to conclude on the basis of the evidence we have collected that the market for technology played a central role in enabling them to specialize in this creative activity.

The Case of Edward Van Winkle

The quantitative evidence thus supports the contention that the use of spe-cialized intermediaries like patent agents and lawyers improved the efficiency of the market for patented technology. Ideally, we would like to collect data on the activities of a broad sample of these specialists so that we can doc-ument the ways in which they facilitated the sale of patent rights, but most patent agents and lawyers have left only fragmentary traces in the historical record. The fortuitous preservation of one set of business diaries, however, has enabled us to track the activities of one such solicitor, Edward Van Winkle, in unusually close detail. Van Winkle resided in Jersey City, New Jersey, but worked in New York City. In January 1905, he moved into a new office in the Flatiron Building in lower Manhattan, and for the rest of that year we are able to analyze the relationships he cultivated with men on both sides of the market for technology and to observe the various ways in which he performed the function of intermediary.[37]

Like many patent agents of the time, Van Winkle's formal training was in engineering rather than law. He was a graduate of Columbia University, and his diary records the pride with which he displayed his certificate of membership in the American Society of Mechanical Engineers, as well as the eagerness with which he sought positions in other engineering societies.[38] By contrast, Van Winkle's legal education was quite casual. In 1905, he enrolled in Sprague's Correspondence School, signed up for courses in contracts, agency, partnerships, corporations, and real property, studied the assigned texts during his spare time, took written examinations in these subjects, and received a Certificate of Law – all in the space of five months.[39]

As befitted his training, Van Winkle earned part of his living as an engineering consultant. For example, in 1905 he was employed by various parties to determine the horsepower needed for a hydraulic pump, design the hub of an automobile wheel, and calculate specifications for a twelve-story apartment house project.[40] By contrast, he did no legal work outside the area of patents and, indeed, hired other lawyers to represent his interests in lawsuits or to process incorporation papers.[41] Even in the area of patents, his legal knowledge seems to have been limited. For example, he asked around and got the name of someone "who is very capable in foreign patent application work" and thereafter subcontracted much of this kind of business to him.[42] He also did relatively little of the more complex side of patent law, such as defending inventors' rights in infringement proceedings. Like other patent lawyers, however, he had long-standing relationships with solicitors in other parts of the country. For example, he routinely used the Washington firm of Evans & Company to conduct searches of patent office records and preliminary interviews with patent examiners.[43] As we will see, he also had extensive dealings with an agent in another city named Zappert.[44]

---

[37] Our main source for the following discussion is Van Winkle's 1905 Diary, but other relevant papers include "Accounts: Personal and Business 1904–1916" and "Reports on Patents, 1905–1907." See Edward Van Winkle Papers, Ac. 669, Rutgers University Libraries Special Collections.

[38] For example, his entry for 22 June, 1905 proudly recorded that the council of the Canadian Society of Civil Engineers "had passed upon my application for associate grade."

[39] See entries for 4 Mar., 6 Mar., 9 Mar., 11 Mar., 3 Apr., 13 Apr., 17 Apr., 10 May, 15 May, 19 May, 10 Jul., 11 Jul., and 24 Jul., 1905, Van Winkle Diary.

[40] 6 Jan., 10 Jan., 18 Jan., 19 Jan., 27 Feb., 15 May, 16 May, and 22 May, 1905, Van Winkle Diary.

[41] See, for example, 24 June, 26 June, and 30 June, 1905, Van Winkle Diary.

[42] 1 May, 1905, Van Winkle Diary.

[43] See, for example, 23 Mar. and 1 June, 1905, Van Winkle Diary.

[44] Zappert's city of residence is unclear, but was certainly not New York because the only contacts between the two men recorded in the diary occurred by letter. See 11 Mar., 27 Mar., 20 Apr., 28 Apr., 1 June, 2 June, and 12 June, 1905, Van Winkle Diary.

Van Winkle's engineering expertise enabled him to provide technical assistance to businessmen interested in purchasing patents. For example, Frank P. Parker and Frederick J. Bosse brought him a "non-refillable bottle" and several other devices invented by John L. Adams and requested that he test the inventions and assess their patentability. When Van Winkle reported positively, the men engaged him to process Adams's patent applications and also papers assigning the patents to themselves.[45] Parker and Bosse seem to have invested in these patents with the aim of reselling them, for Van Winkle's diary includes a couple of entries noting visits by potential purchasers, including one businessman who indicated that, though his company did not want to take up the invention, he himself "would be interested to look at it."[46] It is unclear, however, whether Van Winkle had lined up these potential customers – that is, whether he was functioning as an intermediary in these instances – or whether he was simply providing information to prospective buyers contacted by Parker and Bosse.

On other occasions, however, Van Winkle clearly played the role of intermediary – sometimes on behalf of inventors and sometimes on behalf of purchasers of patents. He noted in his diary, for example, that inventor S. A. Davis "placed in my hands a matter of adjusting royalties + disposing of his drophead patent and said he would give me half of what I collected."[47] A businessman named Kendall dropped by Van Winkle's office to discuss letting him "have the foreign patents in melting furnaces." Later Kendall called again, and "we started the ball a rolling for sale of foreign pats of the Rockwell furnace." Among the first steps Van Winkle took in marketing these patents was to forward information about them to Zappert, an agent in another city with whom he had ongoing contact.[48] Van Winkle also worked from time to time as an intermediary on behalf of parties in other cities. For example, after Zappert wrote and sent him "specimens + literature" about a dry adhesive photographic mounting process, he "took it around to Chas Walsh + he thought it would be a valuable thing to control, he is going to get ideas on the matter and see what he can do towards making some money out of the scheeme [sic]."[49]

In some cases Van Winkle himself took a position in a patent as part of the deal. Thus, an inventor named Pratt "agreed to let me have that patent [for a differential valve motion] on a shop right royalty of 10¢ and

---

[45] See the diary entries for 12 Jan., 2 Feb., 22 Mar., 23 Mar., 29 Mar., 6 Apr., 20 Apr., 28 Apr., and 16 Aug., 1905. On 29 Dec., 1905, the same two men brought in a soap shaving machine invented by a Mr. Luis for Van Winkle to examine and evaluate.

[46] 29 Mar., 1905, Van Winkle Diary. See also 21 July, 1905.

[47] 5 Jun., 1905, Van Winkle Diary.

[48] 28 Apr., 9 May, 1 June, and 2 June, 1905, Van Winkle Diary.

[49] 27 Mar., 1905, Van Winkle Diary.

all over that sum I would have if I sold."[50] Indeed, there is evidence that Van Winkle actively sought such participations. For example, he told one of the officers of the Davis, Redpath Company, that "I would sell him the Canadian patent for 5000^{xx} + if he would assine [sic] me" and do certain other things not specified in the diary entry, "[I] would be willing to go in with him."[51] On still other occasions, he displayed an interest in investing in a new technology long before it got to the patent stage. After "Sol Katz called with a kite proposition," he began to study kites and flying machines and visit the shops of people who were experimenting with the devices. A month late he and Katz agreed jointly to put up money for the development of a promising invention.[52]

As one might expect, Van Winkle's work as intermediary sometimes put him in situations where there was a clear conflict of interest. For example, W. N. Richardson, one of the businessmen with whom he regularly dealt, wanted an option to buy out inventor Edward A. Howe's interest in some patents. Van Winkle recorded Richardson's offer as follows: "He will give $3000 to 4000 for the last two patents and give me a commission of 10%. If I can get the patents for less, will receive a larger fee."[53] Van Winkle called on Howe and "had a hard fight to get Howe to accept terms." Ultimately, however, after a session that lasted two and a half hours, Howe agreed to accept Richardson's terms "provided R will give him a free hand in all future patents."[54] Somehow, throughout all of these negotiations, Van Winkle managed to be completely above board with the inventor about his interest in the deal. He maintained excellent relations with Howe, who continued to do business with him for the rest of the period of the diary. Indeed, after Richardson later decided not to take up the patents, Howe confided to Van Winkle that he had "only signed option so that I [Van Winkle] could collect my fee." Although this statement should probably not be taken at face value, it is an indication of the strength of the relationship that Van Winkle had been able to build with this inventor.

That Van Winkle was able to cultivate relations of trust with a number of inventors is evinced by their willingness to come back to him again with new ideas. For example, Adams, who invented the nonrefillable bottle, subsequently approached him seeking "money on a tooth pick scheme. Saturated wooden toothpicks with spice flavors that are antiseptic auromatic

---

[50] 9 June, 1905, Van Winkle Diary.
[51] 25 May, 1905, Van Winkle Diary.
[52] To Van Winkle's disappointment, the inventor later backed out of the deal. See 7 June, 16 June, 17 June, 18 June, 9 July, 17 July, 23 July, 3 Aug., 4 Aug., 19 Sept., 24 Sept., 12 Nov., 13 Nov., 21 Nov., 4 Dec., 18 Dec., 1905, Van Winkle Diary.
[53] 16 May, 1905, Van Winkle Diary.
[54] 16 May and 17 May, 1905, Van Winkle Diary.

[sic], etc."⁵⁵ Previous work for Pratt involving elevator and escalator devices was what had led Pratt to return and suggest the deal for the differential motion valve.⁵⁶ Similarly, Katz had earlier used Van Winkle to file a patent for a shoe heel.⁵⁷

Not surprisingly, Van Winkle devoted a great deal of his time to cultivating these kinds of personal relationships – not just with inventors but also with businessmen interested in investing in patents. Van Winkle's diary shows that he spent the bulk of each day receiving visitors, calling on people, and talking business over lunch and dinner at the Columbia Club or other similar places. This constant round of face-to-face meetings helped Van Winkle build relationships of trust with parties on both sides of the market. In addition, these meetings became an important source of tips about potential buyers for inventions, new technologies for Van Winkle to explore, and clients he might attract to his practice. Thus, when Van Winkle was handling an elevator safety invention for Pratt, he received information from a friend with whom he often dined "that C. L. C. Howe of the N.Y. Life Co was looking for a safety for Elevators." Van Winkle called on Howe that very afternoon, noting in his diary that "There might be something doing later."⁵⁸ On another occasion, he lunched with Charlie Halsey, who "said he had some cigarette machine patents + papers which he would bring to my office and let me look over."⁵⁹ A similar lunch with Robert E. Booream, an inventor whose work embraced electric bridge hoists, washers for gold mining, and methods of roadway construction, yielded the notation that the two men had "lightly touched on business. We will no doubt be associated."⁶⁰ Van Winkle's use of the word "associated" suggests that he envisioned his work with Booream to encompass more than simply filing patent applications, and the diary entries show him later putting Booream in contact with a mining engineer.⁶¹

A few businessmen appeared over and over again in the pages of the diary as purchasers of, or investors in, patents. One of the most striking things about these men is the wide variety of technologies in which they displayed an interest. Richardson, for example, was involved in patents for hat-frame formers, rails for high-speed railroads, electric railroad systems, and pliers.⁶² Another businessman, Arthur DeYoung, was in frequent contact to discuss technologies as diverse as coin counters, arc lamps, and dry

---

⁵⁵ 28 Sept., 1905, Van Winkle Diary.
⁵⁶ 7 Feb., 17 Feb., 2 Mar., 23 Mar., and 27 Apr., 1905, VanWinkle Diary.
⁵⁷ 4 Feb., 5 Apr., and 22 May, 1905, Van Winkle Diary.
⁵⁸ 31 Mar., 1905, Van Winkle Diary.
⁵⁹ 8 Aug., 1905, Van Winkle Diary.
⁶⁰ 24 Jan., 1905, Van Winkle Diary. See also 5 Mar., 7 June, and 12 June, 1905.
⁶¹ 7 June, and 8 June, 1905, Van Winkle Diary.
⁶² See, for examples, 30 Jan., 16 Mar., 17 Mar., 1 Apr., 1 May, and 7 May, 1905, Van Winkle Diary.

mounting processes for photographs.[63] The most intriguing case is a man who is identified in the records only as Mr. Oliver, although he was closely associated with Van Winkle in a number of important deals. Oliver's investments spanned the full gamut of technologies, from envelopes to drills to arc lamps to sewing machines to signaling systems for railroads.[64]

The wide variety of technologies in which these men were interested suggests that they were not primarily manufacturers seeking to purchase new inventions to improve the efficiency of their enterprises or expand their product lines. Instead, they seem to have been functioning essentially as venture capitalists eager to profit from cutting-edge technologies by getting in on the ground floor. Sometimes getting in on the ground floor simply meant purchasing the rights to promising new technologies. Richardson, for example, typically operated this way. Similarly, Oliver offered an inventor named Peters a note for $100,000 in exchange for the assignment of a patent for a wireless receiver – after Oliver and Van Winkle had thoroughly discussed possible complications from the Deforrest Company, the value of foreign patents, and the likelihood of marketing the device to the U.S. government.[65]

Sometimes, however, getting in on the ground floor meant much more – meant actually organizing companies to develop and exploit an invention's potential. Van Winkle was involved in at least two such promotions during the period of the diary: the Simplex Machine Company and the Automatic Security Signal Company.[66] Both efforts concerned inventions patented by William M. Murphy, and in each case Van Winkle worked closely with Oliver. These promotions suggest that the roles of patent agents as intermediaries could extend far beyond simply matching inventors with potential buyers of their patents. Although Van Winkle did not handle the formal legal work associated with incorporation, he did everything else: He brokered agreements between the inventor and the main investors, arranged for the inventor to assign his patents to the company, arranged for the application and sale of foreign patents, worked to find buyers for the companies' securities and customers for the companies' products, and even helped the inventor

[63] See, for examples, 6 Jan., 28 Jan., and 13 June, 1905, Van Winkle Diary.

[64] See, for examples, 1 Jan., 4 Feb., 16 Feb., 23 Feb., 7 Apr., 11 May, 20 May, and 6 Sept., 1905, Van Winkle Diary. Oliver also financed the invention of a cloth guide for sewing machines by Van Winkle himself. See entries for 24 Aug. and 29, Aug., 1905.

[65] See diary entry for 20 May, 1905. Oliver and Peters subsequently had some disagreement about the terms of the arrangement, and it is not clear from the diary whether the deal actually went through. See also 21 Jan., 24 Jan., 25 Feb., 28 Feb., 2 Mar., 13 May, 22 May, and 27 May, 1905, Van Winkle Diary.

[66] Van Winkle was also involved with DeYoung in a coin-counting venture, but the two men appear to have been shut out of the resulting company and had to negotiate to have their interests in the patents bought out. See 6 Jan., 28 Jan., 23 Feb., 4 Mar., 9 Aug., 16 Aug., 18 Aug., and 14 Sept., 1905, Van Winkle Diaries.

work out knotty technical details.[67] In exchange, he received payment in the form of shares in the new company's stock. In the case of Simplex, for example, he received 25 out of 500 shares; Murphy received 175.[68]

Although we have no basis for assuming that Van Winkle was representative of the general population of patent lawyers, his diary nonetheless offers an intriguing window on the market for patented technology, allowing us to observe in close detail some of the ways in which patent attorneys might improve the efficiency of this kind of trade. The diary provides concrete evidence of the extensive investments that intermediaries had to make in cultivating the trust of participants on both sides of the market – the time and resources that had to be devoted to building personal relations with inventors and also with businessmen who were potential buyers of patented technology. The diary also highlights the very personal nature of many of the channels through which information about inventions flowed during this period. Despite the existence of publications that specialized in reporting new technological developments, the operation of the market for technology depended to a large extent on the circulation by word of mouth of details about new inventions that had not yet been fully worked out – details patent agents and lawyers were uniquely well placed both to obtain and assess. More interesting still, the diary opens a window on a world hitherto largely unknown – a world in which businessmen who were operating in effect as venture capitalists eagerly purchased interests in patents, and where attorneys like Van Winkle not only helped them by assessing the investment potential of new inventions, but also played a vital role in bringing businessmen and inventors together in companies formed to exploit these promising new technologies.

Although much work needs to be done to assess the extent and importance of such activities during the late nineteenth and early twentieth centuries, evidence from interference records and other sources suggests that Van Winkle and his associates were by no means alone. For example, Lansing Onderdonk, a sewing machine inventor, testified that he and patent attorney Henry P. Wells had been part of a group that had organized a business, in the early 1880s, to exploit a combination plaiting and ruffling attachment for sewing machines.[69] The president of the Bonsack Machine Company, Demetrius B. Strouse, was none other than the patent attorney who had

---

[67] See 27 Feb., 22 Mar., 14 Apr., 20 Apr., 11 May, 12 May, 5 June, 15 June, 21 June, 26 June, 17 July, 8 Aug., and 14 Aug., 1905, Van Winkle Diary.

[68] See page inserted by the entry of 27 July, 1905, Van Winkle Diary. Neither of these companies appear to have been successful, but that is a subject for another paper.

[69] See "Deposition of witnesses examined on behalf of Lansing Onderdonk," 32–4, *Onderdonk v. Mack* (1897), Case 18,194, Box 2,521, Interference Case Files, 1836–1905.

filed James A. Bonsack's original cigarette machine patents.[70] To give a final, but very suggestive example, patent lawyer Grosvenor Porter Lowrey played an important role in putting together financing for Thomas Edison's work in electric lighting. Lowrey was a partner in the firm of Porter, Lowrey, Soren, & Stone and also general counsel for Western Union. In this latter capacity, he had handled a number of patents for Edison and had developed a close relationship with the inventor. Edison was thinking of working on electric lighting, but had put the idea aside because he could not see how to come up with the funding he needed for the project. Lowrey came to his aid by putting together "a syndicate of his friends and closest business associates," including some of his legal partners, colleagues from Western Union, and personal friends such as the Fabbri brothers, partners in Drexel, Morgan, & Company. Financing from this group enabled Edison to create the primitive research lab at Menlo Park where he conducted his experiments with incandescent lighting. When the experiments proved successful, Lowrey convinced essentially the same people to organize the Edison Electric Light Company in 1878.[71]

Conclusion

This chapter has investigated the institutions that helped to make the late nineteenth and early twentieth century such a fertile period in U.S. technological history. As we have argued, the creation of a well-developed market for patented technology facilitated the emergence of a group of highly specialized and productive inventors by making it possible for them to transfer to others responsibility for developing and commercializing their inventions. The most basic of the institutional supports that made this market possible was, of course, the patent system, which created secure and tradable property rights in invention. But, as we have argued, trade was also facilitated by the emergence of intermediaries who economized on the information costs associated with assessing the value of inventions and helped to match sellers and buyers of patent rights. Patent agents and lawyers were particularly well placed to provide these kinds of services, because they were linked to similar attorneys in other parts of the country and because, in the course of their regular business activities, they accumulated information about participants on both sides of the market for technology. As our quantitative analysis of assignment contracts demonstrated, patentees whose assignments were handled by these specialists assigned a greater fraction of their patents and

---

[70] See "Testimony on Behalf of Bonsack," 45–46, *Bohls v. Bonsack* (1893), Case 15,678, Box 2,159, Interference Case Files, 1836–1905.

[71] See especially Jocelyn Pierson Taylor, *Mr. Edison's Lawyer: Launching the Electric Light* (New York: Topp-Litho, 1978), 32–4.

also were able to find buyers for their inventions much more quickly than other patentees.

In the case of financial markets, scholars have argued that the emergence of banks and other similar kinds of formal intermediaries not only improved the efficiency with which capital was transferred from savers to investors, but also had a more profound effect on the economy by raising the general level of savings and investment. Although we do not have the evidence we need to test formally whether levels of inventive activity were similarly spurred by the appearance of specialized intermediaries in the market for patents, our results provide at least circumstantial support for such a view. Thus, we have shown that inventors who were most specialized in patenting (that is, had the greatest numbers of patents over a five-year period) and who were most involved in the market (that is, had assigned a higher fraction of these patents at issue) made the most extensive use of registered intermediaries. Moreover, our analysis of the longitudinal "B" sample indicates that inventors who were most involved in the market both had the longest patenting careers and received the highest numbers of patent grants over their careers. In other words, the development of institutions supporting market trade in patented technology seems to have made it possible for creative individuals to specialize more fully in inventive work – that is, it seems to have set in motion the kind of Smithian process that generally has been associated with higher rates of productivity, in this case in the generation of new technological knowledge.

8

Beyond Chinatown: Overseas Chinese Intermediaries on the Multiethnic North-American Pacific Coast in the Age of Financial Capital

Dianne Newell

Studies of capital have expanded beyond examinations of traditional forms – land, labor, and physical capital – to considerations of human capital, and most recently, social capital. Social capital, which Michael Woolcock recently defined as a broad term encompassing "the information, trust, and norms of reciprocity inhering in one's social networks," has become an important contemporary measure of the well-being of individual nations.[1] The concept of social capital is an integral aspect of the field of *new economic sociology*. Its potential to broaden our understanding of the historical interactions between economic and social relations and institutions suggests its relevance also to the field of economic history. Important contributions to the social capital literature, for example, include Naomi Lamoreaux's examination of insider lending in New England banks in the nineteenth century and Avner Greif's studies of reputation and coalitions in medieval trade.[2] Here, I

[1] Michael Woolcock, "Social Capital and Economic Development: Toward a Theoretical Synthesis and Policy Framework," *Theory and Society* 27 (1998): 153–55.
[2] Avner Greif, "Reputation and Coalitions in Medieval Trade: Evidence on the Maghribi Traders," *Journal of Economic History* 49 (1989): 857–82; Greif, "Contract Enforceability and Economic Institutions in Early Trade: The Maghribi Traders' Coalition," *American Economic Review* 83 (1993): 525–49; Greif, "Cultural Beliefs and the Organization of Society: A Historical and Theoretical Reflection on Collectivist and Individualistic Societies," *Journal of Political Economy*, 102 (1994): 912–50; and Naomi R. Lamoreaux, *Insider Lending: Banks, Personal Connections, and Economic Development in Industrial New England*. (Cambridge: Cambridge University Press, 1994).

I am grateful to the volume editors for the opportunity to participate in this publication; to Robert Allen, Michael Bordo, Larry Neal, Angela Redish, Skip Ray, and others for their encouragement and suggestions; and to Brian Elliot, Glen Peterson, Skip Ray, Ed Wickberg, and Henry Yu for commenting on an earlier draft. Two students, Joanne Mei Poon (who provided special assistance with the Yip Sang papers and translated passages of the Chinese-language portions of both the Sam Kee and Yip Sang collections) and Tara Crittenden, and a UBC-Humanities and Social Sciences Research Grant assisted with the work. Special thanks to Lance Davis who, together with the late Robert Gallman, inspired and befriended so many of us over the years.

discuss the complex comprador-like role of the overseas Chinese merchant–contractor on the Pacific Coast of North America in the late-nineteenth and early-twentieth centuries, and I review the business strategies of two Vancouver Chinatown merchant–contractors involved in the (ostensibly) Japanese-owned salt-herring industry in British Columbia. The overseas Chinese are often cited as a prime example of "middleman minorities." In social capital terms, middlemen minorities are those domestic and immigrant minority groups that when faced with adversities have been able to create and exploit disbursed sets of linkages reaching beyond their own communities to tie into the larger economy. This study points to the need to explore more fully a critical economic aspect of the age of finance capital: the functioning of multiethnic business frontiers and the integrative role of social capital in and between ethnic minorities.

Social Capital and Ethnic Minorities

The concept of social capital has a long history but in its recent manifestation, it is, among other things, a refinement of Mark Granovetter's imaginative but rather loose concept of embeddedness. Granovetter has argued that a sophisticated account of economic action must consider its embeddedness in the ongoing structures of social relations.[3] The popular example of traditional social capital, and of embeddedness, is a type of informal credit and loan arrangement that the anthropologist Clifford Geertz first identified in the 1960s as the "rotating credit association."[4] This institution existed among the Chinese at home and abroad, the Japanese in Japan and parts of the United States, and Nigerian and West Indian migrants to the U.S. and Britain, for example.[5] It even survives today among the ethnic Koreans in Los Angeles and New York and the Pakistani in Manchester,

---

[3] Mark Granovetter, "Economic Action and Social Structure: The Problem of Embeddedness," *American Journal of Sociology* 91 (1985): 481–510.

[4] Alejandro Portes and Julia Sensenbrenner, "Embeddedness and Immigration: Notes on the Social Determinants of Economic Action," *American Journal of Sociology* 98 (1993): 1322, 1333. See Clifford Geertz, "The Rotating Credit Association: A Middle Rung in Development," *Economic Development and Cultural Change* 10 (1962): 241–63; also Shirley Ardner, "The Comparative Study of Rotating Credit Associations," *Journal of the Royal Anthropological Institute* 94, pt. 2 (1964): 202–29. Besley, Coate, and Loury observe that these ubiquitous economic institutions "have attracted surprisingly little attention from economists." Timothy Besley, Stephen Coate, and Glenn Loury, "The Economics of Rotating Savings and Credit Associations," *American Economic Review* 83 (1993): 792–810.

[5] Ivan H. Light, *Ethnic Enterprise in America: Business and Welfare among Chinese, Japanese, and Blacks* (Berkeley: University of California Press, 1972), 27–36; Ivan Light and Edna Bonacich, *Immigrant Entrepreneurs* (Berkeley: University of California Press, 1988), Chapter 10.

England.[6] It was and still is a fairly spontaneous arrangement by which members linked by kin and ethnic ties pledge a monthly sum to a common pot that is allocated to members in rotation, sometimes by auction. It exemplifies social capital, because its advantages depended entirely upon the existence of the mutual trust of the members and widespread, institutionalized mutual confidence within the broader ethnic community. Without high levels of trust and confidence, Ivan Light observes, it was not possible to form rotating credit associations in response to spontaneous individual needs quickly and in sufficient size to produce commercially useful proportions.[7] Default problems were circumvented by exploiting the social connectedness of the members, in a process that Alejandro Portes and his colleagues identify as "enforceable trust."[8]

Portes and Julia Sensenbrenner note the frequent use of immigration research to study social capital among minority communities, an observation that is important to our discussions here. The use of immigration studies makes sense, they write, "because foreign-born communities represent one of the clearest examples of the bearing contextual factors can have on individual economic action. With skills learned in the home country devalued in the receiving labor market and with a generally poor command of the receiving country's language, immigrants' economic destinies depend heavily on the structures in which they become incorporated and, in particular, on the character of their own communities. Few instances of economic action can be found that are more embedded."[9]

But if it is also true that an immigrant community's stock of social capital can not only promote but also "derail" economic goal seeking, as Portes and Sensenbrenner, among others, argue, and that "strong intra-community ties, or high levels of integration, can be highly beneficial to the extent that they are complemented by some measure of [extra-community] linkage," as Woolcock explains (drawing on Granovetter's influential idea about the strength, or cohesive power, of "weak" ties), how are immigrant minority groups – often faced with a climate of racism and feared discrimination – able to forge let alone maintain the necessary linkages to the wider business community?[10]

[6] Roger Waldinger, Howard Aldrich, Robin Ward, and Associates, *Ethnic Entrepreneurs: Immigrant Business in Industrial Societies*, Sage Series on Race and Ethnic Relations, Volume 1 (Newberry Park: Sage, 1990), 138.

[7] Light, *Ethnic Enterprise in America*, Chapter 2.

[8] Alejandro Portes and Min Zhou, "Gaining the Upper Hand: Economic Mobility Among Immigrant and Domestic Minorities," *Ethnic and Racial Studies* 15 (1992): 514; Portes and Sensenbrenner, "Embeddedness and Immigration," 1325–27, 1332–38. See also Besley, Coate, and Loury, "The Economics of Rotating Savings and Credit Associations," 794.

[9] Portes and Sensenbrenner, "Embeddedness and Immigration," 1322.

[10] Portes and Sensenbrenner, "Embeddedness and Immigration"; Woolcock, "Social Capital and Economic Development," 174; and Mark Granovetter, "The Strength of Weak Ties," *American Journal of Sociology* 78 (1973): 1360–80.

The classic studies of "minority capitalism" by Light, Portes, Bonacich, and others provide clues to a possible answer. They demonstrate that a set of ethnic and racial minorities – the Chinese in Southeast Asia, the Jews in Central Europe, the Arabs in West Africa, the Indians in East Africa, and more recently, the Koreans in the United States – have occupied a similar position in the social structure: middleman minorities.[11] These older studies produced findings about middlemen minorities that are familiar popular assumptions today. Middlemen minorities have constituted separate and distinct communities within which it was possible to tap into familiar institutions and embedded ties. They have tended to concentrate in trade and commerce as agents, collectors, and contractors who assisted the flow of goods and services through the larger economy. They have been skilled at adapting traditional institutions and practices to new settings, at developing marginal niches and connections in the wider economy, and at capitalizing on their experience and local ties to invest savings in new lines of business (where possible). Whether by design or default, the successful businesses they developed have been small firms, labor-intensive, owned and operated by minority members, and geared to specialized markets.[12] For obvious reasons, they have tended to avoid competition with the host society.

Avoiding competition with the host society not only prevented middlemen minorities from participation in specific economic activities, it usually drove them into intense competition with other ethnic minority communities.[13] Intense competition with other minority communities was not an automatic outcome, however, because entrepreneurial flexibility has been a key to the economic and social success of immigrant middlemen minorities. For example, an alternate strategy for immigrant middlemen minorities in multiethnic societies, in their attempts, as Woodcock writes, "to forge broader and autonomous ties beyond the [resources of family and peers] as their need for larger markets and more sophisticated inputs expands," has been to forge and strengthen ties with other immigrant and ethnic minority communities.[14] Thus, although conventional wisdom suggests that

---

[11] Light, *Ethnic Enterprise in America*; Portes and Zhou, "Gaining the Upper Hand"; Portes and Sensenbrenner, "Embeddedness and Immigration"; and Edna Bonacich, "A Theory of Middleman Minorities," *American Sociological Review* 38 (1973): 583–94. See Bonacich and Modell's list of groups studied (before 1980) as examples of middleman minorities: Edna Bonacich and John Modell, *The Economic Basis of Ethnic Solidarity: Small Business in the Japanese American Community* (Berkeley: University of California Press, 1980), Appendix B.

[12] Bonacich and Modell summarize the older work on middleman minorities in *The Economic Basis of Ethnic Solidarity*, Chapter 2.

[13] See Peter S. Li, *The Chinese in Canada*. 2nd ed. (Toronto: Oxford University Press, 1998), Chapter 4.

[14] Woolcock, "Social Capital and Economic Development," 175, citing Granovetter, "The Strength of Weak Ties," on the social mechanism Granovetter calls "coupling and decoupling."

middlemen minorities simply facilitated the two-way flow of goods and services in an economy, in reality, their social and economic relationships were more complex, fluid, and strategic.

Portes and Min Zhou find importantly that "given the disadvantages that [immigrant] firms face when competing in the mainstream market, the proximity of other minorities that have been unable to develop a strong entrepreneurial presence offers a convenient niche facilitating expansion." They further suggest that certain middleman groups, such as the Cubans and the Chinese in the U.S., have been able "to operate among other minorities with whom they share certain cultural affinities contributing to fictive ethnic solidarity... The diffusion of supra-national ethnicities such as 'Hispanic' or 'Asian' [for example] plays directly into the hands of immigrant entrepreneurs by enabling them to expand their markets without the friction usually confronted by other middleman groups."[15] The potent idea that unexpected, somewhat clandestine, economic relationships might form under the mantle of fictive ethnic solidarity – of supra-national ethnicities – is worth investigating in the case of the economic success of the first generation of overseas Chinese in the developing regional economies of the North-American Pacific Coast.

OVERSEAS CHINESE COMMUNITY FORMATIONS

Michael Godley argues that "of all immigrant peoples, the Chinese in Southeast Asia (known to the Chinese as *Nanyang*) may well have been the most remarkable... the six hundred years or so during which the Chinese have taken up residence... have been marked by a loyalty to the homeland and culture uncommon in other groups beyond the first few generations, and by a paradoxical ability to adapt sufficiently to local conditions to improve economic status through industry and frugality."[16] Ed Wickberg makes the broader claim that wherever the Chinese have migrated, they proved to be among the most adaptable peoples in the world. In the course of their migrations, they have created a great variety of "Chineseness" and in some cases, entirely new ethnic identities.[17] Such appraisals of the dynamic tradition of

---

[15] Portes and Zhou, "Gaining the Upper Hand," 515.

[16] Michael R. Godley, *The Mandarin-Capitalists from Nanyang: Overseas Chinese Enterprise in the Modernization of China 1893–1911*. Cambridge Studies in Chinese History, Literature, and Institutions (Cambridge: Cambridge University Press, 1981), 1–2.

[17] Edgar Wickberg, "Relations with Non-Chinese: Ethnicity," in Lynn Pan, ed., *The Encyclopedia of the Chinese Overseas* (Richmond, England: Curzon Press, 1999), 114–21; Wickberg, "The Chinese Mestizo in Philippine History." *Journal of South East Asian History* 5 (1964): 62–100; and Daniel Chirot, "Conflicting Identities and the Dangers of Communalism," in Daniel Chirot and Anthony Reid, eds., *Essential Outsiders: Chinese and Jews in the Modern Transformation of Southeast Asia and Central Europe* (Seattle: University of Washington Press, 1997), 13–14, 20–21.

the Chinese – as "they rode the waves of capitalism around the world"[18] – have a special meaning in the case of the first influxes of Chinese sojourners to the Pacific Coast.

The vast majority of Chinese sojourners before 1850 migrated to Southeast Asia, and by the end of nineteenth century, 90 percent of the three million Chinese living outside China were to be found in that part of the world. However, of the remaining 10 percent of Chinese sojourners, fully one-third lived in North America: 90,000 in the U.S. and 15,000 in Canada.[19] The early Chinese arrivals in North America tended to concentrate in the Pacific Coast region, drawn there by the economic opportunities created by gold discoveries in the 1850s and 1860s and the ongoing, erratic demand for cheap, largely seasonal labor. They were young male adults who came from South China, from a few counties in the Pearl River delta province of Guangdong (Kwangtung), the capital of which was China's major international trading port, Canton, and spoke some dialogue of Cantonese. North America was a Cantonese frontier.

With the exception of the railroad workers, who entered in the 1870s and early 1880s under temporary labor contracts, most of those who came after the gold rushes arrived without financial means as credit-ticket laborers.[20] Labor recruiters and merchants (often through agents or brokers in Hong Kong), prospective employers, or relatives advanced them their passages and entry fees, debts that they then attempted to work off after their arrival. Employers and labor contractors usually deducted the borrowed funds directly from the employees' wages.

As *relatively* free sojourners, some of them would soon have returned home for good – or at least periodically, if they could afford it. They may have had, or after arriving in North America, acquired, wives in China and started families there. These were "trans-Pacific families;" the men lived abroad as "bachelors" and their wives in China as "widows."[21] The sojourning Chinese were also part of an expanding overseas network that, subject to a nation's domestic laws and regulations, eventually facilitated

---

[18] Gary G. Hamilton, "Hong Kong and the Rise of Capitalism in Asia," in Hamilton, ed., *Cosmopolitan Capitalists: Hong Kong and the Chinese Diaspora at the End of the Twentieth Century* (Seattle: University of Washington Press, 1999), 24.

[19] Edgar Wickberg, "Localism and the Organization of Overseas Migration in the Nineteenth Century," in Hamilton, ed., *Cosmopolitan Capitalists*, 35, 47.

[20] See Shih-Shan Henry Tsai, *China and the Overseas Chinese in the United States 1868–1911* (Fayetteville: University of Arkansas Press, 1983); Li, *The Chinese in Canada*, Chapter 2.

[21] Haiming Lui, "The Trans-Pacific Family: A Case Study of Sam Chong's Family History," *Amerasia Journal* 18 (1992): 1–34. I am grateful to Joannne Mei Poon for this reference. See also Madeline Yuan-Yin Hsu, *Dreaming of Gold, Dreaming of Home: Transnationalism and Migration between the United States and South China, 1882–1943* (Stanford: Stanford University Press, 2000).

the immigration of others – kinfolk and men from the same native place – becoming "links in a long chain."[22] In a process of chain migration, a single male member of a family, once established abroad, might send for or bring back after a visit family members, notably teenage sons or nephews, to assist them in economic enterprises. A prosperous sojourner might eventually send for his wife and filial children, though in the case of sojourners in North America, this was rare before 1900. The practice of maintaining long-distance families through remittances and the process of chain migration of "bachelor" kin and fellow villagers had roots in Southern China, in the migrations of young men from rural areas to towns and cities for work.[23] In all cases, sending money back to families and, if possible, lineages, was an obligation. It was as central to the sojourner ideology as was the notion of eventual return to the family.

The sojourners congregated in overseas Chinese communities – Chinatowns. Chinatowns were crucial nodes in the international sojourning network. By the early twentieth century, Vancouver's Chinatown had become what San Francisco became a few decades earlier: a central way station for the Chinese population in North America, a social and economic center for Chinese traders, consumers, workers, and investors, and a cultural refuge.[24] There were important Chinese enclaves in rural towns and isolated seasonal camps, too, which together with urban Chinatowns would have formed a network of what Ronald Takaki calls "ethnic islands."[25]

The Chinese sojourning activities and bachelor societies in North America operated within various constraints imposed by Canada and the U.S. Both countries instituted prohibitions against Chinese immigration and naturalization and economic controls on those already landed.[26] In the U.S., this

[22] Flemming Christiansen and Liang Xiujing, "Patterns of Migration," in Pan, ed., *Encyclopedia of the Chinese Overseas*, 61–2; Yong Chan, *Chinese San Francisco, 1950–1943: A Transpacific Community* (Stanford: Stanford University Press, 2000).

[23] Christiansen and Liang Xiujing, "Patterns of Migration," 62; Wickberg, "Localism and the Organization of Overseas Migration," 35–55.

[24] L. Eve Armentrout-Ma, "Big and Medium Businesses of Chinese Immigrants to the United States, 1850–1890: An Outline," *Bulletin of the Chinese Historical Society of America* 13 (1978): 1–2, cited in Yee, "Chinese Business in Vancouver," 93, n. 1.

[25] Ronald Takaki, *Ethnic Islands: The Experience of the Urban Chinese in America* (New York: Chelsea House, 1989). See also Kay Anderson, *Vancouver's Chinatown: Racial Discourse in Canada, 1875–1980* (Montreal: McGill-Queen's University Press, 1991); Vic Satzewich, "Reactions to Chinese Migrants in Canada at the Turn of the Century," *International Sociology* 4 (1989): 316–17.

[26] Reviewed in Satzewich, "Reactions to Chinese Migrants in Canada at the Turn of the Century," 311–27; Li, *The Chinese in Canada*, Chapter 3; and K. Scott Wong, "Cultural Defenders and Brokers: Chinese Responses to the Anti-Chinese Movement," in K. Scott Wong and Sucheng Chan, eds., *Claiming America: Constructing Chinese Identities during the Exclusion Era* (Philadelphia: Temple University Press, 1998), 3–40.

institutionalized discrimination began in 1882.[27] Canada, for its part, at first attempted to restrict, rather than prohibit, Chinese immigration; between 1882 and 1923 the state required incoming Chinese workers to pay a stiff entry fee, a "head tax." It eventually introduced exclusion legislation in 1923.[28] The exclusion eras in both countries did not end until shortly after World War II.

The Chinese immigration legislation and regulations on both sides of the border differentiated between Chinese merchants (a category that included traders and contractors and their families), and Chinese laborers. Both countries tended to encourage the merchants to settle permanently with their Chinese families.[29] The status of overseas Chinese merchants as social and economic intermediaries in the larger economy required that they develop and maintain a high level of trust, reputation, and social stability that was not required of the Chinese workers (sojourners).

Despite their rural backgrounds, the initial waves of Chinese arrivals in the U.S. and Canada would have been familiar with the economic practices of the towns and ports of Guangdong. They possessed an understanding of a commercialized, urban economy, an intense drive to make money and contribute to the wealth and status of one's lineage (even from overseas), a strong sense of upward mobility, and refined trading and money-handling skills.[30] Although initially lacking in the language skills and local social connections of many of the European immigrants, the Chinese brought with them kinship and locality ties and, critically, a familiar system of economic middleman activities.[31]

---

[27] Extended and strengthened in 1884, 1892, 1894, 1902, 1904, culminating in the National Immigration Act (1924).

[28] Canada's Chinese Exclusion Act (1923) effectively ended Chinese immigration to Canada. See Patricia E. Roy, "British Columbia's Fear of Asians," in W. Peter Ward and Robert A. J. McDonald, eds., British Columbia: Historical Readings (Vancouver: Douglas & McIntyre, 1981), 658. Canada's head tax for incoming Chinese began at $50 (1885), and over the next few decades doubled (1900), then increased five-fold (1903).

[29] Haiming Lui, "The Trans-Pacific Family"; Satzewich, "Reactions to Chinese Migrants in Canada at the Turn of the Century," 321–24. The preferential treatment of the Chinese merchants encouraged Chinese laborers to set their sights on becoming merchants and labor contractors. See Sucheng Chan, ed., Entry Denied: Exclusion and the Chinese Community in America, 1882–1943 (Philadelphia: Temple University Press, 1991), 94–146.

[30] Maurice Freedman, "The Handling of Money: A Note on the Background to the Economic Sophistication of Overseas Chinese." Man 59 (1959): 64–65, discussed in Paul Yee, "Business Devices from Two Worlds: The Chinese in Early Vancouver," BC Studies 62 (1984): 44–67, and Yee, "Chinese Business in Vancouver, 1886–1914" (MA thesis, University of British Columbia, 1983), Chapter 4.

[31] See Milton L. Barnett, "Kinship as a Factor Affecting Cantonese Economic Adaptation in the United States," Human Organization 19 (1960): 40–46.

The Chinese Comprador System

Chinese agents who assisted European foreigners to set up factories or conduct businesses in the treaty ports of China in the 1840s, once China opened these ports to Western trade and residence, were known as compradors (*mai-pan*).[32] In these ports, "cultural twilight zones between the outside world and the Chinese interior," as Wickberg puts it, compradors recruited and supervised the Chinese staff and workers.[33] They also supplied market intelligence, kept the books, managed native bank orders, and assisted the foreign manager in all dealings with the Chinese. A familiar statement about them is that they dealt with the Chinese customers and suppliers on a Chinese basis and with Western customers and suppliers on a Western basis.[34] Compradors accompanied Western traders and industrialists to Japan and throughout Southeast Asia, to help run their enterprises there.[35]

The British colony and port of Hong Kong was the crucial international cultural and economic link that, like Chinatowns, facilitated international sojourning and the work of the overseas Chinese merchants and labor contractors in the second half of the nineteenth century. Chinese residents of Hong Kong constructed a staging area for the outbound Chinese migrants. The place became a conduit for the flows of remittances, wages, and profits from work abroad (hence, foreign exchange), and an entrepôt for import – export trade between China and the Chinese overseas.[36] Outside China, Hong Kong became a vital source of "Things Chinese."[37]

It would be natural enough for the early Cantonese arrivals in North America to adopt comprador methods, because most of the compradors

---

[32] Comprador is an English term borrowed from the Portuguese word for buyer. See Hao Yen-ping, *The Comprador in Nineteenth-Century China: Bridge between East and West* (Cambridge, MA: Harvard University Press, 1970); Hao Yen-ping, *The Commercial Revolution in Nineteenth-Century China: The Rise of Sino-Western Mercantile Capitalism* (Berkeley: University of California Press, 1986).

[33] Wickberg, "Localism and the Organization of Overseas Migration," 38.

[34] My thanks to Ed Wickberg for this helpful observation.

[35] See Christine Dobbin, *Asian Entrepreneurial Minorities in the Making of the World-Economy, 1570–1940* (Richmond, England: Curzon Press, 1996), 197–213; R. Robinson, "Non-European Foundations of European Imperialism: Sketch for a Theory of Collaboration," in R. Owen and B. Sutcliffe, eds., *Studies in the Theory of Imperialism* (London: Longmans, 1972), 117–141; Sucheng Chan, *This Bitter-Sweet Soil: The Chinese in California Agriculture, 1860–1910* (Berkeley: University of California Press, 1986), 347.

[36] Elizabeth Sinn, "Hong Kong's Role in the Relationship Between China and the Overseas Chinese," in Pan, ed., *The Encyclopedia of the Chinese Overseas*, 105–110; Takeshi Hemashita, "Overseas Chinese Remittance and Asian Banking History," in Olive Checkland, Shizuya Nishimura, and Norio Tamaki, eds., *Pacific Banking, 1859–1959: East Meets West* (New York: St. Martin's Press, 1994), 52–60.

[37] Sinn, "Hong Kong's Role in the Relationship between China and the Overseas Chinese," 107.

on the South China coast were Cantonese and Canton was the center of Western trade. Compradors were valued in the new context for their abilities to facilitate economic relations between the "receiving" society (transplanted Europeans) and the waves of new arrivals of Chinese sojourners.

With their well-developed cross-cultural brokerage skills, Chinese merchants and labor contractors in western North America found employment for Chinese in the service sector, and, for the majority of Chinese, in contract labor gangs.[38] Patricia Cloud and David Galenson have traced the earlier widespread use of labor contracting in nineteenth-century China in industries requiring large gangs, such as mining and agriculture.[39] Chinese agents employed the Chinese contract system throughout Southeast Asia.[40] In both the American West and Canadian West, "Asian" (Chinese, Japanese, and East Indian) labor contracts became common for railway construction and industries with large-scale, seasonal labor requirements, such as lumbering, mining, fruit and vegetable farming and processing, and fish processing.[41] Through the proliferation of labor contracts and the set of reciprocal responsibilities and obligations embedded in them, the floating populations of Chinese "bachelor" workers formed the backbone of the seasonal migratory labor force on the Pacific Coast. Labor contracts were central to the emergent social networks and industrial economy of the Pacific Coast region.

[38] Wickberg, "Relations with Non-Chinese," 115; Anthony B. Chan, "The Myth of the Chinese Sojourner in Canada," in K. Victor Ujimoto and Gordon Hirabayashi, eds., *Visible Minorities and Multiculturalism: Asians in Canada* (Scarborough, Ont.: Butterworth, 1980); and Anthony B. Chan, "Chinese Bachelor Workers in Nineteenth-Century Canada," *Ethnic and Racial Studies* 5 (1982): 513–34; Sucheng Chan, *This Bitter-Sweet Soil*.

[39] Patricia Cloud and David W. Galenson, "Chinese Immigration and Contract Labor in the Late Nineteenth Century," *Explorations in Economic History* 24 (1987): 22–42.

[40] See Godley, *The Mandarin-Capitalists from Nanyang*, for case histories of the successful overseas Chinese capitalists in Southeast Asia in the late nineteenth and early twentieth centuries.

[41] Yuzo Murayama, "Contractors, Collusion, and Competition: Japanese Immigrant Railroad Laborers in the Pacific North West, 1898–1911," *Explorations in Economic History*, 21 (1984): 290–305; Sucheng Chan, *This Bitter-Sweet Soil*; Clarence E. Glick, *Sojourners and Settlers: Chinese Migrants in Hawaii* (Honolulu: University of Hawaii Press, 1980); Chris Friday, *Organizing Asian American Labor: The Pacific Coast Canned-Salmon Industry, 1870–1942* (Philadelphia: Temple University Press, 1994); Jack Masson and Donald Guimary, "Asian Labor Contractors in the Alaskan Canned Salmon Industry, 1880–1937," *Labor History* 22 (1981): 377–97; Dianne Newell, ed., *The Development of the Pacific Salmon-Canning Industry, A Grown Man's Game* (Montreal: McGill-Queen's University Press, 1989); and Newell, *Tangled Webs of History: Indians and the Law in Canada's Pacific Coast Fisheries* (Toronto: University of Toronto Press, 1993). See also Lauren Wilde Casaday, "Labor Unrest and the Labor Market in the Salmon Industry of the Pacific Coast," 2 volumes (Ph.D. dissertation, Economics, University of California, Berkeley, 1938), Chapter 3; Murayama, "Contractors, Collusion, and Competition"; and Cloud and Galenson, "Chinese Immigration and Contract Labor in the Late Nineteenth Century." See also the general discussion of seasonal labor contracts in Warren C. Whatley, "Southern Agrarian Labor Contracts as Impediments to Cotton Mechanization," *Journal of Economic History* 47 (1987): 45–70.

Sucheng Chan refers to the Chinese tenant farmers, harvest labor contractors, and merchants in nineteenth-century California agriculture as "agricultural compradors."[42] Contractors and merchant – contractors based themselves locally in rural Chinatowns, but they could also tap into their network of contacts in the urban Chinatowns to recruit additional labor on demand. The ethnic contract labor system persisted in California through the Japanese, Filipino, and Mexican labor contractors. As argued in Lloyd Fisher's pioneer study of the harvest labor market, it was the most efficient way of bringing about stability, regularity, and reliability in a chaotic market.[43]

The Chinese (or China) contract system for the labor-intensive, highly dispersed coastal salmon-canning industry was similar to but more elaborate than the harvest contract labor system initiated by the Chinese for California agriculture. In salmon canning, the Chinese contract was an essential, complex system for mobilizing, outfitting, organizing, supervising, and remunerating skilled and semi-skilled workers in what was a short-season, cyclical "wild" resource industry with scattered, remote plant locations.[44] The contract outlined a system of "putting up the pack," thus of organizing and supervising all minority plant labor, not just the Chinese workers.[45] In British Columbia (BC), Vancouver-based Chinese merchants and contractors remained in charge of cannery contracts until the system ended following unionization of the fishermen and plant workers during the Second World War. Chinese contract labor was especially critical to developments in BC, which was a staple-exporting region with a persistent shortage of labor. A steady supply of low-paid contract workers enabled the young province to compete in overseas markets. The presence of Chinese merchants, contractors, and traders also held out the tantalizing possibility of large export markets in Asia for Canadian commodities.[46]

In both California agriculture and coastal salmon canning in Oregon, Washington, British Columbia, and Alaska, Chinese labor contractors needed little start-up capital. For one thing, they received cash advances from farmers and cannery men, respectively, to secure an ample workforce

---

[42] Sucheng Chan, *This Bitter-Sweet Soil*, 346.

[43] Lloyd H. Fisher, *The Harvest Labor Market in California* (Cambridge, MA: Harvard University Press, 1953), discussed in Sucheng Chan, *This Bitter-Sweet Soil*, 288–92. See also Edna Bonacich, "Asian Labor in the Development of California and Hawaii," in Lucie Cheng and Edna Bonacich, eds., *Labor Immigration Under Capitalism: Asian Workers in the United States Before World War II* (Berkeley: University of California Press, 1984), 165–66.

[44] See Masson and Guimary, "Asian Labor Contractors in the Alaskan Canned Salmon Industry."

[45] See Dianne Newell, "The Rationality of Mechanization in the Pacific Salmon-Canning Industry before the Second World War," *Business History Review* 62 (1988): 626–55.

[46] The relevant literature on this point is summarized in Satzewich, 'Reactions to Chinese Migrants in Canada at the Turn of the Century,' 311–27.

and to bring workers to a specific locality. For another, they easily obtained credit from their suppliers. Contractors did not pay the Chinese workers until the employers paid them at the end of a season, and only after deducting all the usual contractor's expenses. Expenses were various and large. They included financial penalties for poor workmanship; the cost of room and board, clothing, wine, and opium; gambling debts; cash advances to individual workers; remittance payments (and in BC, head tax payments); and interest on credit and loans. The interest-bearing large, lump sum cash advances that contractors received six to eight months in advance of the canning season were, in effect, short-term loans from cannery owners.[47]

June Mei's review of San Francisco's Chinese community found that labor contracting was a critical source of income for many Chinese mercantile capitalists, in part because of the foodstuffs and other commodities they supplied to Chinese contract workers.[48] Paul Yee's business history of Vancouver's Chinatown reached a similar conclusion.[49] The commerce in remittance transfers, which they handled for hundreds, in some cases thousands, of their Chinese store customers and contract workers was also a capital-raising sideline for Chinese merchants and contractors. It was possible for merchants and contractors to store up remittances before sending them overseas. The remittances went first to a head office in Hong Kong, where the funds were transferred into Chinese currency, then to one of the exchange's branches in South China, and from there to the remitter's family. The overseas letter offices in Hong Kong might also be trading houses, in which case the remittance money could be pooled and used to buy export goods for sale in China and a portion of the proceeds of the sale paid out as remittances.[50]

Through various familiar short- and medium-term capital-raising devices, Chinese merchants and contractors drew on their strong ties to China and the overseas Chinese communities and (weaker) linkages to the surrounding non-Chinese coastal economy to parlay small amounts of finance capital into

[47] This was the case for agricultural labor contractors (see Sucheng Chan, *This Bitter-Sweet Soil*, Chapter 10, especially 348–9) and salmon-cannery contractors (the terms of the cash advance were always included in the terms of the cannery contract).

[48] June Mei, "Socioeconomic Developments among the Chinese in San Francisco, 1849–1906," in Cheng and Bonacich, eds., *Labor Immigration under Capitalism*, 380. Not all of the contractors lived in large urban Chinatowns, however. See Sucheng Chan's brief biography of Lee Bing (1873–1970), one of the wealthiest and most diversified of the Chinese merchants in agricultural California. Sucheng Chan, *This Bitter-Sweet Soil*, 349–57.

[49] Yee, "Business Devices from Two Worlds."

[50] Leo M. Douw, "Overseas Chinese Remittances," in Pan, ed., *The Encyclopedia of the Chinese Overseas*, 108–9. Private postal exchanges ("letter offices") received (and in many cases, prepared) envelopes containing money addressed to the intended recipients; the envelopes were eventually returned to the letter office with a receipt enclosed after the funds were delivered.

important gains. Within Chinatowns, drawing on their own community's stock of social capital, they could raise the initial funds quickly through the informal money-raising associations offering rotating mutual credit to its members. To the Chinese, these associations were known by the particularly Cantonese term for them, *hui*, meaning association or club (*yin-hui*, a money or banking association, and *yi-hui*, literally, a righteous or just association based on [righteous] human ties). The practice in China is 800 years old, possibly the oldest in the world.[51] No collateral was required to secure this credit, and no limits were placed on the number of *hui* that individuals might join. Yee's study found that in the first decade of the twentieth century, some of Vancouver's leading Chinese merchant and labor contracting firms belonged to from ten to fifteen *hui* at a time.[52] Individuals were discouraged from defaulting on their financial commitments by their need to safeguard their reputation and that of their family, and to avoid nastiness for themselves and their families back home at the hands of debt-collecting enforcers.

The *hui* enabled the Chinese overseas to expand independent of the availability and cooperation of conventional lenders and legal sanctions in the host society. The popularity of the *hui* was also cultural: *hui* membership reinforced social and cultural ties (reciprocal obligations and responsibilities) within the Chinese community.[53] Support for *hui* was, for example, a convenient means by which the more established entrepreneurs, such as the two economic leaders discussed in the following, assisted novices with whom they had strong social ties to achieve economic mobility; it was a way of acknowledging a mutual obligation.

Partnerships presented another route to raising capital. There is a general belief – one perpetuated in Francis Fukuyama's recent cross-cultural study of culture as a factor in business – that for the Chinese, as for all intensely familistic societies, the family looms larger than other forms of associations.[54] The fact is, however, that the partnership is as traditional a form of Chinese enterprise as the family firm is.[55] The practice of forming partnerships, that is, of pooling resources for particular ventures, generally on

[51] Discussed by, among others, Light, *Ethnic Enterprise in America*, Chapter 2. I am grateful to Glen Peterson for translating these terms for me.

[52] Yee, "Business Devices from Two Worlds," 51.

[53] Light goes so far as to say that the Chinese may have preferred the *hui* on cultural grounds, but as Yee, Sucheng Chan, and others have demonstrated, it was not likely a question of either/or. Light, *Ethnic Enterprise in America*, 59–60; Yee, "Business Devices From Two Worlds"; and Sucheng Chan, *This Bitter-Sweet Soil*.

[54] Francis Fukuyama, *Trust: The Social Virtues and the Creation of Prosperity* (New York: The Free Press, 1995), 62.

[55] J. A. C. Mackie, "Chinese Business Organizations," in Pan, ed., *The Encyclopedia of the Chinese Overseas*, 93; Yee, "Business Devices from Two Worlds," 52–59; Light, *Ethnic Enterprise in America*, 18; and Waldinger, Aldrich, Ward, and Associates, *Ethnic Entrepreneurs*, chapter 5.

a short-term basis, was widespread among the overseas Chinese. Overseas, as in China, partnerships relied on the social connectedness of partners. The partnerships uncovered in Yee's Vancouver Chinatown study expose the dominance of personal clan, lineage (family of families), and home district ties in business.[56] Chris Friday points out that merchant partnerships were in some cases a means for individuals to get around immigration restrictions by bringing their sons to North America to join their partnership under the favorable category of merchant.[57] Chinatown partnerships were informal, flexible arrangements well-suited to a multitude of enterprises, everything from organizing gambling houses and brothels and launching Chinese restaurants and laundry operations, to purchasing real estate both inside and outside Chinatown, and undertaking mortgages.

Mortgages would also have been familiar to the Chinese in North America, where they engaged them as devices to secure substantial amounts of credit.[58] In undertaking mortgages, the overseas Chinese had to look outside Chinatown and tap into Western legal structures and property regimes that allowed unrelated, autonomous people to cooperate in the creation of businesses and investments. Sucheng Chan's analysis of chattel mortgage records for eighteen counties in the agricultural districts of California 1860 to 1920 found that white individuals were responsible for some loans to Chinese tenants throughout the period. Asian individuals and commission merchants and, to a lesser extent, American banks, lent to them from the 1880s onwards, and Asian banks began lending to them in the 1910s.[59] Similarly, Yee's business study of Vancouver's Chinatown suggests that mortgages available on the Vancouver money market acquired importance as a source of finance capital for many Chinatown entrepreneurs. Vancouver's main Chinatown property owners routinely arranged mortgages at conventional rates in order to purchase real estate in and out of Chinatown, in turn using it as collateral for additional loans for development purposes. Of the forty-five mortgages of Vancouver properties secured by Vancouver Chinese owners over the period 1892–1914, all came from Anglo-Canadian individuals outside Chinatown, including several prominent salmon-cannery owners and managers, and institutions – insurance companies, mortgage firms, and trust companies.[60]

---

[56] Yee, "Business Devices from Two Worlds," 57–58; Yee, "Chinese Business in Vancouver," Chapter 4; Light, *Ethnic Enterprise in America*, 94–95. Dobbin discusses the Chinese partnership, or syndicate, formed in Java called *Kongsi*. See Dobbin, *Asian Entrepreneurial Minorities*, Chapters 3 and 7.

[57] Friday, *Organizing Asian American Labor*, 72.

[58] Sucheng Chan, *This Bitter-Sweet Soil*, 348; William S. Hallagan, "Labor Contracting in Turn-of-the-Century California Agriculture," *Journal of Economic History* 40 (1980): 757–76.

[59] Sucheng Chan, *This Bitter-Sweet Soil*, 348–50; 352–53 (Table 30).

[60] Yee, "Business Devices from Two Worlds," 59–63, 64–67 (Table 3).

The use of property as collateral to secure short- and long-term credit may have been similar to what Winifred Rothenberg observed of the pattern of farm mortgage credit in the emerging capital market in Colonial New England: the pole with which some prominent Chinese entrepreneurs "vaulted over their capital constraints."[61] For the overseas Chinese in the age of finance capital, however, obtaining mortgage credit was also an additional means to stabilize and reinforce important but fragile social and economic (extra-community) linkages to the wider economy. In the case of the mortgages arranged with salmon-cannery men, for example, mortgage credit appears to reflect ongoing reciprocal obligations and responsibilities between Chinese labor contractors/merchant–contractors and their actual or prospective Western clients in the salmon-cannery industry.

The strengthening of ties to the wider economy through labor contracting and credit arrangements did not guarantee success to the Chinatown entrepreneurs when they attempted to invest in mainstream businesses located outside Chinatown, in direct competition with the host society. Westerners closed ranks. Yee cites anecdotal evidence of the early twentieth-century attempts by Chinese merchants and syndicates to own and operate mainstream farms and factories. The attempts usually failed.[62] Despite periodic attempts by the Chinese to enter the all important salmon-canning business, for example, no Chinese are known to have successfully owned or managed a salmon-cannery operation beyond the start-up phase.[63] The Chinese contracts and the China crews were essential to salmon-cannery production, to be sure, but in both the United States and Canada, Chinese entrepreneurs lacked access to the fishing and the distribution and marketing ends of the business. In BC, the Chinese were informally (then after 1923, more formally) blocked from all commercial fisheries. In California and the northwestern states, the Chinese were all but driven out of the commercial salmon fishery, and eventually, every other fishery of prime interest to "Americans."[64]

---

[61] Winifred B. Rothenberg, "Mortgage Credit at the Origins of a Capital Market: Middlesex County, MA, 1642–1770," paper read at the Economic History Association meeting, Durham, NC, September 1998.

[62] Examples summarized in Yee, "Chinese Business in Vancouver," 83, 106.

[63] A wealthy Chinese firm lead by Lam, or Sam, Tung supplied labor to canneries and in 1896 built the Westminster Cannery outside Vancouver. It may have operated for one year, if at all. British Columbia Packers Association acquired it when it formed in 1902 (Newell, ed., *The Development of the Pacific Salmon-Canning Industry*, 57); Yee, "Chinese Business in Vancouver," 82–3 writes of another case (plans to build a cannery never materialized). Chris Friday (*Organizing Asian American Labor*, 71) writes of two aborted attempts to establish Chinese-owned canneries in the U.S.

[64] Newell, ed., *The Development of the Pacific Salmon-Canning Industry*, chapter 1; Arthur F. McEvoy, *The Fisherman's Problem: Ecology and the Law in the California Fisheries, 1850–1980* (Cambridge: Cambridge University Press, 1986), 69, 75–6, 96–9, 113–14; McEvoy, "In Places Men Reject: The Chinese Fishermen at San Diego, 1870–1893," *Journal of San Diego History* 23 (1977): 12–24; Friday, *Organizing Asian American Labor*, 68; and L. Eve

When nativist discrimination blocked their free participation in the larger economy, Chinese middlemen on the Pacific Coast, as elsewhere abroad, devised ways to develop new business niches at the margins without being obvious about it. Publicly they receded behind the scenes, using whatever ways and means seemed appropriate in the context. Anecdotal evidence suggests that in some contexts it would have been sufficient for them simply to adopt conventional, non-Chinese business names for Chinese-owned businesses. This occurred, for example, when in the 1870s Chinese-owned cigar factories in San Francisco masqueraded behind Hispanic names, which were more common in the business, to avoid racial hostility from the city's strong anti-Chinese movement of the day.[65] In other cases, the Chinese had to disguise the official nature of their occupations or businesses.[66] In extreme situations, a Chinese entrepreneur would become an invisible presence operating in the shadows behind a more politically acceptable front man who officially owned the business.[67] What occurred in the case of early salt herring production in British Columbia is an important variation on the theme.

Forging Invisible Links: Chinese–Japanese Salt Herring Production in British Columbia

With so few economic studies of early Chinatowns in North America, the traditional emphasis in the literature on the 'ethnic enclave' nature of these

---

Armentrout-Ma, "Chinese in California's Fishing Industry, 1850–1941," *California History* 60 (1981): 142–57.

[65] Mei, "Socioeconomic Developments Among the Chinese in San Francisco," 377.

[66] For example, a Chinese medical doctor in California disguised his San Francisco practice as an herbal supply business. He operated in a white neighborhood, for white clients, in premises leased for him by a white citizen in his employ. He eventually acquired prime agricultural land for herb growing and brought his son from China to manage the property and the market gardening end of the business. Lui, "The Trans-Pacific Family."

[67] At one extreme was the so-called "Ali Baba" venture of Southeast Asia, which refers to a business fronted by the indigenous sleeping partner (Ali, a nickname for the indigene) and run by the ethnic Chinese (Baba, a name used in Malaysia for a Straits-born person of Chinese descent). "Ali Babas" helped ethnic Chinese businessmen cope with the hostile discrimination that accompanied nationalist policies in countries such as Indonesia, Malaysia, and Vietnam after the Second World War. In Malaysia, the practice of "ethnic by-pass" involved Malay and government collaboration with foreign partners to circumvent the traditional economic control of the ethnic Chinese (K. S. Jomo, "A Specific Idiom of Chinese Capitalism in Southeast Asia: Sino-Malaysian Capital Accumulation in the Face of State Hostility," in Chirot and Reid, eds., *Essential Outsiders*, 250–53). Under Ali Baba arrangements, the indigenous figurehead partners helped the Chinese firm to secure the necessary licenses and contracts for a commission or a share of the profits (J. A. C. Mackie, "Business Relations with non-Chinese," in Pan, ed., *Encyclopedia of the Chinese Overseas*, 127. See also Linda Y. C. Lim and L. A. Peter Gosling, "Strengths and Weaknesses of Minority Status for Southeast Asian Chinese at a Time of Economic Growth and Liberalization," in Chirot and Reid, eds., *Essential Outsiders*, 286–87).

communities supports the notion that the Chinese sojourners were unable to participate in the key economic activities and labor markets. Yet, this was not so for the Chinese middlemen of the developing regions of the Pacific Coast. In British Columbia, the early Chinatown merchants and contractors in Vancouver both constructed and joined existing interracial networks in order to participate to one degree or another in every primary sector of the BC economy. The intricacies of these networks are apparent in the extant business records of two prominent firms – Sam Kee Co. and Wing Sang Co. Through swift increments behind the scenes, the two firms came to control the Japanese herring salteries on Vancouver Island, which the Japanese continued to run. The Chinese economic involvement, which was essential to the beleaguered Japanese operators, amounted to an active but invisible presence of the Chinese in a marginal area of the provincial fisheries, in a racialized environment.

The founder of the prominent Sam Kee Co. was Chang Toy (1857–1920).[68] Sam Kee was Chang Toy's personal alias in business. Most of the company's business correspondence with non-Chinese in North America was signed "Sam Kee" and contained references to Sam Kee as an actual person.[69] A teenager from a peasant family in Guangdong province, he had migrated to BC in 1874 for salmon cannery work. He labored in a New Westminster sawmill, moved to Vancouver to run a Chinese laundry, and in the late 1880s, opened an import–export firm in Vancouver's nascent Chinatown. From China he imported the usual items, Chinese (and Japanese) rice, fish knives (for salmon packing), tea, and dry goods, and to China he exported gold, wheat, barley, salt, and dried seafood. The pattern of imports and exports was similar to that of merchants in San Francisco's Chinatown.[70]

With the help of a clansman merchant in Victoria's Chinatown, Chang Toy's Vancouver Chinatown business spread into retail sales of Chinese foods, medicines, wines, and dry goods. He also undertook labor contracting for the salmon canning, beet sugar, and forest industries. The business contacts he made through his salmon-cannery contracts probably helped him to acquire interests in local herring salteries; those he made through his

[68] Also known as Chen Cai (Chen Dao-zhi, Chen Chang-jin). City of Vancouver Archives (hereafter CVA), add mss. 571, Sam Kee Co. 1888–1935. In addition, see Paul Yee, "Sam Kee: A Chinese Business in Early Vancouver," *BC Studies* 69–70 (1986): 70–96; Yee, "Chinese Business in Vancouver," Chapter 5.

[69] When corresponding in Chinese with overseas agents and clients in Hong Kong and elsewhere, however, he signed himself Chang Toy. These were "middleman" names. Sucheng Chan discovered when she interviewed Joe Lung Kim (born in California in 1900, the grandson of an immigrant who arrived in the 1860s) in 1980 that Chou was his original family name. According to the grandson, white Americans had called his father "Mr. Kim," after the name his father gave to his laundry business: Kim Wing. The family eventually adopted the name Kim. Sucheng Chan, *This Bitter-Sweet Soil*, 487.

[70] Mei, "Socioeconomic Developments Among the Chinese in San Francisco," 379.

forestry industry contracts helped him to branch into sales of cordwood and manufacturing and sales of charcoal (which his firm sold mainly to its salmon cannery clients). His business interests also included steamship ticket sales and cargo trade between Canada and China (he was the Chinese agent for the Blue Funnel Steamship line) and sizable real estate development inside and outside of Vancouver's Chinatown.[71] Details about his family or about his sons' involvement in his various enterprises are scarce.[72]

Yip Sang (1845–1927) was the founder and pioneer Vancouver Chinatown merchant behind the Wing Sang Company.[73] He migrated first to San Francisco in 1864, where he took on various Chinese jobs in that city: dishwasher, cook, and cigar roller. Like many of his countrymen, he panned for gold, following a trail north that led him to the gold fields of British Columbia. He landed in the settlement of Vancouver in the early 1880s, peddling sacks of coal door to door, picking up some English and making contacts in the Chinese community. His early contacts included a Chinese foreman for a leading Chinese labor contractor with the Canadian Pacific Railway (CPR), which netted Yip Sang work as a bookkeeper, time-keeper, paymaster, and eventually superintendent on the southwestern BC portion of the CPR. He returned home to China in 1885 to start a family, then returned to Vancouver alone. From a company store and headquarters in Vancouver's Chinatown he launched a string of lucrative enterprises in addition to his salt herring interests – import–export business, retail merchant, licensed opium dealer, and labor contractor for salmon canneries – under the name Wing Sang Co.[74] The Canadian Pacific Railway and Steamship Line appointed him to the influential, lucrative position of Chinese Passenger Agent. He established his family in Vancouver, and his sons, eventually nineteen of them in all, joined him in business.

When the Chinese Board of Trade formed in Vancouver in 1895, Wing Sang Co. and Sam Kee Co. were already among the handful of wealthiest firms in Chinatown, and their principals were looking to build Asian markets

---

[71] Joining Chang Toy as the second principal in the business was Shum Moon (also known as Shen Man, who in the firm's English-language business correspondence referred to himself by the fabricated (middleman) name: Sam Moon), the firm's comptroller. Shum Moon seems to have specialized in running the firm's Chinese contracts with salmon canneries. He also served as president of the Chinese Board of Trade and Chinese Benevolent Association of Vancouver. CVA, Sam Kee Co., preliminary inventory, notes.

[72] We know that two sons were active in various aspects of the firm (though apparently not involved with the herring salteries in these early years).

[73] He was also known as Yip Ch'un Tien (Ye Sheng, Ye Chun-Tian). Eileen Young Yip, "Yip Sang Alias Yip Ch'un Tien, September 6 1845–July 20 1927," UBC Library, Special Collections, Chinese Canadian Research Collection, Box 25, 1972.

[74] CVA, add mss. 1108, Yip Family and Yip Sang (Wing Sang) Co. Ltd. Note, the company incorporated around 1910 (it was unusual for Chinese firms to incorporate before then); it would appear that the company name Yip Sang Company Limited was adopted in 1950.

for BC products and expand their involvement in what was then the leading industry in the province: the fishery.

From the time they arrived in BC in the late 1880s, Japanese fishermen were salting fish in the off-season for harvesting the commercial grades of salmon. Unlike the Chinese, the Japanese settled with their families and were encouraged to fish. The Japanese quickly became the largest single group of commercial fishers in the Vancouver area. Their presence as fishermen and shore workers (the women and children), like that of the Chinese as shore workers and Indians as fishermen and shore workers (mostly the women and children), facilitated the extraordinary growth of the salmon-canning industry in the 1890s and 1900s.[75] In the marginal fisheries of little commercial value – fall salmon ("chum" or "dog") and herring – the Japanese fishermen developed small crude processing operations for salt-curing the catch. In this early period, BC herring stocks had almost no commercial value. Despite the increasing air of hostility generated by the other commercial fishermen and the population at large, the Japanese managed with the help of the Chinese middlemen–exporters to develop and control the production of dried salt herring for export to China and Chinese communities in a number of Asian countries.[76]

The salt-herring industry at the beginning of the twentieth century centered on half a dozen or so plants located on the islands and harbor around the Vancouver Island coastal coal-mining town of Nanaimo, located approximately twenty-five nautical miles by sea from Vancouver. It involved an inshore seine fishery that operated for approximately four winter months of the year. Herring "dry" salting was a simple process, quite crude by the standards of salmon canning. The fresh-caught fish were soaked in large brine-filled tanks. When sufficiently saturated (that is, when enough salt had permeated the flesh and sufficient liquids driven from it) to preserve the fish for the several months it would take to deliver them to final markets, the salt-herring were dried, boxed, and the boxes crated up for shipping to Asian markets for immediate consumption. Each operation consisted of a seasonal village-like complex dominated by a large barn-like wooden building, called a saltery,

---

75 See Newell, ed., *The Development of the Pacific Salmon-Canning Industry*, 18–19, 133; Newell, *Tangled Webs of History*, 83–86, Canada, Royal Commission on Chinese and Japanese Immigration, *Report. Sessional Papers* (1902), no. 54, 135–64.

76 In 1907 the Asiatic Exclusion League formed in BC to combat what the public perceived as an invasion of the provincial workforce by Chinese, Japanese, and East Indians; citizens in Vancouver rioted against these groups. See W. Peter Ward, *White Canada Forever: Popular Attitudes and Public Policy Toward Orientals in British Columbia* (Montreal: McGill-Queen's University Press, 1978); Gillian Creese, "Exclusion or Solidarity? Vancouver Workers Confront the 'Oriental Problem,'" *BC Studies* 80 (Winter 1988–89): 24–49. Little is known about the BC salt-herring industry but see Newell, ed., *The Development of the Pacific Salmon-Canning Industry*, 18–19; Newell, *Tangled Webs of History*, 93–4; "Nanaimo and the Herring Industry," *BC Magazine* 7 (1911): 235–37.

perched on pilings driven into the tidal foreshore. The saltery housed the curing vats and provided storage for the supplies of boxes, salt, and fish.

In the early years, Japanese fishermen monopolized the salt-herring business. They recruited and organized the fishing crews (Japanese and Indian fishermen) and shore workers (Japanese and Chinese laborers), kept track of the accounts, procured the necessary provisions and packing materials from merchants and lumber mills located within the larger region, and arranged for fishing licenses and freighting.

Although Japanese records of the industry are unavailable, it is known through the surviving records of the Wing Sang and Sam Kee firms that the Japanese fishermen–operators of salteries were plagued by problems of cash flow and marketing, fishing and processing regulations, and the edgy climate of hostility that culminated in the anti-Asian riots in Vancouver in 1907. Although traditionally not natural economic allies, the Japanese fishermen who developed this marginal industry in BC aligned themselves with successful Chinese merchant–contractors in order to maintain a toehold in the enterprise. The Japanese needed access to Asian market information, which the Chinese controlled via their agents in Hong Kong, cash advances and loans, a reliable supply of provisions (on credit), and assistance with securing government fishing and processing licenses. All of this Wing Sang and Sam Kee were in a position to provide.

Chinese involvement in the marginal commercial fishery grew by swift increments. Initially, the involvement of the two Chinatown firms in salt herring production was limited to the local and long-distance shipping and handling arrangements. As early as 1889, Wing Sang Co. was shipping samples of salted dog salmon, known variously as chum and keta, to Asian markets for Japanese fishermen in the salmon-canning district of the Vancouver area. By 1903, the firm was exporting the salt herring output of several of the leading Japanese operations in Nanaimo direct to cities in China and Japan.

Between 1909 and 1913, with the rise of an anti-Japanese movement, Wing Sang entered the industry more directly. The firm also began acquiring Nanaimo-area salteries from English owners and building a handful of their own. However, it operated its own salteries under company names that were Japanese or, in one case, a neutral English name, The Nanaimo Packing Co., Ltd. To each operation Yip Sang assigned an accountant and, eventually, one of his sons as onsite manager, but Yip Sang himself remained in daily contact with the operations from his Vancouver Chinatown base. He retained overall control of these saltery operations until his death in the mid-1920s.

Fish was an important commodity for the Sam Kee Co., too. It was the firm's major export before World War I. At the turn of the century, Sam Kee made trial consignment shipments of canned crab to Hong Kong, salted dogfish (a type of local shark that preys on salmon and herring) to Shanghai, and pickled salmon, canned salmon, and salted dog salmon to Hawaii. In

1903, it began exporting dried salt herring to its agents in Hong Kong, and, later, also to Chinese agents in Shanghai, Singapore, and to two major cities in Japan: Yokohama and Kobe – both cities had substantial Chinatowns.

Sam Kee Co.'s business records provide fuller details about the salt herring business than do those of the Wing Sang Co. To facilitate expansion of the export trade, Sam Kee Co. had to guarantee reliable and adequate supplies of salted fish – packed to the specifications of its various import agents – for the long-distance markets.[77] To live up to its salt-herring contracts with overseas agents, the firm also quickly became involved in the day-to-day decision making of the Japanese producers in Nanaimo. The decisions concerned everything from determining the optimum fishing times to the quality, price, and source of packing supplies such as box lumber and imported salt.[78] Subsequently, the firm bought land and constructed additional saltery buildings, which they in turn leased to the Japanese producers. Thus, it began advancing funds to the consignment packers and supplementing the consignment shipments with additional supplies it purchased outright from nonclient Japanese and English producers. The firm became the financial backer and exclusive purchasing agent, even lobbyist to government, for many of the Japanese packers.

In return for such vital services as these, the Japanese producers provided written guarantees to process a set minimum percentage of the catch for Sam Kee Co., which included the promise not to fish for or to sell fish to others. In the mid-1900s, on the eve of the anti-Asian rioting in Vancouver, Sam Kee Co. had purchased waterfront lots in the Nanaimo area suitable for saltery operations. By the outbreak of the First World War, several Japanese operators rented saltery buildings (possibly newly built) and fishing outfits owned by Sam Kee Co.

The Wing Sang and Sam Kee firms did not publicize their growing involvement in this tiny branch of the provincial fishing industry, actually quite the contrary. The usual Japanese and Indian fishing crews and Japanese and

---

77 One of Sam Kee's three agents in Hong Kong, Sun Tung Chong Co., outlined for Chang Toy the current problems with selling imports of salt cod on the Hong Kong market (a glut of local fish on the Hong Kong market had devalued fish prices) and advised him that there seemed to be a market for "marinated fish, produced in cooperation with our company and Western people ... merchants from Guangdong province are purchasing fish in Hong Kong; if we cooperate with them, business will be good. If we send the fish to stores in other cites, we will make very little money." CVA, Sam Kee, letterbook, v. 2, file 1 (31 December 1909). In turn, Chang Toy supplied information about the herring fishery to the Hong Kong agents: "Since there are many Japanese–Chinese Merchants, the business can be run until the 29th of December ... The Western People also say that Japanese will not be allowed to work in the saltery next year." Sam Kee, letterbook, v. 2, file 1, p. 851 (26 December 1908). Translation by Joanne Mei Poon.

78 Sam Kee tendered extensively among Anglo-Canadian businesses for box lumber, nails, coarse salt, groceries, and other supplies. CVA, Sam Kee, letterbook, 1908–09, v. 1, file 8, pp. 145, 160, 166, 185–89, 199–200; box 7, files 4, 6, and 7 (various dates).

Chinese shore workers looked after the day-to-day tasks. The herring salteries continued to be known by their Japanese or English names. Nevertheless, the participation of the two Vancouver Chinatown firms in salt herring
generated an impressive scattered local network of economic, social, and
cultural relations. All of this took the two firms well beyond familial ties and
Chinatown connections, where trust and norms of reciprocity were present,
and called into play various mechanisms for ensuring agreed-upon rules of
conduct.[79]

The initial contracts between the Vancouver Chinatown firms and the
Japanese salt-herring producers at Nanaimo were simple letters of agreement. The records of Sam Kee Co. reveal the ways in which the Chinese
firms could counter breaches of these agreements with informal economic
punishments. A local Chinese agent secretly monitored the salted-herring
agreements for Sam Kee Co. In the winter of 1908–09, the Chinatown firm
discovered from its agent that some fishermen with the salteries had sold
fresh fish to competitors, even before completing the minimum quota for
Sam Kee Co. Sam Kee wrote to one of them, Charlie Okuri, "you are too
slow putting up fish – we heard your men fishing for other company. Please
don't be fooled by your fishermen."[80] The warning reveals a complication:
The Chinese firm could make agreements with the Japanese operators, but
the latter were either unwilling or unable to extract firm commitments from
the Japanese and Indian fishermen in their employ.

The Chinatown firm's retaliation for such breeches on the part of the
Japanese operators was subtle and strategically timed. First, Sam Kee Co.
simply ignored the routine written instructions it received from the Japanese
operators in question to pay off creditors or to order essential packing supplies on their behalf.[81] Then, at the height of the herring fishing season, when
the Japanese packers were desperate and their operations paralyzed by a lack
of supplies such as boxes and salt to process the catch, Sam Kee finally spoke.
He wrote to the Japanese operator, Makino, that he knew of the Japanese
operator's deception and thus refused to cooperate with him: "You have
to get boxes yourself as we cannot send you boxes, lumber, until the 30th.
We no suppose to supply you with boxes. If you sell fish to other man you
have to get boxes yourself."[82] In a second, more formal, letter to Makino,
Sam Kee outlines an obvious financial penalty for breaching the salt-herring

[79] On the latter point, see Woolcock, "Social Capital and Economic Development," 161; Greif,
   "Reputation and Coalitions," and Greif, "Contract Enforceability."
[80] CVA, Sam Kee, letterbook, v. 2, file 1, p. 315 (10 December 1908).
[81] CVA, Sam Kee, box 7, file 3, Okura to Sam Kee Co., 27, 29, and 31 December, 1908; file 9,
   19, 21, 28 January, 9, 25, February, 1909. U. Makino to Sam Kee Co., 17 and 20 January,
   8 February, 1909.
[82] CVA, Sam Kee, letterbook, v. 2, file 1, p. 350 (nd: but earliest 10 December 1908 and latest
   15 February 1909).

agreement; he also appeals to the man's sense of honor and loyalty. It is a mixed message: "We beg to inform you that we are going to charge you $1 per ton of salt fish for ground rent. Our foreman reports to us that you sold much fish to other person which you might no do. You cannot sell fish before you fulfill our 1000 tons contract. We have been so kind to you by helping you with money and supply and owe so much money since, but we have let you off very easy, but you seem to forget all about it now and you treat other person better than us."[83]

As Greif's work on another but similar case suggests, with these seemingly simple, direct statements, the Chinatown firm identified various means of monitoring and enforcing contracts in long-distance business arrangements where mutual trust is absent. The letters also demonstrate the ability of Chinese merchant–contractors in Vancouver to inflict various penalties on their Japanese suppliers in Nanaimo through the exercise of superior business reputation and economic influence. The Chinese advantage became clearer by the opening of the next herring season, when Sam Kee Co. arranged with an English-owned fishing company client to have the fishing license of another of the errant Japanese packers cancelled, should that outfit dare to breach the contract again. Also, the Chinese firm was willing to pay an agent (an English, not Chinese, agent) full time to monitor agreements with its Japanese salt-fish suppliers. Sam Kee wrote to a potential agent: "We have made an arrangement with Imperial Fish Co. who, if Makino does not act honestly, will influence [the government agent], Mr. Taylor to get his [fishing] license cancelled at once."[84] These sample letters from the Sam Kee Co. archives to and about the errant Japanese salt-herring operators exemplify the sorts of age-old economic punishments used to enforce informal long-distance contracts – despite the commitment problems inherent in their relations.

The ultimate arrangement between Sam Kee Co. and the Japanese salt-herring producers at Nanaimo was a formal, legally binding contract, such as the one signed for the 1912–13 herring fishing season.[85] The terms of the 1912 contract were more comprehensive than the formal Chinese contracts for the salmon-canning industry, and unlike in the case of the salmon cannery contracts, the Chinatown firm dictated the terms. The contents indicate just how far, in a decade marked by a heightening of anti-Asian hostility, a Chinese merchant–contractor such as Sam Kee Co. was able – and allowed – to infiltrate this fringe fishery. The firm had ventured far beyond its original

---

[83] CVA, Sam Kee, letterbook, v. 2, file 1, p. 386 (15 February 1909).

[84] CVA, Sam Kee, letterbook, v. 2, file 1, p. 815 (Sam Kee Co. to George Hannay, 23 November 1910).

[85] CVA, Sam Kee, box 8, file 3 ("Fishing Agreement," November 1912). This document is a rare find.

TABLE 8.1. *Population of British Columbia by Racial Origin, 1870–1941*

Year	% White	% Asian	% Indian	Total Population
1871	24.9	4.3	70.8	36,247
1881	39.3	8.8	51.9	49,459
1891	55.1	9.1	35.9	98,173
1901	74.8	10.9	14.3	178,657
1911	87.1	7.8	5.1	392,480
1921	88.2	7.5	4.3	524,582
1931	89.1	7.3	3.5	694,236
1941	91.8	5.2	3.0	817,861

Source: *Census of Canada, 1871–1941*, in W. P. Ward, "Class and Race in the Social Structure of British Columbia, 1870–1939," *BC Studies* 45 (1980): 28.

role of sales agent and shipper, then purchasing agent and creditor, to become the owner of the land, buildings, and fishing boats and assignee of the all-important fishing and curing licenses. The agreement also illustrates the ongoing problems of contract enforceability among minority communities.

BEYOND CHINATOWN

British Columbia in the age of finance capital underwent an economic transformation from a Native/European staple-based society into a multiethnic industrial one (see Table 8.1). The suppliers of finance capital are usually identified as having been the prime movers in the young provincial economy. Donald Paterson questioned that perspective some years ago. He made the reasonable argument that, despite the scarcity of domestic financial capital and the process of extraregional direct investment in BC before World War I, the role of local entrepreneurs in this industrializing period was critical. He found that British Columbian entrepreneurs "successfully mobilized substantial amounts of European financial capital to expand their participation in the regional economy beyond the limit imposed by domestic savings."[86] The multiethnic, non-European dimension of local entrepreneurship and capital formation in BC has, however, remained largely uncharted.

My study suggests ways in which the overseas Chinese on the Pacific Coast who combined merchant activities with labor contracting also played important roles in advancing the British Columbian economy, as well as

[86] Donald G. Paterson, "European Financial Capital and British Columbia: An Essay on the Role of the Regional Entrepreneur," reprinted in Ward and McDonald, eds., *British Columbia*, 328.

that of the Chinese community within it. In the labor-starved economy of the Pacific Coast, the suppliers of labor had an economic edge. Of all local entrepreneurs, merchant–contractors perhaps were in the best position to grasp the varied economic opportunities on offer. Vancouver Chinatown's Chang Toy and Yip Sang were among the most successful economic and "ethnic" brokers who played this role in development. Their merchant, import–export, and labor contracting activities encouraged strong, extensive, and unique social networks. They developed linkages that stretched deep into their own ethnic community networks, both in North America and abroad, reaching out to other ethnic minority communities in BC and penetrating the dominant society. When they aligned themselves with the Japanese salt-herring operators at the turn of the century, Chang Toy and Yip Sang were both vulnerable to and advantaged by the discriminatory practices against members of the multiethnic Asian minority group. In creating economic entanglements such as these, they and their fellow Chinese merchant–contractors were fashioning a flexible and lasting entrepreneurial web in the regional economies of the Pacific Coast and beyond.

9

Finance and Capital Accumulation in a Planned Economy: The Agricultural Surplus Hypothesis and Soviet Economic Development, 1928–1939

Robert C. Allen

Finance and capital accumulation are closely related, although fundamentally different. "Capital accumulation" refers to increases in productive structures and equipment, while "finance" refers to the borrowing and lending undertaken by and through banks, securities markets, and among private individuals. In market economies, many real investment projects require a corresponding financing plan, so finance is often the complement to capital accumulation. In such cases, a more efficient financial system may increase the pace of capital accumulation or better direct it. Financial transactions, however, need not necessarily lead to capital accumulation, and projects financed out of retained earnings need not involve any new financial dealings.

What about nonmarket economies? Is there a relationship between finance and capital accumulation? In a case like the Soviet Union in the 1930s, there is the possibility of no link. After all, in a market economy where capital formation requires monetary outlay, a lack of money can stop investment, but in a planned economy where investment goods are allocated by fiat, why should money matter? However, even Stalin balanced his budget, so finance was an issue in Moscow as well as New York.

The agricultural surplus hypothesis is the link usually suggested between finance and capital formation in the U.S.S.R. The hypthesis deals with two issues – state finance and farm marketing. So far as finance is concerned, the agricultural surplus hypothesis contends that the investment drive of the 1930s was financed by mobilizing the agricultural surplus. Preobrazhensky (1965) suggested that the state should use its control over prices to turn the terms of trade against agriculture and secure the resources needed to expand the capital stock of the modern, industrial sector. Stalin is supposed to have put this prescription into practice by collectivizing agriculture – the system of compulsory deliveries to state agencies at low prices was the device whereby the state extracted resources from the countryside and used them to increase investment. This is the "standard story" to use Millar's (1974) terminology.

Farm supply is the second issue dealt with by the agricultural surplus hypothesis. Soviet peasants were not willing to sell the volume of grain desired by the Bolsheviks at the price (terms of trade) they were willing to offer. Had the terms of trade been increased, grain sales would have risen (Allen 1997), but such a course was rejected as unacceptable. Higher prices would have exacerbated the state's financing problems – the previous point – and would have also improved rural living standards relative to urban. Such a rise would have reduced rural–urban migration and cut the growth of industrial output. While this chapter is mainly concerned with the financing issue, the impact of alternative financing arrangments on rural-to-urban migration and industrial output growth will also be considered. It turns out that migration is the main avenue by which agrarian taxation affected the real accumulation process, so Stalin's concerns were not entirely unfounded.

Despite its plausibility, the agricultural surplus hypothesis has been strongly attacked (Barsov 1968, 1969, Millar 1974, and Ellman 1975). Barsov, an economic historian, made the key empirical discoveries by working in the Soviet economic archives in the 1960s. He was able to show, contrary to the standard story, that the agricultural terms of trade did not deteriorate – in fact, they improved – during the First Five Year Plan (1928–32). While some state procurement prices were fixed, the free market price of food (i.e., the price on the "collective farm market") was uncontrolled and inflated at a very rapid rate. As a result, agricultural prices as a whole inflated more rapidly than the prices of manufactured goods (Allen 1997, 408). The existence of one free market meant that Stalin was not able to oppress the peasantry in the simple way envisioned in the standard story.

Barsov, Millar, and Ellman made a second calculation that further undermined the standard interpretation – they calculated the trade balance between agriculture and the rest of the economy. Different authors used different prices (1913 prices, 1928 prices, Marxian labor values, etc.) and made somewhat different calculations, but the basic result was the same – sales by the agricultural sector were approximately equal to their purchases. There was no net export surplus and, hence, agriculture made no contribution to national savings.

With peasants out of the running as savers, attention turned toward other candidates. Barsov and Ellman nominated the urban working class whose real wages fell sharply in the early 1930s. A new orthodoxy is emerging, according to which Soviet industrialization was accomplished by depressing urban living standards to produce the savings corresponding to investment. Preobrazhensky is stood on his head.

While Barsov, Millar, and Ellman have undoubtedly corrected one major flaw in the standard story – the finding that agriculture's terms of trade rose is an extremely important one – their research has not settled the matter. The biggest problem lies with their other claim that there was no agricultural export surplus. This is entirely a question of the prices used to value the trade flows, as will be shown. When the full effects of agricultural price inflation (their first point) are taken into account, agriculture emerges as a supplier of capital. Indeed, this result is easier to reconcile with the fact that agricultural taxation financed the state investment budget than is the contrary view that agriculture was not providing savings to the rest of the economy.

More profoundly, however, the Barsov–Millar–Ellman theory of savings should be amended. Theirs is a full employment theory in which the output of consumer goods must be decreased in order *to free resources* to expand the production of producer goods. While consumption did decline during the agricultural collapse of 1933–4, the long run trend was a rise in consumption across the 1930s and a greater (not lesser) utilization of resources in the consumer goods industries. Instead, savings and investment were increased by eliminating structural unemployment. A concomitant rise in the output of consumer and producer goods was, therefore, possible. It is here that the methods of finance enter the story, for the kind of financing policy adopted did affect the rate of rural-to-urban migration and, therefore, the rate of output expansion. When the "agricultural surplus hypothesis" is interpreted as refering to a labor surplus rather than a product surplus, it is much more insightful.

Recomputing Net Agricultural Exports

There are many prices one could use in computing the net export position of Soviet agriculture in the 1930s. Barsov, Millar, and Ellman experimented with 1913 and 1928 prices, but in both cases they used prices received by farmers rather than those paid by consumers. The gap grew substantially in the 1930s; indeed, the rapid inflation of prices on the free market led to the other major revisionist point that agriculture's terms of trade were improving. When the agricultural trade balance is assessed using prices paid by consumers, its net exports rise substantially, and agriculture proves to have financed Soviet investment.

The following examples illustrate the difficulties that arise when prices received by farmers are used instead of consumer prices.

1. As a base case, consider a farmer who sells one kilogram of meat to an urban resident for ten rubles and then spends the proceeds on cloth in a shop. The farmer's trade balance is zero, as is his savings.
2. Suppose there is a bank and the farmer sells his kilogram for ten rubles, deposits four rubles in the bank and buys six rubles worth of manufactures. Now the farmer has a trade surplus of four rubles, which equals his savings. If the bank finances an investment project with the four rubles, then the farmer's personal savings equal the capital formation, and the farmer's net export position correctly equals his contribution to national savings.

3. Instead of a bank lending to a developer, suppose that the state undertakes the investment. If the farmer sells ten rubles worth of meat, the state taxes him four rubles, and the farmer spends the remaining balance of six rubles on manufactures, then his export surplus is four rubles. This will still equal his contribution to national savings and investment.

4. Finally, suppose that the state requisitions one kilogram of meat from the farmer, sells it to consumers for ten rubles, and pays the farmer six rubles of the proceeds, which he spends on manufactures. If the state invests its net gain of four rubles, then the farmer's contribution to national capital formation through *forced* savings (four rubles) equals his trade balance *provided that the agricultural sales are valued at the prices paid by consumers*. Agricultural taxation has also financed a portion of the state investment budget.

On the other hand, if the agricultural sales are valued at the price received by the farmer (six rubles), then the forced savings implicit in the taxation are omitted and only voluntary savings on the part of the farmer are recovered by computing his trade balance.

This example shows that the forced savings implicit in a compulsory procurement system can only be measured by valuing farm sales at consumer prices inclusive of the agricultural taxes. Barsov, Millar, and Ellman, however, value sales at the prices received by farmers exclusive of those taxes. Consequently, their calculations only measure the negligible voluntary savings of Soviet peasants rather than the full contribution of agriculture to national savings.

Table 9.1 shows the flows to and from agriculture in 1937, taking account of turnover tax collections. Retail sales of consumer goods amounted to 126 billion rubles. These sales were mainly processed agricultural products (bread, cotton cloth), so subtracting value added in the consumer goods industries (33 billion rubles) gives the net value of agricultural sales (93 billion rubles). The latter is divided into turnover tax receipts (76 billion rubles) and the income received by farmers on compulsory purchases (17 billion). Farmers also earned 15 billion rubles on their collective farm market sales. Finally, investment in farm equipment equalled 2 billion rubles.

These figures can be used to calculate the net export position of agriculture. Its sales equalled 108 billion rubles inclusive of the turnover tax (93 billion of net sales plus 15 billion on collective farm market sales). Agriculture's purchases equalled 34 billion rubles on the assumption that farmers spent their entire cash incomes (32 billion = 15 billion of collective farm market sales + 17 billion of compulsory purchases) on manufactured consumer goods and including the 2 billion rubles of equipment shipments. By this reckoning, agriculture had a net export surplus of 74 billion rubles (108 − 34 billion rubles). If one followed the lead of Barsov, Millar, and Ellman,

TABLE 9.1. *Sales and Purchases by Soviet Farmers, 1937*

Total retail sales	126 billion rubles
Less value added in processing	33 billion
Net sales of agricultural goods	93 billion
Less turnover tax	76 billion
Farmers' income on sales to state	17 billion
Plus farmer's sales on free market	15 billion
Farm cash income = purchases of manufactures	32 billion
Plus farm equipment purchases	2 billion
Total farm imports	34 billion

Source: Retail sales are from Zaleski (1984, 723), agricultural machinery investment is from Moorsteen and Powell (1966, 429), turnover tax receipts, spending by public agencies, and investment expenditures are from Bergson (1953, 20). Values of agricultural sales are my calculations. Value added in the consumer goods industry is calculated as a residual.

however, and valued farm sales at the prices received by the farmers (i.e., exclusive of the turnover tax), then agriculture would appear to have been a net importer because its sales would only have been 32 billion rubles and its purchases 34 billion rubles. Clearly, it is more insightful to include the turnover tax for the reasons discussed.

Agricultural net exports of 74 billion rubles was very large in comparison to other expenditures in the economy. The total spending of all public agencies was 108 billion rubles, which included investment in fixed and circulating capital of 56 billion rubles. Agricultural taxation financed the state investment budget and much else, besides. (Nove and Morrison [1982, 61–2], in their critique of Barsov, refer to the contribution of the turnover tax to government revenues and raise the question of who bore the tax.)

The figures for 1937 are typical of the mid-1930s but not of the first Five Year Plan (1928–32). The ratio of agricultural taxation (turnover tax receipts plus the yield from the increasingly unimportant agricultural tax) to investment was around 40 percent in 1928, 1929, and 1930. It rose to just over half in 1931 and to about three-quarters in 1932. Only in 1933 – the beginning of the Second Five Year Plan – did agricultural taxation exceed gross investment. Thereafter, agricultural tax revenues grew much more rapidly than investment. By the end of the 1930s, agriculture was paying for the military buildup of those years as well as the investment effort.

There are two reasons why agriculture became the main source of public revenue and national savings only during the mid-1930s. First, the administrative changes required to tax agriculture so heavily were not put into place until the early 1930s. Those changes included collectivization, the system of compulsory deliveries, and the turnover tax. Second, paradoxically, the agricultural terms of trade had to improve enough to allow agricultural taxation to be raised. Very rapid inflation in the free food market in the early 1930s was followed by price reforms in the mid-1930s that raised food prices in state shops to the same level as the prices on the collective farm market. The extra revenue generated in the shops went to the state through the turnover tax rather than to the farmers through higher procurement prices. The improvement in agriculture's terms of trade led directly to the sector's providing savings to the rest of the economy. Far from free markets inhibiting the state's ability to tax agriculture, it was inflation on those markets that made Stalin's system work.

Consumption and Resource Allocation

Although there is much more life in the agricultural surplus hypothesis than Barsov, Millar, and Ellman allowed, it still faces major challenges from other quarters. The history of consumption is a case in point. The agricultural surplus hypothesis implicitly assumes that the Soviet economy was at full employment so that someone's consumption had to fall in order for investment to rise. In the original formalation, peasants were the savers; after the revisions of Barsov, Millar, and Ellman, urban workers were advanced as the main savers. In fact, however, there was no class of savers, as will be shown.

The main reasons for believing that consumption declined in accord with the standard story are because there was a famine in 1933–4 and because urban real wages dropped at the same time. Barsov's figures, which deal only with the first Five Year Plan (1928–32), show these declines. Consumption did, indeed, drop then, but a longer-term view shows that these were unique events. Between 1928 and 1939, farm consumption per head remained constant, urban consumption increased, and total consumption per capita rose over 20 percent. There was no long-run fall in farm consumption or in consumer goods production generally (Allen 1998b).

Also, there was no shift in resources from consumption to investment, as the standard story supposes. This is clear in the case of labor. Kahan's (1959) estimates of Soviet agricultural employment show that the number of days worked in 1933 was 2 percent above the 1926–9 average. From 1934–8, employment increased to 8 to 14 percent more than the 1926–9 level. Kahan (1959, 454) observed that "The most interesting feature of these indexes is the increase in labor inputs during the 1930s, when both the number of producing units and the level of agricultural output were below the 1926–9 level." Before 1950, the policy was to expand collective farm employment to sop up surplus labor in the countryside rather than to cut agricultural jobs.

Employment also increased in the consumer goods industries, the most important of which were processing farm products. In textiles, for instance, employment rose from 1,919,000 in 1927–8 to 2,000,000 in 1933 to 2,568,000 in 1937. In food and allied products, the corresponding figures were 803,000 in 1927–8, 1,094,000 in 1933, and 1,478,000 in 1937 (Nutter 1962, 501–2).

There is no evidence of resource allocation from agriculture – or consumption generally – to investment.

The main reason for the decline in real wages noted by Barsov, Millar, and Ellman was the collapse in agricultural output in the immediate wake of collectivization. As a result, free market food prices shot up (lowering urban real wages) and there was a famine in grain growing areas. Death by starvation, however, is not resource reallocation. The fall in consumption in the early 1930s reflects a disastrous agricultural policy rather than a transfer of farm workers to city jobs.

The Tax Incidence Question

A second challenge to the agricultural surplus hypothesis lies in its ignoring the obvious tax incidence question: Did the tax on bread, for example, lower the incomes of wheat growers by reducing the price they received for their crops or did it lower the income of urban workers by raising the price they paid for their food? The answer to this question bears directly on the link between finance and real economic activity.

In partial equilibrium analyses of tax incidence, the burden of the tax is determined by the price elasticities of supply and demand. In the model used here, the price elasticity of supply in 1930 was about 0.7, whereas the demand elasticity was 1.0. Those figures imply that the tax was shifted onto farmers as Stalin intended. However, a partial equilibrium analysis of this problem is not adequate because the revenues of the agricultural tax were so large relative to other aggregates in the economy. Hence, a general equilibrium analysis has been undertaken.

Simulation Model and Issues

A simulation model of the Soviet economy has been used to measure the contribution of the agricultural procurement system and taxation to capital accumulation in the U.S.S.R. from 1928 to 1939. The role of other policies, including the decision to allocate more resouces to heavy industry, the employment practices of Soviet firms (e.g., soft-budget constraints), and the terrorism that accompanied collectivization are included in the model. In this way, a full accounting of the sources of investment is possible, and the contribution of agricultural taxation can be seen in comparison to the impacts of other policies and institutions.

The model consists of three producing sectors: agriculture, producer goods (machinery and construction), and consumer goods (everthing else including manufactured consumer goods and government activity). Farm output is treated as exogenous because agriculture was a surplus labor sector in the 1930s and because production varied for climatic and political reasons. Farm output is consumed by the peasants, sold as fresh food to urban residents on the collective farm market, and sold to the consumer goods industry for processing. Producer goods output depends on labor and capital employed in that sector, and consumer goods output depends on labor, capital, and the volume of agricultural goods delivered for processing.

There are three souces of demand in the model: (1) urban workers buy manufactured food products, manufactured nonfood products, and fresh food on the collective farm market, (2) peasants buy manufactured nonfood goods, and (3) the state buys consumer goods (including state services) and producer goods for military and investment purposes. The state budget is financed with a tax, which can be changed from one simulation to another.

The model was developed in several forms to represent the alternative policies and institutions. The basic version of the model represents actual practices and was calibrated against Soviet data from the period. This model was tested by simulating economic development with the actual values of exogenous variables to see whether the predicted endogenous variables matched historical experience. Tracking was reasonably good.

The impact of five alternative policies was studied with the model:

1. The Investment Strategy

   A major factor affecting the rate of capital accumulation was the allocation of investment between the consumer goods and producer goods industries. The Soviet Union is well known for having shifted this balance toward producer goods, and that tilt is represented in simulations by increasing the parameter e (the fraction of investment goods going to the producer goods sector) from 7 percent in 1928 to 16 percent in the 1930s.

2. Farm Marketing and State Procurements

   In all models, total farm marketing is treated as a voluntary decision because sales on the collective food market were always at the discretion of the peasants and always positive. In models of collectivization, total sales depend on the collective farm market prices, sales to the consumer goods sector (state procurements) are forced equal to their historical levels, and sales on the collective farm market become a residual. In models without compulsory deliveries, total sales depend on the price received on all sales and a regression model of marketing is used to divide total sales into sales to industry for processing and sales of fresh food directly to urban residents through farmers' markets.

3. Taxes

   A policy of building up the producer goods sector by raising the fraction of investment allocated to it (higher e) implies higher levels of investment than would otherwise occur. More investment increases the state budget and requires tax collections to rise to balance that budget. Because the prices received by farmers equal retail prices less processing costs less turnover tax collections, a high investment strategy implies higher turnover taxes and a greater spread between retail and farm gate prices. This is an important link between the procurement system and economic activity.

To assess the effects of the turnover tax on growth, it is necessary to compare its results with those of an alternative tax. In some simulations, the turnover tax has been replaced with a flat rate tax on cash incomes yielding the amount required to balance the state budget. This tax is explicitly tilted against urban residents because their incomes were entirely in cash while rural incomes included an important component in kind.

4. Terrorism and Rural-Urban Migration

The industrial workforce depends on the urban population, which, in turn, depends mainly on rural-to-urban migration. Migration is made a function of per capita urban consumption relative to per capita rural consumption. One way that tax levels affect growth is by changing that ratio and hence the growth of the urban population. In addition, simulations are done with two migration functions. One reflects the actual experience of the 1930s with its famine, state terrorism, deportations, and high rural mortality. A second function, which implies less migration at any level of relative per capita consumption, is intended to represent what would have happened if "normal" times had continued. Comparison of simulations with the two functions measures the impact of terrorism on growth.

5. Soft Budgets

In the 1920s, Soviet firms were organized in trusts and directed to maximize profits. During the first Five Year Plan, output targets replaced profits as the performance indicator, and firms received extensive loans to allow them to expand employment and meet targets. This replacement of hard budgets by soft budgets meant that employment expanded beyond the profit maximizing point, and the marginal product of labor fell to half of the wage. To measure the impact of this employment policy, simulations were done in two ways. In the first, the full urban workforce was employed irrespective of the marginal product of labor (soft budget constraint), and, in the second, the marginal product of labor was constrained to equal exogenous wages as in the models of Todaro (1968, 1969) and Harris and Todaro (1970). In that case, there was urban unemployment, so rural-to-urban migration was made a function of expected consumption levels.

Table 9.2 shows the results of simulating these policies. The actual nonagricultural capital stock in 1928 was 136.3 billion rubles (1937 prices). If the economy had continued to develop without planning, collectivization, or soft budgets, and with an investment allocation pattern that replicated

TABLE 9.2. *Actual and Simulated Nonagricultural Capital Stock,*
1939 (Billions of 1937 Rubles)

Actual 1928 Nonagricultural Capital Stock	136.3 billion
1939 stock simulated with –	
e = 7%, hard budgets, free food market, no terror	72.5 billion
e = 16%, hard budgets, free food market, no terror	231.4 billion
e = 16%, soft budgets, compulsory sales, no terror	279.1 billion
e = 16%, soft budgets, compulsory sales, terror	302.7 billion
Actual 1939 Nonagricultural Capital Stock	344.7 billion

Source: Allen (1997, 15; 1998a, 585).

the structure of the 1928 capital stock, then the 1939 capital stock would have been 172.5 billion rubles (or 27 percent more). Because the population would have expanded 18 percent that is almost no gain on a per capita basis. This pace of accumulation is what the Soviets were trying to avoid.

Changing the investment pattern to put more new investment into heavy industry (in terms of the model, raising e from 7 percent to 16 percent) would have increased the 1939 capital stock to 231.4 billion rubles for a gain of 158.9 billion rubles. Relaxing the hard budget constraints and replacing profit maximization with output targets would have brought a further substantial gain because the 1939 capital stock would have gone up by another 47.7 billion rubles to 279.1 billion. These two policies were the largest sources of gain.

The policies relating to collectivization and agricultural policy brought additional gains, but they were small. The system of compulsory deliveries of farm products to state procurement agencies in conjunction with the turnover tax would have increased the 1939 capital stock by only an additional 8 billion rubles, reaching 287.1 billion. The terrorism associated with collectivization was more effective than the procurement system in raising capital accumulation because it would have added 15.6 billion rubles to the stock, raising it to 302.7 billion.

The simulated value of 302.7 billion incorporates all of the actual Soviet policies and institutions, so a check on the model is to compare it to the actual value of the 1939 capital stock. That value was 344.7 billion or 14 percent more. The correspondence is not perfect, but the model does replicate most of the growth in the capital stock, so there are grounds for having confidence in the decomposition of its sources.

The simulations allow a dynamic answer to the question of who bore the turnover tax. In this case, a group bore the tax if its consumption was reduced. Comparisons are done using 1936–8 average values to average farm consumption due to weather-induced fluctuations in yields.

Between 1928 and 1936–8, actual farm consumption per head was essentially static (rising from 940 rubles per year in 1928 to 964 rubles in

TABLE 9.3. *Actual and Simulated Peasant Consumption, per head, 1936–8*
(1937 rubles per year)

Actual 1928 consumption per head	940 rubles	
1936–8 consumption per head simulated with –		
	e = 7%	e = 16%
hard budgets, free food market, no terror	1161	1146
soft budgets, compulsory sales, no terror	1208	1016
soft budgets, compulsory sales, terror	1118	1017
Actual 1936–8 consumption per head	964 rubles	

Source: Allen (1997, 15, 1998a, 585).

1936–8), while nonfarm consumption increased from 1,656 to 2,000 – a jump of 21 percent.

Table 9.3 shows farm and nonfarm consumption per head in 1928 and 1936–8 for two investment stragies (e = 7% and e = 16%) carried out in three institutional arrangements – the New Economic Policy (NEP), collectivization and the system of compulsory sales to state agencies, and collectivization as it actually occurred including famine and state terror. With all institutional arrangements, raising e from 7 percent to 16 percent reduced farm consumption per head in 1936–8, while increasing nonfarm consumption. Rural living standards would have been best protected, however, with a continuation of the NEP because the simulated fall in farm per capita consumption was negligible in that case. With collectivization, however it was executed, farm living standards fell more than they would have if rapid industrialization had been pursued within the framework of the NEP. The decline is especially great when the marketing system is the only change from the NEP. In that sense, collectivization shifted the burden of industrialization onto the peasants.

These simulations show that the mobilization of the agricultural surplus made little contribution to capital accumulation in the 1930s, although the policies actually pursued did lower the living standards of peasants. Free markets in food and taxes biased in favor of the peasants would have produced a terminal capital stock only slightly smaller than the one actually achieved, while raising peasant welfare. To the rather small extent that collectivization accelerated growth, its main contribution was through terrorizing and deporting the rural population, which increased urban employment more rapidly than would have otherwise been the case.

The key factor affecting the growth of the capital stock in the Soviet Union was the production and allocation of capital goods. Their production was accelerated by a rapid build up of the inputs in the producer goods industry. The important and effective policies were the ones that accelerated that build-up. Capital increased faster by allocating more investment back into the producer goods sector. This also accelerated employment growth because it created job opportunities in that sector. In addition, the soft-budget constraint allowed the expansion of the industrial workforce. While the marginal product of labor was low, it was still positive, so output expanded.

Finally, more rapid urbanization increased industrial employment. It was here that agrarian policy had its impact. Compulsory deliveries and low procurement prices did increase urban living standards relative to rural ones, and that rise increased migration to the towns. The deportation of the Kulaks (peasant farmers who opposed collectivization), famine, and state terrorism also pushed many more people to the industrial economy. The contributions of these factors was not as large as those due to the investment strategy and the soft-budget constraint, however.

Conclusion

There is much more life in the agricultural surplus hypothesis than the revisionism of Barsov, Millar, and Ellman allows. Agricultural taxation did generate enough revenue to finance most Soviet investment in the 1930s, and agriculture made a substantial contribution to national savings once the rapid inflation in food prices is taken into account. Indeed, it was the improvements in agriculture's terms of trade that provided the revenue that the state sopped up through the turnover tax.

From a broader perspective, however, agricultural taxation was only one factor raising savings and investment in the 1930s and a minor one at that. Simulations of Soviet growth with alternative tax systems show that the turnover tax did lower peasant incomes below levels they might otherwise have achieved and, by the same token, did raise investment by accelerating rural-to-urban migration and thus employment in the capital goods sector. However, the increases were small compared to other Stalinist policies. Allocating more investment to heavy industry and providing firms with the incentive (high output targets) and the means (soft budgets) to hire anyone looking for work greatly expanded the output of producer goods and thus the rate of investment. Indeed, terrorizing the countryside during collectivization was more effective in driving people to the city than the changes in relative incomes implied by alternative tax systems. The Soviet Union would have industrialized rapidly whatever agrarian policy was followed in the 1930s. The one actually chosen made only a small positive contribution to that growth.

This analysis of the agricultural surplus hypothesis highlights the links between finance and real variables in the Soviet Union in the 1930s. Taxation affected capital formation mainly through rural-to-urban migration. The agricultural surplus that was, in fact, mobilized was the labor surplus in the countryside rather than some imagined surplus of hoarded grain. The Soviet Union in the 1930s was a classic labor surplus economy. Vast numbers could leave the countryside without farm output falling. In 1928, the rural population was about 122 million. Perhaps 10 million people died in the famine of the 1930s and another 25 million moved to the cities. Twenty-five million more Soviet citizens died in the Second World War, and by 1950 the pre-war urban population had been regained so the entire wartime population loss was borne by the countryside. Not a great deal of farm capital survived the war either. Despite these losses, farm output had not fallen (Johnson and Kahan 1991).

Bibliography

Allen, Robert C. "Agricultural Marketing and the Possibilities for Industrialization in the Soviet Union in the 1930s." *Explorations in Economic History*, 34 (1997): 387–410.

Allen, Robert C. "Imposition et mobilisation du surplus agricole a l'epoque stalinienne." *Annales: Histoire, Sciences Sociales*, 53 (1998a): 569–95.

Allen, Robert C. "The Standard of Living in the Soviet Union, 1928–40." *Journal of Economic History* 58 (1998b): 1063–1089.

Antel, John, and Paul Gregory. "Agricultural Surplus Models and Peasant Behavior: Soviet Agriculture in the 1920s" *Economic Development and Cultural Change*, 42 (1994): 375–386.

Baran, Paul. *The Political Economy of Growth*. (New York: Monthly Review Press, 1962).

Barsov, A. A. "Sel'skoe khoziaistvo i istochniki sotsialisticheskogo nakopleniia v gody pervoi piatiletki (1928–1933)," *Istoriia SSSR* (1968): 64–82.

Barsov, A. A. *Balans stoimostnykh obmenov mezdu gorodom i derevnei*. Moscow: Nauka, 1969.

Bergson, Abram. *Soviet National Income and Production, 1937*. New York: Columbia University Press, 1953.

Bergson, Abram. *The Real National Income of Soviet Russia since 1928*. Cambridge, MA: Harvard University Press, 1961.

Bergson, A., R. Bernaut, L. Turgeon. "Basic Industrial Prices in the USSR, 1928–1950: Twenty-Five Branch Series and Their Aggregation," Research Memorandum RM-1522, The Rand Corporation, Santa Monica, 1955.

Blomqvist, A. G. "The Economics of Price Scissors: Comment," *American Economic Review*, 76 (1986): 1188–91.

Carter, M. R. "The Economics of Price Scissors: Comment," *American Economic Review*, 76 (1986): 1192–94.

Chapman, Janet G. *Real Wages in Soviet Russia since 1928*. Cambridge, MA: Harvard University Press, 1963.

Cohen, S. F. *Bukharin and the Bolshevik Revolution*. New York: Knopf, 1973.

Davies, R. W. *The Socialist Offensive: The Collectivization of Soviet Agriculture, 1929–1930*. Cambridge, MA: Harvard University Press, 1980.

Davies, R. W. *The Soviet Economy in Turmoil, 1929–1930*. Cambridge, MA: Harvard University Press, 1989.

Davies, R. W. *Crisis and Progress in the Soviet Economy, 1931–1933*. Houndmills, Basingstoke, Hampshire: Macmillan, 1996.

Davies, R. W., Mark Harrison, and S. G. Wheatcroft. *The Economic Transformation of the Soviet Union, 1913–1945*. Cambridge: Cambridge University Press, 1994.

Ellman, Michael. "Did the Agricultural Surplus Provide the Resources for the Increase in Investment in the USSR During the First Five Year Plan?" *Economic Journal*, 85 (1975): 844–63.

Ellman, Michael. "On a Mistake of Preobrazhensky and Stalin," *Journal of Development Studies*, 14 (1978): 353–6.

Erlich, A. *The Soviet Industrialization Debate, 1924–1928*. Cambridge, MA: Harvard University Press, 1960.

Fitzpatrick, Sheila. *The Russian Revolution*. Oxford: Oxford University Press, 1994.

Ghatak, Subrata, and Ken Ingersent. *Agriculture and Economic Development*. Baltimore: The Johns Hopkins University Press, 1984.

Gregory, Paul R. *Before Command: An Economic History of Russia from Emancipation to the First Five-Year Plan*. Princeton: Princeton University Press, 1994.

Gregory, Paul R., and Robert C. Stuart. *Soviet Economic Structure and Performance*. New York: Harper & Row, 1986.

Harris, J. R., and M. Todaro. "Migration, Unemployment, and Development: A Two-Sector Analysis," *American Economic Review*, 60 (1970): 126–142.

Harrison, Mark. "The Peasantry and Industrialization," in *From Tsarism to the New Economic Policy*, ed. R. W. Davies. Houndmills, Basingstoke, Hampshire: Macmillan, 1990, 104–24.

Harrison, Mark. *Accounting for War: Soviet Production, Employment, and the Defence Burden, 1940–1945*. Cambridge: Cambridge University Press, 1992.

Hoeffding, Oleg. *Soviet National Income and Product in 1928*. New York: Columbia University Press, 1954.

Holzman, Franklyn D. *Soviet Taxation*. Cambridge, MA: Harvard University Press, 1955.

Hunter, Holland. "Soviet Agriculture with and without Collectivization," *Slavic Review*, 47 (1988): 203–26.

Hunter, Holland, and Janusz M. Szyrmer. *Faulty Foundations: Soviet Economic Policies, 1928–1940*. Princeton: Princeton University Press, 1992.

Jasny, Naum. *The Socialized Agriculture of the USSR: Plans and Performance*. Stanford, Stanford University Press, 1949.

Johnson, D. Gale, and Arcadius Kahan. "Soviet Agriculture: Structure and Growth," in Arcadius Kahan, *Studies and Essays on the Soviet and Eastern European Economies, Vol. I: Published Works on the Soviet Economy*, ed. Peter B. Brown. Newtonville, MA: Oriental Research Partners, 1991, selection 13, (first published 1959).

Johnson, Simon, and Peter Temin. "The Macroeconomics of NEP," *Economic History Review*, 46 (1993): 750–67.

Johnston, Bruce F., and John W. Mellor. "The Role of Agriculture in Economic Development," *American Economic Review*, 51 (1961): 566–93.

Kahan, Arcadius, "Changes in Labor Inputs in Soviet Agriculture," *Journal of Political Economy*, 67 (1959): 451–62.

Kaplan, Norman M., and Richard H. Moorsteen. "Index of Soviet Industrial Output," Research Memorandum RM-2495, The Rand Corporation, Santa Monica, 1960.

Karcz, Jerzy F. "Soviet Agricultural Marketings and Prices, 1928–1954," Research Memorandum RM-1930, The Rand Corporation, Santa Monica, 1957.

Karcz, Jerzy F. "Thoughts on the Grain Problem," *Soviet Studies*, 18 (1967): 399–434.

Karcz, Jerzy F. *The Economics of Communist Agriculture: Selected Papers*, ed. by Arthur W. Wright. Bloomington: International Development Institute, 1979.

Khanin, G. I. *Dinamika ekonomicheskogo razvitiya SSSR*. Novosobirsk, 1991.

Lewin, M. *Russian Peasants and Soviet Power*. London: Allen & Unwin, 1968.

Lorimer, F. *The Population of the Soviet Union*. Geneva: League of Nations, 1946.

Malafeyev, A. N. *Istoriya Tsenoobrazovaniya v SSSR*. Moscow: Mysl'., 1964.

Mellor, John W., and Mohinder S. Mudahar. "Agriculture in Economic Development: Theories, Findings, and Challenges in an Asian Context," in *Agriculture in Economic Development, 1940s to 1990s*, ed. Lee R. Martin, *A Survey of Agricultural Economics Literature*, Vol. 4. Minneapolis: University of Minnesota Press, 1992, 331–544.

Merl, S. *Der Agrarmarkt und die Neue Okonomische Politik. Die Anfange staatlicher Lenkung der Landwirtschaft in der Sowjetunion, 1925–1928*. Munich: Oldenbourg Verlag, 1980.

Merl, S. "Socio-Economic Differentiation of the Peasantry," in *From Tsarism to the New Economic Policy*, ed. by R. W. Davies. Houndmills, Basingstoke, Hampshire: Macmillan, 1990, 47–63.

Millar, James. "A Reformulation of A.V. Chayanov's Theory of the Peasant Economy," *Economic Development and Cultural Change*, 18 (1970a): 219–29.

Millar, James. "Soviet Rapid Development and the Agricultural Surplus Hypothesis," *Soviet Studies*, 22 (1970b): 77–93.

Millar, James. "Mass Collectivization and the Contribution of Soviet Agriculture to the First Five-Year Plan: A Review Article," *Slavic Review*, 33 (1974): 750–60.

Millar, James. "What's Wrong with the 'Standard Story'?" *Problems of Communism* 25 (1976): 50–55.

Moorsteen, Richard, and Raymond P. Powell, *The Soviet Capital Stock, 1928–1962*. Homewood, IL, Richard D. Irwin, 1966.

Nicholls, William H. "The Place of Agriculture in Economic Development," in *Agriculture in Economic Development*, eds. Carl K. Eicher and Lawrence W. Witt. New York: McGraw-Hill, 1964, 11–44.

Nimitz, Nancy. *Statistics of Soviet Agriculture*. Research Memorandum RM-1250, The Rand Corporation, Santa Monica, 1954.

Nove, Alec. *An Economic History of the U.S.S.R.* London: Penguin Books, 1990.

Nove, Alec, and David Morrison. "The Contribution of Agriculture to Accumulation in the 1930s," in *L'industrialisation de l'URSS dans les années trente*, ed. Charles Bettelheim. Paris: Éditions de l'École des hautes Études en Sciences Sociales, 1982, 47–63.

Nutter, G. Warren. *Growth of Industrial Production in the Soviet Union*. Princeton: Princeton University Press, 1962.

Preobrazhensky, E. *The New Economics*, trans. Brian Pearce, Oxford: Clarendon Press, 1965, (first published 1926).

Sah, R. K., and J. E. Stiglitz. "The Economics of Price Scissors," *American Economic Review*, 74 (1984): 125–38.

Sah, R. K., and J. E. Stiglitz. "The Economics of Price Scissors: Reply," *American Economic Review*, 76 (1986): 1195–9.

Spulber, N. *Soviet Strategy for Economic Growth*. Bloomington, Indiana: University Press, 1964.

Todaro, M. "An Analysis of Industrialization: Employment and Unemployment in LDCs," *Yale Economic Essays*, 8 (1968): 329–492.

Todaro, M. "A Model of Labor Migration and Urban Unemployment in Less Developed Countries," *American Economic Review*, 59 (1969): 138–48.

Vyltsan, M. A. "Obshestvenno-ekonomicheskii stoy kolkhoznoy derevny b 1933–1940 gg," *Istoria SSSR*, 2 (1966): 44–65.

Vainshtein, A. L. *Oblozenia e Platezi Krest'yanstva*. Moscow: Ekonomist, 1924.

Wheatcroft, S. G. "A Reevaluation of Soviet Agricultural Production in the 1920s and 1930s," in *The Soviet Rural Economy*, ed. Robert C. Stuart. Totowa, NJ: Rowman & Allanheld, 32–62.

Wheatcroft, S. G. "Agriculture," in *From Tsarism to the New Economic Policy*, ed. R. W. Davies. Houndmills, Basingstoke, Hampshire: MacMillan, 1990, 79–103.

Zaleski, Eugène. "Les fluctuations des prix de détail en Union Soviétique." *Etudes et Conjunctures* (1955): 329–84.

Zaleski, Eugène. *Planning for Economic Growth in the Soviet Union, 1918–1932*. Chapel Hill: University of North Carolina Press, 1971.

Zaleski, Eugène, *La plantification Staliennes croissance, fluctuations économiques en U.R.S.S., 1932–52*. Paris: Economica, 1984.

IO

Was Adherence to the Gold Standard a "Good Housekeeping Seal of Approval" during the Interwar Period?

Michael Bordo, Michael Edelstein, and Hugh Rockoff

INTRODUCTION

Adherence to fixed parities and convertibility of national currencies into gold served as a signal of financial rectitude or a "good housekeeping seal of approval" during the classical gold standard era from 1870–1914. Peripheral countries that adhered faithfully to the gold standard rule had access at better terms to capital from the core countries of Western Europe than did countries with poor records of adherence (Bordo and Rockoff 1996).[1] In this chapter we extend the approach to ascertain whether the "good housekeeping seal" was also an important institution under the interwar gold exchange standard, which prevailed only from 1925 to 1931.

In simplest terms, the "good housekeeping seal" hypothesis views the gold standard as a commitment mechanism. Adherence to the fixed parity of gold required that members follow domestic monetary and fiscal policies and have other institutions of financial probity (such as having a monetary authority that holds gold reserves) consistent with long-run maintenance of the fixed price of gold. It also signaled to potential overseas lenders that the borrowers were "good people."[2]

An important part of the hypothesis is that the gold standard should be viewed as a contingent rule or a rule with escape clauses. Members were expected to adhere to convertibility except in the event of a well-understood emergency such as a war, a financial crisis, or a shock to the terms of trade. Under these circumstances, temporary departures from the rule would be

---

[1] Also see Flandreau, LeCacheux, and Zumer 1998.

[2] Our approach is similar to, but not the same as, the signaling hypothesis first developed by Spence 1974.

For helpful comments we thank Robert Cull, Larry Neal, and John Wallis. We also benefited from the discussion of of an earlier draft at the Program Meeting of the Development of American Economy group of the NBER, March 6, 1999. For able research assistance we thank Zhu Wang.

tolerated on the assumption that once the emergency passed, convertibility at the original parity would resume (Bordo and Kydland 1995).

An implication of the contingent rule is that the countries that returned to gold parity at a devalued parity after an emergency would be judged as having "weak resolve" and countries that never returned to gold or never adhered would be even worse. In other words, following the gold standard rule served as a signal, other things being equal, to lenders that these loans would be safe, both in the sense that they would not be defaulted on and in the sense that they would not be repaid in a devalued currency. Hence, they would charge a lower risk premium to these borrowers than to borrowing countries that were not good gold standard adherents.

In Bordo and Rockoff (1996) we tested this hypothesis for nine widely different capital importing countries. We found that the risk premium charged on loans in London was lowest for a group of orthodox gold standard countries that never left gold, slightly higher for those countries that temporarily devalued, and still higher for those countries that temporarily left gold and permanently devalued or that never adhered. In this chapter we extend this methodology to the interwar gold exchange standard.

The interwar gold exchange standard generally has a bad press. It only lasted six years before collapsing in the debacle of the Great Depression. It is viewed as a flawed attempt to restore the glories of the classical gold standard. Its flaws included the fact that the principal member, the United States, did not deflate sufficiently after the inflation of World War I to restore the real price of gold to its pre-war level, hence imparting a deflationary bias on the system once other countries restored convertibility (Johnson 1997). It was also flawed because the United Kingdom rejoined gold at an overvalued parity while France did the opposite. Most important, however, was the fact that the United States and France each followed policies of sterilizing gold inflows that exacerbated the underlying disequilibrium.[3]

Despite its flaws and bad press, there is compelling evidence that capital markets in the 1920s were as well integrated between the core countries (the United States, United Kingdom, France, and Germany) as they were before the war (Officer 1996; Hallwood and MacDonald 1996). Also, as we will elaborate, the core counties and most nations attached the highest importance to restoring the gold standard. The gold standard that was restored, however, was based on somewhat different rules than the pre-war variant. It

[3] Other flaws stressed in the literature include: the use of multiple reserve countries; an incipient "Triffin dilemma," that the use of foreign exchange as a substitute for increasingly scarce gold would expose the center countries to a speculative attack as their outstanding liabilities increased relative to their gold reserves; and a lack of credibility compared to the classical gold standard. Because most countries after World War I were concerned with domestic policy goals (the level of real output and employment), their resolve to defend their parities in the face of speculative attack was weakened (Eichengreen 1992).

was a gold exchange standard based on the recommendations of the Genoa Conference of 1922 in which members were encouraged to substitute foreign exchange in dollars or pounds for scarce gold, and the central reserve countries (the United States, United Kingdom, and later France) were to hold reserves only in the form of gold. Also, gold adherence was explicitly a part of a package of financial orthodoxy encouraged for all members. The packages, first imposed as a part of the League of Nations' stabilization arrangements for the former belligerents, included an independent central bank, a balanced budget, and gold convertibility. The package was extended through the efforts of Montagu Norman, Benjamin Strong, and Edwin Kemmerer to many peripheral countries.

In sum, one would expect that the good housekeeping seal hypothesis should hold in the interwar as it did before World War I. Several important differences between the two regimes (aside from the flaws of the gold exchange standard) will influence our approach to testing it. The first change is that the mantle of principal lender was passed from the United Kingdom to the United States, so that most lending to the periphery originated in New York, rather than London. The second difference is that most countries went back to gold at devalued parities. The third is that most countries used foreign exchange as a substitute for gold reserves.

Section 2 of this chapter discusses the restoration of the gold standard in the early 1920s, focusing on the diplomatic efforts by the British, and the development of a new order in international finance. Behind the prodigious effort to restore the status quo ante was the belief in the gold standard as a good housekeeping seal. Following the Cunliffe Report (1918), the official position was to restore the halcyon days of the pre-war period when London was the world's principal capital market. The efforts to return to gold were strongly supported by the United States. The process we describe includes concerted policies by the League of Nations and the financial powers to stabilize many countries and private missions to establish central banks. Although the British were the strongest advocates of a return to the "status quo ex ante," they were faced with the growing reality, based on the fact that to finance World War I they had cashed in their overseas assets and borrowed heavily from the United States, and after they returned to gold at the original parity in April 1925 that they were under continuous balance of payments pressure, that they did not have the resources to restore the lending network that they had before the war. This was manifested in a series of embargoes on foreign lending in the 1920s. For these reasons, and as an extension of its lending activity to the belligerents that developed during World War I, the United States stepped into the breach.

Section 3 describes the evolution of the U.S. role as principal foreign lender. The United States had long been amongst the staunchest advocates of gold standard orthodoxy, and the pattern of overseas lending in the interwar period, as discussed in the following, was clearly tied to adherence to gold by the recipients. The rise of the United States reflected both an extension of wartime lending and its emergence as the strongest economic power. We also consider the indictment that U.S. lending standards were not as strict as those of the British. Although many of the loans issued in the 1920s were defaulted on in the 1930s, the shock of the Great Depression likely was the main reason for the poor performance.

Section 4 presents our empirical evidence for the good housekeeping seal hypothesis. Based on data for forty countries for nine years, we estimated a pooled cross-section, time series regression of the interest rates of countries borrowing in the United States on several measures of gold standard adherence (whether a country adhered to gold, whether it devalued, and whether it was on a gold exchange or gold bullion standard) and a set of macroeconomic and other institutional fundamentals. The results strongly confirm those found for the classical gold standard. They show that countries that adhered to gold at whatever parity received better terms than those that did not, and that countries that did not devalue when they returned to gold did better than those that did.

RESTORING THE GOLD STANDARD

Our historical survey stresses the great importance that the United Kingdom attached to restoring the status quo ante, as a way to recreate the preeminence it held in international capital markets before 1914. The belief in the good housekeeping seal hypothesis was implicit in this strategy and it was strongly supported by the United States and virtually every other country.[4]

Economic, Political and Social Conditions as World War I Ended

At the end of World War I, the United States, Great Britain, France, Germany, and many other nations, belligerents or neutral, had swollen money supplies, large debts, large immediate expenditure needs, and moderate levels of taxation. All of the belligerents had increased taxes during the war, but most of the financing for the war's immense budgets derived from new government debt and money creation. While postwar expenditure needs were lower, even war-time levels of taxation were quite inadequate.

Perhaps the most troublesome element affecting economic life was the demand for reparations. The European Allied victors expected post-World War I reparations would cover government budget gaps, especially the severely war damaged countries of Belgium and France. Reparations were also expected to help pay the inter-Allied loans from the United States as the war's net creditor. For Germany the threat and extent of the highly disputed

---

[4] See Aldcroft and Oliver 1998, Chapter 1.

reparations clouded any attempt by its new government to create a stable fiscal and monetary environment for its economy.

An important new element in post-war European politics of finance was that Europe's working classes had become a much more significant force in national politics. All of the warring states had made great efforts to gain the support of the working classes and their organizations. Having dispropor- tionately suffered in the war's human toll, some political accommodation to these new voices was certain. Perhaps as important, the 1917 Russian Revolution established a communist government, which openly encouraged the working classes of Europe to overthrow their capitalist systems.

Finally, all of the warring states and many of the neutrals had been sub- jected to significant wartime inflation. Except for the United States, the gold standard was suspended by all of the belligerents and many neutrals. From 1914 to 1919 the cost of living multiplied by 1.7 times in the United States, 2.2 in the United Kingdom, 2.7 in France, and 4.0 in Germany.[5] Through a variety of currency and capital controls Great Britain had uniquely managed to maintain the dollar–pound exchange rate very close to the pre–World War I level throughout the war. However, in March 1919, four months after the war ended, Britain was forced to let the pound float.

Considering the Postwar Monetary Standard in 1918–1919

It was thus under these conditions that the question of a post–World War I in- ternational monetary standard was considered by contemporaries. Although there were a few dissenting voices, the dominant view of governments and central banks in Europe and elsewhere was that a return to the pre–World War I gold standard was highly desirable.

The clear expression of this desire in Great Britain was the Report of the Cunliffe Committee. The committee produced an interim report in August 1918 and a brief final report in December 1918, just after the November Armistice.[6]

The August 1918 interim report firmly held that Britain should return to the gold standard without delay. The Committee was concerned with the adverse balance of payments, the "undue" growth of credit, and the prospect of a drain leading to a note issue convertibility crisis. Conditions that the Committee thought would be necessary for a return to the gold standard included a cessation of government borrowing, rehabilitation of an effective Bank of England discount rate, and the restoration of the rules governing

---

[5] B. R. Mitchell 1975, 743–4; U.S. Department of Commerce 1975, Series E135.
[6] *First Interim Report of Cunliffe Committee*, Cd. 9182. The conclusions of the Interim and Final Reports, as well as the Committee's terms of reference, are reprinted in Sayers 1976, 57–64.

the currency and note issues and their required reserve backing in the Bank of England's Banking Department.

With regard to gold, the Cunliffe Committee felt that there was no need for an early resumption of internal circulation of gold or bank gold holdings. Gold imports should be free of restriction while permission for gold exports should be obtained from the Bank of England. The Committee believed that £150 million in gold would be a suitable reserve.[7]

The British balance of payments and fiscal pressures proved too much for the rapid implementation of the Cunliffe recommendations. In late March 1919 official support of the wartime exchange rate of $4.76 to the pound was removed and the next month gold exports were prohibited by law.

Coinciding with the movement to fluctuating exchange rates, the Treasury began to free the capital market from wartime controls. In March 1919 a Treasury notice revised the guidelines for new issues for the still operating wartime Capital Issues Committee. Overseas issues were now permitted, preference being given to those new issues whose proceeds were expended in the United Kingdom, those assisting United Kingdom trade, and Dominion issues. Then, in August and November of 1919 the Defense of the Realm regulations that mandated government regulation of the capital market were repealed.

Yet, in early 1920 Montagu Norman, Governor of the Bank of England, began to use a policy instrument that heretofore had never been a Bank of England peacetime policy tool, that is, privately arranged capital embargoes.[8] Its earliest use seems to have been an embargo on short-term foreign government borrowing, most likely to facilitate the British Treasury's short-term debt refunding operations.[9] This first private embargo proved effective; unlike 1919 and 1921 there were no foreign government issues in London in 1920.[10] Interestingly, some European short-term government borrowers who would have been welcomed in London (or Paris) in the recent past found funding in New York during the embargo year.[11] This development heralded the shifting of the mantle of the world's center for international finance from London to New York in the following years.

---

[7] The final report was issued December 3, 1919; it briefly reasserted the conclusions of the Interim Report. *Final Report of Cunliffe Committee*, Cd. 464.

[8] Atkin (1977, 28) Atkin examines the embargoes throughout the 1920s. See also Moggridge 1971 covering the 1924–1931 years.

[9] In May 1920, Norman's diaries note that he had informally arranged with three principal brokers a queue favoring local authority housing and domestic manufacturing firms first, and then, in descending preference, other domestic firms, Dominion and colonial borrowers and, last, foreign borrowers. Sayers 1976, 288.

[10] Atkin 1977, 155.

[11] According to Lewis 1938, 640–1, the Belgian and Italian national governments obtained short-term funding from the United States in 1920.

Of the major economies of the world, only the United States was on a fully functioning gold standard, as it had been, with very limited restrictions, throughout the war.[12] Britain was with the overwhelming majority of nations in the immediate postwar years in carrying on its international transactions with a floating exchange rate. Like Britain, these other nations were buffeted by variable exchange rates, inflation, and difficult government fiscal problems, and this was a state of financial affairs that did not sit well with their governments or the financial world.

Brussels and Genoa: The International Conferences of 1920 and 1922

In 1920 at Brussels and 1922 at Genoa, conferences were convened to seek solutions for Europe's evolving postwar financial disorders. At these conferences the first attempts were made to reestablish the international gold standard. Neither of these conferences led the participating nations to move together to implement this goal. Yet, the financial policies concerning national fiscal and currency stabilization that were articulated in the resolutions of these conferences represented a strongly held consensus view on how stabilization might individually proceed, if not in international concert. It is also noteworthy that everyone attending these conferences accepted that fiscal and currency stabilization was a necessary preface for the currency link to gold. Thus, it seems fair to suggest that the Brussels and Genoa conferences articulated a path, a set of fiscal and banking principals and practices that, if implemented, would make the restoration of the gold standard much easier.

BRUSSELS. It was the Council of the League of Nations that called for a Commission on Currency and Exchange to meet in Brussels. Given the reluctance of the U.S. Congress to allow the United States to join the League, American participation consisted of an unofficial observer from the United States Treasury. Even so, as the principal postwar international creditor, American views influenced the proceedings and resolutions, especially Washington's negative view toward the establishment of an international central bank or international credit bank. Until Allied debts to the United States were properly scheduled, private, short-term lending from the United States was the method for dealing with European financial needs approved by Washington.

The resolutions of the Brussels Commission viewed the growth of inflation as a key cause of disorganization of business, dislocation of exchanges, the increase in the cost of living, and labor unrest, and thus a phenomena making

---

[12] As of 1919, the United States and Cuba were on a gold standard with circulating gold coins while Nicaragua, Panama, and the Philippines were on a gold exchange standard. China was on a silver standard.

it much more difficult to return to pre-war gold parities.[13] Inflation could be stopped by abstaining from increasing the currency. The chief cause of excessive currency expansion was excessive government expenditure. Governments had to limit their current expenditures to their current revenues and avoid all superfluous expenditures. Banks, especially Banks of Issue, "should be freed of political pressure and should be conducted solely on lines of prudent finance."[14] Additional credit creation and new floating government debt should cease; repayment or funding should begin.

With regard to an international monetary standard, Brussels' Resolution VIII stated that a return to the gold standard was highly desirable, but it was impossible to forecast when the older countries would be able to return "to their former measure of effective gold standard or how long it would take the newly formed countries to establish such a standard."[15] "Deflation, if and when undertaken, had to be carried out gradually and with great caution."[16]

A notable resolution of the Brussels Conference was a call for the creation of central banks in countries where none were currently in place and " . . . if the assistance of foreign capital were required for the promotion of such a Bank some form of international control might be required."[17] This latter phrase was all that remained of the hotly debated ideas for an international bank of issue and an international credit bank, opposed by the United States' unofficial delegate, among others. But, it does foreshadow the idea, if not the specifics, of the League's later financial missions that were to begin in 1922.

GENOA. The Genoa Conference of April–May 1922 was the second international conference called by the Council of Allies to address the continued national and international financial instability. Called with the support of Great Britain, France, Belgium, Italy, and Japan, it was hoped, again unrequited, that the Americans would send official representation. Perhaps the most active planning for the Genoa Conference was undertaken by the Bank of England and the United Kingdom Treasury, with a fairly heavy input from Montagu Norman, the Bank's Governor.[18] Draft proposals brought to

---

[13] Sayers 1976, 69–73. Many of the key international and British monetary documents of the interwar decades are republished in this source, the third volume of Sayer's 1986 (1976) excellent history of the Bank of England from 1891 to 1944.

[14] Sayers 1976, 70.

[15] Sayers 1976, 70.

[16] Sayers 1976, 72.

[17] Sayers 1976, 73.

[18] A draft of proposed resolutions was circulated and shared with, among others, Benjamin Strong, the Governor of the Federal Reserve Bank of New York, 1914–28. Strong was Norman's closest American contact with the Federal Reserve System and New York's financial markets. Strong's links to the Bank of England stemmed from the Federal Reserve Bank of New York's role as the U.S. government's official agent for international transactions from 1916 onward. Norman, in turn, was one of the most knowledgeable Britons in high office

Genoa by the British delegation were among those accepted by the conference's Financial Commission.

A set of widely agreed upon economic and political conditions for national fiscal and currency stabilization, quite similar to the Brussels list, formed an important part of the final conference resolutions. The most controversial Genoa proposals were three important resolutions concerning international monetary arrangements, quickly named the gold exchange standard. These were: (1) central banks should conduct their credit policy so as to avoid undue fluctuations in the purchasing power of gold; (2) central banks were to cooperate continuously with each other; and (3) central banks were divided into two groupings – the central countries, which were to hold their international reserves entirely in gold, and the other nations (unnamed), which were to hold their international reserves partly in gold and partly in foreign exchange, that is, short-term credits on the central countries. International reserves, in other words, could be highly liquid credits placed in the central countries.

In formulating these proposals Norman and the Bank of England saw the world's supply of gold as limited. Britain herself had taken gold coin out of circulation to conserve Britain's holdings. However, it was also the case that these gold exchange standard proposals served national British interests, as was recognized by the United States and France, the other "central" economies.

The British could expect to have a very large share of these short-term credits deposited in London by the world's lesser central banks. Regardless of any temporary embargo on long-term foreign borrowers, Britain remained the dominant market for short-term credit funding of world trade in the early 1920s. Furthermore, these London sterling deposits of foreign banks could be a very accessible source of temporary reserves for the Bank of England when, as happened in the years 1906 to 1910, the Bank was subject to pressures from Britain's balance of payments.[19]

on U.S. monetary and business affairs. Before Norman joined the Bank of England first as Deputy Governor, 1918–20, and then Governor, 1920–44, he had been an associate and then partner of Brown–Shipley, an American mercantile/private banking firm with British partners. His rise through the ranks of Brown–Shipley involved several extended stays in the United States. Norman's American background and contacts must have impressed the Directors of the Bank when he was offered the Deputy Governorship in 1918, a background that could only help in dealing with Britain's principal wartime creditor and the world's largest industrial power. From the beginning of Norman's Bank career, Strong and Norman carried on a frequent and extremely frank correspondence. Indeed, Norman had visited the United States in September 1921 to improve the Bank of England's relations with the Federal Reserve System, both beginning and ending his stay with Strong in New York. Clay 1957; Chandler 1958; and Sayers 1986 (1976).

[19] For example, the Bank of Japan's London reserves were regularly borrowed by the Bank of England at least from 1905 onward. Sayers 1986 (1976), 40–41 and Suzuki 1994, 167–70.

The Return of Gold, 1922–1931

In 1919, there were five nations in the world on the gold standard, the United States, Cuba, Nicaragua, Panama, and the Philippines. Notably, the latter four were closely linked to the United States. By the end of 1922 Costa Rica, Salvador, and Lithuania had restored their link to the standard. Of these seven, Cuba and the United States were on a gold coin standard, the rest were on a gold exchange standard. At the peak of the interwar gold standard in 1929, forty-six nations were part of the gold standard system. China remained on the silver standard while Russia, Turkey, Portugal, and Spain continued to maintain fluctuating exchange rates. Thus, in a much shorter space of time than characterized the spread of the gold standard in the 19th century, most of the world's nation states and their empires had rejoined the gold standard.

Obviously, there were economic incentives for such return. Restoring the gold standard meant the direct and indirect costs of exchange rate fluctuation were sharply minimized, which in turn could have important effects on the costs of short- and long-term finance and the volume of trade. Moreover, a nation on the gold standard was a nation that was likely to keep its government expenditures in line with its tax revenues and thus not meet any large portion of its expenditures with paper money creation. Furthermore, a gold standard government was likely to think that international commerce and finance was a valuable aspect of national economic and social progress. Finally, a gold standard country was not likely to single out foreign businesses for differential treatment in taxation or in courts of contract law.

Even with these advantages for a nation state the immediate economic costs of restoring the gold standard might be quite high, often involving ending an inflationary fiscal policy with significant output and employment effects. It was also politically difficult, particularly in nations where the working classes were finding their voice on matters of taxation and government expenditure and the wealthy classes were unwilling to accept an altered burden. As Eichengreen (1992) makes abundantly clear, new taxes and new expenditures supported by newly widened voting franchises and stronger working class parties were a significant and widespread stumbling block in attempts to restore the gold standard during the 1920s. Indeed these factors, as well as the extent to which the price level had to decline, determined whether countries would return to gold at the pre-war parity or at devalued rates.

When the gold standard was restored in the 1920s it usually involved several stages, with national fiscal and currency stabilization coming first,

During these same years, the Bank of Japan kept foreign currency reserves in New York, Berlin, and Paris.

often accompanied by the creation or reform of the central bank. Then, the nation might move to de facto exchange rate stabilization in terms of gold, with de jure exchange rate stabilization somewhat later.

International Financial Missionaries

In the early stages of national fiscal and currency stabilization and sometimes in the later process of gold standard restoration, the speed and character of the process was frequently and importantly affected by foreign missions. The 1920s must be the most intense decade of financial missionary activity the world had ever seen. The League of Nations sent financial missions to advise Central and Eastern Europe. British, American, and French central bankers officially and unofficially offered advice and financial help. The American economist Kemmerer and other private financial experts were widely used in Latin America and elsewhere.

The common ideology of these missions was forged in the Brussels and Genoa meetings and defined more sharply through each mission's experience. Brown later summarized these ideas, calling them a program of cooperation: "to balance national budgets and stop inflation; to direct the flow of long term capital to countries financially and economically disorganized by the war and to safeguard that capital; to generalize and develop the institution of central banking and safeguard the independence of central banks; to adopt measures of gold economy; to reach a settlement of past debts."[20]

THE LEAGUE OF NATIONS' MISSIONS. In August of 1922 Austria asked the Allied Powers for financial help and was referred to the Council of the League of Nations. A mission was set up to investigate Austria's financial problems and make recommendations. Norman was deeply involved from the start, having a hand in the appointment of several members of the Austrian mission. In March 1923 new statutes for an Austrian central bank emerged and the Bank of England issued a twelve-month loan (March 1923). Three months later in June, a long-term, League-backed loan was floated in London, New York, Paris, and elsewhere, and the Austrian currency was formally linked to gold. Norman saw the Austrian mission as a demonstration of the kind of cooperative international financial help that could work and be replicated elsewhere.[21]

Hungary came to London seeking similar help in March 1923 and was referred to the League. With a settlement of a reparation issue arranged in

---

[20] Brown 1940, 346. The ideas can be repeatedly found in League of Nations reports and annuals. What is equally important is their frequent mention in the correspondence of Norman and Strong in the 1920s. Perhaps the most famous example is Norman's memorandum listing the general principles of central banking, drafted by Norman sometime in 1921, reviewed and amended by Strong. Sayers 1976, 74–5.

[21] Sayers 1976, 168–171.

March 1924, two months later a bridging short-term loan was taken by the Bank of England, a large long-term, League-backed loan was placed internationally, and a fixed link to gold emerged.[22] League long-term loans were also the outcome of stabilization missions to Greece (1924, 1928), Danzig (1925, 1927), Bulgaria (1926, 1928), and Estonia (1927). In total £81.2 million in long-term, League of Nation backed, loans were placed. Britain absorbed 49.1 percent and the United States 19.1 percent. Austria, Belgium, Czechoslovakia, France, Greece, Holland, Hungary, Italy, Spain, Sweden, and Switzerland absorbed shares of 1 to 6 percent.[23] Norman and Strong's support of this type of international cooperation was clearly evident.

KEY COUNTRY SUPPORT FOR KEY COUNTRY RESTORATIONS. The return of the gold standard in the financially troubled principal European economies in the 1920s was also generally supported by international advice and cooperation. However, in these important cases the international aspects of their return were directly in the hands of the principal financial powers. Such was the circumstance for Germany (1924) and Britain (1925). Two financial powers of the second rank, Belgium (1925) and Italy (1927), were also helped by the principal financial powers. The main exception to cooperation among the key monetary powers concerns the French run up to de facto restoration in December 1926 and its de jure restoration in June 1927. As Eichengreen has recently suggested, the particularly acute fiscal and currency crisis in France created a very strong attachment to a purely gold reserve that conditioned their de facto return to gold in December 1926 and de jure return in June 1927 and their attempt to pursue this created riffs with the British and others.[24]

As early as 1919, Strong suggested to Norman that if the principal financial powers first cooperated to stabilize their own government finances and restore the gold standard amongst themselves, it would then be far easier for the other nations to find guidance and resources to stabilize and restore the gold standard following the principal financial powers.[25]

Indeed, American involvement was crucial in the 1923 international commission to help Germany deal with her reparations obligations and get beyond the national and international log jams that produced its devastating postwar hyperinflation. Its outcome, the Dawes Plan, depended critically on official U.S. support and private U.S. participation in the Dawes Loan of 800 million gold marks of foreign currency. Negotiated over the summer of 1924, it was issued in New York, London, Paris, and other European capital markets in October. The United States absorbed half of the loan ($110 million)

---

[22] Sayers 1976, 172–3.

[23] Eichengreen 1989a, 119.

[24] Eichengreen 1992, 172–183, 196–7. See also Clarke 1967, 112–140.

[25] John H. Williams, the Harvard economist who is given credit for originating the key currency idea, was an advisor to Strong. Clarke 1967, 40–41.

and the United Kingdom took a quarter; France, Belgium, the Netherlands, Italy, Sweden, and Switzerland took the rest. In the same month, the new gold mark was repegged to gold.

Britain's own return to gold in April 1925 was vigorously supported by Strong and the New York capital market. A fundamental condition for such a return was a deflation of British prices relative to the United States, which proved elusive despite secularly high unemployment rates, the Bank of England's vigilant positioning of its discount rate, and occasional foreign loan embargoes. However, the longer Britain waited, the more likely it was that the foreign exchange reserves of newly stabilized currencies would be deposited in New York, not London. Indeed, in the winter of 1924–25 first Australia and South Africa and then Switzerland and the Netherlands put Britain on notice that they wished to complete their postwar financial stabilization by restoring the gold standard.[26]

On April 28, 1925, Churchill announced that Britain was back on the gold standard at $4.86 to the pound. The Bank of England had £153 million in gold reserves, virtually the amount recommended by the Cunliffe Committee. Significantly, credits of $300 million had been arranged, if needed, consisting of a $100 million credit from J. P. Morgan and other American banking houses and a $200 million repo line of gold from a number of Federal Reserve Banks for two years.

As things evolved, the American credits were not used, but Norman did find it necessary to arrange a private embargo on foreign loans from November 1924 to facilitate the expected return and an embargo on colonial loans was added two months after the April 1925 restoration. Only in November 1925 was the situation thought sufficiently stable to lift the embargoes.[27] These embargoes most likely hastened the decline of the London international capital markets and the shift to the unfettered environment of New York.

THE MONEY DOCTORS. The third international force for monetary stabilization was the missions of Princeton economist Kemmerer and other private consultants. Because Kemmerer regularly corresponded and met with Strong of the New York Federal Reserve Bank and the State Department concerning his missions, it would appear that he was comfortable operating within the parameters of American monetary and diplomatic policy. Yet, the governments hiring Kemmerer clearly wanted an independent U.S. consultant, not a seconded official of the U.S. central bank or its diplomatic corps. That these governments wanted a foreigner suggests that they were trying to avoid petty

---

[26] Pressnell 1978, Tsokhas 1994, Eichengreen 1992, 190–1. Sweden, Germany, and Hungary had stabilized their currencies in 1924, Sweden and Germany establishing a de jure link to gold.

[27] From June to November 1925 only one Empire loan was issued in London and not one foreign government loan was issued during the whole of 1925. Atkin 1977, 51.

political attacks directed at native experts; that they wanted a U.S. consultant suggests they wanted access to American financial markets. Kemmerer, it was well known, had excellent contacts with the investment banker Dillon, Reed. In the 1920s, Kemmerer headed or jointly chaired missions to Peru (1922), Colombia (1923), Guatemala (1924), South Africa (1924–25), Chile (1925), Poland (1926), and Bolivia (1927), as well as serving on the Dawes Commission to Germany in 1925.

Kemmerer's agenda was virtually the same as the missions of the League of Nations: fiscal stabilization, creating an independent central bank, and stabilizing the currency in terms of gold, de facto, and de jure.[28] Measured by whether Kemmerer's missions resulted in the restoration or establishment of a gold standard, the evidence suggests that it was usually the case that within a year of a Kemmerer mission, the local currency was stabilized in terms of gold.[29] With regard to the effects the Kemmerer missions had on enhanced foreign dollar loans, Eichengreen found a significant effect on national government loans within three years of a Kemmerer mission.[30]

Kemmerer's efforts may have indirectly had a significant effect on the return to gold of a key economy. The advice of the Vissering–Kemmerer commission formed an important basis for the South African government's decision to inform Great Britain that South Africa wanted to return to gold as soon as possible. As was noted earlier, the privately expressed desire of South Africa, Australia, Switzerland, and the Netherlands to return to gold in late 1924 and early 1925 put substantial pressure on Great Britain to speed its own return to the gold standard in April 1926.

Thus, with the efforts of the great powers, especially the United Kingdom and the United States, the League of Nations, and private missions, the gold standard was restored as a gold exchange standard. Many countries accompanied their return to convertibility with deliberate actions to attain fiscal probity including establishing a central bank and a balanced budget. Also because of the severity of the wartime inflation and dislocations and the rising power of labor, many countries returned to gold at devalued parities. The United Kingdom was a principal advocate and architect of the restoration of the gold standard, presumably to restore its position as the world's premier capital market. Yet as events unfolded, she was denied this role and the mantle shifted to New York. This transformation reflected the United Kingdom's weakened financial status after the war, manifested in embargoes on international lending and the decision to return to gold at the original parity that overvalued sterling.

---

[28] Eichengreen 1989b, 60–4.

[29] See Eichengreen 1989b for a list of Kemmerer missions and Eichengreen 1992, 188–90 for Kemmerer's exhaustive list of nations on the gold standard, 1919–1937.

[30] The missions seem to have had little or no effect on short term or nongovernment foreign dollar loans. Eichengreen 1989b, 66–7.

THE MANTLE SHIFTS

Prior to World War I the United States was a debtor nation, similar to Canada, Australia, and other developing countries that were absorbing European capital and exploiting their natural resources. There was, however, considerable U.S. foreign investment, especially toward the end of the nineteenth century. Most was direct investment by American corporations that were expanding their operations abroad. There was also some foreign portfolio investment.[31] The rapid growth in both direct investments and foreign security holdings in the period 1900 to 1914, moreover, suggests that the United States would have become a major foreign investor, and would have changed from debtor to creditor, even in the absence of World War I.[32]

World War I, however, accelerated this transition. The outbreak of the war in Europe brought foreign governments into the American market seeking loans. During the period of U.S. neutrality, these loans were generally short term. Indeed, the volume of short-term lending grew so rapidly that in January 1917 the Federal Reserve felt compelled to warn the banks against acquiring too many foreign short-term loans.

American entry into the war led to massive foreign loans by the U.S. government. The mechanism was simple. The Treasury itself became the purchaser of long-term bonds issued by the Allies. During the war, the Capital Issues Committee controlled sales of foreign securities on private markets.

After the war, U.S. foreign investment boomed. Europe had been devastated by the war and needed capital to restore plants and equipment. Europe also needed capital to reconstruct financial relationships; going on the gold standard meant holding gold or foreign exchange convertible into gold. Britain, although a victor, and possessing lending institutions built up over centuries, was drained by the war. America was ready to replace Britain as the center of lending for developing countries.

Table 10.1 shows the basic dimensions of U.S. foreign lending during the twenties. Over the years 1919 to 1932 some $5.2 billion (at face value) in national and provincial government securities, our focus in this chapter, were floated in the American market. At market prices the figure would be closer to $5 billion. The total, which includes corporate and municipal securities as well as nationals and provincials, was about $9 billion at face value. Most of these were long-term (more than five years) bonds. These were dollar bonds, so that exchange risk was being assumed, at least from a legal point of view, by the borrower.

---

[31] Direct investment rose from $635 million to $2,652 million between 1897 and 1914; security holdings rose from $50 million to $862 million. Lewis 1938, 445.

[32] The surge in U.S. foreign investment and its political ramifications are discussed in Davis and Cull 1994, 92–107.

TABLE 10.1. *Long Term Foreign Dollar Loans Made by the United States (Millions of Dollars, 1919–1932)*

Year	National and Provincial Governments			All Borrowers		
	New Issues	Retirements	Net	New Issues	Retirements	Net
1919	534.4	17	517.4	639.1	25.4	613.7
1920	290.1	3.6	286.5	421.9	20.2	401.7
1921	365.2	44	321.2	526.3	57.1	469.2
1922	509.9	139	370.9	716.1	173.6	542.5
1923	231.9	54	177.9	329.5	72.8	256.7
1924	676.9	57.7	619.2	908.6	103.6	805
1925	551.6	114.2	437.4	918.4	139	779.4
1926	436.7	105.5	331.2	884.1	160.3	723.8
1927	584.8	63.5	521.3	1238.9	157.8	1081.1
1928	486.3	256.1	230.2	1165.1	404.5	760.6
1929	97.4	380.6	−283.2	372.8	440.1	−67.3
1930	432.7	120.1	312.6	757.2	285.8	471.4
1931	75.1	217.9	−142.8	198.8	345.3	−146.5
1932	0	151	−151	0.7	333.6	−332.9
TOTAL	5273.0	1724.2	3548.8	9077.5	2719.1	6358.4

Source: Compiled from Cleona Lewis 1938, 630.
Note: Bonds are at face value.

Issues were substantial even in 1919. National and provincial issues peaked in 1924, while total issues, driven by corporates, peaked in 1927. National and provincial flotations declined sharply in 1929 as investors focused on the soaring returns in the stock market, revived in 1930, and then collapsed as the Great Depression took hold. The purpose of the loans changed over the twenties. The earliest loans were refunding loans needed to finance short-term obligations incurred during the war, and reconstruction loans needed to finance rebuilding of capital damaged in the war, especially railways. Later came stabilization loans, including the Dawes Plan loans to Germany that helped establish the post-hyperinflation German currency. And last came what might be called development loans, directed at a wide range of countries, with the purpose of providing social overhead capital.

The list of countries that sought and obtained dollar loans in the American market in the twenties is a long one. It included major European powers such as France and Germany, smaller European countries such as Bulgaria and Lithuania, South American countries such as Argentina, Brazil, and Chile, and many others. These bonds were distributed by a small number of investment banking houses. J. P. Morgan & Co. was the most important, serving as the lead firm on perhaps half the issues. The others important players were Kuhn, Loeb; Dillon, Read; National City Company; and J. W. Seligman.

The central factor behind the growth of the market was simply that there was good business to be done. Foreigners wanted to borrow; Americans (and few others) had capital to lend. Behind the scenes, the U.S. government offered encouragement. Foreign lending was seen as a way of promoting a stable political equilibrium in Europe, and of extending American influence in other regions. Beginning in 1921, the State Department reviewed proposed flotations.[33] Generally, the Department offered no objection to a proposed loan, but there were a few exceptions based on political considerations. The Department, for example, did not object to Japanese loans if the money was to be used in Japan, but it did object if the money would be used in Manchuria.

During the Great Depression many of the foreign governments that the United States had lent to in the twenties defaulted, including Germany, Bulgaria, Brazil, Cuba, and China. Many municipal and corporate borrowers, of course, defaulted as well. Inevitably, it was argued that lending standards had been lax in the twenties, that they had fallen even further as the lending "mania" progressed, and that the resulting defaults had contributed to the severity of the Depression. On the surface it seemed that although the United States had taken over the role of principal overseas lender from the British, they had not acquired the expertise that the British had accumulated over a century of practice. It also suggests that U.S. lenders may not have followed the same criteria in evaluating foreign loans as the British.

A number of pieces of evidence were adduced to show that standards had been lax. First there was the quantitative evidence. By the end of the 1930s, billions of dollars worth of bonds were in default, and the majority were issues made later in the twenties rather than earlier. There was also an abundance of qualitative evidence. One oft-repeated story concerns the son of the President of Peru who was later convicted of "illegal enrichment" in connection with a Peruvian issue. Another frequently repeated story concerns Cuba. Initially it's foreign borrowing was intended to complete a road running from one end of Cuba to the other, a badly managed project perhaps, but one that could be justified as a productivity-increasing investment in social overhead capital. Later, as the willingness of Americans to lend became evident, the Cubans borrowed for less justifiable purposes – a new Capitol with a gilt dome.[34] And, as with the stock market, one could cite many warnings by wise men that speculation was running wild in the foreign bond market, and that a day of reckoning was at hand.

The problem with this evidence, of course, is that it is hard to know what would have happened in the absence of the Great Depression. Although some borrowers would have defaulted, the number defaulting would have

---

33 Cleveland and Huertas 1985, 147.
34 Lewis 1938, 383–87.

been far smaller, fewer scandals would have been detected, and the warnings of Casandra would have been forgotten. Foreign loans in the twenties did contain substantial risk premiums. To say whether those premiums were "reasonable" would mean knowing a reasonable estimate of the probability of an extremely unlikely event: a collapse of the American financial system in which the Federal Reserve failed to act as lender of last resort followed by a prolonged worldwide depression.

Some attempts have been made to address the standards issue. Friedman and Schwartz (1963, 245–8) provide a perceptive analysis of the standards debate, and of the studies, such as Mintz (1951), available at the time.[35] Friedman and Schwartz argue that the real problem might not have been excessively low credit standards in the 1920s, but rather excessively high standards in the early 1930s, especially at the Federal Reserve.

The critics of U.S. foreign lending in the 1920s, both at the time and since, seem to have assumed that it should have been relatively straightforward for lenders to assess the quality of a foreign issue, a matter mostly of judging the particular project that was to make use of the borrowed capital, combined, perhaps, with some judgment about the weight of the borrowers' total debt burden. Judging the soundness of the issue of a sovereign borrower, however, involves a difficult problem of asymmetric information. The real question is how much a particular country will be willing to suffer in hard times to repay obligations contracted in good times, a piece of information that is hard for lenders to know, whether the borrower is a local businessman or a sovereign nation.

Our research explores how the U.S. capital markets in the 1920s attempted to solve the asymmetric information problem. Our hypothesis is that the U.S. lenders looked at whether a country had made the effort to go on the gold standard, as was the case when Great Britain was the principal lender, and if possible to do so at the pre-war price of gold.

METHODOLOGY, DATA, ECONOMETRIC EVIDENCE

In this section we present evidence for the good housekeeping seal of approval hypothesis for the interwar period. Our approach is to estimate a very simple pooled cross-section time series regression for forty countries and seven years of data.[36] The regression tests to see if adherence to the gold standard affected the interest rate that was charged on dollar-denominated loans to sovereign

---

[35] Mintz computed an annual default index based on the ultimate status of a borrower, rather than of a particular loan, thus adjusting for loans that were not defaulted because they had been substantially repaid before the depression, and concluded that standards had fallen in the late 1920s.

[36] For the data sources and definitions used see the Data Appendix.

borrowers in the U.S. capital market, holding constant other fundamentals. We also ascertain whether in addition to adhering to gold convertibility it mattered whether a country had devalued its currency before restoring the gold standard.

This methodology is somewhat different from that followed in Bordo and Rockoff (1996). That study, which, covered the classical gold standard period 1870 to 1914, had a forty-year sample of data for only nine countries. Most of the variation came from the time dimension in contrast to this study, which relies mainly on the cross-section variation.[37]

The interest rates that we use come from a study by Cleona Lewis (1938).[38] She presented a comprehensive tabulation of new issues in the U.S. markets and the rates charged for approximately forty countries.[39] It's likely that these were not the only countries that were borrowing in international markets. But this was, as discussed in section 3, the most important bond market in the interwar period. The data is organized so that we only use observations for years in which the countries actually borrowed. We do not know why they did or did not borrow. A decision not to borrow might reflect bad credit and an inability to borrow at low rates, or simply an abundance of domestic savings. During this period there were also a number of important stabilization loans offered under the auspices of the League of Nations as mentioned in section 3. In the empirical work described in the following we omit these loans because they do not fit exactly into the framework of our hypothesis – they were made by private lenders but were officially backed on political grounds to help countries stabilize their inflation rates and return to gold. We also did our calculations including these loans in the sample and the results were quite similar.

We used a number of institutional variables to isolate various dimensions of the good housekeeping seal hypothesis. These include dummy variables to ascertain whether it mattered whether a country was on or off gold, whether it had devalued, whether it followed a gold exchange standard or a pure gold standard, and whether it used a gold coin or gold bullion standard.

The third set of variables is a set of macroeconomic fundamentals that one might think would be important in judging a country's ability to service

---

[37] In that study we estimated the Betas from a CAPM regression as well as the simpler regressions reported here.

[38] We thank Barry Eichengreen for drawing our attention to this source.

[39] The countries in our sample are (in Europe) Austria, Belgium, Bulgaria, Czechoslovakia, Danzig, Denmark, Estonia, Finland, France, Germany, Great Britain, Greece, Hungary, Ireland, Italy, Lithuania, Netherlands, Norway, Poland, Rumania, Sweden, Switzerland, Yugoslavia; (in the New World) Canada and Newfoundland, Argentina, Bolivia, Brazil, Chile, Colombia, Peru, Uruguay, Costa Rica, Cuba, the Dominican Republic, Guatemala, Haiti, Panama, El Salvador; and (in the rest of the world), Australia, China, the Dutch East Indies, Japan, Liberia, and the Phillipines.

TABLE 10.2. *Definitions of the Variables*

Variable	Definition
Institutional Variables	
On Gold	A Dummy Variable, 1 if a country fits the criterion
On Gold and Devalued	A Dummy Variable, 1 if a country fits the criterion
On Gold not Devalued	A Dummy Variable, 1 if a country fits the criterion
Gold Coin and Bullion	A Dummy Variable, 1 if a country fits the criterion
Gold Exchange	A Dummy Variable, 1 if a country fits the criterion
Gold Coin and Bullion not Devalued	A Dummy Variable, 1 if a country fits the criterion
Gold Coin and Bullion and Devalued	A Dummy Variable, 1 if a country fits the criterion
Gold Exchange not Devalued	A Dummy Variable, 1 if a country fits the criterion
Gold Exchange and Devalued	A Dummy Variable, 1 if a country fits the criterion
Macroeconomic Variables	
Monetary Policy	Money supply growth rate less real GDP growth rate
Inflation	Rate of change of the CPI
Fiscal Policy	The change in government debt divided by nominal GDP
Foreign Trade	The trade balance divided by nominal GDP
Exchange Rate	The price of the dollar in terms of domestic currency
Gold Reserves/Total Reserves	Gold reserves divided by total reserves
Total Reserves/Imports	Total reserves divided by imports
	* Growth rates are calculated using log differences.
Scale Variable	
Issues/GDP	Bond issues in dollars divided by nominal GDP

its debts. These variables include a measure of monetary policy (the rate of growth of the stock of money less the rate of growth of real output), the inflation rate, a measure of fiscal policy (the ratio of government expenditures less receipts relative to Gross National Product), the ratio of the current account deficit relative to Gross Domestic Product, the rate of change of the exchange rate, the central bank discount rate, the ratio of gold reserves to total reserves, and the ratio of total reserves to imports. The definitions are shown in Table 10.2.

Before we examine the regressions, it is useful to look at the interest rates for our sample of countries, dividing the sample into the countries that were on gold and off gold in the years 1920 to 1929.[40] As can clearly be seen from

---

[40] The sample presented in these figures excludes stabilization loans.

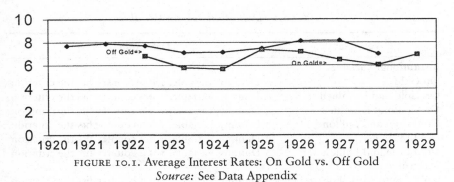

FIGURE 10.1. Average Interest Rates: On Gold vs. Off Gold
Source: See Data Appendix

Figure 10.1, the interest rate for gold standard adherents was less than for nonadherents. Before 1925 the difference is about 100 basis points and afterward closer to 200. A further demarcation, as shown in Figure 10.2, divided the sample into three groups: off gold, on gold and devalued, and on gold and not devalued. From Figure 10.2, if clearly can be seen that interest rates for the last group are considerably lower than for the other groups.[41] Furthermore, after 1925 the interest rates for the on gold and devalued group is about 100 basis points below the off-gold group. These results suggest that good gold standard orthodoxy commanded a very high premium. But even attempting to go back to gold at a devalued parity was better than not doing so.

The advantage to a country of returning to gold can be seen in many individual cases. Thus, for example, Canada paid 5.53 percent when off gold and 4.65 percent when on gold; Australia paid 6.9 and 5.17; Chile 8.05 and 6.75; Denmark 6.93 and 4.8, and Italy 7.8 and 6.25. Indeed, Figure 10.3 shows for the whole sample, the interest rates paid in the two years before going back onto gold and the rates paid in the three years after. As is clearly evident, there is a dramatic decline.

We turn now to the regression results. In Table 10.3 we regress the interest rates on the on–off gold dummy, the dollar amount of the issue scaled by GDP, and a number of macroeconomic variables. All the regressions also include year dummies, which to save on space are not presented. The first equation is the simple benchmark equation, which includes only the gold adherence dummy. As can be seen, this variable is significant and has the predicted negative sign. Equation 2 adds in the size of the issue and the following fundamentals: inflation, fiscal policy, foreign trade, and the exchange rate. As in the first equation, the gold adherence dummy is significant, indeed it is more significant and negative, and two of the other variables are

---

[41] Some new countries did not have a pre-war parity to go back to. They are omitted from the sample at this point.

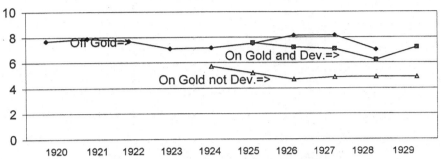

FIGURE 10.2. Average Interest Rate: Off Gold, On Gold and Devalued, On Gold not Devalued
Source: See Data Appendix

significant, inflation and the exchange rate. We have also included the White *t* statistics that adjust for possible heteroskedasticity (the case in which the variance of the disturbances is correlated with the regressors). These results are similar, although the significance of the on–off dummy is higher and the exchange rate is now significant at the 5 percent level, but with a perverse sign. Equation 3 substitutes our measure of monetary policy for the inflation rate. As in the previous regression, this variable is significant.

In Table 10.4, for the gold standard adherence dummy we substitute two dummies: countries that were on gold that did not devalue, and countries that were on gold and did devalue. The on gold not devalued dummy is significant at the 1 percent level and is considerably stronger than the on gold dummy in Table 10.3. Also, as in the previous table, the inflation variable is strongly significant. The only other variable that is significant is the exchange rate in Equation 3.

Finally, Table 10.5 repeats the equations from the previous two tables, except that we add in two additional fundamental variables: the ratio of gold reserves to total reserves and the ratio of total reserves to imports. The

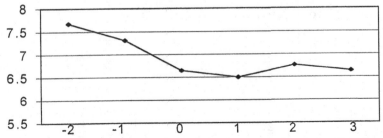

FIGURE 10.3. The Rate of Interest Before and After Returning to the Gold Standard
Source: See Data Appendix

TABLE 10.3. *Pooled Regressions–Dependent Variables: Interest Rates (1920–1929)*

Regressions	Intercept	On Gold	Issues/GDP	Monetary Policy	Inflation	Fiscal Policy	Foreign Trade	Exchange Rate	Adjusted R²	N
(1)	7.85** (9.74)	−1.25* (2.57)							0.23	53
(2)	7.87 [10.65]** [9.03]**	−1.28 (2.72)** [3.73]**	−18.74 (1.37) [1.35]		6.11 (2.33)* [2.80]**	7.91 (1.62) [1.51]	1.25 (0.34) [0.35]	0.14 (1.03) [2.29]*	0.42	53
(3)	8.05 [10.63]** [10.01]**	−1.44 (2.85)** [4.26]**	−20.41 (1.33) [1.62]	4.33 (2.26)* [3.00]**		8.37 (1.47) [1.21]	2.15 (0.56) [0.62]	0.17 (1.36) [2.96]**	0.39	49

Source: See the discussion of the sample in the text and Data Appendix.

Note: Absolute values of *t*-statistics are in parentheses. Absolute values of White *t*-statistics are in brackets. Estimation results of year dummies are omitted in the table.

* significant at 5 percent level.

** significant at 1 percent level.

TABLE 10.4. Pooled Regressions-Dependent Variables: Interest Rates (1920–1929)

Regressions	Intercept	On Gold Not Dev.	On Gold and Dev.	Issues/GDP	Monetary Policy	Inflation	Fiscal Policy	Foreign Trade	Exchange Rate	Adjusted R^2	N
(1)	7.56**	−2.24**	−0.32							0.54	53
	(12.14)	(5.41)	(0.79)								
(2)	7.46	−2.03	−0.35	−3.32		5.74	6.18	2.45	0.07	0.65	53
	(12.83)**	(5.15)**	(0.86)	(0.30)		(2.81)**	(1.61)	(0.84)	(0.66)		
	[15.03]**	[4.87]**	[0.98]	[0.29]		[2.98]**	[1.24]	[0.86]	[1.28]		
(3)	7.43	−1.95	−0.33	2.50	1.82		4.57	4.58	0.13	0.57	49
	(11.34)**	(4.40)**	(0.64)	(0.18)	(1.05)		(0.93)	(1.40)	(0.11)		
	[15.75]**	[5.30]**	[0.85]	[0.19]	[1.13]		[0.76]	[1.35]	[2.13]*		

Source: See the discussion of the sample in the text and Data Appendix.
Note: Absolute values of *t*-statistics are in parentheses. Absolute values of White *t*-statistics are in brackets. Estimation results of year dummies are omitted in the table.

* significant at 5 percent level.
** significant at 1 percent level.

TABLE 10.5. Pooled Regressions-Dependent Variables: Interest Rates (1920–1929)

Regressions	Intercept	On Gold	On Gold Not Dev.	On Gold and Dev.	Issues/GDP	Inflation/ M Policy	Fiscal Policy	Foreign Trade	Exchange. Rate	Gold Reserve Total Reserve	Total Res. Import	Adjusted R²	N
(1)	7.17	−1.16			−38.38	6.66	4.82	−0.15	−0.09	0.95	−0.13	0.28	38
	(4.58)***	(1.27)			(1.73)*	(1.06)	(0.64)	(0.02)	(0.04)	(0.69)	(0.81)		
	[5.01]***	[1.97]*			[1.97]*	[1.36]	[0.71]	[0.02]	[0.04]	[0.75]	[1.33]		
(1)′	7.12	−1.37			−38.24	2.70	−1.08	3.96	−1.27	1.37	−0.15	0.24	34
	(4.68)***	(1.68)			(1.47)	(0.71)	(0.11)	(0.57)	(0.63)	(0.98)	(0.92)		
	[5.29]***	[4.48]***			[1.76]*	[0.80]	[0.17]	[0.72]	[0.52]	[1.10]	[1.53]		
(2)	7.59		−2.24	−0.36	−16.56	7.17	5.16	5.37	0.18	−0.03	0.08	0.59	37
	(6.38)***		(3.06)***	(0.50)	(0.91)	(1.50)	(0.91)	(0.96)	(0.10)	(0.03)	(0.56)		
	[6.45]***		[2.60]**	[0.50]	[0.90]	[1.37]	[0.66]	[0.97]	[0.10]	[0.03]	[0.70]		
(2)′	7.01		−2.11	−0.09	−1.33	−1.39	−5.39	10.44	−1.13	0.55	0.00	0.59	34
	(6.25)***		(3.35)***	(0.14)	(0.06)	(0.47)	(0.79)	(1.95)*	(0.76)	(0.52)	(0.01)		
	[7.73]***		[4.33]***	[0.21]	[0.07]	[0.52]	[0.99]	[2.19]**	[0.55]	[0.55]	[0.01]		

Source: See the discussion of the sample in the text and Data Appendix.

Note: Absolute values of t-statistics are in parentheses. Absolute values of White t-statistics are in brackets. In regressions (1)′ and (2)′, the variable Inflation is replaced by the variable Monetary Policy. Estimation results of year dummies are omitted in the table.

* significant at 10 percent level.
** significant at 5 percent level.
*** significant at 1 percent level.

key finding in this table, as in Table 10.4, is that the on gold not devalued dummy comes in with the right sign, is strongly significant, and large in magnitude (over 200 basis points).[42]

As a test of the robustness of our results, we ran a similar set of regressions (but do not present the results here) on a different set of interest rates. These are long-term bond yields for ten countries used in Bordo and Schwartz (1996). Our results were quite similar to those in Table 10.3, but somewhat weaker.[43]

An important issue that we do not address is that of reverse causality, that regime choice was endogenous rather than exogenous. To do so would require a simultaneous equation approach to explain the choice between being on or off gold as a function of economic and political variables and the link between regime choice and bond yields. Simmons (1994), who studied the interwar period, and Ghosh et al. (1997), who studied the post-1973 period, provide some evidence of a related nature supportive of our hypothesis, that countries that choose to go on gold tended to be politically relatively conservative and fiscally and monetarily prudent and that adherence to gold is associated with lower inflation.

In sum, the results for our measures of gold adherence, especially orthodox gold adherence – that is returning to the pre-war parity – we believe provides strong support for the good housekeeping seal hypothesis. As in our earlier study, the variables that one might at first think should serve as fundamentals, with the principal exceptions of inflation and monetary policy, did not turn out to be that strong.

CONCLUSION

Although this chapter tests the good housekeeping seal of approval hypothesis, we were somewhat skeptical that it would apply to the 1920s. The interwar monetary system generally has received a bad press. It got off to a bad start, as many countries delayed in returning to gold, and many returned at devalued parities. It lasted for only a brief period before ending in the disaster of the Great Depression. Moreover, it was not a true gold

---

[42] We ran regressions similar to those in Tables 10.4 and 10.5 including dummy variables to ascertain whether it mattered if a country was on a gold exchange or pure gold standard and whether it was on a gold coin or gold bullion standard. It did not appear, however, that these further distinctions had a significant impact. Finally, we ran the regressions using one-year lags on the fundamental variables. The results were similar.

[43] Our evidence is based on loans to governments. An important extension of our work would be to determine if private borrowers had better access to capital from the U.S. if their countries adhered to gold. This would require amassing a different database. Evidence that U.S. foreign direct investment accelerated in the interwar and went primarily to those countries that were recipients of sovereign loans in our sample (Wilkins 1974) suggests that our hypothesis would hold for private portfolio investment.

standard, but rather a gold exchange standard that by definition made it more fragile. It has been characterized as having major fundamental flaws that led to a deflationary bias, and most importantly, it has been indicted because members had less of a credible attachment to gold orthodoxy. Yet there is significant recent evidence that suggests that when the gold standard functioned, arbitrage in the short-term capital markets was as efficient as it had been before 1914, and there were substantial long-term capital flows in the 1920s.

Yet despite these reservations, the regression results we report in section 4 were very encouraging for our hypothesis. The on gold – off gold dummy was as significant as what we found for the pre-1914 period, and the fact that the coefficient on the on gold–not devalued dummy was even stronger suggests that adherence to gold standard orthodoxy was highly prized by U.S. lenders. However, the fact that adhering to gold even at a devalued parity was valued suggests that the markets attached importance to being part of the fixed exchange rate system independent of following gold standard orthodoxy.

The general insignificance of the other fundamentals, with the principal exceptions of inflation and monetary policy, echoed what we found in our earlier study. We do not have a ready explanation, but it is possible that the markets preferred the gold standard seal to data that had only recently become available, and that they could not easily evaluate.

Although we believe these results to be compelling, a number of reservations are in order. These include the fact that we could have tested for the influence of other fundamentals such as the political variables considered by Eichengreen (1992) and Simmons (1994) – left wing versus right wing governments, longevity of the government, and so on – or other variables such as prior commercial linkages between the lenders and the borrowers, geography, a common language, and culture.

Although our results show that countries would have received a large gain by going back to gold at the pre-war parity, it is understandable why they chose not to do so. In most cases returning to the pre-war parity would have required substantial deflation and likely declining real activity. In the face of a dramatically changed political economy with the rise of the left and the power of organized labor, the costs of pursuing such a strategy likely outweighed the benefits that we have identified in terms of the spread between the coefficient on the on–off gold dummy and the on gold–not devalued dummy. A case in point is France, which even at the lowest point of postwar inflation in 1919 would have had to deflate by a multiple of the amount that the British and Americans deflated.

Bibliography

Aldcroft, Derek H., and Michael Oliver. *Exchange Rate Regimes in the Twentieth Century*. Cheltenham, UK: Edward Elgar, 1998.

Atkin, John Michael. *British Overseas Investment. 1918–1931*. New York: Arno Press, 1977. [Ph.D. dissertation, University of London, 1968].

Board of Governors of the Federal Reserve System. *Banking and Monetary Statistics*. Washington, DC: Board of Governors of the Federal Reserve System, 1944.

Bordo, Michael D. "The Bretton Woods International Monetary System: An Historical Overview," in *A Retrospective on the Bretton Woods System: Lessons for International Monetary Reform*, eds. Michael D. Bordo and Barry Eichengreen Chicago: University of Chicago Press, 1993, 3–98.

Bordo, Michael D., and Barry Eichengreen. "The Rise and Fall of a Barbarous Relic: The Role of Gold in the International Monetary System," in *Money, Capital Mobility and Trade: Essays in Honor of Robert Mundell*, eds., Guillermo A. Calvo, Rudiger Dornbusch, and Maurice Obstfeld. Cambridge, MA: MIT Press, 2001, 53–151.

Bordo, Michael D., and Finn E. Kydland. "The Gold Standard as a Rule: An Essay in Exploration." *Explorations in Economic History* 32 (October 1995): 423–64.

Bordo, Michael D., and Hugh Rockoff. "The Gold Standard as a 'Good Housekeeping Seal of Approval," *Journal of Economic History* 56 (June 1996): 389–428.

Bordo, Michael D., and Anna J. Schwartz. "The Operation of the Specie Standard: Evidence for Core and Peripheral Countries, 1880–1990," in *Historical Perspectives on the Gold Standard: Portugal and the World*, eds. Barry Eichengreen and Jorge Braga de Macedo. London: Routledge, 1996, 11–83.

Brown Jr., William Adams. *The International Gold Standard Reinterpreted. 1914–1934*. New York: NBER, 1940; reprint, New York: Arno Press, 1970.

Cavallo, Domingo, and Yair Mundlak. "Estadícas de la Evolución Económica de Argentina, 1913–1984," Córdoba, Argentina: IEERAL (Instituto de Estudios Económicos sobre la Realidad Argentina y Latinoamericana), Estudios 9, No. 39 (1986): 103–84.

Chandler, Lester V. *Benjamin Strong, Central Banker*. Washington, DC: Brookings Institution, 1958.

Clarke, Stephen V. O. *Central Bank Cooperation: 1924–1931*. New York: Federal Reserve Bank of New York, 1967.

Clay, Henry. *Lord Norman*. London: Macmillan. 1957.

Cleveland, Harold van B., and Thomas F. Huertas. *Citibank 1812–1970*. Cambridge, MA: Harvard University Press, 1985.

Davis, Lance E., and Robert J. Cull. *International Capital Markets and American Economic Growth, 1820–1914*. Cambridge: Cambridge University Press, 1994.

Eichengreen, Barry. "The U.S. Capital Market and Foreign Lending, 1920–1955," in *Developing Country Debt and Economic Performance. Vol. 1. The International Financial System*, ed. Jeffrey Sachs. Chicago: University of Chicago Press, 1989a, 107–55.

Eichengreen, Barry. "House Calls of the Money Doctor: The Kemmerer Missions in Latin America, 1917–1931," in *Debt, Stabilization and Development: Essays in Memory of Carlos Diaz Alejandro*, ed. Guillermo Calvo. Oxford: Basil Blackwood, 1989b, 55–77.

Eichengreen, Barry. *Golden Fetters. The Gold Standard and the Great Depression. 1919–1939*. New York: Oxford University Press, 1992.

Flandreau, Mark, Jacques Le Cacheux, and Fredric Zumer. "Stability Without a Pact? Lessons from the European Gold Standard, 1880–1914," *Economic Policy* (April 1998): 117–62.

Friedman, Milton, and Anna J. Schwartz. *A Monetary History of the United States 1867–1960.* Princeton, NJ: Princeton University Press, 1963.

Ghosh, Atish R., Anne-Marie Gulde, Jonathan D. Ostry, and Holger C. Wolf. "Does the Nominal Exchange Rate Regime Matter?" NBER Working Paper 5874, 1997.

Great Britain, Parliament, Committee on Currency and Foreign Exchanges. First Interim Report of the Committee on Currency and Foreign Exchanges after the War. [Cunliffe Report.] London: H.M. Stationery Off., 1918.

Hallwood, Paul, Ronald MacDonald, and Ian Marsh. "Credibility and Fundamentals: Were the Classical and Interwar Gold Standards Well Behaved Target Zones?" in *Economic Perspectives on the Classical Gold Standard*, eds. Tamin Bayoumi, Barry Eichengreen, and Mark Taylor. Cambridge: Cambridge University Press, 1996, 129–61.

IBGE. *Estatisticas Historicas do Brasil: Series Economicas, Demograficas e Socias de 1550 a 1988.* Rio de Janeiro: IBGE, 1990.

International Monetary Fund. Annual International Financial Statistics. Washington, DC: International Monetary Fund, various years.

Johnson, H. Clark. *Gold, France and the Great Depression 1919–1932.* New Haven, CT: Yale University Press, 1997.

Lewis, Cleona. *America's Stake in International Investments.* Washington, DC: Brookings Institution, 1938.

Mintz, Ilse. *Deterioration in the Quality of Foreign Bonds Issued in the United States, 1920–1930.* New York: NBER, 1951.

Mitchell, B. R. *European Historical Statistics 1750–1970.* New York: Columbia University Press, 1975.

Mitchell, B. R. *International Historical Statistics: Europe.* New York: Stockton Press, 1992.

Mitchell, B. R. *International Historical Statistics: The Americas.* New York: Stockton Press, 1993.

Mitchell, B. R. *International Historical Statistics: Africa, Asia and Oceania.* New York: Stockton Press, 1995.

Moggridge, D. E. "British Controls on Long Term Capital Movements, 1924–1931," in *Essays on a Mature Economy: Britain After 1840*, ed. D. N. McCloskey. London: Methuen, 1971, Chapter 4.

Officer, Lawrence. *Between the Dollar–Sterling Gold Points: Exchange Rates, Parity and Market Behavior.* Cambridge: Cambridge University Press, 1996.

Pressnell, L. S. "1925: the Burden of Sterling." *Economic History Review* 31 (Feb. 1978): 67–88.

Sayers, R. S. *The Bank of England. 1891–1944. Appendixes.* Cambridge: Cambridge University Press, 1976.

Sayers, R. S. *The Bank of England. 1891–1944. Vol. 1 & 2.* Cambridge: Cambridge University Press, first hardback edition, 1976; first paperback edition, 1986, reprinted with corrections.

Simmons, Beth. *Who Adjusts?* Princeton, NJ: Princeton University Press, 1994.

Spence, A. Michael. *Market Signalling: Information Transfer in Hiring and Related Processes.* Cambridge, MA: Harvard University Press, 1974.

Suzuki, Toshio. *Japanese Government Loan Issues on the London Capital Market 1870–1913.* London: Athlone, 1994.

Tsokhas, Kosmos. "The Australian Role in Britain's Return to the Gold Standard," *Economic History Review* 47 (Feb. 1994): 129–46.

U.S. Department of Commerce (Bureau of the Census). *Historical Statistics of the United States, Colonial Times to 1970, Bicentennial Edition.* 2 vols. Washington, DC: Government Printing Office, 1975.

Wilkins, Mira. *The Maturing of Multinational Enterprise: American Business Abroad from 1914 to 1970.* Cambridge, MA: Harvard University Press, 1974.

APPENDIX: DATA SOURCES

In this study we use 1920–9 annual data for the following forty countries:

Argentina, Australia, Austria, Belgium, Bolivia, Brazil, Bulgaria, Canada, Chile, China, Colombia, Costa Rica, Cuba, Czechoslovakia, Denmark, Egypt, Ecuador, Estonia, Finland, France, Germany, Greece, Hungary, Italy, Ireland, Japan, Mexico, the Netherlands, Norway, Panama, Peru, Poland, Portugal, Romania, Spain, Sweden, Switzerland, the United Kingdom, the United States, and Yugoslavia.

Bond Issues (The value of the issues in million of U.S. dollars): Lewis 1938, 632–6.

CPI (Consumer Price Index): Mitchell 1993, 696–9, 700–2; Mitchell 1992, 848–9; and Mitchell 1995, 930, 935, 939. (For Mexico and Yugoslavia, we use WPI [Wholesale Price Index], Mitchell 1993, 691; and Mitchell 1992, 842.

Devalued or Not (An institutional dummy variable indicating whether or not a country has devalued after returning to the gold standard): Bordo and Schwartz 1996, 11–83.

Exchange Rates (Cents per unit of domestic currency): Board of Governors of the Federal Reserve System 1944, 662–82.

Exports (In domestic currency in millions): Mitchell 1993, 420–31, 435–8; Mitchell 1992, 558–62; and Mitchell 1995, 507, 524, 525, 537.

Foreign Exchange Reserves (In millions of U.S. dollars): Bordo and Eichengreen 2001, 74–5.

Gold Reserves (In millions of U.S. dollars): Bordo and Eichengreen 2001, 74–5.

Gold Type (An institutional dummy variable indicating types of the gold standard – gold bullion, gold coin, gold exchange, etc.): Eichengreen 1992, 188–90.

Government Expenditure (In domestic currency in millions): Mitchell 1993, 653–64, 659–62; Mitchell 1992, 799–801; and Mitchell 1995, 872, 882, 887.

Government Revenue (In domestic currency in millions): Mitchell 1993, 668–77, 680–82; Mitchell 1992, 816–25; and Mitchell 1995, 894, 906, 914.

Imports (In domestic currency in millions): Mitchell 1993, 420–31, 435–8; Mitchell 1992, 558–62; and Mitchell 1995, 507, 524, 525, 537.

Interest Rates (The rates of interest in percent on new issues of dollar denominated bonds): Lewis 1938, 632–6.

Money Supply (Depending on the availability of data, we use M_1 or M_2): Mitchell 1992, 1993, 1995; Bordo 1993; Cavallo and Mundlak 1986; and International Monetary Fund, various years; IBGE 1990.

Nominal GDP (In domestic currency in millions): Mitchell 1993, 748–75; Mitchell 1992, 889–912; and Mitchell 1995, 987–1022.

On Gold or Not (An institutional dummy variable indicating whether or not a country has returned to the Gold Standard): Eichengreen 1992, 188–190.

Real GDP (In domestic currency in millions): Mitchell 1993, 748–75; Mitchell 1992, 889–912; and Mitchell 1995, 987–1022.

Afterword: About Lance Davis

Whether delivering advice to students and colleagues, hiking in the mountains, touring through Europe, or bringing a research program to publication, Lance Edwin Davis has always favored a rapid and sustained pace. And as his many friends can attest, this is the way he has organized and balanced the professional and personal sides of his life. His scholarly writings began with a co-authored book basically completed while in graduate school, continued with two more coauthored books within eighteen months of his Ph.D., and he has seldom paused to rest. Even more impressive, perhaps, is that virtually all of his work has been pioneering and fundamental.

Although Davis has written on diverse subjects, in a sense almost all were of concern to him early in his career: the mobilization and allocation of capital, institutional change, the role of government, and the nature of technical change. The young Davis was also distinguished by a strong belief in the advantages of an economic approach to historical problems and for his proselytizing for cliometrics and the New Economic History. These convictions and commitment are evident in the Davis, Hughes, and McDougall textbook, *American Economic History: The Development of a National Economy*, and in his editorial work on the multiauthored *American Economic Growth: An Economist's History of the United States*. From the first, Davis was interested in building a model of economic growth that would be able to both account for the past and be useful in understanding the present. He aimed economic history at economists (to provide a basis for theoretical analysis and to demonstrate the importance of long-run processes such as institutional change) as well as at historians (to provide more rigor and coherence). Davis, Hughes, and McDougall was an economics text, using history to demonstrate the value of theory, but with the goal of bringing economic history back to the core of economics.

In methodological terms, the combination of new data collection and economic theory is the central characteristic of Davis's work. He has always stressed how new data series permitted formal empirical testing of hypotheses, and showed the way through the meticulous and creative use he made of business records, government documents, newspapers, and many other historical materials. Good theory was of great help to data analysis, but Davis has always insisted that theory had to be grounded in data if it were to be useful. In his frequent division of economists between "those who would rather be clever than be right, and those who would rather be right than clever," there is never any question about which group Davis considers most exalted.

In addition to constructing new data series, Davis has also been a consistent advocate of new methods and approaches. He was among the first economic historians to estimate multivariate regressions, to carry out systematic testing of models, and to champion the use of computers. Anyone wanting a sense of how high expectations were in the early years of cliometrics would do well to read his articles of the period, both to gain perspective on past and present accomplishments as well as some guidance as to the proper direction for the future. Nevertheless, even the young Davis always had much respect for the scholars who came before. The New Economic History permitted greater precision, he suggested, and would make important contributions to our knowledge, but was unlikely to discover many "new revolutionary facts."

The work for which Davis is best known is that dealing with capital markets and the relationships between capital financing and economic growth and structure. His early work was concerned with financial institutions, their operations, and their investment practices. Unlike many other economists who were concerned primarily with capital accumulation and the savings rate, Davis focused on the questions of how and where capital could be mobilized into productive new investments. These studies were enormously influential, not only because he directed attention to the then under-appreciated importance of financial intermediaries, but also because they were based on extensive primary and secondary sources.

Davis began his career-long examination of capital markets with a problem pointed to by M. M. Postan in his 1955 lectures at Johns Hopkins (when Davis was a student there). Postan drew upon an earlier article in which he had argued that:

On the whole the insufficiency of capital [at the start of the Industrial Revolution] was local rather than general, and social rather than material. By the beginning of the eighteenth century there were enough rich people in the country to finance an economic effort far in excess of the modest activities of the leaders of the Industrial Revolution. It can, indeed, be doubted whether there had ever been a period in English history when the accumulated wealth of landlords and merchants, of religious and educational institutions would have been inadequate for this purpose. What was inadequate was not the quantity of stored-up wealth, but its behaviour. The reservoirs of savings were full enough, but conduits to connect them with the wheels of industry were few and meagre.

Writing in the middle of the Great Depression, it is interesting that Postan focused not on the issue of excess savings or of insufficient investment opportunities, but rather on the problem of getting the sufficient savings into the hands of the eager investors. The mobilization process was very slow to start, actually lagging behind the onset of the English Industrial Revolution, as it also did – according to Davis – during early U.S. industrialization. In both cases, however, the pace of economic growth was much accelerated once new institutions of capital mobilization had developed. The ability to move capital into the right sectors required a shift from relying on rather personal relationships between borrowers and lenders, due to problems of information flow, to a financial system that facilitated effective though indirect links between savers and investors.

There have been several different Davis projects on issues of capital mobilization, some with Robert Gallman, some with Robert Cull, and some pursued by Davis alone. The first of these projects was concerned with antebellum textile financing, where Davis points to the early existence of distinct markets by lender type and by occupation of lender, differences reflected in variations in such characteristics as the length of mortgages. Even in the large, early New England textile mills, Davis pointed to the persistence of some capital market imperfections. He also studied the mills's financial structures and the relative importance of equity, loans, and retained earnings as capital sources and how these were related to firm age and to time, in order to understand how the characteristics of the use of capital markets were changing over time. Davis then described, in perhaps his most frequently discussed articles, the interregional flow of funds from east to west, in the period from the Civil War to World War I, with the rise of national markets for short-term and long-term capital. Neither market in the later nineteenth century seemed to include the southern states, a possible change from antebellum times according to some recent work by others, but that issue remains open. Related to the interregional flows of capital were the intersectoral flow of funds, and the interindustry shift of capital to newly expanding industries. Finally, the United States was not a closed economy, and there was an international flow of funds from Great Britain to the United States in most of period studied, but with a net flow of capital out of the United States starting in the decade or two before World War I.

In all of these capital market studies there are several recurring themes: The role of capital immobilities and the restraints on financial flows often persisted, even within a narrow geographic area, and even when there were many new industries needing capital. These immobilities were due, at times, to legal regulations, at other times to different investor preference patterns, patterns that varied by occupation of investor and by their "kinship" networks.

Immobilities were attributed to the impact of market imperfections, a term that has led to some definitional disagreement with others writing on this topic, given that the appearance of so-called imperfections could be related to the presence of transactions costs, to risk differentials, or to uncertainty discounts. To Davis, increasing financial flows required reducing cost differentials, whatever the assigned cause. It might be noted that although Davis often can find examples of market imperfections, particularly in these capital market studies, his customary analysis is one that generally accepts the existence and desirability (if not always the optimality) of a price and market system, with its ability to reduce costs of imperfections when permitted to operate without legislative interference. This would permit inflows to areas and sectors of increased demand for capital from those with greater supply. Given that in the nineteenth century great wealth rents went to financiers more frequently than to entrepreneurs or to developers of new technologies, reductions in the costs of capital transfer also had significant impacts on the structure of wealthholdings and economic power over time. These rents to financiers occurred, it should be noted, even with the quite high savings rate in the United States.

Davis has always been extremely interested in the factors that lead to greater interregional capital flows over time, and his early work on the United States highlighted these developments. In his view, a quite broad range of financial intermediaries developed in response to profit-making alternatives; and, with "saver education" and increased sophistication, they played a major role in accounting for the high savings rates and extensive capital mobility into the appropriate sectors that characterized the late-nineteenth century United States and permitted high rates of economic growth. His analyses of the interregional convergence in interest rates have, in particular, triggered considerable work by others, including a rich complementary set of interpretations about what happened. They have also provided the inspiration for studies of financial markets in other nations and regions, such as France and Latin America.

The comparisons of the United States and British capital markets by Davis, Davis and Gallman, and Davis and Cull, have also been extremely fruitful. The basic argument advanced is that underlying differences in wealth, investment patterns, and institutions led to differences in the way capital markets evolved in the two countries and, thus, to very different industrial structures and patterns of mergers. Britain had a more effective stock market, and this led to more intersectoral flows of funds there than in the United States. Moreover, with capital more accessible through securities in Britain than it was in the United States, there was a lesser need for industrial banks in the former. The greater effectiveness of the British capital market over the nineteenth century also meant that certain U.S. firms in certain sectors found it easier to borrow in Britain than in the United States, despite the latter's higher savings ratio.

In the analysis of the British capital market, Davis was involved in the building up of a time series of financial calls, used to allocate British finance into investment by industry and by location – at home, overseas, or in the empire. This series, along with rates of return then calculated from business records, became one critical base of his subsequent work on the economics of British imperialism. In building up his finance series, Davis found for Britain, as for the United States, that different types of stockholders invested in different industries and areas. Thus, there were differences between those investing in the empire and those placing funds at home or in independent overseas markets. Investor segmentation persisted, even where capital markets were highly developed.

Davis has also been enormously influential in shaping the analysis of the role of the government sector in economic growth. In this regard, several different approaches were pursued. First, there were quantitative studies of government budgets – by level, by revenue and expenditure type, and by taxpayer status. Second, examination of why and how governments do what they do was a fundamental part of the study of institutional change that he undertook with Douglass North, returning political history to a central place in economic history, although within a rational actor framework. Third, by date of publication, is the work with Robert Huttenback on British imperialism in the late-nineteenth and early-twentieth centuries. This project was motivated by a concern with identifying the economic or political logic behind the building and maintenance of the empire and provided considerable detail on the budget revenues and expenditures for Britain and its many colonies, the allocation of British capital financing, the rates of return from corporate accounting records, and on voting both in Parliament and in general elections.

His work on government budgets, beginning with John Legler – his dissertation student at Purdue – has proved seminal. It is only decades later, with the recent work of Richard Sylla, John Wallis, and John Legler that the potential of this project has started to be realized. Davis was the first to recognize that much could be done to quantify and systematically study the important and changing roles of government (federal, state, and local) by exploiting the published and unpublished data that were available. His early, mostly quantitative, articles focused on the regional reallocations involved in antebellum government budgets, the change in the relative importance of different levels of government over time, as well as on the post–Civil War rise in the size of the government sector. The findings yielded new insights, if perhaps not being overly dramatic, but Davis's crucial contribution was in establishing the feasibility of reconstructing local and state budgets and in showing the way to compile a body of evidence that would allow for the investigation of many questions.

The British tax and expenditure studies (with Huttenback) aroused a more passionate response from scholars because they provided budgetary breakdowns for numerous areas and bore directly on the nature and direction of exploitation in the British Empire. The Davis–Huttenback conclusion that on net Britain did not directly exploit, nor benefit from, the colonies in economic terms may not be a surprise to some, but perhaps would have been – judging from their study of parliamentary voting – to British voters. This outcome derives from British taxpayers having borne much of the cost of defense (that is, the financial cost, without delving into the conceptual issues of why defense was perceived as necessary). The argument might well be extended in time and space from the late-nineteenth century British Empire to Britain's pre-revolutionary American colonies or to the United States after World War II as the basic point is that it has always been quite expensive to be a major power. Employing an insightful quotation from Herbert Hoover to add a colorful political complement to their interpretation, Davis and Huttenback suggest that imperialism did not pay for the British as a nation, but it did help British elites to exploit the British middle classes and the local (colonial) businesses to benefit at the expense of those at home.

A second leg of Davis's governmental studies relates to the study of the role of governments in shaping economic institutions, and in forming those institutions that affect economic behavior. The studies of institutions, with Douglass North, also include the analysis of private (individual and cooperative) institutions, such as those that had served to reduce capital market barriers. This joint work served to open up new sets of questions, with an analysis based on a rather neoclassical economic framework, but it seemed less satisfactory, at first, in providing answers to such questions as the optimality of particular outcomes (a question that they call, for some reason, an historian's question). Their approach is, however, better able to describe historical attempts to employ various economic and political methods to seize possible profit opportunities.

In general, this early analysis of institutional change can be considered to have done more to describe the nature of economic forces operating in the political arena, without it being predictive of possible consequences. As the authors noted, this preliminary attempt suffers from being partial and static, with too much of the action exogenous. It was based on a definition of ends that was primarily in terms of narrow financial interest, there being no easy treatment of moral and social values. Yet this approach did ask critical questions: Who gains?; Who wants change?; and Why does the public–private mix vary? The book described what happened and did so by providing stories with real actors, unlike numerous earlier studies of institutional change. To Davis and North the key initiating factors in economic growth and institutional change were economics of scale, externalities, risk, and market failure, all yielding possibilities for private and social gain and for economic growth. They pose their questions with an initial focus on the explanation of economic growth, with less attention given to questions of the extent to which actions chosen were seen to be pure redistribution among groups (as in, for example, imperialism) rather than being growth promoting. This playing down of redistribution is perhaps unexpected for Davis, given his detailed examinations of the behavior of one actual cartel. In pursuing one of his related interests, the behavior of baseball owners, he dealt with a group that certainly sought means of redistribution (away from players and fans). But, perhaps because they seemed to be not too successful, due to either legal or institutional forces or, as Davis likes to suggest, to their own incompetence, the message may have been that most such cartel schemes for redistribution could be downplayed in the long-run, at least if they were private and not government operated.

The second of the two primary questions concerning institutions posed by Davis and North concerned the length of the lag between the initiating disequilibrium and the establishment of the new institutional equilibrium. This is, as their first question, a rather difficult problem, but it is a crucial question for gaining an understanding of many observed institutional changes, and of the general issue of whether it is the nature of the shock or the characteristics of the economic or political frameworks that leads to the institutional change. Clearly, this framework for thinking about institutional change, as well as the set of questions posed by Davis and North, has inspired an enormous subsequent literature. Because the Davis–North tools were drawn from the basic economics toolkit, it is hard to say that they were pioneering in terms of method. Rather, it was the raising of fundamental issues and the demonstration that they can be studied that has led to the major scholarly impact.

Davis's work on the whaling industry, with Gallman and others, flows out of different strands of his own earlier work. The interest in technological change reflects his long-standing concern with economic growth, including both technological change and the ability and ways in which societies adapt to it. The basic framework for understanding the process of technological change is related to the one Davis has used to study institutional change and the role of institutional structures, and he has explored the relationship, as well as the role of externalities in science policy, in several essays. In their book, *In Pursuit of Leviathan*, Davis, Gallman, and Gleiter analyze the rise and fall of the whaling industry over the course of the nineteenth century, with detailed estimates of the sources and patterns of changes in productivity and profits. It is the model study of its kind. The authors map how the major elements of the capital stock evolved over time and contrast the development of the industry in the United States with that in the preceding (Britain) and succeeding (Norway) national leaders. They explore how the difficulty in adapting to a late-nineteenth century technological change was the principal reason why the U.S. whaling industry lost its world leadership position, but also demonstrate how the industry was hampered by the effects of the general expansion of the economy on the quality of labor it could procure. Their work also provides an important analysis of how changes in various substitute, and complementary industries influenced the introduction of new technologies and the change of productivity within whaling (see Figure A.1).

GRAND BALL GIVEN BY THE WHALES IN HONOR OF THE DISCOVERY OF THE OIL WELLS IN PENNSYLVANIA.

FIGURE A.1.

As with Davis's early work, the detailed data and sophisticated issues will attract followers, but to do it well, scholars must be willing to do some extremely hard economic and historical work.

The recent massive tome, also written with Robert Gallman, on *Evolving Financial Markets and International Capital Flows: Britain, the Americas, and Australia, 1865–1914*, uses the analysis of changing capital markets and international capital flows to study the movement of funds from Britain to Canada, the United States, Argentina, and Australia. It has presented much new data from primary sources as well as synthesizing the existing secondary literature. It is, in essence, a study of institutional change and of economic growth in several major nations and does an exceptional job in presenting the relationship between institutional change, financial intermediaries, and economic development in some of the leading nations of the world prior to World War I. The study of the development of financial institutions is currently being extended in a cooperative study with Eugene White and Larry Neal, comparing differences in developments in New York, London, and Paris.

Lance Davis was one of the earliest and one of the most innovative of the new economic historians or cliometricians. Always a leader in identifying and tackling "big" issues, his contributions to knowledge have been based on combining fundamental economic analysis and statistical measurement with the use of new, large-scale datasets, and profoundly shaped our understanding of American and British economic history over the long nineteenth century that ends with the start of World War I, although his recent work on blockades and sanctions extends the period of study to both earlier and later years. His impact on the profession has been broader still, encompassing his service as a co-organizer of key conferences and an important source of encouragement and advice to younger scholars. That he is as active and influential a scholar as he was at his debut more than four decades ago is yet another dimension to his extraordinary achievements.

LANCE E. DAVIS

Date and place of birth: November 3, 1928; Seattle, Washington

EDUCATION

B.A., University of Washington (Magna Cum Laude), 1950
Ph.D., The Johns Hopkins University (Distinction), 1956

POSITIONS HELD

Instructor, Purdue University, 1955–56
Assistant Professor, Purdue University, 1956–59
Associate Professor, Purdue University, 1959–62
Professor, Purdue University, 1962–68
Professor, California Institute of Technology, 1968–80
Mary Stillman Harkness Professor of Social Science, California Institute of Technology, 1980–present

SELECTED HONORS AND AWARDS

Ford Faculty Fellowship, 1959–60
Guggenheim Fellow, 1964–65
President-elect, Economic History Association, 1977–78; President 1978–79; member, Board of Trustees, 1980–82
Research Associate, National Bureau of Economic Research, 1979–present
Fellow, Center for Advanced Study in the Behavioral Sciences, 1985–86
Fellow, American Academy of Arts & Sciences, 1991–present
Sanwa Monograph Prize, Center for Japan–U.S. Business and Economic Studies, Stern School of Business, New York University, 1994

BOOKS

The Savings Bank of Baltimore, with Peter L. Payne. (Baltimore: Johns Hopkins University Press, 1956.)
The Growth of Industrial Enterprise. (Chicago: Scott, Foresman, 1964.)
American Economic History: The Development of a National Economy, with J. R. T. Hughes and D. McDougall. (Homewood, IL: Richard D. Irwin, 1961; revised editions 1965 and 1968.)

American Economic Growth: An Economist's History of the United States,
   with R. E. Easterlin, W. Parker, et al., eds. (New York: Harper & Row,
   1971.)
Institutional Change and American Economic Growth, with Douglass
   North. (Cambridge: Cambridge University Press, 1971.)
Mammon and the Pursuit of Empire: The Political Economy of British Im-
   perialism: 1860–1912, with Robert Huttenback. (Cambridge: Cambridge
   University Press, 1986.)
Mammon and the Pursuit of Empire: The Political Economy of British Im-
   perialism: 1860–1912, with Robert Huttenback. Revised and Abridged
   Edition. (Cambridge: Cambridge University Press, 1988.)
International Capital Markets and American Economic Growth, 1820–
   1914, with Robert Cull. (Cambridge: Cambridge University Press, 1994.)
In Pursuit of Leviathan: Technology, Labor, Productivity and Profits in
   American Whaling, 1816–1906, with Robert Gallman and Karin Gleiter.
   (Chicago: University of Chicago Press, 1997.)
Evolving Financial Markets and International Capital Flows: Britain, the
   Americas, and Australia, 1865–1914, with Robert Gallman, winner of the
   Sanwa International Finance and Public Policy Prize, 1994. (New York:
   Cambridge University Press, 1999.)

PAPERS AND OTHER PUBLICATONS

"Sources of Industrial Finance: The American Textile Industry, A Case
   Study," *Explorations in Entrepreneurial History,* 1st Series, 9 (April
   1957).
"Stock Ownership in the Early New England Textile Industry," *Business
   History Review* 32 (Summer 1958).
"From Benevolence to Business, The Story of Two Savings Banks," with
   Peter Payne. *Business History Review* 32 (Winter 1958).
"The New England Textile Mills and the Capital Markets: A Study of In-
   dustrial Borrowing," *Journal of Economic History* 20 (March 1960).
"A Dollar Sterling Exchange 1803–1895," with J. R. T. Hughes. *Economic
   History Review,* 2nd Series, 13 (August 1960).
"Aspects of Quantitative Research in Economic History," with J. R. T.
   Hughes and Stanley Reiter. *Journal of Economic History* 20 (December
   1960).
"Capital Immobilities and Finance Capitalism: A Study of Economic Evo-
   lution in the United States, 1820–1920," *Explorations in Entrepreneurial
   History* (Essays in Honor of Arthur E. Cole), 2nd Series, 1 (Fall 1963).
"Capital Accumulation Revisited." Paper presented at the Second Interna-
   tional Economic History Conference at Aix-en-Provence, 1962. In *Pa-
   pers of the Second International Conference on Economic History.* (Paris:
   Mouton, 1965.)

"The Regional Impact of the Federal Budget, 1815–1900," with J. Legler. Paper presented at the Third International Economic History Conference, Munich, 1965.

"The Investment Market, 1870–1914: The Evolution of a National Market," *Journal of Economic History* 25 (September 1965).

"Some Aspects of the Economic Development of Great Britain and the U.S.A., 1820–1914." Paper presented at the British American Studies Association, Leeds, 1965.

"Capital Immobilities and Economic Growth: A Study of the Evolution of Two National Capital Markets." Paper presented at the First International Econometric Conference, Rome, 1965.

"The Capital Markets and Industrial Concentration: The U.S. and U.K., A Comparative Study," *Economic History Review*, 2nd Series, 9 (August 1966).

"The New England Textile Industry, 1825–60: Trends and Fluctuations," with H. L. Stettler. Paper presented at the National Bureau of Economic Research Conference on Research in Income and Wealth, September 4–5, 1963, in *Output, Employment and Productivity after 1800*. Studies in Income and Wealth, Vol. 30. (New York: Columbia University Press, 1966.)

"Professor Fogel and the New Economic History," *Economic History Review*, 2nd Series, 19 (December 1966).

"Capital Immobilities, Institutional Adaptation, and Financial Development: The United States and England, An International Comparison," in *Quantitative Aspekte der Wirtschaftsges ch ichte*, edited by H. Giersch and H. Savermann. (Tubingen: Mohr Siebeck, 1968).

"The Government in the American Economy, 1815–1900: A Quantitative Study," with J. Legler. Paper presented at the annual meeting of the Economic History Association, 1966, in *Journal of Economic History* 26 (December 1966).

"Monopolies, Speculators, Causal Models, Quantitative Evidence, and American Economic Growth." Paper presented at the annual meeting of the Organization of American Historians, Chicago, April 1967.

"The New Economic History Re-examined." Paper presented at the annual meeting of the Pacific Historical Association, Palo Alto, 1967.

"And It Will Never Be Literature," *Explorations in Entrepreneurial History*, 2nd Series, 9 (Fall 1968).

"Who's Afraid of Robert Lindner." Paper presented at the annual meeting of the Organization of American Historians, Philadelphia, April 1969.

"Institutional Change and American Economic Growth," with D. North. *Journal of Economic History* 30 (March 1970).

"Specification, Identification, and Analysis in Economic History," in *Approaches to American Economic History*, edited by G. R. Taylor and L. F. Ellsworth. (Charlottesville: University of Virginia Press, 1971.)

"Savings and Investment in Nineteenth Century America," with Robert Gallman. Paper presented at the Fourth International Economic History Conference in Bloomington, IN, 1968, in *Papers of the Fourth International Conference on Economic History*, edited by Ross Robertson. (Bloomington: Indiana University Press, 1973.)

"Self-Regulation in Baseball, 1909–71," in *Government and the Sports Business*, edited by Roger G. Noll. (Washington, DC: Brookings Institution, 1974.)

"The National Research Fund: A Case Study in the Industrial Support of Academic Science," with Daniel Kevles, *Minerva* 12 (April 1974).

"One Potato, Two Potato, Sweet Potato Pie: Clio Looks at Slavery and the South." Paper presented at the MSSB Conference on *Time on the Cross*. (Rochester, NY, November 1974.)

"Institutional Structure and Technological Change," with Susan G. Groth, in *Government Policies and Technological Innovation*. Vol. II. *State-of-the-Art Surveys*. (Washington, DC: National Technical Information Service, National Science Foundation, 1974.)

"Social Choice and Public Welfare: British and Colonial Expenditure in the Late Nineteenth Century," with Robert A. Huttenback. Paper presented to the XIV International Congress of Historical Studies, San Francisco, August 1975.

"The Evolution of the American Capital Market, 1860–1940: A Case Study in Institutional Change," in *Financial Innovation*, edited by W. Silber. (Lexington, MA: Lexington Books, 1975.)

"Tax Writeoffs and the Value of Sports Teams," with James P. Quirk, in *Management Science Applications to Leisure Time Operations*, edited by S. Ladany. (Amsterdam: North-Holland, 1975.)

"Public Expenditure and Private Profit: Budgetary Decision in the British Empire, 1860–1912," with Robert A. Huttenback. Paper presented at the annual meeting of the American Economic Association, September 1976, in *American Economic Review* 67 (February 1977).

"British Imperialism and Military Expenditure," with Robert A. Huttenback. Paper presented at the Anglo-American Conference of Historians, London, July 1978.

"Capital Formation in the United States, During the Nineteenth Century," with Robert Gallman, in *Cambridge Economic History of Europe*, Vol. VII, Part II. eds. by P. Mathias and M. M. Postan. (Cambridge: Cambridge University Press, 1978.)

"Directions of Change in American Capitalism." Paper presented at the First Annual International Seminar on Societies in Transition, Malente, Federal Republic of Germany, July 1978, in *Societies in Transition*, edited by Fischer Apfel. Hamburg, 1979.

"A Bedtime Story: A Comedy in Three Acts," with Robert A. Huttenback. Paper presented at the annual meeting of the Organization of American Historians, New Orleans, April 1979.

"Trends in Recent Scholarship in Institutional Change and American Economic Growth." Paper presented at the annual meeting of the Law and Society Association, San Francisco, May 1979.

"Aspects in Nineteenth Century British Imperialism," with Robert A. Huttenback. Paper presented at the Western Economic Association Annual Meeting, Las Vegas, June 1979.

"Savings and Investment," in the *Encyclopedia of American Economic History*. (New York: Scribner's, 1980.)

"Credit," in the *Dictionary of American History*. (New York: Scribner's, 1980.)

"It's a Long, Long Road to Tipperary, or Reflections on Organized Violence, Protection Rates, and Related Topics: The New Political History." Paper presented at the annual meeting of the Economic History Association, Wilmington, DE, September 1979, in *Journal of Economic History* 40 (March 1980).

"Britain Against Herself: Profits and Empire in the Period of Financial Capitalism." Paper delivered at the annual meeting of the Social Science History Association, Rochester, NY, November 6–9, 1980.

"In Search of the Historical Imperialist," with Robert A. Huttenback. Paper presented at the Purdue Symposium, February 1978, in *Essays in Contemporary Fields of Economics*, edited by George Horwich and James Quirk. (West Lafayette, IN: Purdue University Press, 1981.)

"Some Observations on the Cost of Empire," with Robert A. Huttenback, in *Essays in Honour of Douglass North*, edited by R. Ransom, R. Sutch, and G. Walton. (New York: Academic Press, 1981.)

"The Political Economy of British Imperialism: Measures of Benefit and Support," with Robert A. Huttenback. Paper delivered at the annual meeting of the Economic History Association, St. Louis, September 1981, in *Journal of Economic History* 42 (March 1982).

"The Social Rate of Return," with Robert A. Huttenback, in *Journal of Economic History* 43 (December 1983).

"Imperialism and the Social Classes: Imperial Investors in the Age of High Imperialism," with Robert A. Huttenback. Paper presented at the conference of the 100th anniversary of Marx, Keynes and Schumpeter, Gronigen, The Netherlands, September 6–10, 1983, in *Economic Law of Motion of Modern Society: A Marx-Keynes-Schumpeter Centennial*, ed. H. J. Wagener and J. W. Drucker. (Cambridge: Cambridge University Press, 1986.)

"Institutional Change: New Interpretation." Paper presented at the meetings of the Economic History Association, September 23–25, 1983. *Journal of Economic History* 44 (March 1984).

"The Export of Finance," with Robert A. Huttenback. *Journal of Imperial and Commonwealth History*, 13 (May 1985).

"On the Public Finance of North Carolina." Paper presented at the Conference on Income and Wealth. Williamsburg, VA, March 22–24, 1984. In

Long Term Trends in the American Economy. NBER Studies in Income and Wealth 51, edited by S. Engerman and R. Gallman (Chicago: University of Chicago Press, 1986.)

"Keep the Rascals at Bay or Up the Bureaucrats: North and Wallis and The Transaction Sector." Paper presented at the Conference on Income and Wealth, Williamsburg, VA, March 22–24, 1984, in *Long Term Trends in the American Economy. NBER Studies in Income and Wealth* 51, edited by S. Engerman and R. Gallman (Chicago: University of Chicago Press, 1986.)

"The Structure of the Capital Stock in Economic Growth and Decline: The New Bedford Whaling Fleet in the Nineteenth Century," with Robert Gallman and Teresa Hutchins, in *Quantity and Quiddity: Essays in U.S. Economic History in Honor of Stanley Lebergott*, edited by Peter Kilby (Middletown, CT: Wesleyan University Press, 1986.)

"Clio is Alive and Well in More Places than Oxford, Ohio," with Stanley Engerman, in *The Newsletter of the Cliometrics Society* (April 1986), reprinted in revised form in *Historical Methods* 20 (1987).

"Bureaucracy, Law and Economic Progress: Technical Change in an Institutional Context," The Jacob Schmookler Lecture, University of Minnesota, May 1986.

"Technology, Productivity and Profits: British–American Whaling Competition in the North Atlantic, 1816–1842" with Robert Gallman and Teresa Hutchins. Paper presented at the First International Conference on Productivity, Income, Wealth and Welfare, Bellagio, Italy, March 1986; the Neuvieme Congress International D'Historie Economique, Berne, Switzerland, August, 1986, and at the Southern Economic Association Meetings, New Orleans, November 1986. *Oxford Economic Papers* 39 (December 1987).

"Businessmen, the Raj, and the Pattern of Government Expenditures: The British Empire 1860 to 1912" with Robert Huttenback. Paper presented at annual meeting of the American Economic Association, New Orleans, December 1986, in *Markets in History: Economic Studies of the Past*, edited by David Galenson (Cambridge: Cambridge University Press, 1989.)

"Productivity Change in American Whaling: The New Bedford Fleet in the Nineteenth Century," with Robert Gallman and Teresa Hutchins. Paper presented at the NBER Conference on the Development of the American Economy, July 10–22, 1987, and at the annual meeting of the Social Science History Association, New Orleans, October 30–November 1, 1987, in *Markets in History: Economic Studies of the Past*, edited by David Galenson (Cambridge: Cambridge University Press, 1989.)

"The Decline of U.S. Whaling: Was the Stock of Whales Running Out?" with Robert Gallman and Teresa Hutchins, in *The Business History Review* 62 (Winter 1989).

"Do Imperial Powers Get Rich off their Colonies?," with Robert A. Huttenback, in *SECOND THOUGHTS: Myths and Morals of U.S. Economic History*, edited by Donald McClosky (New York: Oxford University Press, 1993.)

"Call Me Ishmael Not Domingo Floresta: The Rise and Fall of the American Whaling Industry," with Robert Gallman and Teresa Hutchins. In *Research in Economic History*, Supplement 6, *The Vital One: Essays in Honor of J. R. T. Hughes*, edited by J. Mokyr (1991).

"Risk Sharing, Crew Quality, Labor Shares and Wages in the Nineteenth Century American Whaling Industry," with Robert Gallman. Paper presented at the annual meeting of the Social Science History Association, in *American Economic Development in Historical Perspective*, edited by T. Weiss and D. Schaefer (Stanford, CA: Stanford University Press, 1994.)

"The Last 1945 American Sailing Ships," with Robert Gallman, in *The Economics of Informational Decentralization: Complexity, Efficiency and Stability. Essays in Honor of Stanley Reiter*, edited by J. Ledyard (Boston: Kluwer Academic Publishers, 1995)

"Savings, Investment, and Economic Growth: The United States in the Nineteenth Century" with Robert Gallman. Paper presented at the Symposium on Capitalism and Social Progress: Themes and Perspectives; Charlottesville, VA, October 1990, in *Capitalism in Context: Essays in Honor of Max Hartwell*, edited by John James and Mark Thomas (Chicago: University of Chicago Press, 1995).

"One Market, Two Markets, Three Markets, Four? The Network of Finance: Capital Market Integration – the U.S. and U.K. 1865–1913," with Robert Cull. Paper delivered at the International Urban History Group Conference, "Cities of Finance," Amsterdam, May 15–18, 1991. Published in *Annales HHS* 47 (Mai–Juin 1992).

"Sophisticates, Rubes, Financiers, and the Evolution of Capital Markets: U.S.–UK Finance, 1865–1914," with Robert Cull and Robert Gallman. Paper presented at the National Bureau of Economic Research Summer Institute: Development of the American Economy and Franco-American Economic Seminar, Boston, MA, July 1993 and at the 12th Latin American Meetings of the Econometric Society, Tucuman, Argentina, August 1993.

"Institutional Invention and Innovation: Foreign Capital Transfers and the Evolution of the Domestic Capital Markets in Four Frontier Countries: Argentina, Australia, Canada, and the U.S.A., 1865–1914," with Robert Gallman. Paper presented at the 11th International Economic History Congress, Milan, Italy, September 1994.

"Financial Integration Within and Between Countries." Paper presented at the Conference on Anglo-American Finance: Financial Markets and Institutions in 20th Century North America, December 10, 1993, New

York University Center, Leonard N. Stern School of Business, in *Anglo American Finance Systems: Institutions and Markets in the 20th Century*, edited by M. Bordo and R. Sylla (Homewood, IL: Richard D. Irwin, 1995).

"Institutional Investment, and the Evolution of Domestic Capital Markets in Australia and Canada" Paper presented at the 18th International Congress of Historical Sciences, Montreal, Canada, August 1995.

"The Economy of Colonial North America: Miles Traveled, Miles to Go" with Stanley Engerman. Paper presented at A Conference on the Economy of Early British America: The Domestic Sector, Pasadena, CA, October 1995. In *The William and Mary Quarterly* 56 (January 1999).

"Micro Rules and Macro Outcomes: The Impact of the Structure of Organizational Rules on the Efficiency of Security Exchanges: London, New York, and Paris 1800–1914," with Larry Neal. Paper presented at the Third World Congress of Cliometrics, Munich, Germany, July 1997. Published in abbreviated form in *American Economic Review*, 87 (May 1998).

"Lessons from the Past: International Financial Flows and the Evolution of Capital Markets, Britain and Argentina, Australia, Canada, and the United States before World War I," with Robert Gallman. Paper presented at the XII International Economic History Conference, Seville, Spain, August 1998, in *Finance and the Making of Modern Capitalism, 1830–1931*, edited by Phillip Cottrell, Gerald Feldman, and Jaime Reis (Aldershot: Ashgate for the European Association for Banking History, 1999.)

"International Capital Movements, Domestic Capital Markets and American Economic Growth, 1820–1914," with Robert Cull, in *Cambridge Economic History of the United States, Vol. II*, edited by S. Engerman and R. Gallman (Cambridge: Cambridge University Press, 2000).

"The Late Nineteenth Century British Imperialist: Specification, Quantification, and Controlled Conjectures," in *Gentlemanly Capitalism and the New World Order: The New Debate on Imperialism*, edited by Ray Dumett (London: Addison Wesley Longman, 1999).

"Lessons from the Past: Capital Imports and the Evolution of Domestic Capital Markets, 1870–1914," in *Victorian Perspectives on Capital Mobility and Financial Fragility in the 1990s*, edited by Charles Calormis (Washington, DC: American Enterprise Institute, 1999).

"Membership Rules and the Long Run Performance of Stock Exchanges: Lessons from Emerging Markets, Past and Present," with Larry Neal and Eugene White. Paper presented at the annual meeting of the ISNIE (International Society for the New Institutional Economies) Conference, Washington, DC (September 17–19, 1999).

Roundtable on "American Whaling," in the *International Journal of Maritime History* 11 (December 1999).

"Whaling." In *Encyclopedia of the United States in the Nineteenth Century*, ed. Paul Finkelman (New York: Scribner's, 2000).

"Legal and Economic Aspects of Naval Blockades: The United States, Great Britain, and Germany in World War II," with Stanley Engerman. Paper presented at the annual meeting of the Economic History Association, Los Angeles, September 2000.

"International Law and Naval Blockades during World War I: Britain, Germany, and the United States, Traditional Strategies versus the Submarine," with Stanley Engerman. Paper presented at the annual meeting of the American Economic Association, New Orleans, January 2001.

"Formal Estimates of Personal Income are Really Personal," in *Living Economic and Social History*. Essays to mark the 75th anniversary of the Economic History Society, edited by Pat Hudson (Glasgow: Economic History Society, 2001).

"Lessons from the Past: Capital Markets and Economic Growth." Paper presented at the CEPR/Studienzentrum Gernzensee European Summer Symposium in Financial Markets (ESSFM), Gerzensee, Switzerland, July 2000, in *Essays in Honor of Stanley Engerman,* edited by David Eltis, Frank Lewis, and Kenneth Sokoloff (Cambridge: Cambridge University Press, forthcoming).

"Sanctions: Neither War nor Peace," with Stanley Engerman (forthcoming).

"The Long-Term Evolution of the NYSE's Microstructure: Evidence from the Pricing of Seats on the Exchange," with Neal and White. Paper presented at the September 2001 meeting of the Economic History Association, and in revised form, at the January 2002 meeting of the American Economic Association.

WORKS IN PROGRESS

The Impact of the Micro Structure of Rules Governing the NY, London, and Paris Stock Exchanges on the Efficiency of Those Exchanges, 1800–1971, with Larry Neal and Eugene White.

The Economic Effectiveness of Naval Blockades 1700 to 2000, with Stanley Engerman.

Financial Structure and Economic Development in the Long Run: Firm, Industry, and Country Evidence, with Robert Cull and Jean Laurent-Rosenthal.

Index

337